Shurāt Legends, Ibāḍī Identities

Studies in Comparative Religion
Frederick M. Denny, Series Editor

Shurāt Legends
Ibāḍī Identities

Martyrdom, Asceticism, and the Making of an Early Islamic Community

Adam R. Gaiser

The University of South Carolina Press

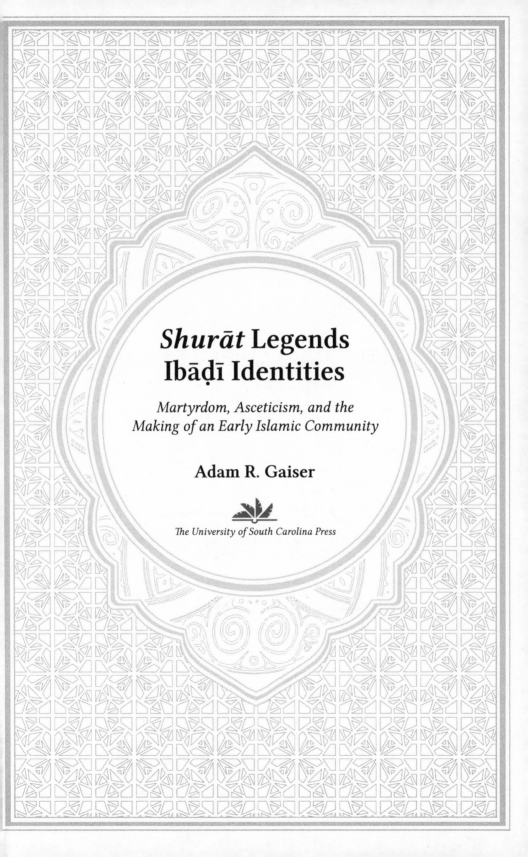

Published by the University of South Carolina Press
Columbia, South Carolina 29208

www.sc.edu/uscpress

Manufactured in the United States of America

25 24 23 22 21 20 19 18 17 16
10 9 8 7 6 5 4 3 2 1

Library of Congress Cataloging-in-Publication Data
can be found at http://catalog.loc.gov/

ISBN 978-1-61117-676-6 (cloth)
ISBN 978-1-61117-677-3 (ebook)

This book was printed on a recycled paper
with 30 percent postconsumer waste content.

For Robin and Gordon Gaiser

What do we care if our souls go out [of our bodies]?
What good to you were bodies and limbs anyway?
We look forward to the Gardens [of paradise],
When our skulls lie in the dust like rotten melons.

Abū Bilāl Mirdās b. Udayya,
from I. ʿAbbās, *Shiʿr al-Khawārij,* 1977

Contents

Series Editor's Preface

This significant book addresses in a detailed and deeply researched manner a subject that is not often found in books about the earliest period of the new Muslim community within thirty years of the death of the Prophet Muhammad and its development from that time. Our author refers to the period in which Islam came into being as "the late antique Middle East" (p. 1). That term is for the attention of modern readers and refers to "greater Syria (that is, the Levant), the Nile, the Arabian Peninsula, Mesopotamia, and Persia between the second and eighth centuries C.E." In his introduction the author continues by acknowledging the importance of the diverse ethnic, political, cultural and religious communities in those regions in that period.

An important focus of the book is the development of the earliest Islamic communities and ways in which they both agreed and disagreed with each other. Adam R. Gaiser addresses his main topic, the Ibadi Muslim community, through studying it in relationship to and in comparison with other early Muslim communities. The author has discovered significant early sources that provide indispensable information about the histories, practices, and convictions of the Ibadis and the roles of martyrdom and asceticism in their personal lives and communities.

This series has been publishing important books, including a fair number on Islam, for many years now. I think that this one will provide valuable information, analysis, and interpretation of the earliest Islamic history for contemporary scholarship and teaching across such disciplines as Islamic studies, comparative religion, and Middle Eastern history.

Frederick Mathewson Denny

Acknowledgments

A host of persons have assisted me in the various stages of this research, and it is my hope that I have not neglected any of them here. Several of my colleagues at Florida State University gave their encouragement, support, and help over the years. Special thanks go to John Kelsay, Tara Baldrick-Morrone, John Corrigan, Matthew Goff, David Levenson, Nicole Kelley, Joseph Hellweg, Harold Short, and Thomas Whitley. Additionally the Florida State University Office of Sponsored Research extended me several internal grants toward the completion of this project.

This book would have been unthinkable without the steadfast encouragement and assistance of Dr. Abdulrahman al-Salimi, who in addition to his unfailing collegiality sent me images of several manuscripts, allowed me access to his family library in Bidiyya, and smoothed the way for me to access manuscripts in the Wizārat al-Turāth al-Qawmī wa'l-Thaqāfa. Thanks also to his brother, Hamza al-Salimi, for his generous hospitality and to the students of the Ma'had al-'Ulūm al-Shara'iyya for their enthusiasm as well as the texts that they so selflessly placed in my hands. My gratitude goes to Hilāl b. Jum'a al-Muqaymī and Muṣṭafā b. Sālim al-Shukaylī at the library of Sayyid Muḥammad b. Aḥmad in Seeb for opening their doors to me and allowing me unfettered access to the manuscripts there.

My colleagues in the Ibāḍī studies community—there are now too many to name—deserve mention for their many helpful comments at conferences over the years. I would be remiss, however, if I did not specifically thank Wilferd Madelung, Josef Van Ess, Valerie Hoffman, Amal Ghazal, Angeliki Ziaka, Ersilia Francesca, Cyrille Aillet, Moez Dridi, Muhammad Hasan, and Douglas Leonard for their encouragement. Special thanks to John Wilkinson for his friendship and for his many insights into the Ibāḍiyya.

To Ahmad Obeidat I owe an immeasurable debt for his countless hours of assistance in translating the poetry that I utilized in this study. Without his expertise in Arabic, this project would have long ago foundered. To Helena de Jesús de Felipe Rodríguez go thanks for tracking down the coloquintida fruit (a.k.a. colocynth, *Citrullus colocynthis,* bitter apple—the *ḥanẓal* mentioned in Abū Bilāl's poem and translated in the epigraph of this book); reserving poetic license, I have translated it as "melon."

Before she passed away suddenly in September 2014, Annie Higgins shared her own translations of some of the *shurāt* poems. We will all miss her ever bright personality. Tom Sizgorich passed away in January 2011 before seeing anything written of this book, but I owe him my thanks for his many suggestions during its gestation. He was an outstanding scholar and a generous colleague; I'm sorry we had such a short time together.

Finally, my thanks to Robin and Gordon Gaiser for their support (both financial and familial) over the years; to my wife, Carolina, a debt of gratitude for the sacrifices she makes to allow our work to continue; and to my daughter, Adela, thanks for her stickers, Little Ponies, and *besitos*.

Notes on Transliteration, Dates, and Qur'ānic Citations

Transliterations from Arabic follow the *International Journal of Middle Eastern Studies* system, which has all but become the standard system in the United States. Each date is given either as a stand-alone date followed by the designator C.E. or as *hijri* year or century first followed by a slash and then common-era year or century. For Qur'ānic citations I use the 1923 Egyptian printed recension of Ḥafs from 'Āṣim, which has become the standard version.

Introduction

The late antique Middle East forms the context in which the Prophet Muḥammad's mission, with the Qur'ān articulating its central message of submission to God, gave way to the early Islamic conquests and then, not thirty years after the death of the Prophet, witnessed the emergence of the Muḥakkima and first *shurāt*. Although the term "late antique Middle East" would have meant little to the peoples living in that region at that time, it is a convenient way of designating the area roughly comprised by greater Syria (that is, the Levant), the Nile, the Arabian Peninsula, Mesopotamia, and Persia between the second and eighth centuries C.E. At this time this region presented a complex tapestry of religio-political entities encompassing Byzantine, Ethiopian, "Nestorian" (that is, Church of the East), "Jacobite" (that is, Syriac Orthodox Church), and so-called "gnostic" Christians as well as Jews, Zoroastrians, Manicheans, stoics, pagans, and others. In the Arabian Peninsula itself Jews and modest numbers of Christians had long lived—not only in the famous and ill-fated Christian community at Najrān but also in Oman, Baḥrayn, and the islands of the gulf. These various groups populated the areas of the world in which the pre-Islamic Arabs held frequent commerce and later, after the coming of Islam and the early Islamic conquests, over which the Muslims exercised political control. It is also amid these various religious affiliations, congregations, and denominations and in this area of the world, initially in Mesopotamia, that the collections of Islamic sectarians known to most as the *khawārij* (sing. *khārijī*, Anglicized as the Khārijites) arose, the first among them being known as the Muḥakkima.[1] The *khawārij*, at least up until the second *fitna* (and probably beyond it), used the term *shurāt* (sing. *shārī*, meaning "exchanger") to refer to themselves.

Initially opposed to ʿAlī b. Abī Ṭālib's decision to arbitrate the battle of Ṣiffīn in 37/657, the Muḥakkima survived their virtual annihilation by ʿAlī's army at the battle of Nahrawān in 38/658 and spread throughout the early Islamic world. They continued to rebel against ʿAlī, and after one of their number murdered him in the mosque in Kūfa, they rose against the ʿAlī's successor (and original opponent at Ṣiffīn), the Umayyad caliph Muʿāwiya b. Abī Sufyān. Indeed, Islamic sources record ten further "Khārijite" (that is, *shurāt*) engagements with ʿAlī and Muʿāwiya and over the following two decades four more significant *shurāt*-inspired rebellions against Muʿāwiya and his son and successor Yazīd.[2] These early conflicts—some fifteen of them in a twenty-three-year period—resulted in the violent deaths of many who fought them and subsequently created a pool of poetry and narrative that circulated among the remaining *shurāt.* As they continued to spread and develop into separate subsects, the stories of their martyrs—or in the style of the *shurāt* themselves, those who had sold their earthly lives to God in "exchange" for his paradise—continued to inspire them and inform their sense of mission.[3] It was also during the second civil war (*fitna*) following the death of Muʿāwiya that, according to Islamic sources, the main divisions of the *shurāt* crystallized into distinct subsects of Azāriqa, Najdāt, Ibāḍiyya, and Ṣufriyya over questions of secession (*khurūj*), the implications of sin and unfaithfulness (*kufr*), and the practice of prudent dissimulation (*taqiyya*).[4]

Although most of the *shurāt* groups that appeared in the late antique and early Islamic Middle East ultimately succumbed to the pressure of the Umayyad and later ʿAbbāsid (and even Fāṭimid) armies, fragments of their literature have survived to the present day, as have one of their quietist offshoots, the Ibāḍiyya.[5] The remnants of the earliest *shurāt* literature can now be found sprinkled throughout the wider corpus of Sunnī, Shīʿite, and Ibāḍī texts. Although later Sunnī and Shīʿa editors and authors remained, on the whole, hostile to the Khārijites, they were forced grudgingly to admire their fierce piety, and they used *shurāt* sources as the basis for their own writings.

For their part, the modern-day Ibāḍiyya do not acknowledge any link to the Khārijites (by which they usually denote the militants, such as the Azāriqa and Najdāt), and they consider it offensive to make such connections.[6] Their aversion is not wholly unjustified: although the early Ibāḍiyya quickly and vehemently opposed those more confrontational Khārijite groups of Azāriqa and Najdāt, whose names became more and more synonymous with Khārijism as a whole, Islamic polemical writings nonetheless classed them all together. Indeed the term *khawārij* has been used in polemical and heresiographical materials over the centuries as a synonym for extremism, brutality, and deviance, such that most Muslims know only this contrived negative image. Yet the Ibāḍiyya have survived for nearly thirteen centuries, creating vibrant societies in the areas where they endured, while the core activities of the militant Azāriqa and Najdāt—two of the chief Khārijite groups that are used to tarnish the image of the Khārijites as a whole—lasted hardly twenty years.[7] Given such manipulations of history, Ibāḍī reactions to being labeled *khawārij* are hardly surprising or unwarranted.

Nevertheless those groups that came to be known as the Ibāḍiyya clearly looked back favorably on certain persons and groups, especially the Muḥakkima and early *shurāt,* who comprised a portion of what would later be recognized by most Muslims as the Khārijites. They preserved their memories in poetry and stories, treated them as authoritative, linked themselves to them in chains of legitimacy, and otherwise fashioned their identity around them. In this way it is equally defensible to say that the Ibāḍiyya are in fact linked to certain currents within the movement dubbed collectively as the Khārijites.

What, then, should be done in the face of such overtaxed taxonomies? As this book is ultimately concerned with the creation of Ibāḍī identity, it proposes to drop *khawārij* as a blanket term for all of the various subgroups usually classed by that term and to use, whenever possible, the specific monikers of the subgroups under discussion. Thus when discussing the Muḥakkima and early *shurāt,* these terms are preferred as the more accurate (and perhaps more value neutral) descriptors of the actual groups. However, as certain of the Muḥakkima also seem to have referred to themselves as *shurāt,* the label *shurāt* is sometimes preferred to refer to the whole of the movement before the advent of the second *fitna.* The term "Khārijite" will be reserved for militant groups (that is, Azāriqa, Najdāt, and so forth) operating during and after the second *fitna,* and for the most part this usage tends to dovetail with how early Ibāḍī authors used the term (albeit polemically).[8] The term also appears in several Azraqite poems as a self-designation with positive connotations.[9] However, "Khārijite" will also be employed in certain cases, especially when non-Ibāḍī authors use the word as a means to paint all of the various subgroups with the same brush.

This book is about the formation of early *shurāt* and Ibāḍī identity through the medium of literature on martyrs and ascetics and in relation to "other" non-*shurāt*/non-Ibāḍīs. In other words, it is a book about how certain groups of people remembered other persons—specifically nobly killed persons (that is, martyrs), those who rejected the world as ascetics, and their enemies—in such a way as to fashion a sense of their own group's uniqueness.[10] Markus notes how the process of identity formation is cumulative: "a continuous biography is the core of our sense of personal identity. This is true no less of a group's sense of identity. It needs to be able to recognize itself as one and the same group enduring through time, the heir of its own past."[11] Broadly speaking, then, the study of early Ibāḍī identity is also a study of tradition and how certain kinds of traditions accumulated and became defined first by the *shurāt* and then by the Ibāḍiyya in such a way as to constitute a sense of their respective distinctiveness in the early Islamic world.

Yet the concept of "tradition" is tricky, as the modern Ibāḍī rejection of the moniker "Khārijite" shows, and much of this difficulty comes from the intricate ways that traditions accumulate among religious groups. How is such a concept of tradition to be imagined? How might scholars responsibly speak of the ways that traditions develop? These are complex questions, but in some senses the amassing of tradition among sectarian groups such as the early *shurāt* and the Ibāḍiyya might be said to resemble (from the outsider's perspective) an avalanche. That is to say, at the beginning of any given sectarian movement events, passions, doctrines, and practices provide an impetuous for the movement of the sectarian group down the proverbial mountainside of their history. As the movement gains momentum, much new material will be picked up along the way and mixed with the older material that remains part of the group's tradition. What began as a movement of relatively modest proportions now carries along with it a tremendous and compelling force, but also one that churns and shifts depending on the terrain in which it finds itself. As such, what constituted this avalanche of tradition at its beginning point cannot be said to be the same as what constitutes it further down the slope of history; and yet the avalanche is still considered to be the same avalanche. Likewise the original momentum of the avalanche continues to propel it down the slope, yet the constantly novel terrain in which such a storm exists may divert its parts down their own particular trajectories; yet the momentum of the avalanche as a whole appears not to have changed.[12]

With this metaphor of the avalanche in mind, a few points might be made about the nature of tradition formation before we turn specifically to how the early *shurāt* and Ibāḍiyya formed crucial aspects of their sectarian identities by fashioning narratives about their martyrs and ascetics. Religious traditions are deceptively conservative in that they claim to preserve an original, unchanged vision for the salvation of humankind. While this claim remains true in some senses, it is equally true that religious traditions accumulate vast amounts of material (doctrine, practices, but also literary genres, themes, and more) as they emerge into and progress through history. Such is the case of the *shurāt* and the Ibāḍiyya, who claimed to preserve the original message of Islam in its pristine form and yet in their literature drew from sources that scholars might not label strictly "Islamic." These sources included pre-Islamic materials as well as ideas, genres, themes, and motifs from the milieu of late antiquity.

How can this aspect of accumulation within a specific religious tradition, such as the *shurāt* or Ibāḍiyya, be responsibly analyzed? It is important to be clear about how they cannot be analyzed: what this study is emphatically *not* saying is that *shurāt* and Ibāḍīs borrowed from their late antique and early Islamic religious neighbors in some crass or simplistic way the complex of attitudes that went into the notions of martyrdom, asceticism, or boundary maintenance. It is a bit fruitless to parse what elements of the concept of *shirā'* might be identified as "early Islamic," "Christian," "Manichean," or indigenously "*shārī*." In addition such a search for "origins" assumes the autochthonous character of images and symbols that had already enjoyed a wide circulation in the world of late antiquity and early Islamdom.

Rather, more organic comparisons are required to describe the subtle ways that traditions take on their shapes and forms within certain cultural contexts. To this end, and in addition to the image of the avalanche, this study employs metaphors of sound, lighting, and location to suggest a complex process whereby geographically proximate religious groups in late antiquity and the early Islamic eras (specifically, Mesopotamia and Persia) lived in a world where the marketplace of religious ideas remained determinedly public and therefore replete with familiar topoi and imagery. Such a culture (writ large) produced religious groups with degrees of overlapping (though not identical) articulations of religious concepts. As participants in this world, *shurāt* (and later Ibāḍī) hagiographical literature must be understood in relation to, rather than in isolation from, the broader world in which the *shurāt,* Khārijites, and Ibāḍiyya operated.

Geography, then, is important. Though scholars will probably never be able to pin down exact texts with which the *shurāt* may or may not have been familiar or draw direct links between *shurāt* and Ibāḍī groups and specific communities of Christians or others, it is possible to see how the forms and depictions of asceticism and martyrdom that predominate in former Sāsānian and Byzantine administered areas seem to have found a profound resonance in early *shurāt* and Ibāḍī expressions of asceticism and martyrdom. Just as certain frequencies of vibration in a string can produce similar resonances in a different string, so too a publically known genre of literature, such as martyrdom, might function in broadly similar ways across different traditions, being intrinsic to none of them. In crafting the stories of their ascetics and "very special dead," the *shurāt,* it seems, took from the local syllabary of signs and symbols that was available to them, and this meant that, in addition to the general Islamic tendency to imbibe late antique narrative forms/structures, they tended to express in their poems and writings (such as they are preserved) an aesthetic more at home with what came to be known as (though is no longer called) "Nestorian" and "Jacobite" forms of asceticism and martyrdom, as well as a spirit-body dualism that recalls so-called "gnostic" and Manichean musings on the subject. This set of images, narratives, and poems was then inherited by the Ibāḍiyya, who put it to their own uses.

At the same time, it is important not to lose a sense of proportion when thinking about the extent to which the various groups of the late antique Middle East may or may not have "influenced" the *shurāt* and Ibāḍiyya. For this reason it is perhaps appropriate to think of the relationship between different traditions of martyrdom narratives in terms of lighting on a stage: our particular stage will be firmly occupied by the stories of the Muḥakkima, *shurāt,* and the Ibāḍiyya (and even at times the militant Khārijites), but other groups' tales will provide backlighting, illuminating the narratives of the *shurāt* and Ibāḍī martyrs and ascetics in ways not previously considered.

Another difficult aspect of describing the process of tradition accumulation involves deciding when such accumulation begins. After all, Islam is as much a product of its pre-Islamic and late antique context as it is the revelations of the Qur'ān and the experiences of the early Islamic community. Likewise the *shurāt* are as much the creation of the early Islamic venture as they are their Arabian, Sāsānian-Mesopotamian/Persian, and later North African contexts. The accumulation of tradition on the grand scale, then, cannot really be said to "begin" at any distinct moment in history. On the scale of discrete movements and subgroups, of course, the historian might indeed find certain moments that define the beginning of a group, as well as those remembered events that give the group some definition. Such a micro-view of history, however, tends to sacrifice the larger contexts in which such groups operate, and so the two approaches—macro and micro—must be balanced. To this end, Boyarin's suggestion that scholars image the relationship between religious traditions as a continuum of practices and identities that exists between poles proves helpful.[13]

Finally, there is the problem of how to describe a tradition that is constantly shifting, changing, and adapting to its ever-evolving context. When looking at now largely defunct medieval Islamic sectarian movements—movements that were despised by some of the authors who wrote about them—the problem is compounded by the issue of sources. Thus a scholar should expect to find (and indeed does find) that Islamic sources (Ibāḍī and other) preserve the stories and poems of the early *shurāt* in a form and manner that suited the needs of the author, editor, or group who preserved them at the moment in time when they were penned. In fact, the nature of the sources on the early *shurāt* is most complicated, presenting the scholar with layers of authors and editors, each of whom had his own agenda in creating the work. Indeed the difficulties of Islamic historiography—layers of authors and editors, obscure motivations, and incomplete or contradictory accounts, to name but a few—are well known to students of Islamic history and must be addressed in some fashion.[14]

This study, then, broadly examines the accumulation of religious traditions by specifically focusing on the theme of identity among the early Ibāḍiyya. It argues that the textual accumulations and doctrinal trajectories that brought into being a distinctive sense of Ibāḍī identity, especially insofar as this identity was constructed and maintained through the inherited stories of the early ascetics and martyrs as well as the tyrants, oppressors, and enemies who persecuted them, must be understood with reference to the *shurāt* narratives that the Ibāḍiyya appropriated and the late antique and early Islamic hagiographical traditions that informed them both. That is, the early *shurāt* as well as the Ibāḍiyya who followed them articulated stories about their ascetics and noble dead in ways that resonated with how such stories were crafted in late antiquity, and as such, their narratives operated, as they did in late antiquity, to create group identity by focusing memory on the martyrs. Of course the *shurāt* and early Ibāḍiyya had their own reasons for crafting hagiography, and this research maintains sensitivity to the distinctive ways that the *shurāt* and Ibāḍīs told the stories of those ascetics and martyrs.

Two aspects of this study should be emphasized from the outset. First, due to space constraints this book focuses primarily on the comparisons that can be drawn between the hagiographical literatures of various Middle Eastern religious groups of late antiquity and those of the *shurāt,* followed by the Ibāḍiyya, in the early Islamic period. As such, it treats but lightly the question of the pre-Islamic Arabian contexts for the early *shurāt* and Ibāḍiyya, just as little space is used discussing the hagiography associated with the Prophetic and early Islamic periods. For example, the issue of tribal affiliations (what Ibn Khaldūn and others identified as *ʿasabiyya*) among the early Khārijites and Ibāḍiyya receives scant attention, though it is certainly an issue of significance in the early Islamic period. Likewise the vast and important literature on asceticism among the wider Islamic community, among those later understood to be Ṣūfī Muslims and those who practiced asceticism as frontier *ghāzī*-warriors (as represented, for example, by Ibn al-Mubārak), has been abbreviated in the interest of space. Happily these and other pre-Islamic/ early Islamic contexts to the emergence of the *shurāt* and Ibāḍiyya have been explored in other works, leaving this study to illumine a relatively unexplored aspect of *shurāt*/Ibāḍī history. It is therefore hoped that this book might be read in conjunction with and complement other works that treat the pre-Islamic and early Islamic heritage of the *shurāt* and Ibāḍiyya.[15]

Second, the book does not delve into the pre-Islamic, and largely Christian, backgrounds of the various North African Berber groups, even though these clearly remain vital to understanding the emergence of Ibāḍism and Ṣufrism there in the mid-second/eighth centuries.[16] In particular, the revival of Donatism in the eastern Maghrib in the sixth century offered important resonances with the widespread *shurāt* and later Ibāḍī notion of removing unworthy leaders. Moreover, Roman Catholic persecution of Donatists created North African martyrs, such as those whose relics were deposited at Jabal Teioualt (near Telerghma in present-day Algeria) in the year 637 C.E.[17] The various Christian populations of North Africa had complex ways of understanding what their traditions meant and (as is common in the history of religions) often incorporated ancient pagan notions into their systems of belief.[18] The religious geography of North Africa (especially in its Donatist Christian guise), then, undoubtedly played an important role in the Berber adoption of Ṣufrism and Ibāḍism, even as the presence of indigenous North African martyrdom traditions likely whetted North African Ibāḍī appetites for the martyrdom stories emanating from Iraq. Nevertheless *shurāt* martyrdom narratives, upon which eastern Ibāḍī authors later built their own hagiographies, clearly originated in the Islamic Mashriq (east) and only later made their way to the Maghrib (west).[19] For this reason this study remains primarily focused on the religious contexts of the Islamic Mashriq.

Cobb argues that human beings create order "by first categorizing the world, then identifying with certain groups, and finally accepting—and when necessary enacting—their behavioral norms."[20] As "identity forming texts," narratives about the martyrs categorized the world into heroes—ascetics, martyrs, and saints, as well as those who recognized, revered, and then followed their example—and enemies, opponents, and oppressors, along with those who supported them. Perkins has drawn attention to how early Christians constructed group identity by participating in the larger, cultural discourses about the suffering human body.[21] These metanarratives "of a meaningful, useable past" accomplished certain work: namely, they remembered the collective suffering of the ascetics and martyrs and in doing so bounded a community around them.[22] Castelli calls this "memory work" a form of "culture making" and highlights its paradoxical natures whereby suffering became salvation, persecution became martyrdom, and powerlessness became power.[23] In a similar vein, Sizgorich has noted how "the histories of local [Christian] communities flowed through the remembered deeds of holy personages, monks, martyrs, wonder workers and zealous defenders of the faith."[24] Ibāḍī ascetic/martyrdom narratives, along with the *shurāt* stories upon which they were based, established *shurāt* and later Ibāḍī identities in a strikingly similar manner: they created meaningful, usable pasts by focusing group memory on the collective sufferings—even the very bodies—of the ascetics and "very special dead."

Following Castelli, Perkins, Cobb, and others, this study treats the *shurāt* and early Ibāḍī martyrdom narratives as "literary creations designed to meet particular communal needs," in particular the need to establish identity. As such, martyrdom narratives are treated as rhetorical devices that need to be appreciated for their literary power and analyzed accordingly in their own specific contexts as well as in the broader context of late antiquity and early Islam.[25] Of course a historical perspective on the texts is important to understanding the persons and authors/editors under investigation, but the materials as they have been preserved must not be confused with "history." The stories and poems of the *shurāt* were written for reasons other than preserving an impartial record of events: martyr narratives could be rhetorical, inspirational, motivational, meant to convey a certain ethical truth, or employed to establish communal identities; poetry eulogizing the *shurāt* necessarily cared to communicate not "what really happened" but rather the poet's emotive response to those he (or she) cared to hold up as exemplary for whatever reason. Moreover *shurāt* material comes mediated through the lenses of one or more medieval editors, many of whom were hostile to the "Khārijites" as a whole. Even silent editors, such as al-Ṭabarī, broke their silence to accuse the *khawārij* of lying, and this fact alone should give pause to consider the sources with extreme care.[26]

This study, then, is concerned with the narratives of the early *shurāt* and then with the Ibāḍiyya who absorbed some of their materials. Hagiographical literature is particularly well suited to the study of tradition accumulation across confessional boundaries because it was prone to crossing (and sometimes recrossing) linguistic boundaries.[27] In other words, hagiography tended to be promiscuous, without being the unique possession of any given religious tradition (even though particular texts are very much the products of specific contexts and are studied as such).

Moreover hagiography and martyrdom literature tended to be public genres of literature. They often served some political or theological purpose—they were "propaganda" of a sort[28]—and therefore needed to be proclaimed for all to hear. Martyrdom texts were, in fact, often read aloud to large audiences, whether at festivals marking martyrs' "birthdays" (that is, the anniversaries of their martyrdom), at the tombs of the martyrs, or in other private venues. The martyrdom of Polycarp, for example, attests to a commemorative celebration held at his tomb on the anniversary of his "birthday."[29] Similarly the martyrdom of Mār Pinḥas exhorts its audience to "listen to the reading aloud of the story of this miraculous man."[30] The aural quality of Christian martyrdom texts has been addressed by several scholars, who point toward the didactic function of the texts in creating Christian identities.[31] For the purposes of this study, what is important is the public quality of martyrdom texts, which, perhaps more so than other kinds of religious texts (with the exception of the liturgies), speak toward a kind of communal culture of martyrdom. In other words, martyrdom texts were known to broader swaths of the late antique Middle Eastern population in a way that, for example, theological texts might not be. Such public access to martyrdom texts is one way to explain continuities in themes and topoi across different religious traditions. It is plausible, then, that late antique hagiographical traditions provide a context out of which *shurāt* and later Ibāḍī ideals on the subject of martyrdom and asceticism developed.

Noteworthy in this regard is how the *shurāt* used the genre of poetry to speak about their martyrs. This poetry betrays a curious mix of Arabian, late antique monotheist (even dualist) themes and images as well as the specifically *shārī*-Islamic ones, many of which present themselves in strange and interesting combinations. While poetry presents its subject in its own way—that is, as idealized, ideological, defiant, and employed to persuade and missionize—in the end poetry is another public genre; in fact many of the *shurāt* poems examined here were publically recited eulogies. Thus, like their Christian counterparts, the early *shurāt* employed a public venue to memorialize their very special dead.

So too ascetic communities in late antiquity and the early Islamic period made the phenomenon of asceticism something eminently public: although individual ascetics and monastic communities desired isolation and separation from the world, it is clear that their ascetic practices were known to and held some value for those living in proximity to the ascetic. Recalling the vast complex outside of present-day Aleppo that sprang up around a figure such as Saint Simon the Stylite, it is clear that ascetic practices were not only well known but also esteemed by broad sections of late antique and early Islamic societies. Again, it is the public quality of these practices that allows for a discussion of the broadly shared nexus of signs and symbols related to them.

Another advantage to the comparative study of hagiography and identity among the early *shurāt* and Ibāḍiyya comes from the fact that the hagiographical tradition of the late antique Middle East is rich with sources and thus ripe with examples for comparison. Syriac preserved an enormous amount of hagiographical material devoted to saints, ascetics, and martyrs—both indigenous and in translation from other languages such as Greek, Armenian, Coptic, Ethiopic, and Georgian. These hagiographical endeavors vary greatly in style, form, and purpose, and many have yet to be properly studied.[32] Arabic too possessed its own Christian literature, which included poetry, hagiography, and liturgy, though almost none of this early material survives.

The tendency of hagiographical material to cross linguistic boundaries, the wealth of hagiographical sources and their public nature, combined with the geographical proximity of Christian, Manichean, "gnostic," and other types of groups to the early *shurāt* and Ibāḍiyya all lend plausibility to a project of comparative hagiography. Based on such comparisons, one can note that *shurāt* notions of asceticism and martyrdom (that is, their conception of *shirā'*) sit comfortably among the various articulations of martyrdom and asceticism in the late antique and early Islamic Middle East and can be viewed as a variant—albeit a variant specific to the *shurāt*—on commonly, though broadly, held themes related to the rejection of the material world. Just as such ideas provided a powerful means by which late antique and early Islamic groups fashioned their sense of identity, so too the early *shurāt* molded a sense of their group around their martyrs and ascetics.

That the milieu of late antiquity served as the context for the early *shurāt* has been proposed by Morony, who suggests that "the Christian background or connections of some of the Khawārij may have contributed to the way their ideas were developed and were expressed."[33] Regarding the *shurāt,* he notes that while the sentiment expressed in Qur'ān 9:111—that God purchases the lives and property of those Muslims who fight in his cause—forms the basis for the notion of *shirā',* the concept mirrors in certain ways the contemporaneous Christian rejections of material values.[34] Morony cites Ephrēm Syrus, who thought of monks as "dead to the material world," as well as the monastic rules of Isaac of Nineveh, wherein the monk is exhorted to die in the "war for God" and to prepare for death beforehand as "one who has no further life in this world," as reflective of the conception of *shirā'* with its attendant connections between asceticism and death.[35]

Indeed the concept of *shirā'* does share a variety of characteristics with specifically Eastern Christian concepts of monastic renunciation as premature death whereby the ascetic became "the successor to the martyr."[36] Accordingly the *shāri,* like the Christian ascetic, could be said to reject the material world in favor of ascetic praxis. But Morony's insight can be pushed yet further and generalized beyond even the Christian communities of the "Barbarian Plain" and the Sāsānian Empire.[37] For example, the description of Ephrēm's model ascetic—the renunciant who lived outside of civilization like a wild animal, letting his hair and nails grow long, eating wild fruits and roots, wearing bundles of straw or leaves or wearing nothing at all—approximates some of what is reported about the pagan ascetics of Syrio-Mesopotamia.[38] Even Socrates, in Plato's *Phaedo,* tells his interlocutor Simmias that "the one aim of those who practice philosophy in the proper manner is to practice for dying and death . . . the soul of the philosopher most disdains the body, flees from it and seeks to be by itself."[39]

Moreover it is clear that Christian writings praising asceticism and martyrdom enjoyed a currency beyond the circles of Christian readers who produced them: the *Acts of Thomas,* an important second-century product of the Syriac-speaking community, was also popular among Manicheans and Marcionites.[40] Models of asceticism and martyrdom, then, as well as the notions that supported them must be viewed as part of a wider syllabary that was, in its broadest outlines, common to many of the confessional communities of late antiquity.

There are, of course, some specific comparisons to be made between the *shurāt* and the world of late antiquity. Regarding the Islamic concept of martyrdom, Lewinstein argues that the Qur'ān speaks of martyrs not with the root *sh-h-d* but with circumlocutions (that is, "those slain in the way of God") and that the Qur'ān does not use the term *shahīd* in a technical sense meaning martyrs.[41] Only in later periods and in conformity with how Christians used the term as "witness" (that is, in Greek, *martyr;* in Syriac, *sāhdā*) did Muslims begin to associate the notion of martyrdom with "witnessing" and to read the idea of martyrdom into the Qur'ānic passages where the root *sh-h-d* appears. Although the specifics of his argument can be debated,[42] this problem, for Lewinstein, points toward a larger issue surrounding the Islamic notion of martyrdom in comparison with that of the Christian: Christians forged their notions of martyrdom under conditions of persecution and political failure, while Muslims enjoyed the stunning successes of the early conquests.[43] Certainly both had their martyrs, but for Christians, martyrdom began as a means by which they asserted "heavenly victory" in the face of earthy defeat and emphasized the "religious value of suffering and death."[44] Because Muslims did not suffer the political humiliations of the early Christians, martyrdom for them took on the strong connotations of striving against idolatry and injustice. For the *shurāt* and Ibāḍiyya, however, the Christian notion of martyrdom resonated still, for the *shurāt* also emerged from catastrophic political failures and suffered the persecutions of their fellow Muslims. In this sense comparisons between *shurāt* and Ibāḍī hagiographies and late antique hagiographical materials remain particularly relevant insofar as the two groups share a similar formative experience.

An ancillary concern remains with the textual sources for the hagiographies of the *shurāt* and Ibāḍiyya. It is the contention of this work that the *shurāt* produced their own hagiographical cycles and that these original works formed the basis for the accounts in later Iraqi non-Ibāḍī, as well as Ibāḍī, sources. That is, the reports on the Muḥakkima and the early *shurāt* that appear in the extant sources (both Ibāḍī and non-Ibāḍī) originated with *shurāt* authors and poets, though the original materials (in whatever form these may have taken) are now lost. This shared source accounts for some of the profound parallels that can be found between Iraqi (non-Ibāḍī) chronicles and North African Ibāḍī prosopographical literature. In proposing the existence of these early *shurāt* cycles, this study hopes to draw attention to their hagiographical nature: often such reports (as they survive in quotations in later sources) are treated as transparent historical records of the early *shurāt*.[45]

By way of balancing the overall focus on the late antique Middle Eastern backdrop to the emergence of the *shurāt* and the Ibāḍiyya, the approach here breaks with the relatively light treatment of pre-Islamic and early Islamic topics to offer a discussion on the relationship of early *shurāt*—even early Khārijite (that is, Azraqite) and Ibāḍī—poetry to the larger tradition of pre-Islamic and early Islamic Arabic poetry. Again in the interest of space, a single theme, that of the wine cup as poisoned cup of death, has been chosen as a means to explore how and to what extent *shurāt* poets elaborated on preexisting themes in Arabic poetry. As the poetry of the *shurāt*/Khārijites has been largely underutilized, a fuller discussion of this poetry in its own cultural and social contexts is appropriate and will augment the otherwise necessarily brief discussions of the Arab-Islamic contributions to the *shurāt* and Ibāḍī traditions.

Also worth examining is just how the *shurāt* fashioned (or were said to have fashioned) their identity in relation to others, especially those considered enemies, opponents, and oppressors. Put another way, this study investigates "boundary themes" in early Islamic writings by and about those labeled the *khawārij*.[46] As the Muḥakkima and early *shurāt* were the first distinct sectarian groups to emerge from the wider Islamic community, the examination of how they differentiated themselves from other Muslims remains vital to understanding their sense of identity. Yet the way that the Muḥakkima and *shurāt* differentiated themselves—specifically how they designated their Islamic opponents using the Qur'ānic terminology of *kufr* (ingratitude, unfaithfulness) and *shirk* (polytheism)—remained one of the most contentious aspects of their movement, generating controversy between later militant and quietist Khārijite groups over the nature and implications of such a designation as well as providing their opponents a basis for their polemics against them. The examination of boundary themes among the Muḥakkima and early *shurāt* shows, through a comparison of boundary themes and terminology in historical and heresiographical sources, that the ways in which the Muḥakkima and early *shurāt* are portrayed to have gone about conceptualizing their opponents appear far more nuanced in historical sources than in Islamic heresiography. By implication the image of the *khawārij* as engaged in *takfīr* (accusations of unfaithfulness) must be questioned: specifically it argues that *takfīr* might have indicated not a theological designation of unfaithfulness proper (that is, *being* a *kāfir*) but rather a polemical designation (that is, *acting like* a *kāfir*), without implying the ensuing legal consequences due to those who were (existentially) *kuffār*. Such a usage corresponds to how Jews and Christians sometimes used accusations of unbelief and polytheism in their own polemical discourses. Even Azraqite poetry contains a fair amount of ambiguity and contradiction when it comes to the actual use (and existential implications) of the term *kufr* as a boundary marker. Thus a measure of uncertainty characterizes the ways that the Muḥakkima and early *shurāt* established communal boundaries in the early period. It is only later, and predominantly with the advent of the militant Khārijites, that the action of *takfīr* more and more amounted to an accusation of existential unfaithfulness and implied the legal consequences of such unfaithfulness.

Ibāḍī narratives shared similar textual sources with their non-Ibāḍī counterparts and thus abound with the same stories and literary tropes—particularly of ascetic practice and martyrdom—that appear in non-Ibāḍī reports on the *shurāt*. Clearly the nascent Ibāḍiyya fashioned their identity, in part, by tracing themselves to the early *shurāt*, and they saw themselves as adopting, in some senses, the *shurāt*'s mantle. In particular, Ibāḍī sources present the figure of Abū Bilāl Mirdās b. Udayya as the epitome of *shurāt*-cum-Ibāḍī qualities. As a pious ascetic and martyr, Abū Bilāl and his followers are put forth as the embodiment of the *shurāt*'s many good virtues. The Ibāḍiyya adapted the inherited *shurāt* image for their own purposes, editing the stories of problematic early *shurāt* and applying the appellation of *shārī* to certain early Ibāḍī figures, such as Ṭālib al-Ḥaqq and al-Julandā b. Mas'ūd, who, as little more than pious administrators, stretch the limits of what was traditionally considered *shirā'*. In this way the Ibāḍiyya added their own novel twists to the notion of *shirā'*, even while they deployed the image of *shurāt* in familiar ways as a means to focus group identity on those considered martyrs and thereby to create a sense of group identity.

Similarly the Ibāḍī imāms and *'ulamā'* adapted the concept of *shirā'* to conditions in Oman, where the once spontaneous act of *shirā'* among the early rebels and martyrs had given way to the *shurāt* as a kind of volunteer army, one that was to fight for the establishment and defense of Ibāḍism. This group, however, seemingly lacked discipline and resolve, such that certain Omani Ibāḍī *'ulamā'* argued for greater control over them. During the first Omani Ibāḍī imāmate, however, the *shurāt* soldiers of Oman could not escape its tribal milieu, aligning themselves with the various factions that weakened the Ibāḍī polity from within and eventually resulted in its dissolution.

Just as Ibāḍīs inherited and enlarged on earlier martyrdom traditions, so too they elaborated on the theme of boundary maintenance and identity in relation to non-Ibāḍīs, especially insofar as the early Ibāḍiyya succeeded to the theologically ambiguous boundary language of the Muḥakkima and early *shurāt*. In particular, the nascent Ibāḍīs enlarged on the concepts of *walāya* (association) with those considered to be true Muslims and *barā'a* (dissociation) from those considered non-Muslims. Part and parcel of this discussion involved the classification and subsequent treatment of non-Ibāḍīs, a topic made more pressing by the need to distinguish the emerging Ibāḍiyya from the militant Azraqites and Najdites. Ibāḍī taxonomies of unfaithfulness from the early period, however, do not possess a high degree of uniformity either in the terminology mustered to classify non-Ibāḍīs or in the categories used to organize them. Early Ibāḍīs seemed to agree on only two points: that non-Ibāḍīs were not full Muslims, but that those who claimed to believe in God and follow his prophet Muḥammad (that is, those who claimed to be Muslims) could neither be treated as *mushrikūn* (polytheists) nor as other types of less-than-full believers (such as the *ahl al-kitāb*). Beyond these two positions, early Ibāḍī authors offered a variety of taxonomical arrangements meant to sort non-Ibāḍīs into recognizable categories and to offer guidance on how members of any given category should be treated.

The importance of viewing Ibāḍī hagiographical depictions of the martyrs and saints, as well as their enemies, opponents, and oppressors, as the result of a process of conscious appropriation of earlier *shurāt* texts—texts that had themselves been formed in resonance with the genre expectations of late antique hagiography—comes through in how such a view allows for early *shurāt* and Ibāḍī identities to be appreciated in their vast historical complexity. This perspective offers a corrective to certain strains of scholarship on the Khārijites, which, whether consciously or not, have perpetuated the assumptions of medieval Islamic historians and heresiographers: namely, that the Khārijites and their subgroups possessed coherent, distinctive theologies;[47] that they represent sui-generous anomalies in Islamic history, unconnected both to the world around them and to what preceded them;[48] and that they find their most characteristic and developed articulations—the logical conclusion of their agendas—in the Azāriqa and Najdāt, who are treated as the most representative of their many subgroups.[49] Placing early *shurāt* and Ibāḍī hagiographical narratives back in the context of late antiquity/early Islam reconnects these traditions to their wellsprings, provides for a richer view of their development and of the motivations attributed to them, and allows for a more nuanced understanding of the discourse of asceticism and noble death among them.

Chapter 1

Late Antique and Early Islamic Contexts

The religious geography of the late antique Middle East set the stage for the eventual emergence of *shurāt* and Ibāḍī hagiographies insofar as the varied Christian and non-Christian groups of the region possessed their own unique notions of asceticism and martyrdom that collectively formed a highly developed and broadly shared syllabary of signs and symbols, and with which the Islamic hagiographical tradition resonated. The genre of hagiography—that is, literature about saints, martyrs, ascetics, and other holy persons—captured the attention of many of the religious communities of late antiquity, just as it found its place among the earliest Islamic authors, the *shurāt* movement, and eventually the Ibāḍiyya. The popularity of hagiographical literature in the late antique Middle East resulted in a vast amount of writings, and thus any author who wishes to draw upon them must necessarily do so selectively. As the concern in this study is ultimately with the Muḥakkima, early *shurāt,* and the Ibāḍiyya, the focus as much as possible is on literature that developed in the areas where these groups were active, especially (though not exclusively) Mesopotamia, Persia, and the Arabian Peninsula. As it is not possible to do so in an exhaustive manner, this work as much as possible looks to narratives that would (or could) have been available to the Arabs and early Muslims, drawing specific attention to certain themes and tropes—such as bodies and boundaries—that did in fact make their way into the literature of the early *shurāt* and Ibāḍiyya. One point should be made clear at the outset: the aim here is not to pin down how specific hagiographical texts were appropriated by Islamic groups, as such an endeavor remains difficult if not impossible given the state of the historical record. Throughout this discussion, hagiography is treated (following Jauss) as a "horizon of expectation" toward which different religious groups fashioned stories of their martyrs, ascetics, and holy persons within a more or less defined genre but did so for their own purposes.[1] Such an approach allows for an appreciation of how certain broadly shared themes resonated among different religious groups even as those groups appropriated them for their own purposes.

The Religious Geography of the Late Antique Middle East

Of the many religious populations that made up the late antique Middle East, the various groups of Christians, with their developed martyrdom and ascetic traditions, form the most verdant context for its study in the early Islamic community and by extension among the Muḥakkima and early *shurāt* movements. The *shurāt*'s presence in Iraq's two main cities of Kūfa and Basra makes the history of the Christians in the Sāsānian realm, especially those Christians at al-Ḥīra (on the Euphrates River south of present-day Kūfa), particularly relevant to the study of early hagiographical literature among Muslims. However, the existence and potential contributions to the genre of Christians from the Byzantine Empire, the Levant, and Ethiopia must not be forgotten, nor should that of the Christians in the Arabian Peninsula, in particular at Najrān. Also vital to the religious geography of the late antique Middle East were the non-Christian communities of Jews, Manicheans, and pagans, though the possible resonance between their hagiographical endeavors and those of the *shurāt* and Ibāḍīs is difficult to determine.

When it comes to the spread of religious ideas to the pre-Islamic Arabs and later to the Muslims, the Byzantine Empire remained, in many ways, the ancient power most removed from the affairs of the Arabian Peninsula. Unlike the Sāsānian, it was not completely conquered and assimilated by the early Islamic state. Nevertheless the Byzantine state remained a powerful player in the late antique world, affecting religious currents in the peninsula indirectly or through their vassals, the Ghassānids, or their Ethiopian allies.[2] While many of the first Byzantine emperors followed Arianism, a form of Christianity that preached a stricter view of the oneness of God and rejected in part the equality of the Father and Son as well as the divinity of Christ, by the end of the fourth century C.E. the second general council of Constantinople (381 C.E.) affirmed the doctrines first put forth at Nicaea (325 C.E.) and set the stage for the eventual ascendancy of what is sometimes called "Chalcedonian" Christianity (at times referred to as Byzantine "Orthodoxy") in the central lands of the Byzantine Empire. Chalcedonian Christianity/Byzantine orthodoxy, however, would have to contend with several offshoots: Nestorius, the bishop of Antioch, had preached that there were two separate natures, one of the Father and one of the Son, coexisting in Christ.[3] He was opposed for his "diphysite" views by the Council of Ephesus in 431 C.E. and condemned as a heretic. Out of Alexandria came the notion, later dubbed "monophysitism," that the two natures of Christ became a unified divine nature at the incarnation, a position that was equally rejected by Rome and Constantinople. The Byzantine emperor Marcian again brought these Christological issues to the fore by convening in 451 C.E. the forth ecumenical council of Chalcedon, where the "orthodox" stressed the two perfect, indivisible, but separate natures of Christ, thus condemning both diphysites and monophysites alike and imagining itself as the "middle way" between them.[4]

Monophysitism and diphytism, even Arianism, however, did not disappear with their condemnation by the "orthodox." In fact, it is not clear when monophysites and diphysites separated into two distinct factions of "Jacobites" (now known as the Syriac Orthodox Church) and "Nestorians" (that is, the Church of the East); Morony, for example, argues that it was late in the sixth century when such a move began, to be completed in the seventh century.[5] When the Nestorian theological school at Nisibis in 540 C.E. closed, it was refounded at al-Ḥīra. This renewed interest in Nestorianism was bolstered by growing Nestorian missionary activities, such that the monophysite monks living in al-Ḥīra seem to have relocated to Najrān.[6] By 592 C.E. the last Lakhmid ruler, al-Nuʿmān III, officially accepted the Nestorian version of Christianity after being miraculously cured by the Nestorian bishop of Mosul.[7] Such were the beginnings of a recognizably Nestorian brand of Eastern Christianity.

While Nestorianism later became the official church operating under the Sāsānian Empire, monophysitism became ever more entrenched in Syria and Egypt as a protest against the orthodoxy emanating out of Constantinople. Such was the case with the Arab allies of the Byzantines, the Ghassānids, a branch of the Azd tribal group who migrated north to settle within Byzantine territory around 490 C.E. and converted to monophysite Christianity.[8] Concluding a treaty with the Byzantines in 502–3, the Ghassānids acted as troops for the empire in its many conflicts with the Sāsānians during the sixth and early seventh centuries. The Ghassānids also protected the borders of the Byzantine Empire from the predations of Arab Bedouins, guarded the trade routes, and raided periodically into the Hijāz.

The Ghassānids, even though formally allied to the Byzantines, staunchly protected and promoted monophysite Christianity among their Arab neighbors, even at the expense of their Byzantine patrons.[9] They sent missionaries to Najrān and maintained good contacts with the Christians there. The Ghassānid king Ḥārith b. Jabala managed to get two monophysite bishops, Theodorus and Jacob Baradaeus (after whom the group was called "Jacobite"), ordained in Syria around 540 C.E. These bishops revived the monophysite church after the Byzantine emperor Justin I (r. 518–27 C.E.) had disestablished it. The Ghassānids also intervened against divisive movements within the church, using their clout to stamp out "heretical" movements and settle scores between patriarchal sees. Their unflinching support ultimately cost the Ghassānids their relations with Constantinople: Ḥārith's son Mundhir was arrested by the emperor in 580 C.E., and his son Nuʿmān was arrested two or three years later. The Jacobite Church, however, survived, spreading eventually as far as India.

As important as the Byzantines and their Arab allies were to the affairs of the Arabian Peninsula, the Sāsānian Empire and its Christians exerted the greatest influence over it. Christianity had early penetrated the territories of what became the Sāsānian realm. Syriac sources, for example, attest to a bishop in Kirkūk as early as 117 C.E. Al-ʿAnbār (Pērōz Shābūr) was another important early site that by 420 C.E. housed a substantial community, so much so that it later boasted both monophysite and Nestorian bishops. Al-Ḥīra, under the control of the Arab Lakhmids (who were themselves Sāsānian vassals), had a bishop as early as 410 C.E. (that is, Hosea, who attended the synod of that year).[10] The first landmark date for the history of Christianity in the Sāsānian realm came in 410 C.E., when the first synod of the *catholicos* Mār Isaac of Seleucia-Ctesiphon established the followers of the bishop of Constantinople, Nestorius (ca. 381–451 C.E.), as a church. By the late fifth century this strand of (the not-yet-called Nestorian) Christianity had become the official, though not the only, Christian church operating in the Sāsānian Empire.[11] A pawn in the ever-growing conflicts between the Sāsānians and Byzantines in the fifth and sixth centuries, the soon-to-be-known-as Nestorian Christians were concentrated in the western parts of the empire: throughout what is today Iraq and parts of Syria. They enjoyed a difficult relationship with the Sāsānian monarchs, at first persecuted heavily and later generally tolerated, with later persecutions being limited to high-class Zoroastrian converts. These Christians also maintained relations with the Arabs of the Arabian Peninsula through their outpost at al-Ḥīra.

The Prophet Muḥammad's contemporaries most certainly knew of the above-mentioned Nuʿmān III, the Christian phylarch of al-Ḥīra who officially brought Christianity to the town around the year 580 C.E. (ten years after the year in which Islamic sources indicate that the Prophet was born).[12] Later sources mention several churches and monasteries at al-Ḥīra, including a theological school.[13] The Christian poet ʿAdī b. Zayd hailed from al-Ḥīra, and many of the Nestorian *catholicoi* were supposed to have been buried there.[14] More important, the pre-Islamic Arabs of the Ḥijāz maintained extensive trade relations with al-Ḥīra.[15] As an Arab center, such relations would have been vital for familiarizing the Arabs of the peninsula with the basic narratives, rituals, and structures of late antique Eastern Christianity. Given that the Arabs of al-Ḥīra celebrated their liturgy in Syriac, it remains noteworthy how many of the possibly Christian loan words that appear in the Qur'ān come via the Syriac, suggesting a strong connection to Syriac-speaking regions.[16] Combining its importance to peninsular trade with its strong Syriac Christian traditions, al-Ḥīra suggests itself as one of the stronger links between Muḥammad's emergent Arabian monotheism and ancient Middle Eastern, specifically Mesopotamian, Christianity.

Al-Ḥīra was also considered part of the so-called "Barbarian plain," the Syrian steppe that spread out around Ruṣāfa (in present-day Syria) and which functioned as a place of meeting and a neutral territory of sorts between the Byzantine and Sāsānian realms.[17] Although al-Ḥīra clearly found itself within the Sāsānaian political orbit and thereby more officially attuned to the emerging Nestorian Church with its attendant diphysite views, monks and other monophysite Christians fleeing Justin's persecution of the Monophysites (518–23 C.E.) found refuge at al-Ḥīra. Monophysite missionaries too were attracted to the city and found fertile ground for conversions to their own brand of salvation.

One Christian group that inhabited al-Ḥīra remains of particular interest, especially because members practiced a peculiar form of social organization that complicated the usual tribal system maintained by Arabs. This group was known as the ʿIbād, a term that referred to the sedentary Christian population of al-Ḥīra.[18] Ibn al-Kalbī mentions two other groups inhabiting al-Ḥīra: the Tanūkh, a conglomeration of southern Arab clans; and the "confederates" (*aḥlāf*), groups of recently immigrated Arab clans from different tribes who sought protection through clientship with a more powerful tribe. The Tanūkh were also Christian but were distinguished from the ʿIbād by the maintenance of their tribal identity. The ʿIbād, on the other hand, were, as al-Jawharī observes, "various tribes from the houses of the ʿArabs who grouped together in al-Ḥīra by their Christianity."[19] The ʿIbād, then, were unique in that they were an amalgam of different tribal groupings welded together by a shared confessional religion. Among the tribes represented in the ʿIbād were the Tamīm, Azd/Mazīn, Lakhm, Ṭayyi', Liḥyān, Rabīʿa, Muḍar, and Iyād.[20] Members of the ʿIbād maintained their tribal affiliation, as was the case with the Tamīmī clan of the Banū Ayyūb, whose members included the poet ʿAdī b. Zayd and several highly placed bishops and political figures in al-Ḥīra. It seems, therefore, as if ʿIbād was something of a title, claimed only by those of established families: Abū al-Baqā' implies as much when he states that the ʿIbād "formed the majority and were the noble people of al-Ḥīra, the people of 'good families' (*buyūtāt*)."[21] They were Arabs who spoke Arabic but had adopted the manners of the local Aramaic population, including the use of Syriac as a liturgical language—enough so to cause confusion to the conquering Arabs, who wondered whether they were true Arabs or not. As Morony has argued, the differences between monophysite and Nestorian Christianity were not well articulated until the late sixth century, so the ʿIbād were probably not solidly for one camp until much later: certainly by the time of the Arab-Islamic conquests the people of al-Ḥīra identified with the Nestorian perspective.

Al-Ḥīra was not alone in introducing Christianity to the pre-Islamic Arabs. In fact several Christian communities existed in the Arabian Peninsula before the coming of Islam. Most famous, perhaps, was the community, an episcopate with several bishops,[22] at Najrān, whose persecution at the hands of Yūsuf Dhū Nuwwās was made famous by early Christian writing in Greek and Syriac but also among Muslims because of its probable mention in the Qur'ān.[23] In addition to the ill-fated community at Najrān, there were several other groups of Christians living in or near the peninsula. Tribes from the north of Arabia boasted Christian converts or even entire subgroups, such as the Ash'ar and the Farāsān branch of the Taghlib that resided in Mukhā. Nestorian Christians lived along the east coast and Persian Gulf: the Banū As'ad b. 'Abd al-'Uzzā, the Kalb, Ṭayy, Tamīm, and 'Ibād; Banū 'Udhra and 'Ijl from al-Yamāma (also between al-Ḥīra and Basra); and Kinda, Taghlib, and Banū Judham. Christians also could be found among the Banū Shaybān in al-Hajar.[24]

In Oman and Baḥrayn, Christianity was solidly established, with a metropolitan see and Christian community at al-Mazūn.[25] Christians could be found among the 'Abd al-Qays of eastern Arabia, the Bakr b. Wā'il of Yamāma and Baḥrayn, as well as the Ḥanīfa b. Lujaym (Yamāma). Wilkinson cites Ka'b b. Barsha al-Ṭāḥī and Ka'b b. Ṣūr as two prominent Omani Arabs who were Christians (the second of whom converted to Islam and eventually became the first *qāḍī* at Basra). The Nestorian metropolitan at Rēv Ardhashīr (in the Bushire area) extended his responsibility for the Christian community from the gulf all the way to Ceylon.[26] Ṭalūn, al-Ḥaṭṭa, and Hajar were also said to have housed Nestorian bishoprics.[27] Just as with the Christians of al-Ḥīra, those of the gulf were more closely tied to their coreligionists in Mesopotamia, a fact borne out by both tribal histories and church architecture: Toral-Niehoff, for example, speaks of an "independent cultural region that included Babylonia, the Gulf area, and probably also central Arabia."[28]

In southern Arabia the church complex at Najrān was certainly vital to the Christian communities who survived the persecutions of Dhū Nuwwās in the 520s. There were three churches in Ẓafār, three at Qānā, one at Ṣana'ā, and possibly more at other places in south Arabia.[29] Later in the sixth century a bishop known as Gregentius was in Ẓafār. The vibrant presence of Christianity in southern Arabia continued until the Persian invasion of south Arabia in 572 C.E., when the Christians of the region again faced some difficulties.

Although Syriac- and Greek-speaking Christians formed the majorities in the late antique Middle East, also present were smaller groups of Christians who were sometimes problematically labeled "gnostic."[30] The polemical writings of Ephrēm Syrus, for example, mention the overtly dualist Marcionites, who held that the creator of this world, a God of justice, was opposed in his attempts to reward the righteous and punish evil by a malevolent God. Beyond them both was a supreme God of goodness, who sent Christ to teach a message of deliverance from the material plane.[31] Marcionites could be found in parts of Mesopotamia and Persia as well as in the Byzantine realms.

Similarly present in the region were the Valentinians, who held that at the beginning of time a state of perfect "fullness" (Pleroma) reigned, guarded by the primal father (Bythos) and his thirty projections until the passion of one of these heavenly archetypes (Aeons) led to her fall and to the creation of the material world. Valentinians identified the God of the Old Testament as the flawed creator of the material world (Demiurge) and human beings as the highest beings in it, beings who participated in both its spiritual and the material nature. Redemption consisted of recognizing the original primal Father as the true source of divine power, achieving divine "knowledge" (gnosis) and freeing the spirit from its material prison, the world. Such gnosis also had positive consequences within the universal order and contributed to restoring it.[32]

Another "gnostic" group in the late antique Middle East was made up of the Messalians (also known as the Euchites), a sect that was first mentioned by Ephrēm.[33] The Messalians apparently held that human perfection consisted of freedom from the world and its passions and that this state could be achieved solely through prayer and not through the church, baptism, and or any of the other sacraments (hence their name, which was taken from the Syriac for "those who pray"). Although radically dissimilar in many respects to other Christians of the region, what these "gnostic" groups shared with their Nestorian or Jacobite coreligionists was a profound interest in ascetic practices, which was often combined with a view of the material world as the lowest realm of existence—at best a stepping stone to the higher planes of spiritual awareness. This is not to imply that the material world was completely rejected; indeed the ascetic body was often the vehicle through which spiritual truth was enacted. Rather, following Brock and Harvey, among the various Christians of the late antique Middle East there was a sense that "religious behavior [was] equivalent to religious belief," a fact reflected in the intense interest in asceticism whether by laypersons or virtuosos.[34]

In addition to Christians, several non-Christian religious communities, such as those of the Manicheans, populated the world of late antique Mesopotamia and Persia. From what can be reconstructed of the teachings of Mani in their broadest outlines, Manichaeism posited a dualist cosmology of God and Satan, of light and darkness, whereby inherently good light had become embedded in the evil, material world of darkness. The proper home of light, which made up the spirit-essence of human beings, then, was not the human body or the world but a realm of pure spirit. With the direction of prophets sent by God, such as Mani claimed himself to be, human beings could free light from its suffering in the material prison on the body, thereby returning it to its original abode.[35]

Bolstering many of these late antique Christian (and especially the "gnostic" Christian) cosmologies lay a strong current of Neoplatonic thinking. The philosophical movement collectively known as Neoplatonism can be traced to the third-century philosopher Plotinus (d. 270 C.E.). This current of thought enjoyed wide popularity in the late antique world and survived into the medieval period in Europe, North Africa, and the Middle East. Consequently, Neoplatonism's specific articulations became many and varied. Nevertheless certain general concepts, many of them found in the writings of Plotinus, can be found across the Neoplatonic spectrum: especially the notion of the One, the ineffable, unknowable first principle of reality, from whom emanated the creation and to whom all beings could hope to return.[36] For many Neoplatonists, the world was conceived as a material prison from which the spirit sought to escape. Such notions, familiar as they were among the communities of late antiquity, provided scaffolding upon which various religious communities would elaborate a cosmology of salvation through ascetic praxis.

Less obvious in terms of their contributions to the broader swath of late antique notions about martyrdom and asceticism as they resonated with later Islamic groups were various Jewish and pagan groups who were, nonetheless, part of the religious geography of the late antique Middle East. Jews formed the oldest organized religious community in Mesopotamia, and Jewish communities could be found throughout the region (including, for example, on the outskirts of al-Ḥīra).[37] Mesopotamian Jews experienced moments of persecution at the hands of the Sāsānians, just as they did at times under the Byzantines and other Christian polities. Likewise various "pagans" survived into the late antique (and even early Islamic) period, including, for example, long-haired, idol-worshipping animal sacrificers in Mesopotamia.[38] Although paganism did slowly disappear under pressure from the confessional monotheisms, its vestiges endured in the magical and astrological traditions as well as in folklore and popular customs.[39] Taken as a whole, this collectivity of late antique Christian and non-Christian groups, and especially their hagiographical literatures, comprised the larger portrait of notions about and writings on asceticism and martyrdom in the late antique Middle East.

Christian Hagiography under the Sāsānians and in the Arabian Peninsula

Martyrdom had become a standard by which the early Christian Church, in part, had measured itself, and it presented one of the primary venues in which Christians articulated their identity.[40] For these reasons the end of the persecutions of Christians by the fourth century C.E. allowed for certain transformations in identity whereby some Christians elided the martyr ideal with that of the ascetic. Indeed, Brock notes that the ascetic was "in many ways the successor to the martyr"[41] and that several early Christian authors, such as Origen, Clement, and Athanasius, regarded asceticism as the equivalent of, even as training for, martyrdom.[42] Clement, for example, in his *Stromata* writes,

> If the confession of God is martyrdom, each soul that has conducted its affairs purely in knowledge of God and has obeyed the commandments is a martyr both in its life and in its speech, no matter how it may be released from the body, by pouring forth the faith like blood during its entire life up to its departure. For instance, the Lord says in the Gospel, "Whoever leaves father or mother or brothers" and the rest "for the sake of the Gospel and my name" is blessed. He indicated not the simple martyrdom, but the gnostic one, in which a person, by conducting his affairs according to the Gospel's rule through love toward the Lord, . . . leaves his worldly family and wealth and possessions for the sake of living without the passions.[43]

Clement considered the main goal of the Christian to be detachment from the world and from the desires of the body, which was to be attained through ascetic practice. Martyrdom epitomized the renunciation of the world, but it was not the only means to bring about detachment.[44]

Regarding the monastic endeavor as the equivalent of martyrdom was also an approach found among Western Christians. For example, a seventh-century Celtic homily reads, "Now there are three kinds of martyrdom which are accounted as a Cross to a man, white martyrdom, green martyrdom, and red martyrdom. White martyrdom consists in a man's abandoning everything he loves for God's sake. . . . Green martyrdom consists in this, that by means of fasting and labour he frees himself from his evil desires, or suffers toil in penance and repentance. Red martyrdom consists in the endurance of a Cross or death for Christ's sake."[45]

Christians were not alone in connecting asceticism and martyrdom, nor were they alone in making this nexus of concepts an integral aspect of their own identity: Manicheans and even pagans possessed ideas of a conceptual spirit-body opposition or of outright dualism that fed into their own unique conceptual systems of martyrdom and asceticism and informed the ways that they wrote their hagiographies. Nevertheless, Christians dominated in both numbers and the volume of hagiographical literature produced.

In the Sāsānian-dominated areas of the late antique Christian world, the maltreatment of Christians had remained a periodic fact of life, and this fact was reflected in the genre of hagiography. For the Christians of the Sāsānian Empire, persecutions of varying degrees of intensity periodically erupted up until the reign of the last Sāsānian emperor, Khusraw II (r. 590–628 C.E.), resulting in a vibrant martyrdom literature in Syriac. The first persecution of a Christian, the martyr Candida, is said to have occurred during the reign of Bahram II (r. 276–93 C.E.), but it was under Shapur II (r. 309–79 C.E.) that widespread persecutions of Christians took place. Brock and Harvey notice that these persecutions tended to conform to periods of Sāsānian-Byzantine hostilities, when Christians in the empire were suspected of helping their coreligionists among the Byzantines.[46] Other periods of persecution followed, such as those under Yazdgard I, Bahram V, and Yazdgard II. Persecutions that occurred later in the Sāsānian era, especially those from the mid-fifth century to the late sixth century, were limited to Christians who converted from high-class or royal families (though many of the shahs attempted to limit the zeal of the Zoroastrian priests).[47]

Commensurate with the continued persecutions of Christians in the Syriac-speaking regions of the Sāsānian realm, hagiographical literature in Syriac narrated the stories of a vast array of martyrs, ascetics, and holy persons from the late antique period. This literature encompassed the wide variety of narrative tropes and topoi that constituted the martyrdom genre in late antiquity. Much of this material is found in *Acts of the Persian Martyrs,* an extensive collection that begins with martyrdom acts under Shāpūr II and extends to those under Khusraw II.[48] Smith notes in regard to this important collection of narratives,

> What all these diverse texts have in common are their various means of remembering and recycling the social and political history of fourth-century Persia for later historiographical or hagiographical purposes. . . . They provide a captivating glimpse into the changing ways that the Christians of Persia conceptualized their religious identity, negotiated an apparently precarious position between the Roman and Persian Empires, and interpreted their own history against the larger backdrop of major religious and political transformations. For this was a period that Christians of the Roman Empire remembered as one of liberation, but that Christians of the Persian Empire recalled as one of violence, destruction, and punitive taxes.[49]

Acts of the Persian Martyrs along with the martyrdom of Mār Qardagh and a bevy of texts—such as the *Acts of Thomas*—that were known to Syriac-speaking Christians of late antiquity thus present some of the most important sources for the social and literary history of the Eastern Christians of late antiquity.

From the literary perspective, martyrdom stories contained certain key elements that made them recognizable as a genre. The story of Candida, for example, whose martyrdom was said to have taken place under the reign of Bahram II (r. 276–93 C.E.), serves to illustrate several of the most important aspects of the genre.[50] Candida was among those Christians taken from Byzantine territory and resettled in the Sāsānian realm under Shapūr I. The story of her trials unfolded, in short, because Candida's beauty drew the attention of the shah, who ordered her to "enter his bedchamber."[51] He loved her so fiercely that she attained the title "King's wife," which stirred the jealousies of the king's other wives and led to her martyrdom. After she confessed her Christianity openly to the king, he repeatedly attempted to win Candida away from it, but to no avail. Eventually he threatened her, put her in chains, and had her stretched and publically humiliated (by showing her naked in the street). Her courage in the face of her shame, however, only encouraged more people to convert. In the end the king cut off her breast, but she continued to rejoice in her martyrdom.[52]

In its basic outline, Candida's narrative betrays the general structure of martyrdom narratives. First, the martyr is brought to the attention of the authorities, who tempt her in one or more ways to abandon whatever form her Christianity happens to take.[53] Often the charge is a refusal to sacrifice or otherwise worship the patron deity of the empire. Likewise persecutions of women for their vows of chastity are widely acclaimed in *Acts of the Persian Martyrs,* as the refusal to marry was seen as a fundamental threat to the family, society, and economy: such was the case with the martyrdoms of Martha, Thekla, Tarbo, Anahid, and others, who were often referred to as "daughters of the covenant."[54] The "interrogation" of the martyr is usually accompanied by her vehement refusal to comply, which insures her fate and leads to the second structural component of the genre: she is tortured and eventually martyred, all of which is usually described in the most vivid language. Third, miracles usually accompany the death of the martyr, signifying that the cosmological order reacts to such a crime. Of course miracles often occur throughout hagiographical narratives, and thus in addition to these basic features of the martyrdom genre, some martyrdom stories might have several added miracles and other acts of piety. Additionally they might contain conversion scenes at the beginning, as when, for example, the narrative of the martyr Mār Ma'in states that he came to faith in God through seeing a monk named Doda skinned alive by King Shapūr,[55] or when Thecla converted by listening to the preaching of Saint Paul.[56]

In addition to the types of martyrdom narratives typically found in *Acts of the Persian Martyrs,* Christian societies of the late antique Middle East remembered and celebrated several soldier-saints. Two of the more famous were Saint Sergius and Saint Bacchus, whose story was preserved in a Greek text known as the *Passion of Sergius and Bacchus.*[57] Set during the reign of Roman emperor Galerius (r. 305–11 C.E.), Sergius and Bacchus, Roman citizens and ranking officers of the Roman army, converted to Christianity but were exposed when they refused to enter a pagan temple. Returned to the emperor, who interrogated them and tempted them to sacrifice to Jupiter, Sergius and Bacchus refused, only to be chained, dressed in women's clothing, and paraded around Rome. Galerius then sent them to Barbalissos (on the Euphrates in present-day Syria) to be tried by its military leader (and an old friend of Sergius). Refusing again to recant their faith, Bacchus was beaten to death, though his spirit afterward appeared to Sergius and encouraged him to persevere. Sergius was then tortured over the course of several days and finally executed at Ruṣāfa, where his death was marked by a miraculous voice welcoming him to heaven. Also a chasm was said to have appeared where his blood fell, protecting the place of his death from the contamination of unbelievers.[58] The cult of Saint Sergius (centered around Ruṣāfa) survived well into the Islamic period, and the saint became an important figure to Christians and Muslims alike. The martyrdom of Sergius and Bacchus, along with equally famous soldier-saints such as Saint George, thus depicts the very special deaths of warriors in particular and speaks to the ability of such stories to cross confessional boundaries.

The Sāsānian realm too produced its share of warrior-martyrs, such as Mār Qardagh, who were commemorated in their own stories. For example, according to the Syriac narrative, the figure of Mār Qardagh was a fourth-century Zoroastrian noble who became a Sāsānian governor. Upon meeting a Christian hermit (Abdisho), Qardagh converted to Christianity, and he subsequently earned the ire of Shapūr II, who ordered him to be stoned. Fleeing to the mountains, where he held out for several months, Qardagh eventually gave himself up and was martyred. Mār Qardagh presents an example of a Christian warrior-saint in the Sāsānian realm whose story was widespread and well known to the Christians of late antique Iraq.

Walker notes the curious addition of a formal debate scene between Abdisho and Qardagh at the beginning of the legend.[59] The story thus interpolates disputation literature into the martyrdom genre, transforming a scene of interrogation "into a narrative space for systematic philosophical discourse."[60] Although unique to Sāsānian martyrdom literature, the Mār Qardagh debate anticipates the *munāẓara* (debate) scenes found within the cycle of stories associated with the Muḥakkima—a debate tradition that found its way into later Ibāḍī depictions of the same events.

Not all warrior-saints were soldiers in the literal sense. For example, the martyr Mār Pinḥas, whose story is preserved among *Acts of the Persian Martyrs,* was described as a "skilled soldier" as well as a "defender of the oppressed, a refuge for the weary, and a comforter to the grieving."[61] Yet one of the Syriac words used to describe him as a "soldier" (*agonesṭā*) was also used more broadly for ascetics, and Mār Pinḥas appears to have had no actual military experience but was described as having fought demons in the wilderness for thirty of the eighty years he spent as a desert ascetic.[62] The war that was fought with the spiritual forces of evil, then, was just as important as that fought with human enemies, and the martyr-soldier did not necessarily need to be an actual soldier. Indeed, Brakke has drawn attention to the importance of "spiritual combat" in the early development of the monastic ideal.[63] The use of military terminology by monks and ascetics, as well as the connections between militant violence and the defense of the faith (whether actual or spiritual), remains especially important when considering the early Islamic conquests, as well as the Muḥakkima, *shurāt,* and Ibāḍiyya.

While the hagiographies of late antique Mesopotamia and Persia remain particularly important for the later appearance of *shurāt* literature, the pre-Islamic Arabian Peninsula possessed an important cult of Christian martyrs and saints that predated even the appearance of Islam. Just as the late antique western Mediterranean was characterized by its cult of the saints, so, as Shahīd notes, "South Arabia was a country of martyrs in the sixth century; the cult of its martyrs and their relics distinguished South Arabian Christianity and its religious architecture."[64] In particular, the story of the martyrs of Najrān (a town in present-day Saudi Arabia near the border of Yemen) stands out as the most salient, not only because of the many versions of the text that survive but also because accounts of the story were likely known in Arabic.[65] In fact the letters used by the author of one of the accounts of Najrān, Simon, the bishop of Beth Arsham, to compose his own account in 524 C.E. (also in letter form) were said to have been delivered to an Arab-Azdite king, Jabala, of the Ghassānids and read aloud at his military camp at al-Jābiya.[66] Also known, though sadly not surviving, is the poetry coming out of Najrān. Both al-Āmidī and Ibn al-Nadīm mention the *diwān* of the Banū al-Ḥārith b. Kaʿb, the main tribal group in the town of Najrān (and also the name of one of the principal martyrs). As the Syriac writer John Psaltes wrote a hymn in Syriac to the martyrs, Shahīd finds it "impossible to believe that the Arab poets of Najrān, who were directly related to these martyrs as their relatives, did not compose them as well."[67] That a Christian Arabic literature from the peninsula surely existed is also borne out by the writings of the Christian poet ʿAdī b. Zayd as well as the existence of an Arabic version of the Christian liturgy.[68] The story of the martyrs of Najrān, then, was well known to the inhabitants of the Arabian Peninsula and available to them in various forms in their own language.

Of course the various versions of the story have their political subtexts, namely those of Byzantine-Sāsānian conflict and the shifting of southern Arabian political alignments; as with other hagiographical traditions, they became a "usable past" for those who employed them. Without a doubt such contexts are important to keep in mind, but more significant for the purposes of this study is how the Najrān cycle existed close to the birthplace of Islam. The martyrs of Najrān narrative remains important as a story that in all likelihood was familiar to the first Muslims and certainly to those of later generations.

Although it exists in several versions, the basic outline of the narrative of the martyrs of Najrān follows a relatively straightforward story line: having already attacked the Ethiopians in Ẓafār, burned their church and killed their priest, and then burned the church at al-Mukhā', the Jewish south Arabian leader Yūsuf Dhū Nuwwās arrived at Najrān in the autumn of 523 C.E. and blockaded the caravan routes in and out of the city. Promising, the story tells, on the Torah, the Tables of the Law, and the Ark of the Covenant and in the presence of the rabbis to guarantee the safety of the Christians if they surrendered, he failed to keep his oath: he exhumed the bodies of the two bishops and placed them in the church along with some three hundred leading Christians, whom he burned alive. Several individual and collective martyrdoms then followed, providing the authors of the various tellings of the martyrdom of Najrān with the raw materials for their accounts.[69]

Of the many stories of individual martyrs at Najrān, several deserve special attention for how they depict a kind of militant resistance on the part of the martyrs. For example, the story of Arethas, also known as Ḥārith b. Ka'b, tells of how this martyr was led before Dhū Nuwwās boasting of always having stood his ground and claiming to have killed one of Dhū Nuwwās's relatives in single combat.[70] In the story Ḥārith claims that he would rather have faced the king and his followers with a sword in his hand but that his fellow Christians had barred the gates and did not let him out. Of course this story speaks to the tribal honor of the Arabs, whose ideal it was to die in battle. It also shows how the prototypical vision of the martyr patiently awaiting his death, and perhaps even forgiving his enemies, was not necessarily the image translated into the Arabian context.[71]

Also of note is the story of Māḥyā, a handmaid of Ḥārith, who is described as largely disliked by her people. She redeemed herself, however, by girding herself with a sword like a man and running through the streets exhorting the Christians there to take up arms against the king.[72] Brought before the king and stripped naked in an attempt to shame her, she boasted that she would have ridden out against the king herself with a sword if her master (that is, Ḥārith) had ordered her to do so. Dhū Nuwwās was said to have tied her legs to a donkey and an ass and dragged her around the city before hanging her upside down from a tree outside the gate.[73]

The martyrs of Najrān cycle survived and became famous in the Arabian Peninsula in part because the Ḥimyarite kingdom of Dhū Nuwwās was reconquered in 525 C.E. by Kaleb (that is, Ella-Asbeha), an Ethiopian ally of the Byzantine emperor Justin I. After Christianity was restored to the region, several churches were constructed, including the church complex at Najrān. The memory of the martyrs clearly framed the identity of the Christian communities of people living in the region, as the *Martyrium Arethae* calls Najrān the "City of the Martyrs," and it later housed an important pilgrimage site dedicated to them.[74] Three churches, including one dedicated to the "Holy Martyrs and the Glorious Arethas," along with the domed *ka'ba* (literally, "cube," probably referring to a cubical structure) of Najrān (likely constructed in the 520s and identical to the Martyrium of Arethas) graced the rebuilt city.[75] Shahīd mentions three different types of Christian communities in sixth-century Najrān: Arians, the result of Emperor Constantius's mission to southern Arabia; Julianist monophysites, whose docetic views may well have formed the basis of the Qur'ān's rejection of Jesus's crucifixion; and Nestorians, the original founders of Najrān, who hailed from al-Ḥīra and returned in force after the Persian conquest of southern Arabia in 570 C.E.[76]

What connections possibly existed between these southern Arabian Christian populations and those of the Arabs to their north? Sizgorich and Cook have detailed the familiarity of later Arab commentators with the story of the martyrs of Najrān, which exegetes commonly associated with the enigmatic events described in *sūrat al-Burūj* (sūra 85), verse 4. This verse describes an accursed "People of the Trench" (*ahl al-ukhdūd*) who killed a group of believers because they believed in God.[77] Sizgorich shows how later Muslim narrators of the story emphasized certain aspects of what was likely a common core narrative of the martyrs of Najrān, and one that shares many elements in common with the Christian versions of the story that survive. In other words, the first Muslims as well as later Arab-Muslim exegetes and historians were well aware of the martyrs of Najrān story in its Christian telling, a fact that bespeaks an extensive awareness of the affairs of the Arabian Christians in the south.

Ascetic Bodies and Religious Boundaries

Another means by which to analyze the ways that the hagiographical genre resonated across the late antique and early Islamic Middle East consists of focusing on specific themes in hagiographical literature. Two themes in particular, bodies and boundaries, are especially fruitful areas of investigation insofar as there is a growing body of secondary literature devoted to both topics. Indeed the topic of the body has become, in the words of one researcher, "problematic and complex" in recent decades, and on its own, the amount of scholarship devoted to the bodies of holy persons in late antiquity is truly impressive.[78] Such studies have presented the bodies of the martyr, the ascetic, and the holy person as "tangible frame[s] of selfhood in individual and collective experience, providing a constellation of physical signs that signify relations of persons to their contexts."[79] As a means of exploring how the narratives of martyrs and ascetics played into the identities of those who wrote and remembered them, the theme of the body remains particularly potent: as a focal point of the community and its narratives, ascetics and the "very special dead" offered means by which various religious groups of late antiquity articulated their unique relation to that which they considered sacred.[80] In addition, because the theme of the martyred and ascetic body likewise can be found amid the writings of the early Muslims, *shurāt,* and Ibāḍiyya, such scholarship provides a stepping-stone to understanding the ways that certain themes appear in the hagiographical literatures of late antiquity and the early Islamic period.

Likewise the theme of boundary maintenance among the various religious sects and groups of late antiquity and the early Islamic period is a fruitful avenue for investigation. For as much as the late antique hagiographies shared certain broadly recognizable features, each distinct religious group nevertheless appropriated and articulated them in their own unique fashion. Maintaining the distinctive religious identity of any discrete religious group was a task that concerned monks and heresiographers of all confessional stripes. The notions of martyrdom and asceticism played their part in establishing boundaries between groups insofar as the martyrs, ascetics, and holy persons of the hagiographical stories became a "usable past," and one that established insiders and outsiders, believers and heretics, righteous and tyrannical.[81] Hagiography as a boundary theme, then, is also vital to the understanding of how identity formed (in part) in the late antique Middle East.

One characteristic feature of the late antique nexus of signs and symbols related to martyrdom and asceticism was a complex rejection of the material world, a denunciation that manifested itself in sometimes extreme ascetic attitudes toward the human body.[82] Although Christians of late antiquity were by no means the only group to articulate this attitude, without a doubt the Christian expression of it more and more became the paramount model, especially as Christianity became the ascendant religion of the region. Christian asceticism, especially as it was practiced among the Syriac-speaking communities of greater Syria and Mesopotamia, was based in biblical passages that express the extremity of the so-called "world-denying" aspect of Christian thought. For example, Luke 12:33 states, "Sell your possessions and give to the poor. Provide purses for yourselves that will not wear out, a treasure in heaven that will not be exhausted, where no thief comes near and no moth destroys." Likewise, Luke 14:33 says, "In the same way, any of you who does not give up everything he has cannot be my disciple." In addition John 15:19 states, "If you belonged to the world, it would love you as its own. As it is, you do not belong to the world, but I have chosen you out of the world. That is why the world hates you." Such passages formed the basis for renunciation of the world and the adoption of certain practices that transported the ascetic out of the world of everyday experience and into a sacralized world of blessing.

The gospels emphasized that disciples of Christ should renounce material possessions, leave their homes, break with their families, and take up the burdens of Jesus (that is, "bear their cross").[83] Many late antique Middle Eastern Christian ascetics took these prescriptions literally and added some practices of their own, such as fasting, celibacy, and tonsure. Abstaining from eating meat and keeping a simple diet were important to the early ascetics, as were periods of extended fasting. Many Syriac-speaking Christians in particular subscribed to the view that John the Baptist was a model ascetic, explaining away his apparent consumption of locusts (*akrides*) in the desert as a corruption of "wild fruits" (*akrodrua*). Likewise, Brock finds the issue of celibacy in Syria-Mesopotamia to have been especially stringent: in certain Eastern communities, for example, celibacy was seen as an essential condition for baptism.[84] The origins of tonsure—the shaving of part or all of the head as a sign of religious devotion or humility—in the late antique Middle East remains unclear, but by the seventh and eighth centuries C.E. and among Eastern Christians it had become common to shave the entire head (the so-called "Eastern" rite) in imitation of the Apostle Paul.[85] Saint Germanus I, patriarch of Constantinople (715–30 C.E.), cites the imitation of the Apostle Peter as well as James, the brother of Jesus, as the sources for the practice.[86] Controlling the body through fasting and celibacy or marking it through tonsure were some of the ways that early Christian ascetics expressed their conviction that the materiality of the world—even of their own bodies—must be somehow overcome in order to live the true and pure life of the spirit.

Such attitudes toward the human body often found their expression in literary form. The *Acts of Thomas*, for example, posited a robust dichotomy between the corruptible body and the (potentially) incorruptible soul, between the ever-degenerating material world and the eternal world of the spirit. For this reason the *Acts* mentioned "deeds that profit not," "pleasures that abide not," "riches and possessions that perish on the earth," "garments that decay," "beauty that becomes old and is disfigured," in addition to the body "which becomes dust."[87] Souls, on the other hand, are "not ended by dissolution" and possess the potential to return to God and to live in his paradise for eternity.[88] Because all things on earth are subject to corruptibility, the *Acts* maintained that activities related to the world should be rejected for that which partakes of the spirit and therefore abides eternally. The *Acts* condemned, for example, engaging in sexual intercourse, eating, and drinking.[89] Beauty, riches, and human dignity, which the text assured will become dust, likewise belong to the "transitory things" of this world.[90] In contrast, the "incorruptible Bridegroom" (that is, Jesus) awaited the believer in paradise, as did heavenly riches and sovereignty.[91] The *Acts* thus taught that those things connected to the body should be rejected so as not to hinder the soul's progression toward perfection, making asceticism a vital aspect of salvation.

Attendant to the rejection of the world, the *Acts of Thomas* portrayed the hero of the story, the Apostle Thomas, as passively unperturbed by the happenings of the world around him. In the first section of the work, Thomas refused his Lord's command to go to India, whereupon Jesus (who was believed to be Thomas's twin brother) appeared to an Indian merchant and sold Thomas as a slave.[92] Having found himself thus sold into slavery, Thomas woke in the morning, prayed his prayer of "thy will be done, Lord," and commenced loading the merchant's wares aboard his ship, signaling his acceptance of his fate.[93] Thomas's last act in this world was to goad the soldiers of King Mazdai into stabbing him with their swords, saying, "Come, fulfill the will of him who sent you," whereby Thomas was killed and achieved his martyrdom.[94] As the product of Syriac speakers the *Acts of Thomas* remained an important gauge of early Syriac Christian ideals of asceticism.[95]

The impassivity of Thomas characterized some later Eastern Christian writings about saints, martyrs, and ascetics: Theodoret of Cyrrhus (d. 457 C.E.), for example, wrote of an ascetic named Salamanes, who in his quest for seclusion left his home village of Kefarsana (*Kapersana*) on the west bank of the Euphrates and bricked himself into an abandoned hut in a village on the east bank.[96] When the bishop heard of his sanctity and came to ordain Salamanes, the ascetic said nothing, eventually forcing the bishop to leave (and repair the wall that he had destroyed). Later the people of Kefarsana, jealous to have their local saint back, crossed the river, pulled down the hut, and stole Salamanes. A few days after that, the rival villagers entered Kefarsana and recaptured the saint, returning him to his (presumably rebuilt) hut. In his writings Theodoret praised the ascetic for not having said a word during these activities nor shown the slightest concern over what was happening to him: "thus did he behave as completely dead to the world, and could truly say the words of the Apostle—'I have been crucified with Christ and I no longer live, but Christ lives in me. The life I live in the body, I live by faith in the Son of God, who loved me and gave himself for me.'"[97] In this way Salamanes expressed an extreme form of *apatheia*—that originally Greek concept of dispassionate equanimity toward the world (often associated with the Stoics) that would become adapted throughout Christendom in various ways.[98] Another means of expressing *apatheia* was to compare the ascetic to "strangers" or "foreigners" in the world—a trope that became extremely important in early Syriac writing. Thus the fourth-century Syrian ascetic writer Aphrahat wrote, "We should be aliens from this world, just as Christ did not belong to this world. . . . Whoever would resemble the angels, must alienate himself from men."[99] In this way the notion of being a stranger in the world found strong support in late antique Syriac writings.

Extreme attitudes toward the human body often resulted in its being considered a locus of divine power. Transforming their bodies through their asceticism, many holy persons were held to have pushed themselves toward the perfection enjoyed by Adam. This "exemplary embodied self" was often described with metaphors of light: according to the *Apophthegmata Patrum,* the face of Pambo shone like lightning, in the glare of which was seen "the glory of Adam"; the same text described Sisoes's face shining as the sun; Silvanus shone like an angel, and an old ascetic appeared as a flame; the *Historica Monachorum* described Or's radiant face to be like an angel's.[100] In death as in life, the ascetic's body, just as the martyr's, was treated as a locus of sacred power, providing relics to repel evil and contain blessing.[101] Tombs likewise served as spaces where the spiritual power of the martyr or ascetic could be accessed in various ways: Gregory of Nyssa described the dust from the tomb of the martyr Saint Theodore as a "treasure" and considered the saint "whole and present" at his tomb, able to receive the petitions of those who came to him there.[102]

In comparison with Egyptian monasticism, Syrian-Mesopotamian asceticism appeared highly individualistic and extreme in its practice. Yet for writers such as Ephrēm and Aphrahat, the imitation of Christ "taking up the cross" meant sharing in the sufferings of Christ through asceticism and mortifications.[103] For the Syrian-Mesopotamian ascetics, theirs was a life of mourning for and participating in the passion of Jesus. Later, in the fifth and sixth centuries, more traditional forms of cenobitic monasticism became established in Syria. Yet certain writers, such as Isaac of Antioch, continued to praise the older, more zealous, and individualistic form of asceticism, even as monastic orders more and more became the norm.[104] The practice of older, more dramatic forms of asceticism continued, of course, if only among those deemed "heretics," even as the ideal of asceticism in its extreme form remained as a literary device.

Though "Nestorian" and "Jacobite" Christians remained the most prominent among the late antique Middle East's Christian populations, they did not enjoy a monopoly on the ideas of asceticism or martyrdom, and rejection of the material world in favor of ascetic praxis and/or martyrdom can be seen among "gnostic" Christian groups. The Marcionites, for example, practiced asceticism as a response to their imprisonment in the material plane. Trapped as human begins were in the material world by a malevolent God, the Marcionite response was to reject as much of it as possible: for example, Marcion forbade baptism except to those who foreswore marriage and sexual intercourse, and he envisioned celibacy as a deliberate "abandonment" of the alien God and "withdrawal from his company."[105] To further extricate themselves from the material world, the Marcionite elite fasted extensively, and when not fasting they refrained from all meat except fish.[106] Likewise they prepared themselves for martyrdom, with excessive prayers to keep them pure so as to escape the material world. In fact Marcion envisioned the crucifixion as the means by which Christ purchased humankind from the malevolent God, modifying the above-mentioned quote from Galatians to read, "The life I live in the body, I live by faith in the Son of God, who *purchased* me and gave himself for me."[107]

Manicheans joined the Syriac-speaking Christians of late antique Mesopotamia and Persia in wedding a world-denying ethos to ascetic practices. Because light suffered from its entrapment in human bodies, plants, soil, and rocks, the Manichean Elect chose not to till the soil, pick fruit, harvest plants, or kill animals; they even refused to step on tilled ground for fear of harming the light caught within the budding plants. In addition they did not bathe so as not to defile the light imprisoned within the water.[108] They did not eat meat or drink alcohol; the *Kephalaion,* for example, instructed the holy person to "punish his body with fasting."[109] Sexual intercourse imitated the demonic fornications that bound the light to its material prison in the first place, and so it was strictly avoided.[110] Manichean ascetics also adopted a lifestyle of extreme poverty, exalting in their rejection of the body: a Coptic Manichean psalm proclaimed, "I left the things of the body for the things of the Spirit; I despised the glory of the world, because of the glory that passes not away."[111] For the Manichean laity, the chatechumens (that is, *sāmi'ūn,* "auditors"), fasting, prayer, and almsgiving were expected, as was supporting the Elect. Such actions were considered compensation for marriage and procreation.[112]

Moreover certain Manichean texts implicitly connect notions of asceticism and martyrdom in ways similar to that done in Christian texts. One Manichean homily, for example, compared Mani's death (known as his "crucifixion") in the prison of Bahram I to the sufferings and martyrdom of the Christian apostles.[113] Another hymn, this one composed by a Manichean ascetic, counseled endurance in the face of suffering by detailing the pains endured by Jesus, Andrew, John, and James (that is, John and James, the "two sons of Zebedee"), Thomas, Paul, Thecla, Drusiane, Maximilla, and Aristobula, and, finally, Mani himself.[114] Indeed the Coptic account of the martyrdom of Mār Sīsin (Sisinnios), Mani's immediate successor, stressed the bodily suffering of the martyr. Thus for Manicheans as for Christians, the pain endured by ascetics as a result of their praxis was viewed as similar to that borne by the martyrs.

In this fashion the myriad of religious groups that populated the late antique Middle East articulated a vision of their bodies that reflected their commitments to the notions of martyrdom and asceticism. These articulations found their way into the literatures of these various groups, creating a broadly shared nexus of signs and symbols that could be drawn upon by specific authors. As the hagiographical genre was one of the more "public" genres of literature in late antiquity, such a syllabary became, in many ways, the purview of any group or author willing to take it up. In such a way the genre of hagiography entered the early Islamic and then the *shurāt* and Ibāḍī corpora.

Also vital to understanding the dynamics of martyrdom and asceticism in the late antique Middle East is the intersection between identity, hagiography, and group boundaries. As Castelli and others have shown, the memorialization of the martyrs and ascetics in late antiquity was bound up with the complex process of identity formation.[115] To rally around these narratives, to retell them, listen to them, and to witness the visual representations of them, was to embrace a complex of signifiers that, among other things, helped to define communities. As a complement to the ways that hagiography provided saintly figures, homiletic inspiration, and exhortations, it also created group identity by delineating believers from enemies and heretics. The stories of the martyrs and ascetics remained a particularly poignant means by which religious groups established a sense of boundary: after all, martyrs often debated or bore witness to the true faith before an enemy dispatched them, thus offering in condensed form (and often through powerful imagery) a vision of self and other. Likewise the bodily mortifications of the ascetic, or her tomb and bones, signified the true worth of the afterlife, even as they called attention to the world-bound excesses of those considered outsiders, enemies, or oppressors. The late antique syllabary of martyrdom and asceticism thus remained indelibly and profoundly intertwined with the ways that late antique religious communities imagined their groups in relation to others.

As a method of boundary maintenance, hagiographical literature existed in relation to other types of writing that also aimed at shoring up and defining a community in relation to others. In this sense hagiography can be seen alongside and sometimes blending into other types of boundary literature such as polemic, debate, and heresiology. Indeed polemic and even debate (in the case of Mār Qardagh) sometimes formed part of the hagiographical narrative. Heresiology, in contrast, tended toward its own discrete styles, especially that of the catalog, typified by Epiphanius of Salamis's fourth-century *Panarion,* or "Medicine-Chest," a work that conceived of error in terms of inoculating the faithful against the sickness of heresy. Other well-known works of heresiology included Irenaeus's "Against Heresies" (*Adversus Haeresus*), Theodoret of Cyrrhus's "Compendium of Heretical Fables" (*Haereticarum fabularum compendium*), and his "Remedy for the Diseases of the Greeks" (*Græcarum affectionum curatio*).[116] All of these genres played into the ways that late antique religious people articulated a sense of their own identity in relation to those considered outsiders.

One specific aspect of boundary maintenance in late antiquity should be mentioned as it bears particular relevance for the ways that the Muḥakkima, *shurāt,* and Ibāḍiyya were said to have envisioned their group over and against others by using the language of *kufr* (unfaithfulness) and sometimes *shirk* (polytheism/idolatry) to describe their opponents. Such practices may have a late antique and early Islamic context, and indeed Hawting has drawn attention to how intramonotheist polemics used accusations of idolatry as shorthand for improper belief and practice.[117] Such accusations were fairly common among rival Jews, Christians, and even among Muslims of later periods, without implying actual disbelief, polytheism, or the worship of idols. Hawting notes, for example, that Muslims can label other monotheists such as Jews and Christians *kuffār,* and yet this label does not refer to their having abandoned their beliefs and entered into idol worship. Thus among the various classes of *kuffār* outlined by later Islamic theologians are those whose "monotheism is in some sense less than perfect." Similarly, Jewish rabbis employed the term *kōfēr bā-'iqqār* ("rejecter of the principles of faith") to refer to those who "accepted the existence of God, but whose behavior or faith in some way fell short."[118] Given these observations, Hawting states that "the force of the accusation of idolatry is often that the opponents are no better than idolaters, that their beliefs or practices are inconsistent with monotheism as it ought to be understood and that the opponents, therefore, have made themselves equivalent to idolaters."[119] If indeed the Muḥakkima, early *shurāt,* and Ibāḍiyya should be seen against the background of late antiquity, then Hawting's observations remain important to understanding the possible usages and motivations behind such accusations.

Asceticism and Martyrdom at the Birth of Islam

Such, then, was the world into which the Qur'ān was revealed and upon which it frequently commented. Indeed the Qur'ān's obvious familiarity with monotheistic themes, stories, and tropes (including those of martyrdom and asceticism) makes it almost certain that the first Muslims possessed a sophisticated knowledge of late antique religions, if only from their relations with al-Ḥīra and Najrān (and most certainly from other sources).[120] Whatever the extent of this familiarity, the early Islamic conquests brought Muslims in direct contact with the communities of Mesopotamia, Persia, and Byzantium and placed them in positions of protection and authority over the kinds of religious communities mentioned above.

The exact nature of the first Islamic community's contact with Christians is difficult to ascertain. While the Prophet Muḥammad's interactions with the Jews of Madīna are well documented in the *sīra* literature, there is limited evidence for actual contacts between the Prophet and Arabian Christians. Shahīd has speculated about the existence of an Ethiopic Christian community living in Makka during the Prophet's time there. He points toward the mention of two Ethiopians, Jabr and Yasar, who would read the Torah and Gospels aloud in Makka; the Prophet's Ethiopian wet nurse Um Aymān; his close associate Bilāl; as well as the affinity in the Qur'ān between certain Ethiopic Christian terms and names and those same terms as found in the Qur'ān.[121] Shahīd even goes so far as to postulate the existence of an Ethiopic bible in Muḥammad's Makka. On firmer ground, Shahīd also notes that Muḥammad had contact with Quss b. Sā'ida al-Iyādī, the Christian bishop of Najrān, having heard a sermon of his at the fair of 'Ukāz.[122] Likewise the *sīra* literature mentions how Muḥammad was recognized as a future prophet while still a youth on caravan with his uncle in Bosra by a Christian Monk (Baḥīrā), as well as his Christian maternal uncle, Waraqa b. Nawfal, who was credited with recognizing the first Revelation to Muḥammad as a message from God.[123] Later in his career as a prophet at Madīna he was said to have received a delegation of Christians from Najrān—an episode known to the *sīra* compilers and said to be alluded to in the Qur'ān.[124] In addition there is evidence that pre-Islamic Arabs had contact with Christians living farther afield from the peninsula, including dealings with some of the more famous ascetics of late antiquity: "Ishmaelites" (among others, including Iberians), for example, are said to have visited Simon the Stylite at his monastery outside of present-day Aleppo.[125]

Muḥammad's contacts with Christians, then, while not as extensive as his relations with the Jews of Arabia, nevertheless appear to have presented him—as well as the early community around him—with ample opportunities to deepen his knowledge about Christians and Christianity. The exact nature of this interaction with Christians, however, is elusive: beyond the Qur'ānic references to the martyrs of Najrān and the Sleepers of Ephesus story (which also exists in several Syriac versions), the Qur'ān does not allude to specific hagiographical narratives with which Muḥammad and the early Islamic community may or may not have been familiar.[126] Moreover the historicity of several of the events that are mentioned in the Prophetic biographies can be challenged, leaving scholars to wonder about the extent of the early community's contact with Christians. Likewise the extent of the early community's contact with Manicheans, "gnostics," or other religious groups from the late antique Middle East is difficult to pin down.[127]

While it is difficult to identify the nature of early Islamic-Christian interactions or which hagiographical narratives the early community might have known, general ascetic practices among the first Muslims are easier to recognize. Acknowledging the fact that the Prophetic biographies were written and collected several decades, if not centuries, after Muḥammad's death, the Prophet as presented in these narratives seems to have been acquainted with Christian styles of monasticism. However, if the references in the Qur'ān are any indicator of the general early Islamic feeling toward monks, then the early Muslims must have possessed a complex picture of them. Several verses present them in a poor light. For example, 9:31 claims that certain Christians made their scholars and monks into "lords" (*arbāban*) beside God, though it does not indicate what the monks themselves might have thought of this action; and 9:34 accuses Christian scholars and monks of unjustly taking wealth and of diverting people from the worship of God. Still, 5:82 assures Muslims that the Christians are nearest "in affection" among the monotheists, in part because of the priests and monks among them.

Whatever the view toward monks among the early Muslims, it is clear that several of the practices that Muḥammad was said to have adopted before his calling as a prophet resonate strongly with certain ascetic practices of late antiquity: notably fasting, extended seclusion in a cave, and night prayers. Of course the mysterious group known as the *ḥanafiyya,* indigenous Arabian monotheists, may have introduced or at least familiarized the peninsular Arabs with such practices. From the little information that survives about them, it is possible to discern an ascetic strain paralleling that found outside of Arabia. For example, a rival of Muḥammad in Madīna, one Abū Amīr ʿAbd Amr b. Ṣayfī, reportedly belonged to the group, practiced *tarahhub* (monkery), wore a coarse hair garment, and was known as "the monk" (*al-rāhib*).[128] According to several accounts, Muḥammad was affiliated with the *ḥanafiyya:* in an exchange with the above-mentioned Abū Amīr he claimed to have purified the practices of the *ḥanafiyya* with his mission.[129] That these monotheists existed in Arabia and practiced certain familiar ascetic or monastic actions speaks toward the general late antique milieu of asceticism and piety that permeated the late antique Middle East in the late sixth and early seventh centuries C.E.

Moreover the Prophetic biographies attest to an attitude toward Muslim bodies, especially that of the Prophet, that recalls, in some senses, the general late antique tendency to ascribe power and sanctity to the body of the holy person. An account of al-Zuhrī's in Ibn Hishām, for instance, records that ʿUrwa b. Masʿūd al-Thaqafī, sent by the Quraysh to speak with Muḥammad, observed that "whenever [Muḥammad] performed his ablutions [the Muslims] ran to get the water he had used; if he spat they ran to it; if a hair of his head fell they ran to pick it up."[130] Such a notion reflects the late antique idea of holiness and power as concentrated in the body (and thus the body parts and leavings) of the holy person. Alternately, ʿAṣim b. Thābit was said to have taken a vow not to touch or be touched by polytheists so as not to be defiled. When he was killed at Uḥud, his body was said to be protected by hornets from falling into the hands of Sulāfa bt. Saʿd b. Shuhayd (who wanted to drink wine from his skull) and then washed away in a flood.[131] Such miracles underscore the notion of the sanctity of the holy person, and ʿAṣim's story would have been understood just as readily if it had appeared in a Christian hagiography. Of course the Prophetic biographies were penned long after Muslims had come in extensive contact with the non-Muslim communities of the Middle East, and in part they may have been written with the conversion of these communities—mostly Christians and Jews—in mind: in other words, such scenes as those mentioned above may have been specifically interpolated into the narrative precisely because they made sense to a late antique audience. Moreover one of the earliest and most important extant biographies, that of Ibn Hishām, was based on a prototype disseminated by his teacher Ibn Isḥāq, the son of a converted Christian. Nevertheless the appearance of recognizable late antique tropes related to asceticism and the body in the narratives of the early community points toward either a growing awareness of late antique narrative styles or the continued interpolation of them. In either case, when the early Islamic community set about narrating the life of their Prophet and his companions, it was from the syllabary of late antiquity that they drew many of their images, topoi, and even genres.

The Qur'ān is perhaps a better indicator of the attitudes that became authoritative for and in all probability were adopted by the early community. Indeed underlying the many instances of ascetic behavior that dot the Prophetic biographies is a Qur'ānic approach toward the world that is replete with reminders of its intransient nature as well as exhortations to asceticism: "Wealth and children are adornments of the worldly life. But the enduring good deeds are better to your Lord for reward and better for [one's] hope";[132] "And they rejoice in this world's life, yet this world's life is nothing compared with the Hereafter but a temporary enjoyment";[133] "Say: The enjoyment of this world is short, and the Hereafter is better for him who obeys God's commandments in fear of Him";[134] "This life of the world is but a pastime and a game, but the home of the Hereafter, that is Life if they but knew."[135] These verses remain telling of the late antique context into which the Qur'ān was revealed and how certain Muslims understood piety as encompassing ascetic practice. Indeed a Qur'ānic verse seems to indicate that a group from among the early Muslims contented themselves with extended prayers and possibly with other practices of an ascetic nature: "And keep yourself content with those who call on their lord morning and evening seeking his face."[136] Later Sufi tradition associated this verse with the impoverished early Muslims known as the *Ahl al-Ṣuffa,* the "people of the bench," so-called because they were homeless and slept on a bench in Madīna and shared their scant food and belongings.[137]

Certainly not all among the Islamic community were contented with every aspect of asceticism. For example, some Muslims later expressed considerable discomfort with the notion of celibacy. Reflective of this "antimonastic" trend among later Muslims are ḥadīth that connect marriage and procreation with the proper behavior of Muslims: "He who is able to marry and does not marry is not one of us";[138] "I am not commanded [to practice] monkery."[139] In part some of the unease surrounding celibacy can be traced to anxieties about demarcating the differences between Christians and Muslims.[140] Nevertheless some early Muslims did, in fact, choose to remain celibate. For example, a band of early Islamic warriors (*ghaziyīn*) in al-Azdī's *Futūḥ al-Shām* are described as chaste.[141] In addition several early Sufis, such as Rābi'a al-Adhawiyya of Basra, were known to have refused marriage.

As Muslims of later eras endeavored to understand the function of asceticism within the Islamic community, figures such as the *ghāzī*-scholar 'Abdullāh b. al-Mubārak emphasized the link between asceticism and *jihād.* Ibn al-Mubārak's *Kitāb al-Jihād* (Book of *Jihād*), a work that reflects the independent and ascetic frontier mentality of its author, presented several ḥadīth that explicitly linked fighting with the idea of asceticism: "every community has its monasticism (*rahbāniyya*), and the monasticism of my community is *jihad* in the way of God"; "God gave us in place of [wandering monasticism] *jihād* in the path of God and *takbīr* from every hill."[142] Significantly, Ibn al-Mubārak also wrote a work on *zuhd,* asceticism.[143]

Participants in the early conquests were likewise shown to have conflated asceticism and *jihād.* Sizgorich, for example, has shown that the early Muslim authors depicted the participants of the conquests in ways similar to how late antique Christians depicted the monks who patrolled (often violently) the borders of proper Christian identity. That is, early Muslim *mujāhidūn* were frequently shown to be (in the words of a Christian monk sent to scout the advancing Muslim army in al-Azdī's *Futūḥ al-Shām*) "monks by night, lions by day," to have fasted, remained chaste, prayed throughout the night, and otherwise eschewed the riches of the world.[144] No less than 'Umar b. al-Khaṭṭāb—idealized by the early *shurāt* and Ibāḍīs alike as a model leader—was famous for his ascetic piety.[145] In this manner late antique tropes of asceticism and violence became entangled in the narratives that shaped how Muslims viewed their early history—an image reflected in Ibn al-Mubārak's idealized ascetic warrior as well as in al-Azdī's depiction of the early Islamic *ghāziyīn.*

Along with such associations between asceticism and fighting came a nexus of concepts surrounding those who had been killed—martyred—in the process. Just as with ascetic practice, the early Islamic community had embraced the concept of martyrdom and militant piety from the beginning. Images of martyrdom dot the Qur'ānic pages: "God has purchased from the believers their persons and their wealth in return for paradise; they fight in the way of God, kill and get killed";[146] "And do not say of those who are slain in the way of God, 'they are dead.' No! They are living, though you perceive it not."[147] Similarly, early martyrs such as Ḥamza, Ja'far al-Ṭayyār, and Sumayya were remembered in the Prophetic biographies, along with other martyrs who had died in the "way of God," and these Islamic narratives often preserved in depictions of these figures the link between piety and fighting. Al-Ṭabarī, for example, preserved the poetry of 'Umayr b. al-Ḥumām, famous for having rushed into the battle of Badr after hearing the Prophet's promise of paradise for any who fought and were killed:

> I hasten to God without provision,
> Except for fear of God (*al-tuqā*) and working for the Hereafter,
> And patience in God in the struggle (*al-jihād*),
> For every other provision is liable to be exhausted
> Except for fear of God (*al-tuqā*), piety (*al-barr*) and right
> guidance (*al-rashshād*).[148]

Such an attitude of "working for the Hereafter" by abandoning the temporal "provision" of the world and attaining martyrdom sits easily among late antique hagiographical tropes surrounding the martyrs.[149]

Elsewhere, Islamic literature preserved martyrdom stories that probably were taken directly from earlier (and, for some versions at least, Arab Christian) hagiographies. Islamic sources, for example, preserve a widely attested cycle that Islamic exegetes related to the "People of the Trench" (*aṣḥāb al-ukhdūd*).[150] Though the details of the story are exceedingly varied (even to the point of contradiction), it is clear that the story was broadly known and contained some of the common elements of the martyrdom genre. In the version of the story in the ḥadīth collection of Muslim, for example, a king's magician (*sāḥir*) wishes for an apprentice, and the king sends him a young boy.[151] On the way to the palace the young boy meets a monk (*rāhib*), who begins to instruct him. From the monk the boy learns to treat blindness and to cure leprosy and other diseases, converting all whom he cures to the worship of God. The king becomes suspicious and eventually tortures the monk as well as a converted courtier (by sawing their heads in half) to find the culprit. The boy miraculously survives being thrown from a mountain and dropped into the ocean, and he informs the king that he can be killed only if the king hangs him from a tree in front of all his people and then shoots him with an arrow while pronouncing the *basmalla* (that is, *bismillāh al-raḥmān al-raḥīm,* "In the name of God, the Compassionate, the Merciful"). This the king does, and the boy dies, but all of the king's subjects convert, forcing the king to martyr all of his subjects by digging ditches, lighting fires in them, and throwing in his people. The ḥadīth ends with a young child encouraging his mother to endure the ordeal for the sake of truth (*ḥaqq*). Not only does the ḥadīth contain many of the structural elements of martyrdom narratives (that is, conversion, interrogation, trial and martyrdom, miracles), but it also contains several topoi that would have been familiar to a Christian or Islamic audience (that is, a king, a monk, a magician, curing of diseases, and even the burning trenches). From a narrative perspective, then, Muslims seem to have quickly become (if they were not already) familiar with the martyrdom genre.

Similarly, Islamic hagiographical narratives preserve an image of the body that reflects, to an extent, the ways that late antique Middle Eastern religious groups expressed their desire to escape from the materiality of this world by devaluating their own lives and bodies. Ibn 'Arfā', for example, having asked the Prophet during the battle of Bakr about what makes God "laugh with joy at His servant," received the answer, "plunging his hand into the enemy without armor," whereupon Ibn 'Afrā' threw down his coat of mail and fought until he was killed.[152] Likewise, Khubayb b. 'Adī, taken prisoner by the Quraysh after the battle of 'Uhud and executed in Makka, is said to have mused in his death poem that God would "bless the limbs of a mangled corpse" and "count them by number, and take them one by one."[153] Indeed the Prophetic biographies contain copious examples of mangled Muslim bodies, and there are strong continuities between the various late antique Middle Eastern articulations of martyrdom, with its attendant attitude toward the human body, and the kinds of early Islamic depictions of martyrdom and asceticism that became part and parcel of the Prophetic *sīra* and *futuḥāt* genres.

Along with notions of asceticism and martyrdom, the early Islamic community also developed several ways to distinguish itself from other religious groups. This process of boundary articulation, however, seems to have taken considerable time, and it is not entirely clear that early Muslims initially placed importance on the confessional identities of other monotheists (that is, Jews, Christians, and possibly even Zoroastrians) as such. Rather there is a strong possibility that members of the early community emphasized their common belief in God, and in the impending Day of Judgment, and saw themselves as urgently "building with other Believers a righteous community of those hoping to be saved when the Hour came."[154] To be clear, there is no doubt that the earliest Muslims knew the differences between Jews, Christians, Zoroastrians, and other religious groups: the Qur'ān's obvious familiarity with these groups makes it certain that the first Muslims knew these distinctions. The point, rather, is that the earliest Muslims might have chosen to downplay such differences in favor of their common belief in God and in their commitment to overcoming injustice in the world before the Judgment came.

Holding to the common goal of creating a just society on earth would have had two strong implications for the early Muslims; just as differences between monotheists of different confessional groups were downplayed in the interest of common goals, so too differences within the community of believers had to be managed. First, the Qur'ān had warned Muslims—quite clearly—not to divide their religion into sects: "And Lo! This your *umma* is one *umma,* and I am your Lord, so keep your duty to Me. But they have broken their religion (*amrahum*) between them into pieces (*zuburan*), each party (*ḥizb*) rejoicing in its tenets."[155] Other Qur'ānic verses concerning sectarianism express a similar sentiment: "Lo! As for those who sunder their religion (*farraqū dīnahum*) and become partisans (*shī'an*), no concern have you at all with them. Their case will go to God, who will then tell them what they used to do";[156] "And be you not as those who divided (*tafarraqū*) and disputed (*akhtalafū*) after the clear proofs had come to them."[157] These verses offer clear warnings against intrareligious division, using words that denote splitting, fracturing, differing, or pieces (*farraqa, tafarraqa, akhtalafa, zubur*) to characterize sectarianism as a separation from an original unified *umma.* Such verses would have served as powerful warnings to Muslims and discouraged the kind of divisiveness that could lead to the creation of sects.

Second, the believer's project of building a just social order would have meant that those considered outsiders, or enemies, could be defined not only by a rejection of the central tenets of monotheism but also by their resistance to the endeavor. In other words, the idea of who might be the opposite of the believer (that is, an unbeliever) might be as broad as the category of believer. It would certainly encompass polytheism, as well as those who rejected the notion of God and the last day, but it would also include the notion of active resistance—of tyranny, oppression, possibly even "cardinal" sinfulness. In fact a term often set against *mu'min* (believer) in the Qur'ān is *kāfir,* a concept whose expansive meanings are difficult to pin down. Using Blachere's version of Nöldeke's Makkan/Madīnan Qur'ānic classificatory system, Waldman argues for a fourfold development of the concept of *kufr* in the Qur'ān.[158] According to her, the concepts of *kufr* and *imān* in the early Makkan *sūra*s describe (often in conjunction with several other terms such as *kadhb* or *istighāna*) those who remain "inimical to the call" and "ungrateful" by denying God's message.[159] Thus, rather than simply describing accepters and rejecters of the message, the *kufr/imān* dichotomy referred in the early periods to those "who do certain acts out of a proper state of the heart" as well as those who "fail to do them" out of deficiency or sickness.[160] By the second Makkan period, the term *kufr* became more and more connected to the concept of polytheism (*shirk*), and by the third Makkan period it denoted an active kind of rejection, one given resolve by God.[19]

Finally, by the Madīnan period the *kuffār* referred to "the class of people to be fought by the *mu'min*."[162] Such an expansive notion of unbeliever would have suited the early community as Donner describes it: that is, as a community that strove to live in righteousness, in accordance with the guidance provided by God's law (*dīn*), any who actively worked against such an endeavor would become an unbeliever, the very notion of which would be broad enough to encompass a variety of transgressions, all of which were tied in some way to the idea of rejecting God's laws.[163] Indeed the parallelism between verses 5:44, 5:45, and 5:47 seems to equate *kāfirūn,* sinners (*fāsiqūn*), and oppressors (*ẓālimūn*), all of whom share the refusal to judge by what God has revealed. Thus not only is the notion of *kufr* conceptually expansive, but in addition it sits alongside (and is often linked to) other terms of transgression such as *kadhb, shirk, fisq, ẓulm,* and *dhanb.* From a Qur'ānic perspective, then, proper belief was synonymous with righteous behavior: as Donner notes, "in addressing those who believe the Qur'ān was exhorting them to act in a certain manner, . . . rather than to 'possess' an abstract substance (to 'have' faith)."[164] Faith was proper action, and thus its opposite was improper action, variously defined with the terms for sin, unfaithfulness, and polytheism.[165]

Unfortunately there is little evidence beyond the Qur'ān for how the earliest Muslims (as a believers' movement) might have characterized outsiders, enemies, and unbelievers in this early period. According to Bonner, the early conquests seem to have been directed against broadly defined "enemies of God," and he notes that it is not altogether clear who these "enemies" were at the beginnings of the *futuḥāt.*[166] That these enemies were not Jews, Christians, or other monotheists as such is made clear from non-Islamic sources, among them the comments of the Nestorian monk Yohannan bar Penkayê, writing in Syriac in northern Mesopotamia in the 680s: "Their armies used to go in each year to distant lands and provinces, raiding and plundering from all peoples under heaven. And from every person they demanded only tribute, and each could remain in whatever faith he chose. There were also among them Christians, not a few, some of them with [that is, belonging to] the heretics [that is, the monophysites] and some with us [that is, Nestorians]."[167] When the armies did attack Jews, Christians, or other monotheists, then, it can be assumed that in accordance with the above-defined Qur'ānic understandings of transgression, they did so because they regarded them in some way as tyrants, oppressors, or as otherwise opposed to the business of establishing the just society. That these "enemies" were likewise depicted as being engrossed in worldly matters (as opposed to being focused on the hereafter) is equally probable: a common trope of later *futuḥāt* literature is the image of the early Islamic warrior-ascetics resisting powerful officials and kings, rebuffing their bribes, and remaining nonplussed by their displays of wealth.[168]

In the period following Muḥammad's death, during the so-called Ridda Wars when Muslims confronted Muslims whom they considered transgressors for refusing to pay the *zakāt,* the terminology of *ridda/irtidād* ("going back" but later "apostasy") was mustered to describe them. This term clearly struck some later Muslim authors, and quite possibly the original characters about whom they were writing, as uncomfortable. ʿUmar, for example, was said to have questioned Abū Bakr's insistence on using the language of reversion/apostasy by quoting a ḥadīth guaranteeing the safety of those who cleaved to monotheism.[169] And if the notion of a broadly defined nucleus of believers dedicated primarily to the creation of a just order was plausible, then the notion of "belief" as a theological concept would have been less important to these early believer-Muslims than its practical manifestations. As such, labeling someone a *murtadd* in the early period might not have been a statement about that person's lack of belief per se but would have pointed to his/her refusal to comply with revealed law, interpreted in this case by Abū Bakr to mean paying *zakāt* to the Islamic polity as represented by him, the successor to the Prophet. This is, in fact, how the term seems to have functioned for Abū Bakr.[170]

By the time of the Muḥakkima and early *shurāt,* the Islamic syllabary was becoming rich with symbols and images of asceticism and martyrdom that resonated with those found among the various confessional groups of the late antique Middle East. Muslims had begun to remember their "very special dead" as well as their ascetic-warriors in ways that established the sanctity of their slain or emaciated bodies, even as they sometimes devalued the world in which those bodies were entrenched. Muslims had already begun to stake out a religious identity and to draw boundaries between themselves and others—identities and boundaries initially based not on a strict understanding of confessional distinctiveness but on the idea that monotheism and its praxis were intimately joined, if not inseparable. Such a spirit undoubtedly fired the first Islamic conquests and gave later hagiographers and historians added material about which to refine further the identity of the still-emerging Islamic community. Insofar as the Muḥakkima and early *shurāt* preserved the "spirituality of the conquest society," an aspect of this preservation involved writing down and preserving the memories of their martyrs and saints as well as establishing the boundaries of proper Islamic behavior—all of which had been indelibly shaped by the context of late antiquity.[171]

Chapter 2

Shurāt Battles, *Shurāt* Bodies

The stories of the Muḥakkima and early *shurāt,* preserved as they are in non-Ibāḍī sources, contain themes that resonate profoundly with certain aspects of late antique Middle Eastern hagiographies, and they provided the basis for an emerging *shurāt* identity. Specifically an account of the Muḥakkima movement and early *shurāt* rebellions following the theme of *shirā'* exemplifies the kind of "exchange" that encompassed the idea of dying in battle for the sake of God's order as well as the pursuit of asceticism in this world.[1] The concept of *shirā'* is an essential aspect of how the mission of the Muḥakkima and *shurāt,* their place in the world, and their relation to God were understood. *Shirā'* sits comfortably among the various articulations of martyrdom and asceticism in the late antique Middle East (especially what is today Iraq-Iran) and can be viewed as a specifically *shārī* variation on broadly held themes related to the rejection of the material world.

In examining the narratives and poetry of the so-called *khawārij* that can be found in non-Ibāḍī—that is, proto-Sunnī and pro-ʿAlīd—sources, despite their late dates and overtly polemical authors and editors, it is nevertheless possible to see reflected in the pages of these works some aspects of how the early *shurāt* were remembered as martyrs and ascetics. This is possible, in large part, because later authors and editors clearly had access to sources written about and possibly by the *shurāt* and later Khārijites. Al-Ṭabarī, for example, quotes at great length the work of the Kūfan (and pro-ʿAlīd) historian Abū Mikhnaf, who had access to and preserved in his writings some material related to the Muḥakkima, early *shurāt,* and later Khārijites. Likewise some of al-Balādhurī's sources seem to have come via Kūfaen-Abū Mikhnaf, though they are not stated to be as such. In addition, although it is impossible to untangle what might or might not be "authentic" from what might have been edited and despite the fact that editors such as al-Ṭabarī remained openly hostile to the *khawārij* as a whole, there are numerous instances when they appear in a positive light or when the structure of their narratives mimics the kinds of hagiographical genres that were familiar to those of the late antique Middle East.[2] It is unlikely that a hostile editor such as Abū Mikhnaf or al-Ṭabarī would consciously frame narratives in ways that valorized the Muḥakkima and early *shurāt,* and so it can be assumed that the stories appearing as such in non-Ibāḍī sources reflect in some fashion the original *shārī* narrator or author. This "reflection," of course, will be neither precise nor wholly trustworthy from the perspective of the modern historian, but it will provide a basis from which to compare the narratives of the Muḥakkima and early *shurāt* with what can be found about them in Ibāḍī sources.

What can (or cannot) a historian learn from early *shārī* and Khārijite poetry? Arabic poetry is, of course, a complex genre of writing and one that the denizens of the late antique and early Islamic worlds used extensively for a wide variety of purposes.[3] Arab poets worked within several fixed genres, and their poems were expected to follow the form and meter of those genres, as well as include certain moods, and reference the various images associated with the genres.[4] The value of any given poem came from the aesthetic of its language as well as the way the poet creatively played with or even transgressed the boundaries of the genre in which she wrote. Given the semifixed nature of the poetic genres and their imagery and the qualities that were often associated with certain types of poems, a certain amount of hyperbole should be expected from them. For example, *shārī* and Khārijite poets often penned eulogies and battle poems in which the figures of the eulogized or the warriors were infused with the nostalgia of memory or the heroic bravado of battle. In both cases poets idealized their subjects to some degree; indeed in battle poems the quality of *fakhr*—boasting of one's achievements—was a recognized poetic trope.[5] *Shurāt* and Khārijite poems therefore can be treated not as history per se but as romanticized visions of history that operated according to certain fixed narrative expectations. Poems were presented according to the rules of their genre, and therefore they focused on certain subjects at the expense of others. Nevertheless, as martyrs and heroes were often the subjects of poems par excellence, *shurāt* and Khārijite poetry ended up having quite a lot to tell about those figures who embodied the ideal of *shirā'*.

An examination of the poetic imagery of the "poisoned cup," an image that hearkens back to the pre-Islamic Arabian poetic genre, illustrates that while *shurāt* and Khārijite (and even later Ibāḍī) poetic imagery does fit into the larger late antique Middle Eastern landscape, it also appropriates specifically Arabian poetic themes. In these poetic articulations, the poisoned cup becomes the image of death on the battlefield and is thus related to the nexus of martyrdom, asceticism, and so forth insofar as it expresses the Arabian poetic tropes of *fakhr* or of poetic resignation to the inevitable fate of death. The imagery has been changed, however, from that of the pre-Islamic wine cup, which leads the poet to muse upon the vagaries of life to that of outright death in battle—a theme that recalls usage by the pre-Islamic poet ʿAntara b. Shaddād. In other words, *shurāt* and later Khārijite poets took a common poetic image and turned it to their own uses but did so in a recognizable fashion and firmly within the tradition of Arabic poetry. Thus, while the notions of *shirāʾ* and their expressions do locate the *shurāt* and later Khārijites in the wider literary world of the late antique Middle East, their poetry is no less "Arabian" by being placed within it.

Shirāʾ—Asceticism and Rebellion among the Early Khārijites

For all of the many subsects later grouped under the rubric of *khawārij,* the formative moments—the instances that defined their beginnings—commenced at the battle of Ṣiffīn in the year 37/657 and culminated in the battle of Nahrawān in 38/658. These events gave rise to the first Khārijites, a group labeled by the heresiographers as the Muḥakkima, the Ur-sect of all subsequent Khārijite offshoots. The historical record contains several accounts of the Muḥakkima, few of which are entirely free of discrepancies and contradictions. Nevertheless the general outline of the incidents that led to their emergence can be sketched in broad strokes, and this narrative opens with Muʿāwiya b. Abī Sufyān's call for arbitration during a crucial moment at the battle of Ṣiffīn.[6] Having found himself nearly outfought by ʿAlī b. Abī Ṭālib's army, Muʿāwiya's counselor ʿAmr b. al-ʿĀṣ suggested that their soldiers hoist up copies of the Qurʾān (*maṣāḥif*) on the ends of their lances. This act signaled their desire to arbitrate the dispute between Muʿāwiya and ʿAlī by the Qurʾān, and it caused confusion in the ranks of ʿAlī's army. Many, ʿAlī among them, wanted to continue fighting. Others from ʿAlī's army pressured him to arbitrate (some from this group were later to repent of their actions and become Muḥakkima), and ʿAlī agreed to do so. The announcement of the arbitration (*taḥkīm*) provoked one or more of ʿAlī's soldiers to utter what would become the slogan of the dissenters, *lā ḥukm illā li-lāh* ("No Judgment but God's"), a phrase that expressed rejection of the arbitration agreement. This phrase would also provide this group with their name, the *muḥakkima,* or those who utter the phrase *lā ḥukm illā li-lāh.*

Upon returning to Kūfa, the faction within ʿAlī's army opposing arbitration grew, as did their frustration with ʿAlī. A portion of them decided to secede from (*kharaja ʿan*) ʿAlī's camp and removed themselves to a site outside of Kūfa known as Ḥarūrāʾ (hence another name for the Khārijites was the *ḥarūriyya*). Although the reports of this incident are especially confusing, the dissenters seem to have elected provisional leaders and to have debated with ʿAlī's representative, ʿAbdullāh Ibn al-ʿAbbās, and with ʿAlī. According to some accounts of this debate (*munāẓara*), ʿAlī convinced them (or some of them) to return to Kūfa. However, after it became clear that ʿAlī was proceeding with the arbitration, the Muḥakkima removed themselves to a place called al-Nahrawān, to the northeast of the Tigris. On their way some were said to have randomly attacked and killed Muslims, incidents that either gave ʿAlī the excuse or forced him to attack the Muḥakkima there assembled.

The battle of Nahrawān is described in every source as a disastrous defeat for the Muḥakkima, and it provided their first, though certainly not the last, martyrs. For example, an early poem mentions one of the Muḥakkima's leaders, Zayd b. Ḥisn al-Ṭā'ī, in a eulogy:

> I complain to God that from every tribe
> of people, battle has annihilated the best [of them].
> May God requite Zayd so long as the Sun rises in the East,
> And may He establish their dwelling in the Gardens of Paradise.[7]

Mention of the "Gardens of Paradise" makes it clear that the poet, al-ʿAzīz b. al-Akhnas al-Ṭā'ī (himself a Ṣiffīn veteran and martyr at Nahrawān), viewed the deaths of the Muḥakkima as worthy of God's reward. Likewise no less than Abū Bilāl Mirdās b. Udayya, the doyen and hero of the early *shurāt,* is said to have uttered the following during his own uprising some twenty or so years after the battle of Nahrawān:

> After Ibn Wahb, the pure and pious,
> And those who [faced death] in those battles,
> Can I desire to remain or hope for health
> After they have slain Zayd b. Ḥiṣn and Mālik?
> Oh Lord purify my intention and my perception,
> And give me piety until I meet them.[8]

Remembering the Muḥakkima killed at Nahrawān in poetry and in practice became, in accordance with how such figures tended to be valorized in the hagiographical literature of the late antique Middle East, an essential part of what seems to have been originally *shurāt* sources for the stories as they are preserved now.

Additionally it is clear that from the very outset the notion of *shirā'* seems to have been associated with the Muḥakkima. If the reports of their early activities and their poetry are to be believed, then the concept of *shirā'* formed an essential piece of how the Muḥakkima imagined their relation to God, their struggle against Muʿāwiya and ʿAlī as a righteous fight, and the reward that awaited them for engaging in it. Linguistically the root *sh-r-*[hamza] has connections to the ideas of buying, selling, and exchanging.[9] Thus, Qur'ān 2:16 speaks of those who "exchanged guidance for error" (*al-ladhī ashtarū al-ḍalāla bil-hudā*). Given the Muḥakkima's reported association with the "Qur'ān reciters" (*qurrā'*)[10] in ʿAlī's army, the Qur'ān probably set the tone for how they understood *shirā'* as martyrdom. For example, 2:207 states, "And there is a kind of person who exchanges his life to earn the pleasure of God; and God is full of kindness to his devotees." Similarly 9:111 states, "God has purchased (*ashtarā*) from the Believers their persons and their goods; for theirs [in return] is the Garden [of Paradise]: they fight in His way, and slay and are slain: A promise binding on Him in truth, through the Torah, the Gospel, and the Qur'an: And who is more faithful to his covenant (*bi-'ahdihi*) than God? Then rejoice in the bargain (*bi-bī'kumu*) which you have concluded: That is the achievement supreme." Several points of interest emerge from these verses. First, *shirā'* is presented as an exchange, covenant (*'ahd*), or bargain (*bī'*) that is made between God and a certain "kind" of person, implying that not everyone engaged in it. The exchange involved fighting and possibly dying, with the exchangers giving their lives as well as their worldly goods (*amwāl*) in return for God's pleasure and for entry into paradise. Qur'ān 9:111 also mentions that the act of exchange involves a "promise" (*wa'd*) that God had revealed to previous monotheistic communities—by implication Jews and Christians—in their own scriptures as well as to Muslims in the Qur'ān. The verse extols *shirā'* as something to be celebrated as a "supreme achievement." In light of Lewinstein's contention that the Qur'ān does not seem to use the term *shahīd* in the meaning of martyr, it is noteworthy how profoundly the notion of *shirā'* does, in fact, seem to approximate the idea of martyrdom, even to the point of the Qur'ān mentioning previous monotheistic communities to which the promise of *shirā'* was made.[11] Given that the early Islamic community was surely familiar with the notion of martyrdom, the concept of *shirā'* presents itself as an early (and thoroughly Qur'ānic) means by which they might have understood it.

Scattered reports—mostly poetry—from the early Muḥakkima indicate that the idea of *shirā'* as a willingness to die for the cause of God was known to or associated with them from the outset. For example, an early Muḥakkimite leader, Ma'dan b. Mālik al-Iyādī, who was said to have been deposed for expressing in verse his dissatisfaction with those who "stayed behind" and did not participate in the fight at Nahrawān, sang, "Peace upon those who pledge allegiance to God as an exchanger (*shārīan*), / and no peace on the party remaining."[12] Although this report in which the poetry is embedded appears anachronistic—the report uses the term "Ṣufriyya" to describe those who deposed al-Iyādī, and its author, al-Mubarrad, was an Azdī from Basra and probably used Ibāḍī sources in his *al-Kāmil fī'l-Lugha wa'l-Adab*—it nevertheless expresses the sentiment that "exchange" (*shirā'*) was something that the early Muḥakkima valued (even if some of them valued it too highly). Al-Mubarrad's report continues, explaining how the Muḥakkima looked to 'Abdullāh b. Wahb al-Rāsibī as their imām. Poetry attributed to him likewise expresses his commitment to *shirā'*:

I am Ibn Wahb al-Rāsibī, the exchanger (*al-shārī*),
I strike among the enemy to gain vengeance,
Until the state of the evil ones (*dawlat al-ashrār*) vanishes,
And the truth returns to the righteous (*al-akhyār*).[13]

For al-Rāsibī, *shirā'* seems to have been intimately connected with the idea of fighting those who promoted a state of evil, as well as returning the "righteous" to their place of truth.

Likewise al-ʿAzīz b. al-Akhnas al-Ṭā'ī connected *shirā'* to piety when he intoned, "They swear [to practice] *taqwā,* and do not follow a whim, / So God will not exclude one who was an exchanger (*man kān shārian*)."[14] If these poems can be accepted as genuine in some capacity (even if the reports in which they are embedded are not), then the notion of *shirā'* as an analogue to the late antique concept of martyrdom may well have already been current among certain members of ʿAlī's army, and it certainly became something of a trope among those who later remembered and wrote about the Muḥakkima. Moreover *shirā'* clearly possessed strong associations with fighting injustice as well as following a life of piety (*taqwa*) in conformity with God's revealed ordinances.

It is clear that authors on the Muḥakkima described them, in conjunction with their commitment to *shirā',* as possessed of an attitude of rejection toward the present world and a preference for the hereafter. Such sentiments can be found in numerous reports on them. Thus, upon accepting the leadership of the Muḥakkima, Ibn Wahb al-Rāsibī is said to have commented, "I do not accept it out of desire for this world, and I will not abandon it out of fear of death."[15] Similarly in a report from Abū Mikhnaf he is said to have orated, "Pleasure in this world, confidence in it, and love for it, is an occasion of distress and destruction."[16] In the same report Ḥurqūs b. Zuhayr stated, "The delights of this world are few, and separation from it is imminent. Do not let its fineries and delights tempt you to stay in it or turn you from seeking what is true, and rejecting evil."[17] In this way a familiar late antique Middle Eastern nexus of martyrdom and world denial, in its particular Muḥakkimite articulation, made its way into descriptions of the Muḥakkima.

The process of remembering the Muḥakkima in ways quite similar to those by which other late antique martyrs and ascetics were evoked seems to have begun quite early. If the poetry attributed to Muḥakkimite authors is, in fact, authentic, then al-ʿAzīz b. al-Akhnas al-Ṭā'ī's lamentations on the martyrdom of Zayd b. Ḥiṣn found its continuation some twenty years later in the eulogies of Abū Bilāl on Zayd, Ibn Wahb, and Mālik. Such valorizations represent the first glimmerings of a concept of *shurāt* identity, and it is no accident that such an identity was anchored in the bodily sufferings and "very special" deaths of those slain at Nahrawān. The ascetics among the Muḥakkima and the martyrs of Nahrawān provided the founders of what was becoming a movement, while the concept of *shirā'* offered a central tenet for those that followed. Unsurprisingly those who looked to the Muḥakkima as their predecessors and embraced the idea of *shirā'* in the face of evil, tyranny, and oppression became known collectively as the *shurāt.*[18]

Several *shurāt* rebellions would follow the battle of Nahrawān, providing yet more martyrs and ascetics as models of *shirā'*. In an immediate aftermath of the battle, for example, three persons who are described as Khārijites—ʿAbd al-Raḥmān b. ʿAmr b. Muljam al-Murādī, al-Burak b. ʿAbdullāh, and ʿAmr b. Bakr al-Tamīmī—are reported to have conspired to assassinate ʿAlī, Muʿāwiya and ʿAmr b. al-ʿĀṣ in the name of revenge and fighting tyranny. According to al-Ṭabarī's report, they said, "What if we 'exchange our selves' (*sharaynā anfusanā*) and go to the imāms of error, seek to kill them, deliver the land from them, and thus achieve vengeance for our brethren?"[19] Ibn Muljam was the only person among them to succeed, killing ʿAlī as he exited the mosque in Kūfa.[20]

Sources from the early *shurāt* exalt Ibn Muljam for the killing of ʿAlī, as is shown by several poems that praise the event. For example, the first of two poems attributed to Ibn Abī Mayyās al-Murādī reads,

> You upon whom be blessings, we have struck Ḥaydar ["the lion"]
> Abū Ḥasan (that is, ʿAlī) with a blow to the head and he was
> split apart.
> We have removed kingship from his concerns
> with the blow of a sword, since he waxed high and haughty.
> We are noble and powerful in the dawn
> when death puts on and wraps itself in death.[21]

The reference to "kingship" in the first hemistich of the second line is meant as a criticism, as the idea of kingship was something looked down upon in the Qur'ān, and it became something of a trope among later *futuḥāt* literature for the *ghāzīyīn* to reject the sumptuous offers of the kings they encountered.[22] ʿAlī is accordingly described as "high and haughty" in a manner similar to how such figures would later be described.

Ibn Abī Mayyās's second poem references the demand made of Ibn Muljam by a certain Qaṭamī bt. ʿAlqama of the Taym Ribāb that in order for her to consider marriage to him he should bring her the head of ʿAlī as part of her dowry:[23]

> I have not seen a dowry, brought by a generous man,
> neither from Arab nor foreigner, like the one of Qaṭāmī's;
> Three thousand *dirhams*, a servant and a singing girl,
> and the stabling of ʿAlī with the piercing blade.
> [There is] no dowry, however costly, more costly than ʿAlī,
> And no killing above that performed by Ibn Muljam.[24]

Another, anonymous poem likewise commends Ibn Muljam's act:

> We buried Ibn Muljam under the [cover of] darkness,
> Successful, when to each soul comes its reward [lit. its book].
> Abū Ḥasan took a blow to the head
> by a blessed hand, and after death, the recompense.[25]

Praise of Ibn Muljam thus comes from several sources, making it likely that his memory was widely preserved among the early *shurāt*.

Chronologically the *shurāt*'s hagiographical imagination next turned to the martyrs of Nukhayla. The battle of Nukhayla was said to have occurred after Muʿāwiya declared himself caliph in 41/661. At this time many of the Muḥakkima who had left the battlefield at Nahrawān repented their desertion and gathered at a place called Nukhayla outside of Kūfa, following Farwa b. Nawfal al-Ashjaʿī as their leader.[26] Muʿāwiya sent his army against them, and after it was repelled, he threatened the Kūfans into joining the attack against the Muḥakkima. When Farwa's tribe, the Ashjaʿ, captured and imprisoned him, ʿAbdullāh b. Abī al-Ḥawāʾ al-Ṭāʾī assumed command, and he died in the fighting.[27] Ḥawthara b. Wadāʿ al-Asadī then arrived to take over. Refusing to desist from battle, even when Muʿāwiya sent to him his father and son, Ḥawthara was said to have uttered, "I yearn more for a sharp stabbing that makes me wallow among spearheads than for my own son."[28] He would shortly die as well.[29] Only fifty of the Muḥakkima who fought at Nukhayla were said to have survived. Farwa b. Nawfal lived only to later perish fighting the new governor of Kūfa, al-Mughīra b. Shaʿba.[30]

Like their brothers at Nahrawān, the early rebels at Nukhayla were remembered for their piety and their willingness to give up this world for their cause. For example, a poem attributed to ʿAbdullāh b. ʿAwf b. Aḥmar, Muʿāwiya's general and the man who killed Abū al-Ḥawāʾ in battle, expresses his regret at having killed a man of piety and prayer, someone who kept the night vigil with sadness and who eschewed the things of this world.[31] The same report describes Ḥawthara's prayer calluses and alludes to his devotion.[32] The battle at Nukhayla likewise assumed importance in the later martyrology of the *shurāt* and Khārijites. For example, al-Aṣam al-Ḍabbī, an Azraqite, sang,

> I profess the religion to which the *shurāt* adhered
> on the day of Nukhayla, by the ruins of Jawsaq.[33]
> Those who mustered on the path of their forebears from the Khārijites,
> before doubt and suspicion [befell them].
> A people, who if reminded of God or if they mention [His name]
> Prostrate themselves in fear, chin and knees [to the ground].
> They proceeded towards God until they were lodged in rooms
> With thrones, in a house made of gold.[34]

The poem mentions the profound fear of God that the *shurāt* were supposed to have felt at the very mention of God as well as their willingness to martyr themselves for their heavenly reward (in this case heavenly apartments).[35]

This "fear" at the mention of God, of course, was commonly known to and associated with Christian monks of all stripes, who were exhorted in Philippians 2:12 to work toward salvation with "fear and trembling." It became something of a trope in *shurāt* and Khārijite poetry, as when the Azraqite poet ʿĪsā b. Fātik al-Khaṭṭī sang in memory of those killed with Abū Bilāl:

> At nightfall they are submerged [in prayer],
> and when the darkness is dispersed they are still prostrated, praying.
> Fear of God has put their sleep to flight, their nights spent in vigils,
> while those who live a tranquil worldly life lie asleep.
> In the darkness, kneeling in prayer,
> A sigh from which their ribs cleave;
> In daytime, it is as if they are mute from a long silence,
> From the tranquility (*sakīnathum*) of their devoutness.
> They cry aloud, longing for Him,
> But if they whisper, their Lord is Hearing.[36]

The fear and longing that characterize the *shurāt*'s worship in this poem could just as easily have been attributed to pious Christian ascetics, monks, or laypersons, among whom a similar fear was said to have taken hold.

Following Nahrawān and Nukhayla, scattered *shurāt* rebellions continued to plague Muʿāwiya's reign. Thus, for example, Ibn Muljam's companion Shabīb b. Bajra al-Ashjaʿī rebelled outside of Kūfa and was killed by the governor's men.[37] Another *shārī,* Muʿayn b. ʿAbdullāh al-Muḥāribī, was captured by al-Mughīra, imprisoned, and later killed. According to the accounts in al-Balādhurī and Ibn al-Athīr, Muʿāwiya sent instructions that Muʿayn could be released if he bore witness that Muʿāwiya was the caliph.[38] When presented with the opportunity, Muʿayn was said to have defied his captors by testifying that God was the Truth and that the Day of Judgment was approaching. He is further shown antagonizing them by putting down the tribe of Tamīm, at which point one of their members killed him. Muʿayn's death was later avenged by another of the *shurāt.* In this fashion his story betrays many of the elements of a typical late antique martyrdom tale, including a trial, the *shārī*'s staunch refusal to accede to the demands of his tormentors (that is, his "witness"), and his death. It simultaneously contains the Arab/tribal element of vengeance, exacted by later *shurāt* on behalf of their slain brother in faith.

Al-Balādhurī and Ibn al-Athīr likewise recorded *shurāt* rebellions from the early period involving non-Arab "clients" (*mawālī*): a *mawla* of the Banū Ḥārith b. Kaʿb known as Abū Maryam was said to have rebelled along with two women, Qaṭṭām (perhaps referring to the same Qaṭamī bt. Alqama who demanded ʿAlī's head from Ibn Muljam) and Kuḥayla—an act that posthumously earned him the condemnation of Abū Bilāl.[39] Similarly, Abū Layla, described as tall and black (that is, not an Arab), rebelled in Kūfa in 42/662 along with thirty horsemen from the *mawālī*. He was killed along with his followers in the outskirts of the city.[40] The presence of *mawālī* among the earliest *shurāt* is most intriguing as it begs the questions as to the origin and influence of non-Arabs in the movement. Although the evidence is slight and does not yield a definitive answer, later Khārijite movements, such as the Azāriqa, likewise contained significant numbers of *mawālī* among them, making their presence among the earliest *shurāt* as tantalizing as it is difficult to decipher.

Other recalcitrant pockets of Kūfan *shurāt* continued to resist Muʿāwiya and his governors into the 40s/650s. One, Ḥayyān b. Ẓabyān al-Sulamī, wounded at Nahrawān and among those forgiven by ʿAlī after the battle, had left for Rayy with some of his companions, but upon hearing of ʿAlī's death he decided to return.[41] In Rayy he was reported to have called some of his companions to his house, where they praised ʿAlī's killer. The group included Sālim b. Rabīʿa, al-Mustawrid b. ʿUllafa of the Taym Ribāb of Tamīm, Muʿādh b. Juwayn al-Ṭāʾī (said to be the cousin of the Nahrawān martyr Zayd b. Ḥiṣn), and ʿItrīs b. ʿUrqūb, among others. According to several sources, Ḥayyān, Muʿādh, and al-Mustawrid became the leaders of the Kufan *shurāt* after their return, though formal allegiance (that is, the *bayʿa*) was given only to al-Mustawrid.[42]

According to Abū Mikhnaf's report in al-Ṭabarī, Ḥayyān b. Ẓabyān was said to have addressed the group gathered in his house in Rayy:

> By God, no one lives forever. Nights and days and years and months will not continue indefinitely for a son of Adam until he tastes death and will part from the virtuous brothers and leave the world over which only weaklings weep, a world which is always harmful for whoever has concern and worry. Then let us be off, may God have mercy on us, to our city [that is, Kūfa]. Let us join our brothers and summon them to command the good and to forbid evil, and to strive against the factions (*ʿalā jihād al-aḥzab*). For we have no excuse sitting out the fight (*al-quʿūd*) while our rulers are oppressive, and while the guiding *sunna* is abandoned and our vengeance remains unexacted against those who killed our brothers at our gatherings (*al-majālis*). If God gives us victory over them, let us turn afterwards to that which is more correct and satisfying and upright. God will thereby heal the bosoms of the believers. If we are killed, we would have repose in parting from oppressors, while our predecessors have set an example for us.[43]

Ḥayyān's speech articulates the fleeting and ultimately unsatisfactory nature of the world, while simultaneously affirming the duty of the *shurāt* to fight against oppression and impiety and to exact revenge for Nahrawān. It likewise gives the precedent of his predecessors (*aslāf*) for the action of *shirā'*, though it does not name it as such, preferring the term *jihād*. Another poem, attributed to Mu'ādh b. Juwayn, expressly identifies Ḥayyān b. Ẓabyān's group as *shurāt*.[44] Ḥayyān's desire to avenge those fallen at Nahrawān is corroborated by a poem attributed to him, in which he states,

> Friends, I have no solace, nor patience
> Nor need [for the world] after those fallen at an-Nahr
> [that is, al-Nahrawān],
> Except fighting a myriad of armies
> that neither call on God nor wield a sword for His sake.[45]

Al-Mustawrid expressed a similar sentiment when, before being elected as the leader of the assembled Kūfan *shurāt*, he said, "We do not seek the glory of this world, and there is no way to remain in it. We desire only immortality in the abode of immortality."[46] In this way the early leaders of the Kūfan *shurāt* were said to have articulated a vision of martyrdom that combined a devaluation of the present world with a desire, possibly even the duty, to fight against tyranny and oppression. As such, this vision resonates not only with the early Islamic *ghāzīyīn* but also with the nexus of martyrdom and world-rejection that permeated the late antique Middle East.

Al-Mustawrid's election as *amīr al-mu'minīn* signaled the beginning of the Kūfan *shurāt*'s desire to resist the Umayyads. They prepared to rebel in 43/663, but after Ḥayyān b. Ẓabyān and several members of the group were arrested by al-Mughīra, al-Mustawrid decided to leave Kūfa for safer refuges. After a brief stay in al-Ḥīra, they returned briefly to Kūfa, only to be driven out again as the governor pressured the tribes and whipped up sentiment against the *khawārij* among 'Alī's supporters. Al-Mustawrid's group escaped in small bands first to Sura, then to Ṣarāt, and then to Bahurasīr, where the Umayyad general Simāk b. 'Ubayd al-'Absī destroyed the bridge over the Euphrates and prevented their crossing. According to the firsthand account of al-Mustawrid's nephew 'Abdullāh b. 'Uqba al-Ghanawī (preserved by Abū Mikhnaf), al-Mustawrid wrote a letter to Simāk b. 'Ubayd calling on him to disavow 'Uthmān and 'Alī for their misdeeds (*iḥdāth fī'l-dīn*) and for abandoning the judgment of the Qur'ān. The letter promised a battle if he refused, and it outlined how the *shurāt* fought in order to "take revenge on behalf of our folk for tyranny in judgment, failure to enforce the *ḥudūd*, and monopolization of the *fay'*."[47] It is striking in these passages how profoundly revenge for those fallen at Nahrawān and the notion of fighting to restore justice in the face of injustice drove al-Mustawrid and his band of *shurāt;* it is a sentiment that matches that attributed to Ḥayyān b. Ẓabyān as well as earlier *shurāt* luminaries such as Muʿayn b. ʿAbdullāh al-Muḥāribī and Ibn Muljam.

Simāk b. ʿUbayd, of course, refused al-Mustawrid's conditions, and the *shurāt* prepared for combat. Continuing the theme of rejection of the world in favor of the hereafter, al-Mustawrid was said to have used the following words to goad his followers to fight: "I did not go forth seeking the temporal world, nor its renown, glory or survival in it. I do not want any of it for myself, and that goes double for the things people compete for in it. I value such things less than the toe of my shoe. I went forth seeking only martyrdom (*al-shahāda*), and that God would guide me to honor by humbling some of those who err."[48] He decided, however, to exhaust the pursuing Umayyad army by withdrawing and forcing pursuit, thus dividing their forces. Eventually a small band of the Umayyad army under the direction of Maʿqil b. Qays caught up with al-Mustawrid in Madhār and resisted their attacks until the main Umayyad force arrived. During the ensuing battle, al-Mustawrid called upon the *shurāt* to seek martyrdom, saying that "paradise belongs to whomever is killed with the genuine intention of *jihād* against these oppressors and their expression of enmity."[49] Ultimately the *shurāt* were duly routed, and al-Mustawrid was killed.[50]

As with earlier Kūfan *shurāt,* al-Mustawrid seems to have entered the hagiographical roll call of *shārī* martyrs. Not only were his story and speeches preserved (and ultimately collected by Abū Mikhnaf), but in addition al-Mubarrad preserves several sayings of al-Mustawrid and describes him as a person "frequent in prayer, strong in *ijtihād.*"[51] That his sayings survived might indicate that for some of the Kūfan *shurāt,* al-Mustawrid was even considered a person whose actions were worthy of emulating to some degree.

After al-Mughīra died, many of the Kufan *shurāt* who had supported al-Mustawrid emerged from prison, and they later rebelled under Ḥayyān b. Ẓabyān and Muʿādh b. Juwayn. Like al-Mustawrid before them, these agitators were said to have articulated a vision of asceticism and martyrdom in the name of fighting injustice and tyranny. Exhorting his companions, Ḥayyān described how God had "decreed the *jihād* for us" and how for those who engaged in it, God would "grant . . . the reward of this world and the better reward of the other world."[52] Echoing Ḥayyān, Muʿādh is recorded as saying, "By God if we knew that when we gave up *jihād* against oppressors and the rejection of injustice, we would have some excuse with God for doing so, then abandoning it would be easier for us and lighter than undertaking it. But, since we have been created with hearts and ears, we knew and were convinced that there will be no excuse for us until we reject oppression and change injustice by *jihād* against the oppressors."[53] Against those who counseled gathering their strength outside the city of Kūfa, Ḥayyān argued for fighting within it: "by God, there are not enough of you to expect victory in the world against the aggressive oppressors thereby. Rebel beside this city of yours [i.e., Kūfa] and fight according to the command of God against whoever violates obedience to Him."[54] Before raising their rebellion in 58/678, Ḥayyān addressed the Kūfan *shurāt* with the words, "I would never take pleasure in anything in the world after I abandoned my pleasure in order to make this revolt of mine against the sinful oppressors. By God, I do not want the world in its entirety for myself, nor for God to deprive me of martyrdom in this revolt of mine."[55] Ḥayyān b. Ẓabyān, Muʿādh b. Juwayn, and their small band of Kūfans were not to be disappointed: they were surprised by the Kūfan army at Jawkhā and martyred.[56]

With al-Mustwarid, Ḥayyān b. Ẓabyān, and Muʿādh b. Juwayn the concept of *shirā'* as a particular form of Islamic martyrdom comes into sharper focus. On the one hand, *shirā'* seems to have been indelibly tied to fighting injustice and oppression, and as such those who wrote about the early *shurāt* considered it a duty that could not be lightly abandoned. That is not to imply that the early *shurāt* considered *shirā'* an absolute duty in all circumstances; there is but scant evidence that the early *shurāt* rejected *quʿūd* or *taqiyya,* and even those who called for an activist approach engaged in *quʿūd* and *taqiyya* when their circumstances required it: Ḥayyān b. Ẓabyān's above-quoted statement that the *shurāt* "have no excuse sitting out the fight (*al-quʿūd*) while our rulers are oppressive" was made after Ḥayyān spent years in hiding in Rayy and thereby expresses at best a strong preference for *shirā'* over *quʿūd.* Thus, while *shirā'* remained the highest goal and that to which the early *shurāt* aspired, *quʿūd* was not completely discounted. As an ideal to which the *shurāt* aspired, *shirā'* was conceived as a rejection of the world, expressed as ascetic practice while in the world or in the "exchange" of this life for the next, for which the *shārī* was guaranteed paradise through martyrdom.

Such sentiments surrounding the notion of *shirā',* incorporating as they do some of the familiar trappings of late antique Middle Eastern hagiographical narratives, point toward the conscious crafting of the early *shurāt* narratives in the interests of preserving the memory of the preceding martyrs and ascetics and rallying group identity around their persons. Such identity construction can be witnessed within the sources, as when Ḥayyān b. Ẓabyān invoked the example of his "predecessors" or lamented the fallen at Nahrawān. Moreover, fashioning an image of the *shurāt*'s very special dead as having fought tyranny and oppression provided a focal point, a rallying cry, and a justification for engaging in the same struggle. It positioned the nascent *shurāt* as participants alongside the prophets in the unfolding cosmic mission to establish a just and good society on earth before their Judgment. In addition, just as Christian and other late antique narratives of the martyrs turned defeat into ultimate victory, shame into honor, and criminal insurgency into righteous rebellion, so too the narratives of the early *shurāt* valorized death as the ultimate "exchange" through which the *shārī* purchased paradise as he humbled the tyrants of this world.

From a textual standpoint, it is clear that a Kūfan "cycle" circulated in various forms among the early *shurāt* of that city (and certainly beyond). Although the original source or sources for this cycle are missing, the fact that the conceptual framework of *shirā'* as found scattered throughout the poetry of the early *shurāt* matches what is preserved in the historical sources makes it likely that *shārī* authors and poets were consciously crafting a narrative, replete with fixed actors, that articulated the stories of those who had "exchanged" this world for the hereafter in the pursuit of justice. This postulated source or sources acted as the basis for later proto-Sunnī and pro-ʿAlīd accounts (for example, Abū Mikhnaf's) of the early *shurāt* and eventually made their way into Ibāḍī literature as well. *Shurāt* groups outside of Kūfa, it seems, engaged in similar processes, creating (or appending to the Kūfan cycle) their own hagiographical stories of local martyrs and heroes.

After Ibn Ẓabyān and Ibn Juwayn's rebellion, little was heard of the Kūfan *shurāt*. A certain Ziyād b. Kharrāsh al-ʿAjalī was said to have rebelled against Ziyād b. Abīhi with three hundred persons in 52/672 as well as Muʿādh al-Ṭā'ī (called "the second" so as not to confuse him with Muʿādh b. Juwayn al-Ṭā'ī) in the same year with thirty rebels. Beyond these, however, no further uprisings of note were recorded from the city.[57] Certainly, quietist strains of *shurāt* continued to exist: the sources attest to a proto-Ibāḍī community in Kūfa, which produced the likes of ʿAbdullāh b. Yazīd al-Fazārī;[58] al-Masʿūdī reports that Hishām b. al-Ḥakam, the Imāmī Shiʿite disciple and contemporary of Jaʿfar al-Ṣādiq, shared a store in Kūfa with him.[59] But the further history of the early Khārijite *shurāt* was written farther south, in Basra, from whence the next host of *shurāt* martyrs, ascetics, and heroes emerged.

The first recorded uprising of Basran Khārijites was that of Sahm b. Ghālib al-Ḥujaymī and Yazīd b. Mālik al-Bāhilī, known as al-Khaṭīm ("broken nose") because of a blow he had taken to the face.[60] Ibn al-Athīr and Ibn Khayyāṭ place their rebellion in 41/661, al-Balādhurī in 44/664, and al-Ṭabarī in 46/667.[61] They were said to have rebelled near Basra and to have been beaten back into the reeds and captured by the army headed by the Basran governor ʿAbdullāh b. ʿĀmir, who offered them amnesty and protected them when Muʿāwiya ordered them killed. However, when Ziyād b. Abīhi became governor (in 45/665), Sahm and al-Khaṭīm feared that he would not honor their amnesty and rebelled again. Decamping to Ahwāz, they supposedly killed a *mawlā* of Qudāma b. Maẓʿūn al-Jumaḥī. Nothing came of their rebellion, and Sahm returned to Basra hoping that the governor would grant him another pardon, but Ziyād crucified him on the door of the governor's palace. Al-Khaṭīm initially faced exile in Baḥrayn but returned to Basra and was ordered under house arrest. Upon breaking his house arrest, he was killed in 49/669 by Muslim b. ʿAmr, the leader of the Bāhila.[62] According to al-Balādhurī, Ziyād also arrested and killed two women, Arāka and Um Sarī, who attempted to rebel with al-Khaṭīm.[63] Only a single anonymous line of poetry remembers Sahm b. Ghālib: "If the parties will admit to crucifying him, God will not abandon Sahm b. Ghālib."[64] Nevertheless their story was recorded and appears in several places, making it likely that on some level the local *shurāt* of Iraq honored them.

Other scattered, small rebellions plagued the Umayyad governors of Basra. A group of *shurāt* under ʿAbbād b. Ḥuṣayn attacked Ziyād's governor of Basra, Shaybān b. ʿAbdullāh al-Saʿadī, and killed his son. Shaybān sent Bishr b. ʿUtba al-Tamīmī and the Basran authorities (*shurṭa*) to attack them, slaying them all.[65] One of Muʿāwiya's men, Ḥāritha b. Ṣakhr al-Qaynī, was said to have adopted "Khārijite views" on his way to Egypt and decided to go to Iraq to rebel against Ziyād. Ziyād searched for him but was unable to nab him as the people of Quḍāʿa prevented Ziyād from doing so. Ḥāritha was granted amnesty at the intervention of the Quḍāʿa and eventually went to Madīna, where he was killed fighting alongside the armies of ʿAbdullāh b. al-Zubayr at the battle of al-Ḥarra (in 63/683).[66]

The next major Basran uprising was that of Qarīb b. Murra al-Azdī and Zuḥḥāf b. Zaḥr al-Ṭāʾī, two cousins, with sixty to eighty persons in 53/672–73.[67] Reports of both Wahb b. Jarīr (in Khalīfa b. Khayyāṭ and al-Ṭabarī) and al-Balādhurī emphasize the violence of their rebellion, with al-Balādhurī mentioning that they engaged in *istiʿrāḍ* (random violence)—an act that reportedly earned them the condemnation of Abū Bilāl Mirdās b. Udayya.[68] Killing a *shaykh* from the Banū Ḍubayʿa whom they mistook for the leader of the Basran *shurṭa* (*ṣāḥib al-shuraṭ*), Qarīb and Zuḥḥāf proceeded to cut a bloody swath through several neighborhoods and mosques in Basra before Sayf b. Wahb as well as youths from the Banū ʿAlī and Banū Rāsib engaged them in battle. Before long the Basran authorities arrived, and according to al-Balādhurī's report, the *shurāt* retreated to a house, where they were surrounded and then killed in the morning as the governor's forces broke in.[69] A certain ʿAbbād b. Ḥuṣayn al-Ḥabaṭī (in al-Ṭabarī's version it is ʿAbdullāh b. Aws al-Ṭāḥī) killed Qarīb and brought back his head to Ziyād. His body and those of Zuḥḥāf and their companions were crucified.[70]

After Qarīb and Zuḥḥāf's rebellion, Ziyād and his governor in Basra, Samura b. Jundab, treated the Basran *shurāt* with particular harshness, crucifying them along with a woman who was said to have addressed Qarīb and Zuḥḥāf's dead bodies, saying, "the peace of God, and his mercy, 'well have you done, enter [here, that is, paradise] to dwell forever.'"[71] Ziyād was reported to have threatened to withhold the stipends of the tribes if they allowed any *khawārij* to escape, causing the people of Basra to murder many of them, including Shaqīq b. Thawr, Ḥajjār b. Abjar, and ʿAbbād b. Ḥuṣayn al-Ḥabaṭī.[72] In addition it is reported that several women associated with Qarīb and Zuḥḥāf were drowned. Ziyād's threat to crucify any woman who rebelled reportedly terrified the female *shurāt* into submission.[73]

The harsh treatment of the *shurāt* continued into the governorship of ʿUbaydullāh b. Ziyād. Al-Mubarrad mentions one of the "ascetics of [the

Khārijites]" (*min nussākihim*) named Khālid b. 'Abbād (or 'Ubāda), who was brought before Ibn Ziyād and questioned as to his whereabouts. Khālid answered, "I was with a people who mention God, and who speak of the Imāms of Tyranny, and who dissociate from them (*fayatabarra'ūna minhum*)!"[74] After Khālid refused to speak well of 'Uthmān and Mu'āwiya, Ibn Ziyād ordered him to be killed. However, the Basran *shurṭā* refused to kill a man whose prayer marks were evident on his face until a certain al-Muthallam b. Masrūḥ al-Bāhilī did so. The *shurāt* then planned their revenge against al-Muthallam, luring him into a house in the Banū Sa'd area, where Ḥurayth b. Ḥajl and Kahmas b. Ṭalaq al-Ṣarīmī killed him. They buried him, along with some money that he was carrying, in the house. Later during Abū Bilāl's uprising, Ḥurayth addressed the Bāhila in Ibn Zur'a al-Kilābī's army, telling them where al-Muthallam's body could be found along with the money.[75] Such an anecdote was meant to underscore Ḥurayth's piety.

With the narrative of Khālid b. 'Abbād, al-Mubarrad's account returns to the hagiographical structure and themes of earlier *shurāt* stories. It not only contains an interrogation scene of a pious ascetic and his defiant refusal and martyrdom, but it also goes out of its way to describe the devoutness of the martyr—virtues recognized even by the Basran authorities. Moreover, even after the *shurāt* exacted their revenge on al-Muthallam, they were shown to uphold the basic requirements of Islamic piety by insuring (on the verge of a battle!) that the monies found with him were returned to their rightful owners. Although Khālid b. 'Abbād's story is not found among those preserved by al-Ṭabarī, al-Balādhurī, and others, its structure is similar to them, and it certainly hailed from a *shārī* source. As al-Mubarrad was a native of Basra and a member of the Azd tribe (which ultimately came from eastern Arabia), his sources represent an independent Basran/Arabian tradition on the *shurāt*—one parallel to that found in Kūfa.

The background events that led to the penultimate, pre-Azraqite Basran *shurāt* rebellion occurred in 58/677, when Ibn Ziyād arrested an assembly of *shurāt* who used to gather near a wall and curse the ruling powers.[76] He prevailed upon the twelve Arabs, among them Ṭawwāf b. 'Allāq and Aws b. Ka'b, to kill the other twelve *mawālī*. The killers were freed, and they pleaded coercion as they faced the censure of their fellow Basran *shurāt*. After a Basran named 'Uqba b. al-Ward al-Bāhilī killed a certain Ḥujayr al-Bāhilī for speaking ill of their slain brethren (and was himself then seized and slain), the murderers, filled with regret and weeping over their actions, proposed retaliation and then payment of blood money. Both were refused, until Ṭawwāf met his cousin al-Hathāth b. Thawr al-Sadūsī, who said, "I will not answer you except with a verse from the Book of God, which says (in 16:110) 'Then surely your Lord, to those who emigrated after they had inflicted persecutions [on Muslims] (*min ba'di mā fatanū*)[77] and thereafter strove (*jahadū*) and patiently persevered, surely your Lord after all this, is Forgiving, Merciful.'"[78] Taking the verse to mean that they would be forgiven the murder of their brethren if they rebelled, Ṭawwāf accepted the pledge (*bay'a*) of leadership from seventy of his followers from the 'Abd al-Qays, and they agreed to attack Ibn Ziyād. Even when one of their number gave them up, thus forcing them to rebel sooner than they had wished, they felt themselves committed (*ma'khudhūn*), killed a man from the Banū Ḍubay'a, and decamped to an area called al-Jalḥā. The Basran authorities caught up with them, routing them and forcing them back to Basra, where they were outnumbered and eventually killed. Ṭawwāf was forced into the river, where he was slain with arrows.[79] Ibn Ziyād ordered his body crucified, but he was taken at night and buried by his family and some of the 'Allāq tribe.

On the whole, Ṭawwāf and his companions seem to have been remembered in a positive light by their contemporary *shurāt*. Not only does the story as it is presented in al-Balādhurī and Ibn al-Athīr highlight their commitment to *khurūj* (even after they are betrayed), but also an anonymous line of poetry valorizes their bravery: "there were not, in the religion (*dīn*) of Ṭawwāf and his brothers, and the people of the Wall, gatherers of cotton and grapes."[80] In addition another poem, from a later period, mentions Ṭawwāf among other early *shurāt* figures as someone whom the poet wishes to emulate:

> Oh Lord! Grant me piety and sincerity in trustworthiness;
> and I will be satisfied with serious matters, for You are the Sustainer
> and the Complete;
> until I sell (*ḥattā ubī'a*) that which passes [away] for the afterlife;
> and remain in the religion (*dīn*) of Mirdās and Ṭawwāf;
> and Kahmas and Abī al-Sha'thā` when they hasten to God,
> and [also] the possessor of humility, Zuḥḥāf.[81]

Moreover, Abū Bilāl was supposed to have remembered Ṭawwāf in a line of poetry: "my self is uncertain, and I don't feel security from fate (*al-dahr*), after [the deaths of] Ka'b, Ṭawwāf and Ghassāl."[82] Although Ṭawwāf here functions as a reminder of the inconstancy of life, Abū Bilāl's evocation of him appears favorable. Ṭawwāf and his companions thus entered the hagiographical imaginary of the early *shurāt*, becoming a model for action and a martyr to be remembered.

However, despite the general tone of praise among *shārī* poets for Ṭawwāf and his followers, other *shurāt* clearly had reservations about them. For example, 'Īsā b. Fātik al-Khaṭṭī, who later rebelled with Nāfi' b. al-Azraq, supposedly responded to al-Hathāth b. Thawr al-Sadūsī, Ṭawwāf's cousin and the one who quoted 16:110 in order to inspire Ṭawwāf in rebellion, with the following words:

> You were ignorant of Ṭawwāf and ornamented his doings,
> But Ṭawwāf began to tear [people] with arrows.

So say to ʿUbaydullah: if you were seeking
Those of greed, vehemence, blame and stinginess,
Then there are some people whose father is Sadūs.
And indeed Sadūs is the disease of religion and reason.[83]

Not only, then, did Ibn Fātik insult al-Hathāth's tribe, the Sadūs, but he also clearly had a bitter attitude toward Ṭawwāf and his actions. Given that Ibn Fātik later rebelled with the Azāriqa—a group known for their violence toward any who did not share their views—it is to be assumed that it was Ṭawwāf's murder of his fellow *shurāt* and not his act of rebellion that garnered Ibn Fātik's censure. In fact many Muslims in the early period held that the murder of a fellow Muslim was a sin that God would not forgive; it is therefore likely that Ibn Fātik found Ṭawwāf's sin unpardonable.[84]

The crowning rebellion of the pre-Azraqite *shurāt*—for later Ibāḍīs the paradigmatic uprising—was that of Abū Bilāl's beginning in 58/678. Abū Bilāl Mirdās b. Udayya along with his brother ʿUrwa enjoyed the highest esteem in the narratives of the early *shurāt:* they were Ṣiffīn veterans, original members of the Muḥakkima, and participants in the battle of Nahrawān;[85] ʿUrwa was sometimes credited for the first use of the phrase *lā ḥukm illā lilāh* at Ṣiffīn as well as having drawn the first sword in rebellion against it;[86] and Abū Bilāl was described as serious in his worship of God (*ʿābidan*) and a leader who commanded the respect of his companions.[87] Indeed so widespread was Abū Bilāl's fame that he was later claimed as a follower even by Muʿtazilites and Shiʿites.[88]

As befit figures of such stature, their stories were crafted so as to accentuate their ascetic qualities as well as their deaths as martyrs. ʿUrwa was said to have met his end at the hands of ʿUbaydullāh b. Ziyād during his persecution of the *shurāt* in 58/678.[89] According to the story in al-Ṭabarī (on the authority of Wahb b. Jarīr) and Ibn al-Athīr, ʿUrwa approached Ibn Ziyād when the latter was outside of Basra, and he mentioned five faults that he found with Ibn Ziyād.[90] Although Wahb b. Jarīr neglects to mention two of these sins in his narrative, ʿUrwa was said to have quoted to Ibn Ziyād Qur'ān 26:128–30, the words of the prophet Hūd to the people of ʿĀd: "Do you build a landmark on every high place to amuse yourselves? And do you get for yourselves fine buildings in the hope of living therein [forever]? And when you exert your strong hand, you do so as tyrants?" Ibn Ziyād, assuming that ʿUrwa would not say such things if he did not have his companions close to him, fled but later hunted down ʿUrwa, who had escaped to Kūfa. Once ʿUrwa was captured, Ibn Ziyād cut off his hands and feet, at which ʿUrwa was said to have retorted, "I think that you have ruined this world for me, but ruined the other world for yourself." Ibn Ziyād then killed him along with his daughter. A variant account by al-Mubarrad of ʿUrwa's killing places it at the hands of Ziyād b. Abīhi, who interrogated ʿUrwa as to his views concerning Abū Bakr, ʿUmar, ʿUthmān, ʿAlī, Muʿāwiya, and himself.[91] 'Urwa was said to have accused 'Uthmān and 'Alī of *kufr*, to have vehemently cursed Mu'āwiya, and to have said to Ziyād that he was the "first in fornication (*zinya*) and the last in proselytization (*da'wa*)" and that after Ziyād's disobedience he would meet his Lord.[92] Narratives on 'Urwa b. Udayya thus fashion his story along familiar hagiographical lines: all of the versions have some sort of interrogation before 'Urwa's martyrdom, and all show him as standing up to the oppressive Umayyad governors.

Accounts of Abū Bilāl's life are likewise filled with anecdotes that paint him as standing up to the powerful and tyrannical Umayyads. He is credited, for example, with publically shaming Ziyād with a Qur'ānic verse, of threatening Ghaylān b. Kharsha when he maligned "those who sell their lives and exchange the hereafter for this world," and of censuring Murra b. 'Āmir for wearing a long-sleeved shirt (that is, for dressing in wealthy clothing).[93] Such narrations established Abū Bilāl's credentials and set the stage for his eventual rebellion against Ibn Ziyād.

The inspiration for Abū Bilāl's uprising is said to have come from the martyrdom of a woman named al-Balthā', one of the Ḥarām b. Yarbū' of the Tamīm, at the hands of Ibn Ziyād.[94] Al-Balādhurī's narrative describes her as "one of the Khārijite *makhābīt*," a term that probably refers to "those who are humble [before God]" and may have been a particular group among them.[95] Al-Balthā' is said to have publically maligned Ibn Ziyād and recounted his misdeeds, so much so that the governor began to mention her name in the court. As her associate, Abū Bilāl was warned and approached al-Balthā' and counseled her to hide herself or to practice dissimulation (*taqiyya*), but al-Balthā' demurred, saying, "I would hate for someone to meet with misfortune because of me if [Ibn Ziyād] demanded me."[96] Refusing to escape, she was seized by the governor, who cut off her hands and feet and displayed her dead body in the marketplace. Abū Bilāl passed by her and is reported to have uttered, "This is a better person in death than you, oh Abū Bilāl! There is no death more precious to me (*aḥabba ilay*) than the death of al-Balthā', and every demise other than the demise of al-Balthā' is doubtful."[97] As with the martyrdom narrative of Mar Ma'īn, Abū Bilāl's narrative established his desire to die fighting oppression through the observation of another who was willing to do so. As a narrative device, Abū Bilāl's witness of al-Balthā''s martyrdom models the type of identity that was established through these stories, for just as Abū Bilāl resolved to rebel by the example of al-Balthā', so too those who heard the story of Abū Bilāl—who embraced it and held up its main character as a paragon of virtue—placed the highest value on "exchanging" themselves for paradise and in so doing embraced the identity of the *shurāt*.

Abū Bilāl's narrative further portrays his piety with anecdotes that accentuate his fear of God—his *taqwa*—and his absolute devotion. For example, the narratives speak of how his resolve to engage in *shirā'* was strengthened when he passed by a well that was being repaired and his garment was spattered with pitch. Abū Bilāl fell to the ground, and the Bedouin who was repairing the well thought that he was having an epileptic fit, but Abū Bilāl explained that he thought that the pitch was the pitch of hell mentioned as part of the sinner's punishment in Qur'ān 14:50.[98] Similarly in al-Balādhurī and Ibn al-Athīr's versions, the pitch caused Abū Bilāl to recite the verse "their garments of liquid pitch."[99] Such evocation of Qur'ānic verses is meant to portray Abū Bilāl as ever mindful of the Qur'ān and alert to the consequences of his own actions. Such praiseworthy characteristics are unlikely to have come from the pen of a non-*shārī* author and in all probability reflect the original telling of the narrative.

Moreover al-Mubarrad mentions how, according to reports from the *shurāt* (probably meaning Ibāḍīs), after taking the pledge (*'aqd*) from his companions and resolving to rebel, Abū Bilāl raised his hands in the air and asked God to give them a sign confirming the truth of their decision. Some reported that the house shook, while others said that the roof was raised.[100] Other signs are reported from Abū Bilāl's followers. Ḥabība al-Naṣrī's thoughts about his daughters weakened his resolve to rebel, and so he decided to check them to make sure that they would be all right without him. In the middle of the night, his youngest daughter asked for a drink, but Ḥabība did not answer her. When she asked again, her older sister fetched it for her. At this, Ḥabība knew that God would not cause them distress, and his resolve to rebel was strengthened.[101] Similarly, Kahmas worried about his mother should he rebel, but she said, "I have given you to God," thus releasing him of his responsibility to her.[102] As with other stories of the martyrs and saints, miracles and signs accompany their actions, signaling divine favor for their mission.

Despite Abū Bilāl's resolve, it is reported that he and his fellow Basran *shurāt* were imprisoned before being able to rebel.[103] This event became another cause for celebrating Abū Bilāl's moral rectitude: an anecdote found in many sources tells of how Abū Bilāl's jailer, a milk-brother of Ibn Ziyād (that is, he and Ibn Ziyād were of different parents, but were nursed simultaneously by the same woman—presumably a wet nurse), admired Abū Bilāl's zeal in worship and allowed him to return to his home during the night.[104] At dawn Abū Bilāl would return to the prison. One night Ibn Ziyād decided to kill his Khārijite prisoners the next morning; according to the account in al-Mubarrad, some of their number had murdered a member of the authorities.[105] A friend of Abū Bilāl rushed off to his home to warn him of his impending execution. The jailer too heard the news and worried that Abū Bilāl would escape and that the jailer would be rebuked for letting him leave during the night. However, Abū Bilāl returned as usual to the prison and said, to the astonishment of the jailer, "you would not be rewarded for your kindness if you were punished because of me."[106] In al-Mubarrad's version Abū Bilāl states that he would not want to meet his Lord having committed deception (by not honoring his promise to return).[107] When Ibn Ziyād began to kill the Khārijite prisoners, the jailer intervened on Abū Bilāl's behalf, and he was spared.

When Ibn Ziyād once again decided to persecute the *shurāt,* Abū Bilāl and his followers commenced their uprising. Reportedly, Abū Bilāl addressed his companions, saying that both patience and fighting were weighty matters and that therefore they should retreat, drawing their swords against only those who drew their swords against them. In this way he hoped to be able to put an end to whatever oppression (*ẓulm*) it was in their power to end.[108] Al-Mubarrad mentions that thirty *shurāt* joined Abū Bilāl's group, including Ḥurayth b. Ḥajl and Kahmas b. Ṭalq al-Ṣarīmī.[109] On their way out of town, Abū Bilāl and his group met ʿAbdullāh b. Rabāḥ al-Anṣārī, whom they assured they would not harm.[110] Coming to Āsik (a district of al-Ahwāz between Arajān and Rāmhurmuz), they intercepted someone carrying the stipends (*ʿaṭā*) to Ibn Ziyād. Abū Bilāl's group now having reached forty persons, they took only the share due to him and his group, telling the carrier to return with the rest.[111] Another anecdote tells how Abū Bilāl refrained from killing two associates of Ibn Ziyād who met him on their way to Khurasān.[112]

In 60/680 Ibn Ziyād sent an army of two thousand under the command of Aslam b. Zurʿa to bring back Abū Bilāl and his group.[113] They met at Āsik, where Abū Bilāl routed them and a *shārī* named Maʿbad nearly captured Ibn Zurʿa. So disastrous and shameful was Ibn Zurʿa's defeat that he was heckled in the marketplace of Basra with the taunts "Abū Bilāl is behind you!" and "Oh Maʿbad, capture him!" Ibn Ziyād was even forced to send the *shurṭā* to the marketplace to stop it.[114] A poem attributed to the *shārī* poet ʿĪsā b. Fātik al-Khaṭṭī valorizes the Khārijites at the battle of Āsik:

When they woke, they prayed and rode out
On noble horses with stubbly hair.
When they gathered, they assailed them,
and the hired ones fell; they attacked us
For the rest of the day until
the dark of night came, when they engaged us in ruses.
The one watching them said when he saw them
that they have fled from us.
Two thousand believers—as you claim,
and forty defeated them in Āsik.
You lie—it is not as you claim!
The Khawārij were the believers!
They are a small company, with no doubts,
Who over the many were victorious.
You all have obeyed the commands of an obdurate tyrant,
[but] there is no obedience to oppressors.[115]

The reference to the "small company" (*fi'a qalīla*) who were rendered victorious over the many is likely a reference to Qur'ān 2:249: "But those who were certain that they would meet God said, 'How many a small company has overcome a large company by permission of God?' And God is with the patient." The poem likewise makes reference to the notion of resisting oppression and tyranny, a potent theme in late antique and early Islamic narratives on the saints and martyrs.

Continuing the narrative, Ibn Ziyād was said to have sent 'Abbād b. 'Alqama al-Māzinī with an army of three or four thousand against Abū Bilāl.[116] Finding the *shurāt* either at Tawwaj (that is, ancient Taoke on the Shirīn River in the province of Fars) or Darābjird (also in Fars, near modern Dārāb, Iran), they began to fight on a Friday.[117] Abū Mikhnaf's account in al-Ṭabarī mentions that after finding themselves surrounded, Abū Bilāl said to his followers, "Whoever of you has come out in pursuit of worldly things, let him go, but whoever of you only wants the Hereafter and to meet his Lord, that was decreed earlier for him," and then he recited Qur'ān 42:20.[118] Although they were offered the choice to flee, Abū Mikhnaf's report mentions that none of the *shurāt* abandoned the fighting. When the time for prayer arrived, Abū Bilāl called for a temporary cessation so that the two armies could perform their Friday prayers.[119] Although Ibn 'Alqama agreed to the truce, when the *shurāt* began to pray, he and a group from his army fell upon them when they were between the full prostration and the sitting position (that is, when their faces were to the ground). With this deception Ibn 'Alqama killed them all and took Abū Bilāl's head. Al-Mubarrad's report mentions that the skulls of these Khārijites were displayed (*ṣulibat,* lit. "crucified") on posts; this included those of the *shārī* ascetic (*nāsik*) Dāwūd b. Shabath and the *mujtahid* Ḥabība al-Naṣrī of the Qays.[120] The *shurāt*'s bravery and piety were underscored by Ibn 'Alqama's perfidy, and by the heads of the pious worshippers displayed so shamelessly in public.

As is typical of *shurāt* narratives, several reports include the story of how the *shurāt* avenged Abū Bilāl's killing by waiting for Ibn 'Alqama in Basra.[121] There they reportedly asked him what they should do about a brother of theirs who had been unfairly slain. Ibn 'Alqama told them to ask that the governor punish the man, but the *shurāt* said that the governor had not acted, at which point Ibn 'Alqama replied, according to Abū Mikhnaf's account, "then kill the man, may God destroy him!" At this the *shurāt* fell on him uttering their cry and also killed his son.[122]

As with other narratives of the early *shurāt,* Abū Bilāl's revolt became the focal point for *shārī* and later Khārijite identities. His exploits remained some of the most celebrated among *shurāt* poets, and eulogies to Abū Bilāl and his followers were quite common. Thus, for example, a woman of the Banū Salīṭ intoned,

May God recall Mirdās and his first companions,
who exchanged (*sharū*) [their lives along] with him,
  a rain full of yelling
[that is, who gathered lots of soldiers ready to fight].
Each of them has given generously and sincerely to God
their hearts, upon the meeting of the soldiers.[123]

Accordingly martyrdom through *shirā'* remains a theme of these poems, as shown by the following from Ka'b b. 'Amīra:

God has bought (*sharā*) Ibn Ḥudayr's soul
and he has embraced the Paradises of Firdūs with its many blessings,
He was made happy by a people with faces like
The stars in the darkness when their clouds have cleared
Forward they rode—with Indian swords and with lances
On charging horses given to running.[124]

Ibn 'Amīra's poem takes up the theme of fighting in exchange for paradise, drawing upon the traditions of Arabic battle poetry to embroider the image of Abū Bilāl's companions riding toward their deaths.[125] Inevitable death, another stock poetic image, informs 'Imrān b. Ḥaṭṭān's eulogy:

If death is hateful to you, then depart
And seek a land where people do not succumb!
You will not find a land in which people
Do not come and go in droves
Toward their tombs; [and] the four [grave diggers] do not cease
To lower a bier towards the grave.
Oh Jamra, Mirdās and his brothers have died.
And before them, Prophets died.
O Jamr, if a pure soul is safeguarded
From adversity, that still, oh Jamra, wearies us.
Then Mirdās would yet be safe and sound,
And mourners would not have lamented his death at Dhāt al-Ghuṣn.
If only I could annihilate myself for you who are cast in a desolation,
You would not become, this day, buried in graves.
He was a rightly guided man through whom God chose to guide
  others;
He prayed at all times and had no liking for those who did not.
He who is . . . does not forget the hereafter, nor is he
Distracted when the heedless deny it.
You have left us like orphans whose father had died,

And who have not since seen any comfort or ease.
May God reward you, Oh Mirdās, with paradise
Just like you used to point us toward guidance.[126]

Ibn Ḥaṭṭān's poem likewise touches on the themes of piety, holding up Abū Bilāl as a model of devotion and guidance while lamenting the poet's inability to have fought alongside him. Abū Bilāl here becomes a father who guides his children, constantly praying, mindful of the hereafter, and yet destined for death as all others.

In Abū Bilāl, then, *shurāt* authors found a model saint and martyr, and they crafted their stories and eulogies of him accordingly. Filled with miraculous signs, pious actions, and brave deeds, the narrative of Abū Bilāl and his companions offers profound parallels with other late antique and early Islamic hagiographical literature and can be viewed as a particularly *shārī* variant on the familiar themes of martyrdom and sainthood. Crafted in familiar ways, the story of Abū Bilāl clearly functioned as a focal point for early *shārī* identity, providing a martyr of impeccable piety and integrity, a model for those who cherished his memory. Although the figure of Abū Bilāl closes the chapter on the early *shurāt,* he continued to serve as an inspiration for many subsequent Khārijite groups, among them the most notorious and perhaps most violent, the Azāriqa.

For Islamic heresiographers, the Azāriqa constitute the first recognizable subgroup of Khārijites. They reportedly took their name from their first leader, Nāfiʿ b. al-Azraq, who according to an anonymous report in al-Mubarrad at first "followed the people of Nahrawān, and Mirdās [b. Udayya] and those who rebelled with him." However, according to many sources Nāfiʿ did not keep to the careful tactics of Abū Bilāl. Al-Mubarrad's narrative tells how a *mawlā* from the Banī Hāshim convinced Nāfiʿ that his enemies along with their wives and children were *kuffār* with whom no intermingling was permitted and that they were to be fought as the *mushrikūn* of the Prophet's era. The Azāriqa likewise did not permit *taqiyya* or *quʿūd* and considered those who practiced them or refused to make the *hijra* to their camp unbelievers (*kuffār*) who could be legitimately fought.[127] Such actions, along with reports of *istiʿrāḍ* and the administration of a "test" (*miḥna*) for potential members, indicate that the Azāriqa in many ways had moved beyond what earlier Muḥakkima and *shurāt* had deemed appropriate or permissible.

Many accounts of the emergence of the Azāriqa relate how the supposed "founders" of the three main divisions of later Khārijites—Nāfiʿ b. al-Azraq, ʿAbdullāh b. Ibāḍ, and ʿAbdullāh b. Ṣaffār—split in 64–65/684 over the question of the treatment of their enemies.[128] Although this *tafrīq* narrative as it is presented in the sources smacks of anachronism in its clean doctrinal and historical divisions between Azāriqa, Ibāḍiyya, and Ṣufriyya, the Azāriqa do seem to have formed a coherent and separate grouping when those willing to fight the approaching Zubayrid general Muslim b. ʿUbays left Basra to regroup in Khuzistān in the Ahwāz under the leadership of Nāfiʿ b. al-Azraq. Although Nāfiʿ was killed at the battle of Dūlāb (on the east bank of the Dujayl/Kārūn River) in 65/685, Azraqī activities would last some fourteen years in and around the environs of Basra, the Ahwāz, Fars, and Kirmān. Relentlessly pursued by the Zubayrid and later the Umayyad governors and in particular by the Azdite Basran general al-Muhallab b. Abī Ṣufra, the Azāriqa fought numerous battles under different imāms. Their most capable leader after Nāfiʿ, Qaṭarī b. al-Fujā'a, was even able to threaten Basra again in 71/690, only to be beaten back by al-Muhallab into the mountains of Fars and then Kirmān in a series of attacks that commenced in 75/694. The end of the Azraqites came about in 78–79/698–99 after the *mawālī* in the Azraqite camp under the leadership of ʿAbd Rabbihi al-Kabīr forced the Arabs under the direction of Qaṭarī from their home base of Jīruft (that is, Jiroft, in the Kirmān province). Al-Muhallab's army finished the Azraqite *mawālī* at Jīruft, while Sufyān b. al-Abrad and the governor of Ṭabaristān pursued and killed Qaṭarī's followers in the surrounding mountains. Qaṭarī fell from his horse and was discovered and killed. A remaining contingent of Azāriqa under the command of ʿAbīda b. Hilāl waited out a siege in the town of Sadhawwar (near the province of Qūmis) and there perished in a final attack.

Despite the deviations from earlier *shurāt* practice, the core concerns of the Azāriqa, at least as far as these can be discerned from their poetry, nevertheless fell more or less in line with those that occupied some of their predecessors. The perceived duty to fight injustice and tyranny, for example, remained a constant theme among them. In fact a variant report in al-Mubarrad locates the impetus for Nāfiʿ b. al-Azraq's rebellion in Abū al-Wāzaʿ al-Rāsibī, who supposedly castigated Nāfiʿ and his companions in Basra when they cursed the "tyranny of the Sulṭān" but remained unwilling to take up arms against him. Abū al-Wāzaʿ rebuked Nāfiʿ with the words, "You were given a sharp tongue and a weak heart. I wish that your heart had the sharpness of your tongue, and your tongue had the weakness of your heart!"[129] Abū Wāzaʿ is reported as reciting the following:

> You cannot harm people with your tongue;
> It is only with your hands that you can be saved from anxiety.
> Fight those people who fought against God and persevere,
> For God may confound the evil course of the Banū Ḥarb.[130]

Not content simply to censure Nāfiʿ, Abū Wāzaʿ then purchased a sword, had it sharpened and polished, and attacked the people of Basra. This event reportedly impressed Nāfiʿ and his followers, inspiring them to open revolt.[131] Although Abū Wāzaʿ apparently attacked at random—and this does not fit with what is reported, for example, about Abū Bilāl's tactics—the core concern of fighting against perceived tyranny (and Basra was a military outpost under the control of the Umayyads) underlies the actions of both Abū Wāza' and then Nāfi'.

Azraqite poetry likewise attests to the conception of fighting for the creation of a just order as the primary Khārijite duty; the main difference is that unlike earlier *shurāt* groups, the Azāriqa did not tolerate "sitting out" the fight (*al-qu'ūd*). Thus, Qaṭarī b. al-Fujā'a was said to have uttered to Abū Khālid al-Qannānī, one of the "sitters,"

> Abū Khālid, get up! For you will not [live] forever!
> And the Merciful has not made an excuse for the sitter (*qā'id*).
> Do you hold that the Khārijī is on the path of guidance,
> While you remain among thieves and no-goods?[132]

Similarly al-Aṣam al-Ḍabbī praises in a poem "those who mustered on the path of their forebears from the Khārijites, before doubt and suspicion [befell them]";[133] and Sumayra b. al-Ja'd intoned, "There is no good in the world when religion is not true, and not directed toward the aim of rebellions (*al-makhārij*)."[134] Accordingly the Azāriqa adopted the mantle of *shirā'*, as when al-Aṣam al-Ḍabbī referred to those killed with 'Abīda b. Hilāl in Sadhawwar as *shurāt* who looked down on their waiting bothers from the heavenly "land of the exchangers" (*balad al-shāriyyīn*).[135]

The Azāriqa, then, joined the long litany of early *shurāt* rebellions whose storied were crafted along familiar late antique Middle Eastern hagiographical lines. Along with those that preceded them, the poetry and narrative from and about the Azāriqa show a propensity to reject the world for the hereafter (that is, to engage in *shirā'*), a decision that manifested itself in an intense piety as well as the willingness to martyr themselves standing up to tyrants and oppressors of all stripes. The Muḥakkima and early *shurāt* undoubtedly held *shirā'* in high esteem, and it is only insofar as the Azāriqa took the duty to battle tyranny as absolute, leaving no leeway for those who would practice *taqiyya* or not fight with them, that they strayed from the ways that most of the earlier groups practiced *shirā'*.

Shurāt Bodies

The Muḥakkima, early *shurāt,* and first Khārijites, then, inherited a late antique/early Islamic syllabary filled with images of piety in life and martyrdom in death, even as they shared geographical spaces still abounding with Eastern Christians, Marcionites, Manicheans, and other groups who articulated similar notions. Crafting the stories of their own "very special dead" in ways that profoundly resonated with other late antique and early Islamic hagiographical literatures, early *shurāt* literature, such as can be found between the pages of the texts in which it now survives, displayed profound structural and thematic parallels with the hagiographical genre as a whole and must be considered as another iteration of that genre.

In addition to the structural and thematic parallels, another means by which to investigate the parallels between early *shurāt* and late antique/early Islamic hagiographical literature is to examine how narratives and poetry by and about the Muḥakkima and early *shurāt* wrote notions of asceticism in life and martyrdom in death onto the human body. Just as with late antique Christian groups, as a locus of the tortures inflicted on the martyr, and of ascetic practice—in short, as a locus for travail—the suffering body became a point upon which early *shurāt* and Khārijite identity could be focused and through which the confession of truth could be enacted. In other words, *shirā'* was marked on the human body, whether in life or in death, and such physical signs provided the *shurāt* and later Khārijite communities with the embodied truth of their movement, concentrating their attention on the ascetic piety and fearless martyrdom of the early *shurāt* saints and, in so doing, providing a locus for group identity.

From the beginnings of the Muḥakkima movement, the notion of *shirā',* insofar as it was conceived as a kind of piety, also seems to have been intimately connected to ascetic practices that were visible on the human body. The familiar trope of indicating piety through descriptions of its physical marks on the body initially comes into focus from several of the descriptions of the first Muḥakkima. For example, ʿAbdullāh b. Wahb al-Rāsibī was said to have been so callused from his frequent prayers that he earned himself the nickname "he of the calluses" (*dhū al-thafināt*).[136] An alternate report in al-Baghdādī gives a similar nickname (*dhū al-thidiyya*) to the Nahrawān martyr Ḥurqūṣ b. Zuhayr.[137] Ibn al-Jawzī described how Ibn al-ʿAbbās, entering the Muḥakkima's camp in the middle of the night, said of them, "I have never seen [a group] so strong in effort (*ijtihād*); their faces [were] bruised from their prostrations, and their hands [looked] as if they were the pads of camels, their shirts were worn, and they busied themselves in night vigils [with] faces wasted away [from fasting]."[138] Ibn al-ʿAbbās's description highlights night prayers, excessive praying, fasting, and an adopted lifestyle of poverty (for example, worn-out shirts) as characteristic traits of the early Muḥakkima.

Prayer marks as well as yellowed faces and feeble bodies from fasting were attested in several other descriptions of later *shurāt:* Ibn al-Jawzī described the bearded and shaven-headed man who was prophesied to be the progenitor of the early Khārijites as *dhū al-khuwayṣra* ("he of the slender waist"), presumably from fasting;[139] several reports mention Ḥawthara b. al-Wadāʿ's prayer marks as visible on his body;[140] Ibn Muljam was described as possessing a yellowed face (from fasting), with the marks of prayer clearly visible on it;[141] and al-Mustawrid was described as praying often (*kathīr al-ṣalāt*).[142] The poet ʿĪsā b. Fātik al-Khaṭṭī mentions the practice of night vigils in his poem:

At nightfall they are submerged [in prayer],
and when the darkness is dispersed they are still prostrated, praying.
Fear of God has put their sleep to flight, their nights spent in vigils,
while those who live a tranquil worldly life lie asleep.[143]

Moreover, ʿUrwa b. Udayya's *mawlā* was said to have described him to Ibn Ziyād with the words, "I did not bring his food to him during the day, nor did I ever make his bed for him at night."[144] So too the early *shārī* poet and hero Farwa b. Nawfal al-Ashjaʿī spoke of slain *shurāt* corpses as "decaying carcasses; shaded by the fledged birds who hop about them, indulging in the little flesh that their bodies possess; thin bodies, emaciated from fasting."[145] Ḥujiyya b. Aws's poem evokes the common images of birds of prey, or vultures, feasting on the dead bodies of those slain in battle:[146]

When I remember Rajā' and his companions
I almost blame myself for some things.
How lucky are the eyes of those who have seen the like of this group
That has come to support Ibn al-Zubayr.
You see birds of prey hopping around them,
Turning over bodies with little flesh.
Oh grief for not having seen them
In Makka as the wounds of horses bled![147]

Later Khārijite groups were reported to have continued the ascetic practices of their predecessors: the Ṣufriyya were said to "wear themselves out in devotions" (*nahakathum al-ʿibāda*), and as a result their faces turned yellow;[148] and Abū Mikhnaf describes the Iraqi Khārijite Ṣāliḥ b. al-Muṣarriḥ's face as yellowed from his prayers (*muṣaffar al-wajh*).[149] Additionally the theme of night vigils appears in two lines from the Azraqite poet Sumayra b. al-Jaʿd: "in the daytime they are battling lions of the woods / but at nightfall they keep vigil, standing up in prayer, like sobbing mourners."[150]

General descriptions of *shurāt* asceticism are also quite common in the sources; for example, Ibn al-Aʿtham's description of the first Muḥakkima describes them as "ascetics in practice, and wearers of the burnouse" (*nussāk al-ʿibād aṣḥāb al-barānis*).[151] A burnouse was a long woolen cloak often associated with ascetics and mendicants, especially in the Christian and Sufi traditions.[152] Similarly, ʿAlī b. Abī Shimr b. al-Ḥusayn of the Taym Ribāb, a follower of al-Mustawrid, is described as one of their "pious ascetics" (implying that there were more than one);[153] Abū al-ʿAbbās's report in al-Mubarrad mentions Khālid b. ʿAbbād (or ʿUbāda) as an ascetic (*nussāk*);[154] and Abū Bilāl's group included the Khārijite ascetic (*nāsik*) Dāwūd b. Shabath.[155]

Qaṭarī b. al-Fujā'a declares in a poem, "[I swear] by your age that I am in life an ascetic (*zāhid*)."[156] Similarly the terms *ijtihād* and *mujtahid* when applied to early *shurāt* seem to indicate extraordinary effort and earnestness in religious practice (rather than acumen in the field of Islamic law), as when al-Mubarrad's report describes al-Mustawrid as *shadīd al-ijtihād* ("strong in effort").[157] Abū Bilāl is characterized as "a worshipper of great effort" (*kāna 'ābidan mujtahidan*),[158] as were his follower Ḥabība al-Naṣrī of the Qays[159] and Abū al-Wāza' al-Rāsibī.[160] An anonymous source in al-Malaṭī's heresiography calls the Khārijites "the people of night [vigils], piety and effort" (*aṣḥāb layalin wa war'in wa ijtihādin*).[161] Indeed, Ibn al-'Abbās's abovementioned description of the Muḥakkima's asceticism opens with his declaration that he had never seen such "effort" (*ijtihād*).

Added to the abundant references to excessive prayers, night vigils, fasting, and intentional poverty is a singular allusion to the practice of celibacy. Abū Bilāl was said to have uttered,

> Oh you seeker of good, the river of tyranny hampers
> spending nights in vigils, if no one comes to cross it.
> I do not deserve to live if I do not abstain from every
> beautiful woman,
> Until the flash of tyranny turns to rain.[162]

Abū Bilāl's celibacy is obliquely corroborated by a comment in Ibn Qutayba to the effect that he did not have any offspring.[163] Later among the Ibāḍiyya the issue of celibacy would become contested; yet this reference remains the only one to the practice among the early *shurāt*, and it is difficult if not impossible to determine the extent of celibacy among them.

Similarly oblique passages imply the practice of tonsure among the early *shurāt*, hinting that it was widespread among them. Indeed a curious passage in the anonymous early Iberian-Islamic chronicle the *Akhbār Majmū'a* rhetorically asks about the polity that the early "Khārijite" rebels in North Africa and Iberia established and describes some of their actions as based in the precedent of earlier Khārijites. Specifically the passage mentions "the raising of copies of the Qur'ān [on lances]; [and] the shaving of heads, which was done in emulation of the followers of al-Azraq and the people of Nahrawān, and those of al-Rāsibī 'Abdullāh b. Wahb and Zayd b. Ḥisn [*sic*]."[164] In addition a reference to the so-called Ṣufriyya of Mesopotamia mentions that before they would rebel, they would visit the tomb of Ṣāliḥ b. al-Musarriḥ and shave their heads there.[165] In a similar fashion, two ḥadīths from the collection of Abū Dāwūd imply that tonsure is a designation by which the Khārijites were known:

> [The messenger of God] said: there will be among my community differences and splits, and a people who speak beautifully but act

> evilly; who recite the Qur'ān but it does not pass their collar-bones; who will fly from religion [like the] flight of an arrow from the bow—they will not return until the arrow comes back to its notch. They are the worst of people and animals; happy is the one who fights them, and is killed by them; they call to the Book of God, but they have nothing to do with it; whoso fights them will be nearer to God than they. They asked: oh messenger of God, what is their sign (*sayyimāhum*)? He replied: Shaving the head (*al-taḥlīq*) and eliminating the hair (*al-tasbīd*); if you see them, you should kill them.[166]

Later in the same ḥadīth Abū Dāwūd clarifies the meaning of *al-tasbīd* as "eliminating the hair" (*isti'ṣāl al-shi'r*). In a second ḥadīth, also from Abū Dāwūd's collection, 'Alī is shown to have confronted a man with a long beard and shaven head and commented, "From this one's stock there will be people who recite the Qur'ān, but it will not pass down their throats; they will fly from religion [like the] flight of an arrow from the bow."[167] It is clear that the Khārijites are intended, as both of these ḥadīth come from the "chapter on fighting the Khārijites" (*bāb fī qatl al-khawārij*) in Abū Dāwūd's *kitāb al-sunna* ("book of the Sunna") portion of his ḥadīth collection; moreover the arrow and bow metaphor is usually associated with descriptions of the Khārijites.[168] Tonsure, then, was associated in some fashion with the image of the *shurāt* and later Khārijites, and it was tied up with the piety by which they were known.

As with their Christian counterparts, there is some evidence that these ascetic practices were believed to infuse the dead bodies of the ascetics/martyrs with sacred power, thus making their burial places sites of special importance. Mention has already been made to the Ṣufrī-Khārijite pilgrimage to the tomb of Ṣāliḥ b. al-Musarriḥ. In addition al-Mubarrad reports that the Banū Yashkur of Basra were displeased when the body of Abū al-Wāza' was interred in their cemetery, saying that they "were afraid that the Khārijites would make his tomb a place of visitation (*taj'al al-khawārij qabrahu muhājiran*)."[169] These reports indicate that to some extent the dead bodies of *shurāt* and Khārijites were considered powerful and that visitation to their tombs was an action deemed important in some way.

The *shurāt*'s ascetic practices were undergirded by a world-denying ethos that was manifested in an opposition between the temporal and impermanent body and the eternal world of the spirit. Early *shurāt* poetry, for example, abundantly attests to such an attitude among them.[170] Abū Bilāl Mirdās b. Udayya, the doyen of the early *shurāt* and model for later Ibāḍī conceptions of *shirā'*, compared the temporary and therefore worthless life in this world with the hereafter, "which has no price" and for which he was willing to exchange his life:

Surely I have weighed what remains of the life of this world.
It will pass away imminently, indeed, by God, it does not incite us.
Piety before God and the fear of the flame sent me out
To exchange my soul for that which has no price.[171]

Similarly an anonymous (probably Azraqite) poet drew attention to the dashed hopes of this world, counseling piety, which included fighting:

Oh seeker of truth, do not be lured by hope,
For the span of life falls short of your hopes.
Work for your Lord and ask Him for forgiveness,
Fearing Him, you know, is the best of works.
So assault the effeminate (*al-makhānīth*), marking their white breastplate,
Lest you become by morning the fart of a camel![172]

Often the opposition between the temporal and the eternal was expressed with the imagery of dead or decaying *shurāt* bodies. Thus, in a different poem, Abū Bilāl was credited with saying,

What do we care if our souls go out [of our bodies];
What did you do with bodies and limbs [anyway]?
We look forward to the Gardens [of paradise],
When our skulls lie in the dust like rotted melons (*al-ḥanẓal*).[173]

Here the graphic imagery of rotted heads sits opposite the imagery of the gardens of paradise, the true home of the *shārī* soul. Abū Bilāl's rhetorical question, "What did you do with bodies and limbs [anyway]?" further signaled the dichotomy between the temporal world in which bodies were useless and the eternal world where the *shurāt* will live in the gardens of paradise. A similar opposition, signaled by the heads of Abū Bilāl's followers, exists in ʿIsā b. Fātik al-Khaṭṭī's eulogy:

It is for the sake of God, and not for people that the beams were raised
With [the heads of] Dāwūd and his brothers.
They died, murdered, torn to pieces and tormented
Birds of prey hovering around them.[174]

Likewise al-Aṣam al-Ḍabbī counterpoises the imagery of Khārijite heads carried away on camels with the "supreme" otherworldly "goal" of the Khārijites:

I profess the religion to which the Khārijīs adhered
On the day of Nukhayla, by the ruins of Jawsaq . . .
They did not remain long facing
every white pure-colored sword
before they perished, and the spectator saw their heads
carried away by young, noble she-camels of red color.
The world thus became severed from them,
and they attained the supreme goal of their quest.[175]

Here the *shurāt*'s "supreme goal," paradise, comes from being severed from the world (and in this poem the severing is quite literal).

The willingness of the *sharī* to "expose" their bodies to violence is another means by which this poetry communicates a rejection of the material world. Farwa b. Nawfal al-Ashjaʿī—the early rebel at Nukhayla—included a description of emaciated bodies when he wrote of the *shurāt*'s willingness to face death:

They exposed their bodies to arrows and spears,
  And [now] nothing remains of them but decaying carcasses
Shaded by the fledgling birds who hop about them
  Indulging in the little flesh that their bodies possess.
Thin bodies, emaciated from fasting, as if they are
  Swords when the horses' wounds bleed [during battle].[176]

Similarly, Abū Bilāl boasts of his followers,

We do not—if a group of our enemies
Come at us like the waves of the sea—
Stop if their seas rage toward us;
Nor are we fearful, swerving from the cutting sword.
Instead we meet the lances with our chests,
And with our heads meet every glittering white sword.[177]

Likewise, Qaṭarī b. al-Fujā'a viewed himself as a target for spears and boasted of his exposure to death,

No one is inclined to retreat
On the day of battle, in fear of death.
I see myself a target for spears,
Once at my right, and in front of me.
Till I infused—with what was shed of my blood—
The sides of my saddle or the reins of my bridle.
Then I left, having inflicted injuries, but not being injured myself,
With renewed insight and sure footedness.

Exposed to death, I hit war-marked men—
Valiant in war, and famous.
I call upon the brave to fight and do not hold
that the killing of noble men is forbidden.[178]

In another poem Qaṭarī compares death to a necklace that he wears: "So long as martyrdom (*shahāda*) misses me, death is a necklace around our necks."[179] Certainly these poems articulate the common Arabian, poetic trope of bravery in battle, but they also signal a careless attitude toward death—an attitude resonating in many senses with the *apatheia* of the Christian monk.

In similar fashion, a narrative preserved by Ibn al-Jawzī describes the captured Ibn Muljam as unconcerned when ʿAlī's supporter ʿAbdullāh b. Jaʿfar cut off his feet and hands and when he put out his eyes. Ibn Muljam became anxious only when Ibn Jaʿfar prepared to cut out his tongue, when he said, "I would detest being in this world inanimate, not remembering God."[180] Not only does this report contain a gruesome description of Ibn Muljam's dismemberment, but it also takes note of his indifference to the tortures visited on his body in a manner reminiscent of the late antique notion of *apathea*. Whatever its source, this report likely came from a *shārī* origin; it is unlikely that an ʿAlīd or proto-Sunnī source would so valorize ʿAlī's killer.

This uncaring outlook with which the *shurāt* met death is matched by the imagery used to describe their dead bodies. The irreverent—almost flippant—metaphors employed to portray these corpses underscore a belief in the transience of the world. Thus, ʿUbayda b. Hilāl al-Yashkurī (Abū al-ʿAyzār) sings,

He [that is, the *shārī*] draws near and lances lift him as if he were
A piece of meat caught in the claws of a starving [beast].
Dead, he drops while spears hoist him [again].
Indeed, the lifespan of the *shurāt* is short.[181]

In this poem the *shārī*'s body is merely a piece of meat, to be dropped and picked up again by the spears that hoist it. Here it is the imagery that communicates the fleeting nature of the world by its conflation of the Khārijite corpse with a mere bit of meat.

Similarly, Qaṭarī b. al-Fujāʾa sings of the battle of Dūlāb:

I haven't seen a day with more stabbed bodies,
Exploding with blood from dead and injured persons.
Many glorious blows, hitting the cheek of a young man
With a forelock, strong in motherly descent.
He was struck at Dūlāb, but Dūlāb was not his homeland,
Nor was Dayr al-Ḥamīm.

If you witnessed us that day, and our horses
Conquering from the *kāfirs* every valuable thing (*ḥarīm*),
You would see young men who sold their souls to God
For the gardens of Eden with Him, and blessing.[182]

In Ibn al-Fujā'a's poem, stabbed bodies and the blood that gushed from them are to be celebrated, as they signaled the successful exchange of the temporal world for the hereafter.

Such casual comparisons with death seemed to come easily in Khārijite poetry, as it was something, in the words of an anonymous Khārijī poet, "inevitable and true; whoever it does not greet by day, it comes to by night."[183] Death was therefore to be welcomed as the release from life. In fact for many Khārijite poets, death was eagerly desired. Thus, Qaṭarī b. al-Fujā'a's wife Um Ḥakīm intones,

I bear a head I'm tired of bearing.
I'm bored of oiling and washing it.
Is there no man who will relieve me of its weight?[184]

Dissatisfaction with the temporal world, expressed as extreme "boredom" with it, also pervades this poem by Abū Bilāl: "My God, give me access and closeness / To you, for I have become bored of Fate (*dahr*) [that is, weary of living]."[185] Similarly, and with Abū Bilāl as his explicit model, the poet 'Imrān b. Ḥaṭṭān expressed outright disdain for the world as well as a desire to leave it in the manner of his heroes:

Abū Bilāl caused me to hate this life
and revolt became dearer.
And 'Urwa after him . . .
May 'Urwa, the virtuous and brave, flourish.
I am afraid to die in my bed.
I hope for death under the points of spears.
Even if I were certain that my end
would resemble Abū Bilāl's, I would not care.
There may be some who take thought of this world,
As for me, I hate it, by God, the Lord of the House.[186]

These expressions of "boredom" with the world and other statements rejecting the material world thus elided easily with the *shurāt*'s desire for martyrdom.

This nexus of symbolism expressing the rejection of the material world through a dismissive attitude toward the human body and the simultaneous desire to "exchange" this world for the hereafter place the concept of *shirā'* comfortably among the same signs and symbols of the late antique Middle East that animated Eastern Christian, Manichean, and other "gnostic" conceptions of asceticism and martyrdom. Just as this fixation with the bodily marks of ascetic piety and with the suffering, mutilated, and dead bodies of the martyrs operated as a focal point for late antique Christian (and other) communities, so too the ascetic and martyred bodies in the narratives and poetry on the Muḥakkima, early *shurāt,* and later Khārijites displayed the symbols of the model Muslim and offered figures around which the early *shurāt* and Khārijite groups could rally. As a locus for identity, the *shurāt* martyrs and saints embodied the spirit of worldly rejection in favor of the hereafter, thereby turning their deaths into the ultimate triumphs, their humiliations into dignities, and their defeats into victories.

The Poisoned Cup: Arab-Islamic Imagery in the Poetry of the Shurāt

By way of providing a fuller context for the poems heretofore examined, this section turns toward a consideration of the ways in which Arabian (especially pre-Islamic) and early Islamic poetic themes became embedded in the poetry of the *shurāt* and those who followed after them. Such an investigation is meant to underscore the pre-Islamic Arabian and early Arab-Islamic contexts for the production of *shurāt* poetry and thus to round out the study of the late antique Middle East as the soil from which sprang the *shurāt,* Khārijite, and Ibāḍī movements. Of course the themes of pre-Islamic/early Islamic poetry are vast and varied, and thus, as a means of keeping this task contained, this section traces one specific image, that of the wine cup/poisoned cup, from its pre-Islamic roots to its manifestations in the poetry of the *shurāt* and Khārijites and even in some Ibāḍī poems.

The wine/poisoned cup image is particularly well suited to this task for several reasons. First, wine imagery occupies a significant place in pre-Islamic poetry. Numerous poems allude to wine (in the *dhikr al-khamr* or *al-qawl fī'l-khamr* sections), and some are exclusively devoted to the theme of wine (that is, *khamriyya* poems).[187] This prevalence of wine imagery did not necessarily abate with the advent of Islamic strictures against wine drinking. Second, wine imagery in pre-/early Islamic poetry was varied enough so as to lend itself to a wide range of expression within the poetic tradition.[188] One of these expressions involved the transformation of the wine cup into a poisoned cup symbolizing death on the battlefield. Third, and unsurprisingly, it is this battlefield imagery of the poisoned cup that appears in the poetry of the *shurāt,* early Khārijites, and Ibāḍiyya, thereby connecting the image of the poisoned cup to the matrix of concepts that were associated with martyrdom and asceticism. Thus the poisoned cup imagery in *shurāt* poetry is not unrelated to the overall expressions of martyrdom and asceticism traced earlier, and yet it remains a distinctly Arabian image. In this way it is possible to view this poetry as a complex intersection of resonances, simultaneously connecting these groups to their proximate (that is, Arab-Islamic) and wider (that is, late antique Middle Eastern) contexts.

The theme of wine in Arabic poetry has a long history stretching from the Jāhilī poets up through the ʿAbbāsid-era poems of Abū Nuwwās and beyond. Wine themes in the pre-Islamic and early Islamic periods were common in Arabic poetry and often expressed the mood/theme of *fakhr* (self-vaunting or tribal boasting) or even *ḥikma* (poetic wisdom).[189] *Fakhr* was generally of two types: individual and tribal. Typical of the individual boasting associated with wine might be the lines by Labīd (that is, Abū ʿAqīl Labīd b. Rabīʿ b. Mālik al-ʿĀmirī, d. ca. 34/661) from his *muʿallaqa* ("hanging") poem:

> You do not know, no, how many nights
> Bright faced, with drinking company and delicious entertainment
> I have spent in talk! Showing up at the innkeeper's banner
> at the moment it is raised, when the wine is choice,
> paying any price for every vintage aged in blackened skins
> and tar-smeared jugs, seals broken,
> for a pure morning draught and the play of a singing girl
> upon her lute, fingers slipping softly across the strings.[190]

In this selection Labīd boasts about his drinking as a way of showing both his generosity and his struggle to enjoy life in the face of its vicissitudes. The mood of *fakhr* is perpetuated in later sections of the poem in which Labīd brags of his prowess in battle as well as of the courage and virtues of his tribe.

References to wine in Arabic poetry likewise made their appearance in sections devoted to the poet's wisdom (*ḥikma*). Often drinking became a trope whereby the poet expressed the fleeting nature of life, the inevitability of death, and the attitude attendant to such a philosophy. Representative stanzas of this type might be those of Ṭarafa (that is, Ṭarafa b. al-ʿAbd b. Sufyān b. Saʿad Abū ʿAmrū al-Bakrī al-Wāʾilī, d. late sixth century C.E.), for example,

> Let me quench the owl's thirst whilst I live since I fear
> the drink of death which will leave me thirsty.
> A noble man satiates himself in life, for you will know
> if we die tomorrow which of us is thirsty.[191]

Here the poet links wine drinking to the fear of death, claiming that the "noble" person is one who fulfills his desires while he is still alive. Such attitudes expressed the poetic *ḥikma* of the pre-Islamic era, conveying as it did a kind of desperate hedonism that accompanied a belief in the finality of death.[192]

Of course there can be found in the Arabian poetic tradition plenty of instances of poets—even pre-Islamic poets—refraining from drinking, expressing in their poetry the pre-Islamic quality of self-control known as *ḥilm* (a quality associated in the Islamic period with God).[193] For example, ʿAntara b. Shaddād, a pre-Islamic warrior-poet from the sixth century whose name means "the valiant," often expressed in his verses outright disdain for wine and drinking.[194] Although little is known of the historical ʿAntara, and his legend grew into a large and popular genre in the medieval Islamic world, it was his martial prowess that distinguished him and his poetry.[195] In line with ʿAntara's "spartan and heroic spirit," his verses (or those verses attributed to him) transform the wine cup into the cup of death: for instance, "God protect you my friend! Get up and sing about the cup that I drink—the cup of death (*ku's al-manāyā*), filled with blood. / Spare me a draught of wine which sets the mind of a brave man on an errant [trail]."[196] In ʿAntara the boastful utterances of the poet turn away from drunkenness and toward the heroic deeds of battle in the face of death. Consistently ʿAntara's poems transform the imagery of the wine cup into that of combat:

> I long for the clash of sharp swords
> and I pine for the jabbing of spears.
> I yearn for cups of death (*ka'sāt al-manūn*) when they are pure
> and the arrows of misfortune pass over my head.[197]

Such poems possessed, according to Kennedy, a "quasi-lyrical heroism" as well as a "mock-*khamriyya*" quality: "The spear is my basil and the skulls of noble men who have striven for glory are the wine-cups (*kāsāt*) of my *majlis*."[198]

With the continual mention of death and the heroic deeds that ʿAntara proposed in the face of it, the common poetic wisdom trope of finding pleasure in wine was transmuted into the noble pursuit of the "cup of death":

> Go to what you know!
> I see that fate (*al-dahr*) does not allow anyone to escape from death.
> Let me give my sword its due in war,
> and quaff a pure drink from the cup of death (*ka's al-maniyya*).[199]

In this way ʿAntara's transfigurations of the wine poem imagery into something more akin to the mood of battlefield invectives (that is, *hijāʾ*) placed his wine poems on one end of a large spectrum encompassing many different kinds of attitudes toward wine. Instead of poetic *ḥikma* coming through the poet's enjoyment of wine in the face of inevitable death and the fleeting nature of the world, ʿAntara articulates *ḥikma* through the warrior-poet's bravery in the face of death on the battlefield. ʿAntara would not be alone in doing so: *shurāt* and later Khārijite and Ibāḍī poets likewise employed the image of the cup of death as a means to articulate their battlefield prowess as well as their willingness to die as martyrs.

Given the *shurāt*'s and Khārijites' strong associations with asceticism and the seriousness with which they apparently took Qur'ānic piety, it is not surprising that outright wine imagery does not figure prominently in their poetry. Rather, and in line with Qur'ānic articulations of the just and ethical life, the evanescence of human life was to be disregarded in favor of the life to come.[200] Nevertheless, as with ʿAntara, there are traces of wine imagery in some poems, albeit transformed into the quasi-lyrical heroism that converts the cup of wine into the cup of fate/death and transmutes the drinker into a hero on the battlefield. In this sense the imagery of the cup of death became a means for *shurāt* poets to signal their willingness, even desire, to die as martyrs fighting their enemies, and thus ties this poetry to the matrix of asceticism/martyrdom discussed above. For example, Muʿādh b. Juwayn, exhorting his fellow Kūfan *shurāt* as they rebelled with al-Mustawrid outside of Kūfa, boasted from al-Mughīra's prison,

Indeed, Exchangers (*shurāt*), the time has come for one
Who sells himself to God to depart.
Will you remain out of ignorance in the house of those who err
(*khāṭi'īn*),
While every one of you is hunted down to be killed?
For the enemies assaulted the folk and they
Set you up for slaughter by a mistaken opinion.
Indeed, oh folk, strive for a goal which
When it is mentioned is more righteous and more just.
If I were with you on the back of a swimmer (*sābiḥ*)
Powerful, short-legged, armored, not defenseless.
If only I were with you opposing your enemy,
For I am given first the cup of death (*ka's al-maniya*) to drink.
It is hard for me that you are afraid and driven out
When I draw out [my sword] unsheathed among the violators
(*muḥillīn*),
When every glorious person scatters their group,
When you would say he had turned away and fled, he would
come back
Showing the blade of the sword in the heat of the tumult.
He regards steadfastness as exemplary in some places.
It is hard for me that you are wronged and decrease
And I become sorrowful like a prisoner in chains.
If I were with you while they headed for you
Then I would stir up dust between the two factions

For many a group have I broken up, and many an attack
Have I experienced, and many an opponent have I left dead
on the ground.[201]

Ibn Juwayn's mention of the "cup of death," which he wishes to drink by joining his brethren on the battlefield, stands easily amid other battlefield imagery of horses, swords, dust, and tumult. In a similar manner Thābit b. Wa'la al-Rāsibī, weeping for his slain comrades, was said to have declared, "I will follow my brethren [that is, I will die like them] and drink of their cup with a cleaving, two edged, Indian sword in hand."[202] In these poems the "cup" becomes conflated with the imminent death of the poet/warrior in an impending (or missed) battle. It remains an object of desire and as such expresses well the *shārī*'s aspiration to martyrdom. At the same time, classic Arabian tropes of warfare—horses amid a sea of enemies, drawn swords, the dust of battle—place these poems comfortably within the Arabian poetic tradition.

Later Khārijite poetry likewise places imagery of the "cup" amid classic pre-Islamic/early Islamic poetic battlefield tropes. The Azraqī poet Qaṭarī b. al-Fujā'a, for example, captures the mood of *fakhr* in his poem:

How many days of recreation for those that lead comfortable lives,
While my recreation was the fury of battle's flaming fire?
I stood firm on a well-exposed place, while war rejected her veil
And the waves of death flowed equal, without end.
Through how many torrid noonday hours did I plough the desert
At the serried trot of the raiders' horses?
They safely crossed the terrible ravines,
Like lions guided by other lions.
Even if I must die in my bed, I will not die afraid by thoughts of
warfare,
A dismay which is the last resort of the weak.
I will not say that I have never poured death into the cup of its
drinker,
When fatal doom descended, like spears who reach out to slake
their thirst in blood.[203]

Even more confrontational is Qaṭarī's battlefield challenge:

You rebellious one who wishes to contend [with me in a duel],
approach!
That I may hand you the poisoned beverage of death.
There is no shame in passing one another the cup which slays
Those who put their lips to it; pour it out for me, and drink.[204]

In fact this poem was included in the *diwān al-ḥamāsa,* a collection of mostly pre-Islamic poetry on the theme of courage and bravery in battle—an inclusion that speaks volumes to Qaṭarī's use of classical poetic themes and images, such as the cup of death.

Later, quietist Khārijite and Ibāḍī poets would likewise incorporate the image of wine/the cup into their poetry. Thus, ʿImrān b. Ḥaṭṭān's elegy for Abū Bilāl claims,

Oh my eye, weep for Mirdās and for his passing.
Oh Lord of Mirdās, make me succeed Mirdās.
He left me in dismay to weep over the loss
In a lonely dwelling that was once frequented.
After you, I disavowed those who [*sic*] I had known.
There are no people after you, oh Mirdās.
If you have drunk from a cup whose first round
Was for the chiefs, and they enjoyed the drink,
Then all those who have not drunk from it yet
Will soon drink from it recurrently.[205]

Ibn Ḥaṭṭān first invokes the familiar image of the lonely dwelling, usually reserved for images of the lost beloved but here replaced by longing for the slain Abū Bilāl. The final stanzas of the poem transition to the theme of the "cup," which here stands for death that was "enjoyed" by those who tasted it. The poet's *ḥikma* is expressed through the reminder, also familiar to pre/early Islamic poetry, of the inevitability of death that is couched in the image of drinkers quaffing the cup in succession. Such an image matches another line from Ibn Ḥaṭṭān in which he states that "whoso does not die young will die senile, for death is a cup, and man is its drinker."[206]

Returning to the theme of battlefield poems, the Ibāḍī poet ʿAmr b. al-Ḥuṣayn al-ʿAnbarī, a companion of the Ibāḍī rebel Abū Ḥamza al-Mukhtār b. ʿAwf (companion of Ṭālib al-Ḥaqq), eulogized several of his slain comrades in a long poem replete with battlefield imagery. Of his companion Abraha b. al-Ṣabbāḥ al-Ḥimyarī (Abū Ḥamza's deputy in Makka, later killed at al-Abṭaḥ) he sings,

And your brother, Abraha, the camel-rider,
The friend of the raging war, and the kindler of embers.
With a wide, spattering thrust, causing blood to flow copiously,
As the transgressor (*al-ghawī*) causes the flow of the choicest
wine.[207]

Instead of the imagery of the cup, ʿAmr b. al-Ḥuṣayn simply conflates the blood flowing as a result of Abraha's thrusts with the flow of wine. As the poet earlier contrasted his righteous companions with those "covetous souls" who "call for wine," it is perhaps unsurprising that this poem eschews the image of the cup.[208] Elsewhere, however, ʿAmr b. al-Ḥuṣayn is not averse to the image of the cup, as in his eulogy for those slain at the battle of Qudayd (in 130/748):

> Watch, lest your fated death come suddenly.
> I did not fulfill my desires [for sacrifice] with the *shurāt*'s followers.
> So, going with them toward the enemy, I will conduct my tight-muscled steed,
> The well-built, strapping, spirited one,
> Descending like a wolf whose solid color
> Suggests the sticky sap of the prickly herb.
> With my horse I will throw off a tyrannical, disgraceful contingency of boors
> Away from my people, gathered together.
> With it I wander among the resolute youths
> Like gaming arrows or a rambling gambler hitting its mark.
> Thus we and they and whoever is between us circulate
> The cup of death (*ka's al-manūn*), which asks, "Is there a drinker?"
> We keep on drinking and giving them drink from a ruddy jug
> As well-honed sword blades deliver severing blows.[209]

Returning to the now-familiar theme of the "cup" as death on the battlefield, not only does the poem conflate the passing of the cup with sword blows, but it also personifies the cup by making it ask if there are any "drinkers."

Such imagery, coming as it does from early *shurāt* poets, Azraqites, and later Ibāḍīs, clearly draws from a well-established tradition in pre/early Islamic poetry that uses the image of the wine cup as a metaphor for death on the battlefield. As such, and in conjunction with the employment of common battlefield images, *shurāt* poetry is located firmly within the Arabian poetic tradition, albeit within the part of that tradition associated with wine-eschewing poets such as ʿAntara. At the same time, such imagery fit well with the common late antique and early Islamic themes of martyrdom that were simultaneously deployed by the *shurāt* in other poems. Thus wine imagery (such as it is) in *shurāt* and later Khārijī and Ibāḍī poetry bespeaks of a complex relation of resonances that bring together the late antique and Arabian contexts for these groups. This transposition serves as a powerful reminder that Arabian and late antique Middle Eastern "influences" on the *shurāt* should be considered not as separate but as integrated hues in the broader spectrum of backlighting that illumines them.

Examining the narratives of the Muḥakkima and early *shurāt* points out the structural and thematic resonances with other late antique and early Islamic hagiographical literatures and shows how the concept of *shirā'* sat comfortably among other late antique and early Islamic rejections of the material world in favor of the hereafter, the devaluation of the human body, and the consequent desire for martyrdom. Put another way, narratives on the *shurāt* as well as specific expressions of *shirā'* are best viewed in relation to the late antique and early Islamic nexus of signs and symbols that articulated the genre of hagiography as a rejection of the temporal world for that of the hereafter. As was common in the late antique Middle East, notions of asceticism and martyrdom were fundamentally integrated into this syllabary and provided a powerful focal point for establishing group identity around the figures of the saints and martyrs. Through the crafting of hagiographical tales and poetry, the early *shurāt* and the Khārijites who followed them engaged in a familiar process of late antique and early Islamic identity creation, concentrating the collective memory on the suffering of those "very special dead" who had preceded them and giving their resistance to tyrants and oppressors continued meaning. Remembering the heroes and martyrs was but one aspect of how the early *shurāt* and Khārijites articulated a sense of their own identity: remembrance of the martyrs entailed the subsequent devaluation of the enemies as tyrants, oppressors, sinners, or other deviants such that the idea of *shirā'* was fundamentally tied to dichotomies of piety and impiety.

Chapter 3

Shurāt Boundaries

From the Muḥakkima to the Azāriqa

The Muḥakkima, early *shurāt,* and first Khārijites created or were said to have created a sense of their identity in relation to those they considered outsiders, enemies, and other opponents. "Boundaries" in this sense refer not to physical or geographical markers but, following Donner's definition of boundary themes in the early Islamic narrative traditions, to "events that define the community or group in relation to others."[1] Such a definition is well suited to the purposes of examining early *shurāt* notions of boundaries: the Muḥakkima and early *shurāt* as well as the later Khārijite and Ibāḍī groups that followed them interpreted the events of the battle of Ṣiffīn and the behavior of their later enemies as proof of their status as not fully Muslim in some sense. In other words, among those later labeled "Khārijites," the conversation about who was and who was not a member of the community involved taking a stance on the event of arbitration (*taḥkīm*) at Ṣiffīn as well as recognizing and resisting the tyranny and oppression of certain Muslims (especially ʿUthmān, the Umayyads, and their governors). The boundaries so established thus marked an intra-Islamic identity.[2]

Although the *shurāt* and Khārijites and later the Ibāḍiyya all rejected the notion that any other than themselves were Muslims in the full sense, the degree to which a non-*shārī,* non-Khārijī, or non-Ibāḍī fell short of being a full Muslim and the extent to which such a person retained or lost the right to be treated as such remained a heated question among them. The question of boundaries, then, established not only intra-Islamic identities but intra-Khārijite/Ibāḍite identities as well. The question of the sinner, her status as less than fully Muslim, and the proper stance toward such a person became, in part, the issues that marked the militants from the quietists, giving rise to groups such as the Azāriqa, Najdāt, Ibāḍiyya, and Ṣufriyya. Such self-definition, of course, developed over several decades—a fact that is largely missing from the flattened presentation of Islamic heresiographers, whose interest in delineating "proper" Islamic theology from that which they considered deviant led them to reify the groups they were discussing into fixed taxonomies, simplify their stances in the interest of comparison, and to anachronistically project doctrines back into earlier periods.[3]

As is common in the field of medieval and early Islamic studies, the state of the sources on the Muḥakkima, *shurāt,* and early Khārijites frustrates, for the most part, a firsthand portrait of how these groups characterized various "others." Although some early poetry survives—notably from the Azāriqa—most of the reports about how these groups may have created boundaries between themselves and others come from secondhand accounts, especially Islamic histories and heresiographies.[4] Thus, for the most part what survives is how non-*shurāt* authors and editors framed and fashioned *shārī* boundary themes for their own purposes. Compounding these difficulties is the fact that there are limited means to discover the purposes of non-*shurāt* authors and editors.[5]

Despite these issues, textual comparison offers one means by which the predilections and prejudices of various non-Muḥakkima and non-*shurāt* authors can be exposed, allowing a sense of early *shārī* and early Khārijite boundary themes to emerge. That is, by setting heresiographical and historical texts against each other and then analyzing and comparing what can be found in early *shurāt* and Khārijite poetry, it is possible to read between the sources toward an idea of how these early groups might have defined enemies and outsiders, and how this notion might have changed over time.

As a means of anchoring this textual comparison, the focus here is especially though not exclusively on poetry and reports about the Muḥakkima's, early *shurāt*'s, and Khārijites' use of *takfīr.* The choice of *takfīr* is particularly relevant to the discussion of boundary themes, as most heresiographies draw specific attention to the ways that the "Khārijites" used the language of *kufr* to describe enemies and outsiders, to the extent that the use of *takfīr* has come to define the Khārijites in many heresiographical texts. Likewise, Islamic historical texts contain numerous reports of the use of *takfīr,* and *shurāt* and Khārijite poetry employs the term *kufr/kāfir* in various ways to establish boundaries. That the Muḥakkima, early *shurāt,* and Khārijites used the term *kufr/kāfir* in labeling enemies, sinners, or other types of non-Khārijites is beyond a doubt. However, what they meant when they employed it presents a host of difficulties.

While *shurāt* and Khārijite poets' use of the term *kufr/kāfir* tends to be, on the whole, more abstruse, Islamic heresiographers and historians working decades or centuries after the demise of the initial *shurāt* and Khārijites have far more reified notions of what *kufr* was supposed to mean and tend to invest it with theological-legal importance. Yet the Qur'ān contains several senses of *kufr,* one of which tends to merge and conflate the rejection of belief in God and the last day with sinful, tyrannical, or oppressive actions. It also draws attention to how members of the early community, as a "believers movement," may have downplayed between themselves and other monotheists the importance of theological tenets in favor of working toward the creation of the just order on earth. As they were early Muslims closer in time to the era of the "believers movement," therefore, the Muḥakkima's and other early *shurāt*'s uses of *takfīr* and other accusations of misdoing should reflect an earlier, and more Qur'ānic, understanding of outsiders and enemies. As such and in conjunction with Hawting's observations that accusations of polytheism (*shirk*) and unfaithfulness (*kufr*) among monotheists could be understood as metaphor or hyperbole put toward polemical uses, the Muḥakkima's and early *shurāt*'s uses of *takfīr* should denote enemies who oppressed and tyrannized those who cleaved to God's mission, rather than designating, as Islamic heresiographers would have it, a reified theological-legal infraction that renders the offender outside the realm of belief altogether and therefore worthy of violence.

Indeed an analysis of the ways that heresiographers, historians, and early *shurāt* poets portray the activity of creating boundaries will, on the one hand, draw attention to how heresiographers and historians chose to distort the issue of "Khārijite" boundary maintenance in their own interests. On the other hand, it will show how the language of *takfīr* in reports and poetry by and about the *shurāt* must be understood as related to early Islamic concepts of social justice and piety and as intimately (and organically) connected to other concepts such as tyranny and oppression, which the *shurāt* saw themselves as opposing. Put as a question, what is the extent to which heresiographers and historians have simplified the issue of *takfīr?* The answer will reproblematize and recomplicate the possibilities of what the early Muḥakkima and their successors among the *shurāt* may have been doing when they accused 'Alī and other enemies of *kufr, shirk,* or a number of other sins.

That significant ambiguity surrounds the use of *takfīr* among the Muḥakkima and that the result of *takfīr* was the same for those considered oppressors as well as those considered theological-legal deviants (that is, they were all to be fought) explain, in part, why so many of the subsequent Khārijite and Ibāḍī subsects set about trying to clarify the implications of *takfīr.* How might boundary themes have developed among those who came after the Muḥakkima, especially among those later Khārijites known as the Azāriqa? The Azāriqa present a particularly interesting case as they are said to have adopted the strictest stance vis-à-vis non-Khārijite Muslims, employing the language of *kufr* (and even *shirk*) as a means to establish absolute boundaries between themselves and those they considered outsiders. They subsequently held these outsiders, Islamic heresiographers and historians assure their audience, to be the equivalent of disbelievers (*kuffār*) and even polytheists (*mushrikūn*) and therefore outside the community altogether. Comparisons with boundary themes in Azraqite poetry show that although the Azraqī Khārijites do indeed seem to have been moving toward a more reified definition of outsiders as *kuffār*, their poetry presents a range of boundary themes that link accusations of *kufr* to a web of other concepts that evoke oppression, tyranny, and impiety. Thus, while Azraqite accusations of *kufr* do tend to imply the theological-legal consequence of such an accusation, Azraqī poetry shows their stance on *takfīr* to be in the process of development and far from uniform.

Heresiographical Treatments of the Muḥakkima

Islamic heresiographers tend to subsume the Muḥakkima under the general rubric of "*khawārij*," offering blanket statements on what the Khārijites—presumably all of them—claim to be true. This level of generalization also holds when it comes to the Muḥakkima's use of *takfīr*, with heresiographers on the whole portraying a more or less uniform portrait of it. Al-Ashʿarī, one of our earliest extant examples of heresiography among the nascent Sunnīs, reports that the Khārijites agreed on anathematizing (*ikfār*) ʿAlī when he opted for arbitration but that they disagreed over whether or not this *kufr* was also *shirk*. Al-Ashʿarī also mentions that they held major sins to be *kufr* but claims the Najdāt as an exception to this rule.[6] Al-Baghdādī, a pupil of al-Ashʿarī, further elaborates on this point, preserving his master's opinion as well as giving that of al-Kaʿbī. Al-Baghdādī takes al-Kaʿbī to task for claiming that all of the Khārijites held major sinners to be *kuffār*: quoting al-Ashʿarī, al-Baghdadī informs us that the Najdāt did not anathematize those who committed *ḥudūd* crimes from their own group but preferred to use for them the term *kufr ni'ma* and not *kufr dīn*.[7] Of course the terminology of *kufr niʿma* and *kufr dīn* seems to parallel that attributed to Ibn Ibāḍ—more specifically with the attempt to differentiate between non-Ibāḍīs and those who disbelieve or otherwise deny God (as through the actual practice of idolatry, for example).[8] However tantalizing and/or confused these reports may be with respect to the Najdāt and Ibāḍiyya, al-Ashʿarī and al-Baghdādī's implication remains that the other Khawārij used *takfīr* to indicate *kufr dīn*, or disbelief/rejection in the tenets of monotheism, which these heresiographers show to be a nearly universal principle among those whom they label Khārijites.

Another Ashʿarite heresiographer, al-Iṣfarā'inī, is equally explicit in his characterization of the Khārijites as holding a notion of *kufr* as reified disbelief. He claims that they agree on two points, the first being that ʿAlī, ʿUthmān, the people of the Battle of the Camel, the two arbiters, and all who agreed with the arbitration are *kuffār* (*kaffarū kuluhum*); and the second point being that those who commit sins are thereby considered *kāfirs*.[9] Here the exception again is the Najdāt, who according to al-Iṣfarā'inī say that the *fāsiq* is a *kāfir* but meaning that he is "ungrateful for the blessings of his Lord" (*kāfir ni'mat rabbihi*). Al-Iṣfarā'inī then adds that the Najdāt "used that designation [that is, *kāfir*] for those among them to indicate denial (*kufrān*), not in the meaning of disbelief (*kufr*)."[10] Again, even though he allows for the Najdāt as an alleged "exception" to the rule, he proposes that the majority of the Khārijites held their opponents to be disbelievers because of their sins.

Other heresiographers are equally as explicit in their characterization of the Khārijites as equating the notion of *kufr* with disbelief proper: al-Shahrastānī, for example, begins his Khārijite chapter by claiming that the Khārijites declare major sinners to be *kuffār* (*yukaffirūn aṣḥāb al-kabā'ir*) and then explicitly contrasts this stance with that of the Murji'ites and others.[11] In his section on the Muḥakkima, al-Shahrastānī claims that they held 'Alī at fault (*akhṭa'a*) for permitting arbitration and also held him to be a *kāfir*.[12] Likewise al-Malaṭī, after claiming that the Muḥakkima held that it was *kufr* to appoint Abū Mūsā al-Ash'arī to the arbitration and that the *shurāt* collectively anathematized sinners (*yukaffirūn aṣḥāb al-ma'āṣī*) as well as those who differed from the claims of their *madhhab*, goes into an extensive refutation of this "stance" with ample reference to the ideas of the Murji'a as well as the notion that God has made the category of sinner different from that of *kāfir*.[13] It seems fairly clear that al-Malaṭī also conceptualizes the notion of *takfīr* among the first Khārijites as connecting sin and disbelief; indeed his refutation makes little sense otherwise.

Shi'ite heresiographers similarly imply that the Khārijites connect the notions of belief and action, disbelief and sin. Al-Rāzī, for example, casts the Khārijites as those who treat Muslims as if they are *kuffār* and *mushrikūn* (except those who accept their path), claiming that they anathematized (*ikfār*) 'Alī and 'Uthmān and every imām after Abū Bakr as well as major sinners (*al-ikfār bi-irtikāb al-kabā'ir*).[14] So too Abū Tammām portrays the Khārijites as those who "agree that acts of obedience (*al-ṭa'āt*) are all components of faith," quoting the Khārijites as also saying, "we are quite certain of the *kufr* of whoever commits a major sin."[15]

When it comes to treatments of the Muḥakkima specifically, heresiographers for the most part leave the consequences of such a conflation between sin and *kufr* unstated. Al-Baghdādī and al-Iṣfarā'inī offer an exception: these two explicitly include two incidents—which also appear widely in historical accounts of the Muḥakkima—that are meant to illustrate the legal ramifications of the accusation of *kufr*. In the first event, a group of Khārijites are shown to have murdered a pious Muslim known as Ibn Khabbāb for holding views contrary to theirs.[16] In the second case, the Muḥakkima are portrayed in the course of their debate (*munāẓara*) with 'Alī accusing him of forbidding the taking of spoils at the Battle of the Camel, to which 'Alī asks which one of them would receive 'Ā'isha, thereby silencing them.[17] In this way both heresiographers depict the consequences of the Muḥakkima's stance toward sinners, resulting either in random violence or in absurd legalism.

The heresiographical portrait of the Khārijites' use of *takfīr*, then, is fairly standard across the genre: subsuming the Muḥakkima under the general rubric of "*khawārij*," the heresiographers characterize them as employing the language of *kufr* (though al-Ash'arī mentions *shirk* and al-Shahrastānī *khaṭī'a*) to anathematize sinners as fully reified disbelievers (with the exception, some Ash'arī-Sunnīs claim, of the Najdāt or Ṣufriyya), thereby conflating sin and disbelief. In addition, although most heresiographers do not provide explicit accounts of the consequences of this presumed early Muḥakkimite stance toward sinners (the exceptions being al-Baghdādī and al-Iṣfarā'inī), their subsequent chapters on the Khārijite subsects (such as the Azāriqa) are filled with examples of Khārijites killing non-Khārijites (an act known as *isti'rāḍ*) as well as deposing their leaders for minor infractions. In the pages of the heresiographies, then, such actions are clearly meant to connect the dots between holding a sinner to be a *kāfir* and the consequences of such a stance.

Historical Treatments of the Muḥakkima

Portrayals of the Muḥakkima in Islamic historical sources provide significantly different caricatures from those given in heresiographical sources. Most profoundly, historical texts attribute to the Muḥakkima a wide range of terms used to castigate 'Alī and his followers for agreeing to arbitration. The terminology of *kufr*, of course, does tend to dominate in these portrayals, but its intended meaning is far from certain. For example, Abū Mikhnaf (in al-Balādhurī) reports a meeting outside of Kūfa between 'Alī and the "Khārijites" in which 'Alī gives certain assurances to them, who then take these assurances to mean that 'Alī had repented his decision to appoint arbiters and admitted it to be an act of *kufr* and an error (*ḍalāla*).[18] Al-Sha'bī contains a similar report but uses only the term *kufr*.[19] Al-Ṭabarī preserves a related version of this story, claiming that it comes from the Khārijites themselves, wherein the Khārijites admitted to forcing 'Alī into the arbitration, but that they subsequently considered the action *kufr* on their part, repented from it, and demanded that 'Alī do the same.[20] Although the time line of events after the battle of Ṣiffīn is muddled and reports differ significantly, other historians place this sequence (that is, the Khārijites admitting their part in the arbitration as *kufr* and demanding that 'Alī then repent and admit the act as one of *kufr*) in different contexts: for example, another account of Abū Mikhnaf's (in al-Ṭabarī and al-Balādhurī) puts the event at Nahrawān; while yet another version places it in a letter responding to 'Alī's request to return to fighting.[21] In Ibn A'tham al-Kūfī's *Kitāb al-Futūḥ*, the Khārijites ask Ibn 'Abbās if he has "engaged in *kufr* toward his Lord (*akafarta bi-rabbika*) just as your companion 'Ali has engaged in *kufr*."[22] Moreover, when in Abū

Mikhnaf's text 'Alī's supporters take an oath of allegiance to him, the Khārijites quip that "the people of Iraq and Syria are competing with each other in *kufr* like two racing horses."[23] Likewise in al-Sha'bī's account, when the Khārijites met in the house of 'Abdullāh b. Wahb al-Rāsibī before decamping to Nahrawān, they "anathematized those who accepted the arbitration" (*kaffara man raḍā bi'l-ḥukūma*).[24] In Ibn Qutayba's version of this same story, the Khārijites quote Qur'ān 5:47 to make their point.[25] 'Urwa b. Udayya is quoted as bearing witness to the *kufr* of 'Alī and 'Uthmān before Ziyād b. Abīhi.[26] In this way accusations of *kufr* make up the lion's share of those accusations leveled against 'Alī and his supporters after they agreed to arbitration. If it is assumed that the term *kufr* refers to an act of disbelief, then such portrayals seem to fit with how later heresiographers have interpreted the meaning of the Muḥakkima's accusations against 'Alī.

However, the language of *kufr* is not the only language used to reproach 'Alī and his followers. In fact historical sources preserve several other terms used in conjunction with or even as replacements for terms related to *kufr*. For example, the terminology of *shirk* appears in several places: al-Minqarī and al-Dīnawarī both preserve a report about Ṣāliḥ b. Shaqīq, the leader of the Murād tribal grouping, who at Ṣiffīn upon hearing of the arbitration agreement is reported to have uttered, "no judgment but God's, despite the *mushrikīn*!"[27] Al-Ṭabarī (via Abū Mikhnaf) and al-Balādhurī (via Wahb b. Jarīr and al-Zuhrī) report that when 'Alī's army returned to Kūfa to await the arbitration, the Khārijites heckled 'Alī by quoting Qur'ān 39:65, which reads, "And it was already revealed to you and to those before you that if you should associate (*la-in ashrakta*) [anything] with God, your work would surely become worthless, and you would surely be among the losers."[28] In addition Abū Mikhnaf preserves an exchange between Qays b. Sa'd b. 'Ubāda and the Khārijites in which Qays berates them for accusing 'Alī and his supporters of *shirk:* "you have done a terrible thing, bearing witness against us that we have committed *shirk*."[29] Likewise al-Minqarī states that the Khārijites bore witness to 'Alī's *shirk,* and Wahb b. Jarīr describes a group of Khārijites who, after their brethren returned to their houses with assurances from 'Alī, remained belligerent and bore witness to the *shirk* of 'Alī and his companions.[30] Last, a report in Ibn al-Jawzī indicates that the Khārijites said to al-Ḥasan b. 'Alī, "you have committed *shirk* (*ashrakta*) just as your father committed *shirk* (*kamā ashraka Abūka*)."[31] Of course the concepts of *kufr* and *shirk* can be associated with one another, as they sometimes are in the Qur'ān, and so it is indeed possible to read such accusations of *shirk* as interchangeable with those of *kufr*.[32] Such readings explicitly follow the later heresiographical construal of what *takfīr* meant to the Muḥakkima. However, it must be admitted that the historical sources alone do nothing to clarify whether or not such an interpretation is accurate.

Yet other terms over and above *kufr* and *shirk* appear in historical sources in conjunction with the Muḥakkima's accusations against 'Alī—a fact that complicates the heresiographical interpretation of the meaning of *takfīr*. Thus in a story that is widely reported, a group of Khārijites including Ḥurqūṣ b. Zuhayr al-Saʿdī and Zurʿa b. al-Burj al-Ṭāʾī (and sometimes Zayd b. Ḥiṣn al-Ṭāʾī) came to ʿAlī and demanded that he repent his mistake (*khaṭīʾa*); later in al-Ṭabarī's version of the narrative they used the word sin (*dhanb*).[33] In al-Zuhrī's account (in al-Balādhurī) Zurʿa accuses ʿAlī of "desiring this world."[34] Yazīd b. ʿĀṣim al-Muḥāribī accuses ʿAlī of introducing "the things of this world into our religion" (*iʿṭāʾ al-dunya fī dīninā*), something that Ibn ʿĀṣim finds to be a "smearing of the affairs of God" (*idhān fī amr Allāh*) and a "disgrace" (*dhull*).[35] In al-Zuhrī's account of the Khārijite demand for ʿAlī's repentance, the Khārijites accuse ʿAlī of "doubt" (*shakk*) and demand that he bear witness to his own error (*tashhad ʿalā nafsak bi-ḍalāla*).[36] Yet other Khārijites use the language of reverting/apostasy to describe ʿAlī's acceptance of the arbitration: at Ṣiffīn one of the Banū Yashkur is reported to have asked ʿAlī, "did you revert/apostatize after belief? Did you doubt after certainty?"[37] Still other Khārijites are reported to describe the actions of ʿAlī as innovations and as acts of oppression: Abū Mikhnaf preserves an account of the Khārijite meeting in ʿAbdullāh b. Wahb al-Rāsibī's house, wherein the Khārijites denounce "this hateful *bidʿa*" and, quoting Qurʾān 4:75, express their desire to "leave this town whose people are oppressors."[38] Later in this version, Ḥurqūṣ b. Zuhayr gives a speech in which he voices his abhorrence to "*bidʿa* and oppression."[39] In one version of ʿAbdullāh b. Wahb al-Rāsibī's reply letter to ʿAlī, he accuses ʿAlī of doubt in his religion and asks him to repent and acknowledge his sin (*dhanb*).[40] Historical sources thus preserve a proliferation of terms—all of which are negative in some way—to describe ʿAlī's acceptance of arbitration. While most of these accusations involve the language of *kufr* and *shirk*, this language is often coupled with that of sin, mistake, *bidʿa*, error, or oppression—a fact that complicates the idea of *kufr* as a reified theological infraction.

Of course in historical sources there is a concerted effort to portray the Muḥakkima's accusations of *kufr* against ʿAlī as implying a serious theological-legal infraction. However, such attempts are usually problematic in one way or another, be it in their inconsistencies, open polemic, or anachronisms. Thus, for example, in one of Abū Mikhnaf's accounts (on the authority of Shurayḥ b. Yūnis), when the Khārijites demanded that ʿAlī repent and bear witness to his action as *kufr*, he responded by rhetorically asking if he should admit *kufr* after his belief (*imān*).[41] In Ibn Qutayba's version of this same exchange, ʿAlī asked if he should admit to *kufr* after his belief, his emigration, and fighting (*imān, hijra,* and *jihād*) with the Prophet Muḥammad.[42] Such exchanges are clearly meant to frame the Khārijite uses of the term *kufr* in terms of later dichotomies of belief/disbelief.[43] However, the pro-ʿAlīd leanings of Abū Mikhnaf, a likely source for his fellow Kūfan Ibn Qutayba, should introduce some doubt as to the impartiality of this report.

Similarly al-Dināwarī's version of this event remains historically questionable as it reflects an obviously anachronistic *kalām* exchange. In a debate with the Khārijite leader Ibn al-Kawwā' before the battle of Nahrawān, 'Alī responded to the accusation that he had committed *kufr* by pointing out that he had merely appointed Abū Mūsā al-Ash'arī as an arbiter, to which Ibn al-Kawwā' replied that Abū Mūsā, then, was a *kāfir.* 'Alī then asked when Abū Mūsā became a *kāfir:* when 'Alī sent him to the arbitration or when he engaged in arbitration? Ibn al-Kawwā' replied that he became a *kāfir* when he engaged in arbitration. 'Alī then trapped his opponent by reasoning that he had sent him as a Muslim and that (according to the faulty reasoning of Ibn al-Kawwā') Abū Mūsā became a *kāfir* only afterward.[44] Such structured arguments reflect the debate style of *kalām* and thus probably reflect a later argument interpolated into the narrative.

Another tactic used in some reports is to present the Khārijites as randomly killing those who do not hold their position. The implication, of course, is that the Khārijites believe that they can treat non-Khārijites as *kuffār* in the legal sense because they understand the term as referring to disbelievers proper. Thus a report in al-Ṭabarī casts 'Abdullāh b. Wahb al-Rāsibī as desiring to kill 'Adī b. Ḥātim al-Ṭā'ī on his way to Nahrawān.[45] This is, however, the only report that attributes the intention of killing to 'Abdullāh al-Rāsibī, and his motive may have been to prevent 'Adī b. Ḥātim from informing the Muḥakkima's enemies of their position.

A far more common and far more condemning narrative concerns the Khārijite killing of Ibn Khabbāb and his family. This story is found in virtually every source on the Muḥakkima, and its basic outlines include Ibn Khabbāb's questioning and murder, 'Alī's subsequent demand at Nahrawān that the Khārijites hand over the killers, as well as their refusal to do so, which usually involves an admission of collective responsibility for the act.[46] Several versions of the story explicitly use the language of *isti'rāḍ* to describe the motivations of the killers,[47] such that one of Abū Mikhnaf's accounts even portrays 'Alī as berating the Khārijites for *isti'rāḍ* and pledging safety to those who have not engaged in it.[48] As a whole, the story is clearly meant to portray the Khārijites as treating their opponents as theologically non-Muslims who can be licitly killed, and thus it represents a backhanded attempt to identify them as holding to the legal consequences of what *kufr/shirk* might mean for the Muslims whom they so accused.

However, there are several reasons to doubt this story as it appears in Islamic histories. First, the language of *isti'rāḍ* is plainly anachronistic, reflecting a later vision of the Khārijites heavily influenced by the actions of the Azāriqa and Najdāt. Second, the details of the story vary considerably across accounts, to the point that only the vague outlines of the story can be accepted as historically accurate.[49] Thus, for example, in Ya'qūb's account (in al-Ṭabarī) the Khārijites kill Ibn Khabbāb because he quotes a ḥadīth that predicts *fitna* and instructs Muslims not to be the killers (but to be the ones slain).[50] In a version of Abū Mikhnaf's (via Ḥumayd b. Hilāl), Ibn Khabbāb gives a different ḥadīth but is slain because he praises 'Alī.[51] In yet a third version attributed to Abū Mikhnaf (in al-Balādhurī), after the Khārijites capture Ibn Khabbāb, he witnesses them censure one of their own for eating a date illicitly and then for wrongfully slaughtering a pig that belonged to a *dhimmī.* When Ibn Khabbāb points out that his own blood is far more illicit than that of a pig, the Muḥakkima kill him mercilessly.[52] Still more variations on these three basic versions of the Ibn Khabbāb story can be found in the historical sources, with their details equally muddled or obviously modified.[53]

Moreover al-Balādhurī claims that Sahm b. Ghālib al-Ḥumaymī and 'Abdullāh b. Yazīd al-Bāhilī (that is, "al-Khaṭīm") were the first Khārijites to label "the people of the Qibla" (that is, professing Muslims) as *kuffār* and that Sahm and al-Khaṭīm killed a certain 'Ubāda b. Qurṣ al-Laythī as well as his son and cousin between the bridges near Basra in 44/644.[54] The story as given by al-Balādhurī describes how these Khārijites rebels accused Ibn Qurṣ of being a *kāfir,* whereby Ibn Qurṣ described how he had entered Islam in front of the Prophet. Denying his claim, Sahm and al-Khaṭīm then killed him and his group. This narrative matches in structure descriptions of the Muḥakkima's alleged killing of Ibn Khabbāb and his family, and it is entirely possible that their stories have been conflated.

Whatever the case, the general outlines of the Ibn Khabbāb story are likely to be true to an extent: some Muḥakkima who were on their way to Nahrawān probably killed Ibn Khabbāb and perhaps a few others, and the larger group at Nahrawān may have decided not to give them up to 'Alī (who, after all, they did not consider the rightful imām). But this is the extent of what can be surmised without entering into the realm of polemics; the real motives for the killing remain unknown, as is the wider reaction to it of the Muḥakkima gathered at Nahrawān. The stories as they appear in Islamic historical works have clearly been shaped to portray the "Khārijites," all of them collectively, as endorsing the unprovoked killing of their opponents. The strong implication, of course, is that the attribution of *kufr* allows the Khārijites to treat their opponents according to the legal status of *kuffār.* Such a rendering not only possesses a strong whiff of polemic but also conveniently provides an excuse for 'Alī to fight the Muḥakkima at Nahrawān, just as it relieves him of any responsibility for their virtual annihilation there. Given these problems, it is doubtful that the portrayal of the Muḥakkima as intentionally engaging in random killing is trustworthy. More likely it reflects later attempts to cast the Muḥakkima, and by implication all Khārijites who followed them, in a certain polemical mold.

Still other problems arise from the assumption that the Muḥakkima held 'Alī's blood to be licit because they considered him outside of the realm of belief. If such were the case, then the historical sources could be expected to portray 'Alī's killer, Ibn Muljam, as articulating this claim as one of the reasons for assassinating ʿAlī. However, the accounts of ʿAlī's murder fail to do so, citing rather the motive of revenge as well as a desire on the part of the conspirators to be rid of "the imāms of error."[55] Ibn al-ʿAbbās's version of this event accuses ʿAlī of committing "corruption in the earth" (*fasad fī'l-arḍ*).[56] Several versions of the story add that Ibn Muljam desired the hand of a Muḥakkimite woman, Qaṭamī bt. ʿAlqama of the Taym Ribāb, who in revenge for her father and brother killed at Nahrawān demanded ʿAlī's head as part of her dowry.[57] Thus revenge, desire for a woman, and ʿAlī's corrupt actions, and not accusations of *kufr*, are given as Ibn Muljam's motivations to murder ʿAlī.

In fact the only time in the sources that Ibn Muljam mentions *kufr* is in a poem that is attributed to him and in which he expresses his distaste at a Muslim and a Christian participating in the same funeral and his desire to attack the offenders.[58] The sources relate how on his way to kill ʿAlī, Ibn Muljam passed the funeral procession of a certain Abjar in which a Christian priest and Ḥajjār b. Abjar were in attendance. On viewing this scene, Ibn Muljam is reported to have recited,

> If Ḥajjār b. Abjar is a Muslim
> The bier of Abjar would have been kept away from him
> But if Ḥajjār b. Abjar is a *kāfir* (*in kāna . . . kāfiran*)
> Then this sort of *kafūr* is inappropriate.
> Do you accept this? That a priest and a Muslim
> Are together before a bier? Shameful spectacle![59]

Ibn Muljam further states in the remainder of the poem that he would attack the group if not for his mission against ʿAlī. Thus, obviously, Ibn Muljam sees a boundary being crossed and considers its crossing as *kufr* worthy of his violent attention.

However, it is not ultimately clear what—exactly—so raises Ibn Muljam's ire, and several possibilities present themselves. Overall the problem seems to be the mixing of Muslims and priests, but here is where the ambiguity sets in. Does Ibn Muljam mean that Muslims should not mix with Christians or just Christian priests? Does he imply that Muslims should not mix with Christians and/or priests only at funerals or in general? Or is it that he objects to a Muslim carrying the bier of a Christian? In al-Dīnawarī's version of the story (which does not include the poem), the priests are said to be chanting the New Testament (*al-Injīl*), so perhaps it is this chanting to which Ibn Muljam objects.[60] A further problem arises when we note that Ḥajjār b. Abjar is the son of the deceased Abjar: does Ibn Muljam mean to imply that a true Muslim would not attend the funeral of his unconverted father?[61]

What is clear is that Ibn Muljam contrasts the term "Muslim" with *kāfir*, thus setting up a dichotomy between those who submit to God and thereby act accordingly and those who remain ungrateful (one meaning of *kufr*) and therefore misbehave. This contrast refers not to belief and disbelief proper but rather to those who act righteously out of submission to God and those who do not, and thus it approximates some of the ways that the Qur'ān speaks of *imān* and *kufr* as well as how the early "believers movement" might have thought about the relation between belief and action. However, unlike Donner's hypothesis of the "believers movement," which posits close cooperation between monotheists, Ibn Muljam's poem creates stark boundaries between Muslims and Christians—so stark that those who violate them, according to Ibn Muljam, become legitimate objects of violence. This position, if authentic, clearly represents a break with how the hypothetical early "believers" were to have acted. Evidently with Ibn Muljam something has changed.

Sizgorich sees in the poem evidence for Muslims attempting to establish boundaries between themselves and Christians, and such an explanation is certainly plausible except that Ibn Muljam's poem is the only example in which such a stark boundary between Muslims and Christians appears.[62] Usually the Muḥakkima and early *shurāt* are portrayed as enjoying especially good relations with the *ahl al-kitāb*, though it may have been that they maintained such relations precisely because the boundaries between the two groups were known and respected.[63] Also conceivable is that, given the ambiguities surrounding the use of the term *kufr*, some Muḥakkima—Ibn Muljam among them—had early on adopted a harder line, seeing *kufr* as implying the theological-legal implications that it would later assume with a vengeance among the Azāriqa and Najdāt. Wahb b. Jarīr's comment that there existed three groups among the Muḥakkima—one of whom considered 'Alī's actions *shirk*—might point toward such a conclusion.[64] But if this explanation is to be accepted, why would Ibn Muljam not have applied such language to his main enemy, 'Alī? Equally plausible is that the poem is anachronistic.[65] Whatever the case, it is clear that while Ibn Muljam's poem remains unique in how it establishes boundaries between Muḥakkima-Muslims and Christians, its dichotomy of *muslim/kāfir* is thoroughly Qur'ānic and may reflect the ways early "believers" conceptualized the connections between proper action and proper monotheism.

On the whole, then, reports in the historical sources about the Muḥakkima's use of *takfīr* as a boundary theme remain considerably more varied and ambiguous than what can be found in heresiographical materials. Historical narratives portray the Muḥakkima as employing a wider assortment of terms to describe 'Alī's actions, ranging from *kufr* and *shirk* to *khatī'a, dhanb, ḍalāla, bid'a, shakk, idhān, dhull,* and even *irtidād*. The fact that alternate reports sometimes substitute general terms such as *dhanb, khaṭī'a,* and *ḍalāla* for *kufr* should at least give scholars pause before concluding that *kufr* denotes a reified theological infraction, as Islamic heresiographers would have it. Without a doubt the early Muḥakkima regarded the acceptance of the arbitration as a serious violation, but that they viewed it in the fully reified manner of later heresiographers is highly doubtful. Rather the range of associations between *kufr, shirk,* and other terms relating to sin, oppression, and misguidance that appear amid the historical reports about the Muḥakkima imply that accusations of *takfīr* imprecated the accused as those who showed their ingratitude toward God and his true followers by refusing to observe piety and work for the just social order. As such, their understanding of *kufr* may have had something in common with how the early Islamic community, as a "believers movement," imagined themselves as working to build God's society on earth before the impending apocalypse.

Moreover, and operating under the assumption that the first Muḥakkima's deployment of the concept of *kufr* owed something to the Qur'ānic understandings of the term, it is noteworthy how Qur'ānic usages of the term tend to elide the notion of *kufr* as rejection of the ideas of God and the last day with sinful, tyrannical, or otherwise improper action.[66] Historical accounts of how the Muḥakkima tarred their opponents appear to do the same: that is, they also seem to run together the idea of *kufr* as improper action stemming from "ingratitude" toward God with sin, error, injustice, tyranny, and other impieties.[67] Judging from historical reports, the Muḥakkima appear to have applied an earlier, unreified, and thoroughly Qur'ānic conception of *kufr* to their enemies. As such, the heresiographical portrait of the Muḥakkima's use of *takfīr* proves anachronistic, reflecting much later understandings of what *kufr* meant in relation to *imān.* The same can be said, to an extent, of many of the reports on the Muḥakkima that are found in Islamic historical sources.

Last, and following Hawting, if accusations of *kufr* and *shirk* can be viewed as polemic and hyperbole on the part of the Muḥakkima, then the heresiographical assertion that the "Khārijites" conflated *kufr* and sin and thereby treated their opponents as the legal equivalents of *kuffār* can be further questioned, at least as far as the Muḥakkima are concerned. The point here is that *takfīr* need not necessarily be a statement about the sinner's state of faith and subsequently of his membership in the community of believers but could merely be a rhetorical statement about the amplitude of the sinner's sin without the subsequent equation of the sinner with the *kāfir* (that is, the difference between *acting like* a *kāfir* and the existential state of *being* one). Without sources from the Muḥakkima this question cannot be answered definitively. Nevertheless it is enough to introduce alternate possibilities, including the strong one that the motives and reasons later attributed to the Muḥakkima by their ideological opponents might not be accurate.

Boundary Themes after the Muḥakkima

The few poems that are attributed to post-Muḥakkima *shurāt* seem to bolster the conclusion that the notion of *kufr,* when used as a boundary theme, denoted something less than the polar opposite of belief. For example, in a poem attributed to Abū Bilāl Mirdās b. Udayya, doyen of the early Basran *shurāt,* the term *kufr* appears but with an ambiguous meaning and alongside other terms that more specifically indicate the nature of the boundaries being established. For example, Abū Bilāl is said to have uttered,

> The rulers have made plain their tyranny, and agreed
> Upon oppressing the people of truth with deceit (*ghadr*) and *kufr.*
> It is with you, my God, if you wish it, to change
> All that the Banū Sakhr have brought to us.
> They have constrained the world around us in its vastness
> And have left us restless in fear.
> Oh Lord, do not hand over your friends (*wulātak*) to ruin,
> But support them, oh Lord, with victory and perseverance.
> Open for us a good way, and do not forbid us
> From a meeting with large numbers of those deviants (*dhawī al-ilḥād*).[68]

Here the term *kufr* does not seem to function directly as a boundary marker. Rather, Abū Bilāl pairs it with deceit as something that is part and parcel of the tyrannical ruler's "oppression" (*ẓulm*). In this sense *kufr* here might indicate what the tyrant does because of his ingratitude toward God's blessings. It is certainly a serious transgression, but its precise nature is ambiguous, seeming to share in the language of tyranny and oppression. Later in the poem Abū Bilāl describes his enemies not with the term *kāfirūn* or *kuffār* but with *dhawī al-ilḥād*—a word implying deviation and desertion of the true community (after its Qur'ānic usage) but not disbelief proper or atheism (as *ilḥād* would later come to mean).[69] Certainly the concepts of *kufr* and *ilḥād* share the idea of being outside of the true community, but the point here is that these terms seem to lack the theological precision that is attributed to them by later heresiographers. They function, it seems, more to generally stake out insiders and outsiders, *ilḥād*'s meaning being specifically suited to such a purpose. Such usages are not surprising: Abū Bilāl became the hero of the moderates, and later the Ibāḍiyya, and is remembered by them for his restrained stance toward non-*shurāt.*

Other early *shurāt* employ still different language to express the difference between themselves and their enemies. Muʿādh b. Juwayn b. Ḥiṣn al-Ṭā'ī al-Sanbīsī, the early Kūfan Muḥakkimite who survived the battles of Nahrawān and Nukhayla and was finally killed fighting al-Mughīra b. Shaʿba (the governor of Kūfa) in the army of the *shārī* leader Ḥayyān b. Ẓabyān, states,

Indeed, Exchangers, the time has come for one
Who sells himself to God to depart.
Will you remain out of ignorance in the house of those who err (*khāṭi'īn*),
While every one of you is hunted down to be killed?

. . . It is hard for me that you are afraid and driven out
When I draw out [my sword] unsheathed among the *muḥillīn,*
When every glorious person scatters their group,
When you would say that he had turned away and fled, he would come back,
Showing the blade of the sword in the heat of the tumult.[70]

Two terms indicate boundary themes in Mu'ādh b. Juwayn's poem. The first offers the metaphor of error and matches some of the ways that the Muḥakkima were said to have spoken about 'Alī and his followers as those who had committed "errors." The second term, *muḥillīn,* refers literally to "those who make lawful [what is unlawful]" but here seems to function as a general epithet for sinners.[71] In addition Ḥāritha b. Ṣakhr al-Qaynī, one of Mu'āwiya's men, who later became a member of the *shurāt,* in his poems accuses the Iraqi governor Ziyād b. Abīhī of being a tyrant (*ẓālim*) and "afflicted to the utmost in misguidance" (*al-munā ṭuraf al-ḍalāli*).[91] Clearly the post-Muḥakkimite usage of boundary themes closely resembles the ways that the Muḥakkima were said to have tarred their adversaries.

Historical sources likewise contain scattered reports of post-Muḥakkimite *shurāt* employing the term *kāfir* to describe their enemies. For example, Ḥawthara b. Wadā' al-Asadī is said to have chided his father, who was sent by Mu'āwiya to tempt Ḥawthara away from his rebellion with memories of his son, with the words, "We are under attack by the hand of a *kāfir* with a spear, shall I be turned from him in an instant [because] I desire for my son?"[73] As with the early reports of the Muḥakkima's usage of the term, the sense of *kāfir* in this phrase remains ambiguous; indeed a variant report from al-Mubarrad does not contain the term at all.[74]

At some point, of course, Muslims in general and the *shurāt* in particular began to regard the accusation of *kufr* as more than polemic and hyperbole and as more than staking out a hazily defined notion of ingratitude toward God. When this transformation occurred and how remain somewhat obscure, but a curious report in al-Balādhurī seems to imply that the Muḥakkima and immediate successors did not employ *takfīr* at all. Rather it was the Baṣran Khārijite Sahm b. Ghālib al-Hujayrī, who rebelled in the year 44/664 (six full years after the battle of Nahrawān), who first did so: "he was the first who designated (*sammā*) the people of the *qibla* with [the label] *kufr;* the Khārijites before him did not bear witness to [a person's] *kufr* or faith (*imān*)."[75] The text adds that Sahm held the "views" of the *mustabṣirīn*—the term's exact referent is obscure, but it seems to denote a particular subset of early *shurāt* who held distinct opinions.[76] Given the abundance of reports that point to the Muḥakkima's employment of *takfīr*, this singular report that attributes it to Sahm b. Ghālib remains an oddity. However, the report could be taken to mean that Sahm b. Ghālib was the first to use the label *kufr* in its emerging theological-legal sense, suggesting that at some point after the demise of the Muḥakkima at Nahrawān, some groups of *shurāt* began to reify the meaning of *kufr* to imply its "harder" theological-legal ramifications.[77]

In addition reports in the historical sources of random killing among post-Muḥakkimite *shurāt* suggest the possibility that among some *shurāt* any outsider was considered a legitimate target of violence (a stance that implies the application of *takfīr* in its reified sense to non-*shurāt*). Al-Balādhurī, for example, reports that Ibn Muljam's companion Shabīb b. Bajra al-Ashja'ī (who was said to have been with Ibn Muljam when he killed 'Alī) killed any woman or child he encountered as he escaped from Kūfa (the text does not use the term *isti'rāḍ*).[78] Of course such reports might easily have been contrived in the interest of anti-Khārijite polemics. However, most of the narratives about Qarīb b. Murra al-Azdī and Ẓuḥḥāf b. Zaḥr al-Ṭā'ī describe how their engagement in random killing (in this instance the texts use the term *isti'rāḍ*) gained them the censure of Abū Bilāl, who is quoted as saying, "God will not bring Qarīb close (*lā qarrabahu Allāh Qarīb*) to all good [things], and God will not forgive Ẓuḥḥāf, for they have committed a senseless injustice (*'ashwā' muẓlimatan*)."[79] As this report quotes Abū Bilāl and expresses horror at *isti'rāḍ*, it likely hails from a quietist *shārī* (possibly an Ibāḍī) source, and as such there is less likelihood that it is entirely fabricated, despite the fact that Qarīb and Ẓuḥḥāf later became heroes to the Ibāḍiyya.[80] Furthermore it is noteworthy that Qarīb's and Ẓuḥḥāf's rebellions took place in 50/670, nearly twelve years after the demise of the Muḥakkima at Nahrawān, a fact that points toward the spread among some *shurāt* of the practice of what was to become known by the term *isti'rāḍ* (if indeed it was a conscious practice and not simply random killing later labeled as such).

The early *shurāt*, then, more or less mirror the varied and often ambiguous means by which the Muḥakkima conceptualized their enemies, using a range of terminology that encompassed the notions of *kufr, ilḥād, ḥulūl, khiṭ'a, ẓulm,* and *ḍalāla* to indicate that their opponents were something less than full Muslims. For the most part, it seems as if the early *shurāt* continued using the label *kāfir* in its early, and unreified, Qur'ānic sense, and in line with how the Muḥakkima seem to have used it, but that later a group (following Sahm b. Ghālib) among them began to apply it in a theological fashion, even as other early *shurāt* began to randomly attack non-*shurāt*. It is worth noting, however, that such actions come across as exceptions to the general rule, such that al-Balādhurī's source singles out Sahm b. Ghālib as the first of the *shurāt* to dichotomize *kufr* and *imān,* and Abū Bilāl is shown to have roundly condemned Qarīb and Zuḥḥāf's acts of random killing.[81] On the whole and from what little evidence can be found, it seems as if the early *shurāt* cleaved, more or less, to a vision of boundaries that was as vague as that of their predecessors among the Muḥakkima.

Boundary Themes among the Azāriqa

It is with the Azāriqa, who are believed to have emerged as a distinct Khārijite subgroup with the rebellion of their eponym Nāfiʿ b. al-Azraq in Basra in 64/683, that boundary themes among the Khārijites are said to be the most starkly drawn. Accordingly, with the Azāriqa the practices of *takfīr* and *istiʿrāḍ* supposedly found their most extreme expressions. Al-Ashʿarī in his *Maqālāt al-Islāmīyyīn* outlined what would, with few exceptions, become the standard heresiographical portrait among the Sunnīs of Azraqite doctrines: dissociation from (*barāʾa min*) those who did not fight (*al-qaʿada*), or who practiced *taqiyya* in either word or deed; anathematizing as *kuffār* all Muslims who did not make the *hijra* to their camp; administering an examination (*miḥna*) of those who came to them; allowing the killing of the women and children among their enemies (that is, of *mushrikūn*); and believing that these enemies, along with their women and children, were also in hell.[82]

From the Ibāḍī perspective, a similar portrait of Azraqī boundary maintenance emerges. Sālim b. Dhakwān censors the Azāriqa for classifying their *qawm* (that is, non-Ibāḍī/*shārī* Muslims) as idolaters (*ʿabadat al-awthān*) and subsequently severing inheritance relations and refusing to intermarry with them or to grant them protection.[83] He reports that they deemed it permissible to enslave their *qawm,* take their women and property as spoils, kill their children, and indiscriminately slaughter them (*istiʿrāḍuhum*). Ibn Dhakwān also mentions the "test" (*miḥna*) administered to non-Azraqīs and that the Azāriqa anathematized those who did not fight (*al-qaʿada*), declaring their lives and property licit and refusing to associate or even to pray for forgiveness for them.[84]

Historical reports on the Azāriqa present a picture extraordinarily similar to that found in Islamic heresiographies. Al-Madāʾinī's report in al-Balādhurī, for example, describes how Nāfiʿ b. al-Azraq found *istiʿrāḍ* licit, along with the killing of the non-Azraqī children and those who refused to fight. This report also gives the Qurʾānic verses that Nāfiʿ supposedly used to justify his actions, mentions how the Azraqites would administer the *miḥna,* and quotes Nāfiʿ forbidding marriage, inheritance, and eating the slaughtered meat from non-Azraqites.[85] It also clarifies that Nāfiʿ classified the status (that is, the *dār,* "abode") of non-Azraqites as that of *kufr.*[86] Similarly al-Mubarrad and others preserve an exchange of letters between Najda

b. ʿAmr al-Ḥanafī, the eponym of the Najdites, in which Najda censors Nāfiʿ for anathematizing those who did not fight, for deeming it permissible to kill children, and for refusing to honor the trust (*amāna*) of a non-Azraqite. Nāfiʿ replies with Qurʾānic verses justifying his positions.[87] What becomes abundantly clear from the similarities between heresiographical and historical reports on the Azāriqa is how later authors understood them to have unequivocally committed themselves to the fully reified notion of *takfīr* as an accusation of theological-legal import, carrying with it all the implications of how an idolater was to be treated. If such reports are to be trusted—and their sheer volume alone makes it difficult to doubt that the Azāriqa did not in some capacity engage in what they were accused of doing—then a more fully reified notion of what *kufr* meant and implied had made its appearance with the Azāriqa.

In fact several historical reports emphasize how the Azāriqa broke from past traditions of the *shurāt:* in the words of an anonymous report in al-Mubarrad, "they followed the people of Nahrawān, and Mirdās [b. Udayya] and those who rebelled with him" until a *mawlā* from the Banī Hāshim convinced Nāfiʿ b. al-Azraq differently.[88] Of course, as an Azdī of Basran origins, al-Mubarrad may well have had access to Ibāḍī sources, citing them in his assessment of the Azāriqa. In fact Ibn Dhakwān's condemnations of the Azāriqa hinge on the similar contention that they followed a different path from that of their predecessors, the very same people with whom they professed to associate.[89] Likewise, Najda b. ʿAmr in his letter to Nāfiʿ b. al-Azraq comments on how Nāfiʿ "strayed from the right path" after having been a model Muslim ("a merciful father to the orphan, a kind brother to the weak").[90] Azraqite boundary themes, particularly their stark definition of *kufr* and its implications, then, were viewed by some as a novel interpretation that broke with what many *shurāt* (and possibly later Ibāḍīs as the sources for such reports) considered to be the proper understanding and implications of *takfīr.*

Azraqī poetry provides a more nuanced glimpse into the creation of boundary themes among them: while these boundary themes are indeed marked by the language of *kufr,* as with the Muḥakkima this terminology is by no means the only method of establishing boundaries between insiders and outsiders; and furthermore the precise nature of the boundary so created by the term *kufr* (and its variants) is not altogether clear and unproblematic. It is more accurate to say that the language of *kufr* in Azraqī-Khārijite poetry serves as one strand in a conceptual web indicating enemies to be fought, and that this strand is linked to other concepts that express boundary primarily in terms of piety/impiety, guidance/deviance, and justice/tyranny. As such, it is not terribly different from how earlier Muḥakkima and *shurāt* expressed boundaries, and the poetry of the Azāriqa therefore affords a view into developing notions of boundary that were neither fixed nor universal among them.

In fact there are several ways that Azraqī poets denote the boundaries between themselves and others. Unsurprisingly, invocations of tribe and family—that classic means of establishing Arab identity—sometimes make their appearance in their poems. Thus, for example, Yazīd b. Ḥabnā' states,

> The wretched is the one whose abode is the Fire,
> And the victorious is he who is saved from the Fire.
> God protect me from that which procures
> The blame of my clan or draws me near to disgrace,
> And from worldly goods that makes one forget the evil to come,
> When the Mighty will inform me of my deeds.
> I do not approach the house from the rear [in suspicion]
> Nor do I slander my cousin.[91]

In this poem Ibn Ḥabnā' mixes the standard tropes of respect for tribe and family with that of Islamic piety such that, for him, there is no tension between them.

Yet the Azāriqa from whom Ibn Ḥabnā' hailed were known for breaking—sometimes violently—with their tribes in favor of their group. Therefore, perhaps, a more typical attitude is that expressed by 'Īsā b. Fātik al-Khaṭṭī (an early comrade of Nāfi' b. al-Azraq) when he sings,

> My father is *islām,* there is no father aside from it.
> When they boast of the deeds of Bakr and Tamīm,
> Both of these help the claimant
> To be on a par with the possessor of poisoned glory.
> There is no glory, even if [one is] ennobled with a hereditary
>   disposition [toward it],
> But *taqwa* is the most ennobling.[92]

Al-Khaṭṭī regards the glory gained from boasting about tribal connections as a type of poison, preferring piety alone and symbolically subverting tribal norms by claiming Islam as his only father. The contrast with Ibn Ḥabnā''s easy mixing of piety and tribal sentiment shows how boundary themes, such as the theme of tribe and family, in Khārijite poetry can be quite complex and anything but straightforward.

Ibn Ḥabnā''s sentiment that true community is based in religious ties, of course, is echoed in several passages in the Qur'ān that speak about the concept of the *umma* as a religiously based community, ideally beyond tribal and even familial ties.[93] It is no surprise that early *shurāt* and later Khārijite groups found inspiration in the Qur'ān for such idealized notions of religious community. However, just as the Qur'ānic notion of the *umma* supplemented (rather than supplanted) preexisting notions of tribal and familial identity, so too the idea of tribal affiliation among the early *shurāt* and their successors the Khārijites did not utterly diminish in importance (for example, Ṭawwāf's murder of the *mawālī,* as well as the split between Arabs and *mawālī* in Qaṭarī b. al-Fujā'a's army). Indeed several scholars have noted the prominence of certain tribes among the *shurāt* and Khārijite movements.[94] Also noteworthy in this respect are the various religiously based social units of late antiquity, the most familiar to the Arabs likely being the 'Ibād of al-Ḥīra, in which tribal ties were not utterly eclipsed but subordinated to the religious mode of identification. Without attributing a direct line of "influence" to the 'Ibād of al-Ḥīra and while recognizing the strong Qur'ānic component in *shārī* notions of community, it is safe to assume that the early *shurāt* and Khārijite movements tended toward the idealized religious community but remained nevertheless in a world where tribal affiliation was the main currency of social interaction.[95] While many early *shurāt* and Khārijite groups did, in fact, affiliate on the basis of tribe, explicit boundary themes were more often than not established through the use of religious language.

As with the Muḥakkima and early *shurāt,* when Azraqī poets described their enemies, they used a variety of terms to establish the boundaries between them. Thus a poem from 'Umra Um 'Imrān b. al-Ḥārith al-Rāsibī eulogizing her son killed at the battle of Dūlāb with Nāfi' b. al-Azraq states,

> God supported 'Imrān and purged him,
> For 'Imrān used to call upon Him at dawn.
> He called on Him in secret and in public so that He might grant him
> Martyrdom at the hands of deceitful deviants (*milḥāditin ghudar*).[96]

Likewise, 'Īsā b. Fātik al-Khaṭṭī, one of Nāfi' b. al-Azraq's companions, sang,

> I fear the punishment of God if I die contented
> With the rule of the treacherous and oppressive 'Ubaydullāh [b. Ziyād].
> I fear that I will meet my Lord without terrifying
> Those rebels and deviants (*dhawī al-baghī wa'l-ilḥād*) with an immense army.[97]

In these poems it is the term *ilḥād* (*dhawī al-ilḥād,* and so forth)—the above-cited term implying deviation and desertion of the true community—that sets the boundaries between insiders and outsiders. Ibn Fātik, of course, pairs *ilḥād* with *baghī* (rebellion), painting the portrait of the outsider as both rebel and deviant. It is important to note that in another poem attributed to Ibn Fātik, the poet is perfectly willing to use the language of belief to make a point for his imagined interlocutor:

Two thousand believers—as you claim,
and forty defeated them in Āsik.
You lie—it is not as you claim!
The Khawārij were the believers!
They are a small company, with no doubts,
Who over the many were victorious.[98]

Ibn Fātik, then, was not averse to using the language of belief, and it must be concluded that his preference for the terms *ilḥād* and *baghī* was on some level intentional.

Ibn Fātik is not alone in employing the language of rebellion to describe his enemies, as one of Qaṭarī b. al-Fujā'a's poems similarly employs it: "You rebellious one (*ayuhā al-bāghī*) who wishes to contend [with me in a duel], approach! / That I may hand you the poisoned beverage of death."[99] The language of rebellion recalls Qur'ān 49:9, in which Muslims are instructed in the case of believers (that is, insiders) fighting one another to fight "the [group] that transgresses" (*al-latī tabghī*) until that group submits or is defeated. Later Ibāḍī tradition provides this verse as part of the Muḥakkima's argument against 'Alī at the battle of Ṣiffīn: that is, that Mu'āwiya's band was the "rebellious party" alluded to in the verse and mentioned in later Prophetic ḥadīth in connection with 'Ammār b. Yāsir, and that 'Alī had contravened a clear Qur'ānic command to fight when he accepted the arbitration.[100] It is not hard to imagine this Ibāḍī line of reasoning as stemming from an earlier *shurāt* position and simultaneously being shared by the Azraqites. Alternately the Azāriqa may simply have been using the term as a means to insult their enemies. In either case the language of rebellion provides another example of the variety of boundary themes that appear in Khārijite poetry.

Other Azraqī Khārijites employed still different language to express the difference between themselves and their enemies. A line of 'Ubayda b. Hilāl al-Yashkurī (that is, Abū al-'Ayzār), one of the leaders of the Azāriqa along with Qaṭarī b. al-Fujā'a, says of his fellow Azraqite Ḥuṣayn b. Mālik, "There were no horsemen among the *muḥillīn* / Who would contend with him for death, except Ḥabīb [b. al-Muhallab]."[101] As noted above, the term *muḥillīn* refers literally to "those who make lawful [what is unlawful]," but here it seems to function as a general epithet for enemies. Specifically it is a general insult against al-Muhallab's soldiers.

Elsewhere the same Abū al-'Ayzār sings,

There is attainment for the *shurāt* at night.
For those gone astray (*al-ghawā*) there is distress;
In their group [you find] whims (*hawā*) and [bad] tendencies (*mayl*),
And sins (*fitan*) as if they were like a torrent.[102]

Here the boundary metaphor involves guidance and misguidance and employs the Qur'ānic notion of whim as well as "corruption" (*fitna*) to mark the difference between Khārijites and others.

Yet a fourth method of establishing group boundaries is drawn by the Azraqite poet al-Ḥārith b. Ka'b al-Shannī:

> Indeed the mention of 'Awn b. Aḥmar has tested my bones and thinned them,
> And made my nights sleepless.
> A youth who feared only God, the One
> And whose favor every needy man sought.
> Ibn Aḥmar fought sincerely for God,
> When every neglecter (*muqaṣṣir*) was content with injustice.[103]

The boundary here is with those who fight, such as Ibn Aḥmar, and those who neglect the duty and are therefore content, in the eyes of the poet, to live with injustice. Ibn Ka'b's employment of this term tallies nicely with reports that describe how the Azraqites rejected *qu'ūd* (not participating in the fight).

As with the historical reports on the Muḥakkima and early *shurāt*, Azraqite poetry contains several methods and terms by which the poetry creates boundary themes, thereby placing the language of *kufr* as a boundary theme among other terms that indicate deviance, rebellion, impiety, and neglect of the duty of battle. Coming to the Azraqite poems that use the term *kufr* and its variants as boundary themes, it becomes apparent that when Azraqī poets employ the language of *kufr*, the nature of the boundary so indicated is not always clear, mimicking the ambiguities of the term among reports of the early Muḥakkima and their successors. An example is the Azraqite poet 'Amr al-Qanā b. 'Umayra al-'Anbarī al-Tamīmī's use of the term *kufr* when he sings,

> We met you the morn of Immolation Day,
> With horses swift as lances,
> Led by 'Amr al-Qanā at dawn,
> Toward a people accustomed to *kufr* (*lahajū bi-kufrin*).
> Today I fulfill my vow to my enemies,
> And, through revenge, attain my desire.[104]

Kufr in this poem appears to be an attitude or action to which people can become accustomed. In this sense it might resonate with the Qur'ānic notion of *kufr* as ingratitude as well as the actions that spring from it. The poet's use of the term also recalls how, according to the Qur'ān, God strengthens the resolve of those so bent on rejecting the message.[105]

Another interesting usage of the term can be seen in some lines from Qaṭarī b. al-Fujā'a's poem about the battle of Dūlāb:

If you witnessed us that day, and our horses
Conquering from the *kuffār* every *ḥarīm.*
You would see young men who sold (*bā'ū*) their souls to God
For the gardens of Eden with Him, and blessing.[106]

Determining the sense of the term *kuffār* in this poem depends in large part on the interpretation of the term *ḥarīm,* which can refer to valuable things in general and especially to wives and concubines or to an area that must be defended.[107] Is the poet then saying that the Azraqī warriors took territory from their enemies or that they took their wives, concubines, and possibly even children as spoils? Given the Azraqites' reported tendency to treat the women and children of their enemies also as *kuffār,* it is entirely possible that the latter reading is justified. However, two points complicate this interpretation. First, the poem refers specifically to spoils taken on the day of the battle of Dūlāb, and it stretches the imagination to think that the Zubayrid army under the command of Muslim b. 'Ubays brought along their wives and concubines for the taking. Second, the next line of the poem mentions the exchange of the soul for paradise, and as has been shown, *shirā'* often concomitantly involved ascetic practices such as celibacy. Thus the term *ḥarīm* in this poem might not refer to women, and thus the *kuffār* of this poem are not necessarily disbelievers in the theological-legal sense of the term (which would imply that their women could be taken) but rather are generic "enemies" to be fought.

Other Azraqī poets provide a few more clues as to the nature of *kufr* in Azraqī-Khārijite discourse. The following poem is said to have been uttered during the siege of the Azāriqa at Jiroft during which Qaṭarī b. al-Fujā'a was said to have counseled escape and to have killed a certain 'Āmir b. 'Amr al-Sa'adī for threatening to dissociate from him. 'Āmir's cousin Ḥuṣayn b. Ḥafṣa al-Sa'dī, incensed at his cousin's death, was said to have recited,

Oh Qaṭarī b. al-Fujātī [*sic*], do we not get anything from justice
Except the deeds of tyrants?
Do you not feel ashamed, Oh Ibn al-Fujāti,
Of that which has clothed you in dishonor while you were away?
Every day your lips expose
Your mouth to al-Muhallab, while your heart is aflight.
How far is your guarded escape from him?
When you are an associate (*walī*) whilst he is a *kāfir*?[108]

The boundary distinction here is between insiders as "associates"—*awliyā'*— and *kuffār.* The boundary is clearly marked, with *kuffār* as the definite outsiders, but the nature of what distinguishes Qaṭarī as a *walī* from al-Muhallab as a *kāfir* is unclear. Ibn Ḥafṣa's rhetorical device implies that Qaṭarī's desire to flee from battle would make him the equivalent of such a *kāfir*—a sentiment that underscores the importance of fighting for the Azāriqa.

Another Azraqite poem, from Qaṭarī b. al-Fujā'a, seems similarly to bear out the heresiographical observation that the Azāriqa considered the refusal to fight—*qu'ūd*—as tantamount to *kufr.* However, the boundary so established is not without its problems from the standpoint of Azraqite doctrine. Qaṭarī's poem is said to be addressed to a fellow Khārijite, Sumayra Ibn Ja'd, who instead of fighting sought out al-Ḥajjāj:

> What is the difference between Ibn Ja'd and ourselves?
> While we stride in our double-textured curiass,
> Fighting al-Muhallab's horsemen,
> each of us facing the blows of sharp swords,
> Ibn Ja'd goes off in search of truth to his *amīr,*
> An *amīr* who does not command piety toward God!
>
> . . . Make amends, Abū Ja'd, do not shut
> Your eyes in a darkness that blinds every eye.
> Repent a repentance that will guide you to martyrdom,
> For surely you are a sinner (*dhū dhanbin*), not a *kāfir.*
> Come to our way and you will get in *jihād* spoils
> That which will give you profitable rewards and no loss.
> This is the goal, the desired recompense,
> While every merchant obtains his riches in this world.[109]

Ibn Ja'd's refusal to fight has made him, in the eyes of Ibn al-Fujā'a, a sinner but not yet a *kāfir,* and presumably it is this distinction that leaves room for Ibn Ja'd to respond to Ibn al-Fujā'a's call and return to the Azraqite fold through fighting. In other words, the sin of *qu'ūd* has not yet excluded Ibn Ja'd definitively from the Azraqite fold as a *kāfir.* From this poem it seems fairly clear that a *kāfir* is an absolute outsider and that *kufr* is something more serious and damning than sin, which can apparently be redeemed through *jihād.*

Yet Qaṭarī's division between sinners and *kāfir* is problematic in another sense: the position that sinners from within one's group are not fully *kuffār* but occupy the status of sinner is not supposed to be the doctrine of the Azāriqa, who according to the heresiographers firmly equated major sins such as *qu'ūd* with *kufr,* anathematizing any who would not join their camp.[110] It is true that other Khārijite groups were said to have softened their stance toward sinners, as when the founder of the Najdāt supposedly excused his followers from sins that they committed in ignorance or when he similarly refused to consider the refusal to fight (*qu'ūd*) as the equivalent of *kufr,*[111] but not so the Azāriqa. Qaṭarī's poem, then, presents a fascinating exception to the supposed Azraqite line and might represent a glimpse beyond the reconstructed categories of the heresiographers into the actual development of Azraqī doctrines. It has been argued elsewhere that the numismatic evidence from the Azāriqa does not entirely square with what Islamic heresiographers have written about them.[112] Likewise, Qaṭarī's poem seems to indicate that the Azāriqa either did not hold a single view on the question of *qu'ūd,* sin, and *kufr* or that their view developed over the nearly twenty years of their operations.

Thus the Azāriqa do, on the whole, seem to have been moving in the direction of treating *kuffār* as the legal equivalents of unbelievers, but, as with the Muḥakkima and early *shurāt,* the language of *kufr* is by no means the only way that Azraqī poets marked the boundaries between themselves and those they considered outsiders. Accusations of *kufr* sit alongside other terms for outsiders, such as *dhawī al-ilḥād, al-baghī/bughāt, al-muḥillūn, al-muqaṣṣirūn,* and *al-ghawā.* It is possible, then, to see how *kufr* and *kāfir* sit among a constellation of terms that range from general slurs ascribing rebellion and deviance to specific imputations of neglecting the duty of battle or misguidance. Given this range of boundary themes in Azraqite poetry, it is possible to question the heresiographers' tendency to emphasize the language of *kufr* as the main means by which the Azāriqa imagined the difference between themselves and others.

This leads to another point: looking across the different boundary themes in Azraqite-Khārijite poetry, it is noticeable how they all indicate in one way or another persons (such as al-Muhallab) whom the Azāriqa found (and from whom they were possibly taking spoils) or qualities (such as *kufr* on other impieties) associated with those whom the Azāriqa fought, or those who would flee or refuse to fight (and thereby become enemies). With the exception of this last point (that is, equating *qu'ūd* with *kufr*), such a stance lines up more or less with one of the ways that the Qur'ān speaks of *kuffār* as the enemies of the believers in battle.[113] And if the Azraqites more often than not employed accusations of *kufr* in the unreified Qur'ānic senses, then it is worth remembering that in the Qur'ān it is God who ultimately knows the state of the *kuffār*'s faith, while the believers can usually know only the outward signs of it (that is, refusal to pray, transgressing the limits of God, fighting the believers, and so forth). In light of this observation, the description of Azraqite enemies as impious tyrants, deviants, oppressors, or rebels takes on added weight and implies that for the Azāriqa, their enemies were fought not necessarily because they were unfaithful, ungracious, or unbelievers but because they manifestly and variously opposed and oppressed those who were trying to effect God's rule on earth and in so doing became unfaithful, ungracious, and the equivalent of unbelievers.

This is a fine point to be sure, and in fairness it cannot be said that heresiographers such as al-Ash'arī have it all wrong. The Azāriqa do, after all, tar their opponents with the label of *kuffār* and seem to have treated them accordingly. Yet in doing so the Azāriqa persisted in accordance with how the hypothetical early "believers movement" interpreted the Qur'ānic notions of *kufr* and *imān:* that is, that actions and beliefs were intimately associated with one another, and that those who would not work for the creation of the just society were outside of the community. But the ground was shifting beneath the Azraqites' feet: the community of "believers" was moving to define itself more precisely as Muslims. Whereas the early "believers movement" valued the common goal of justice on earth over theological differences among confessional communities, the new sense of Islamic identity demanded that the hazily defined early notions of *imān* and *kufr* give way to more-specific concepts. As the recently settled sons of the *ghazīyīn,* the Azāriqa remained convinced that like their fathers, they had a duty to root out oppression and tyranny in the name of Islam. Finding this persecution in their own lands and at the hands of ostensibly Muslim leaders, they came to understand the Qur'ānic term *kuffār* as referring to all who opposed or would not join their fight.[114] They were the righteous remnant of believers, engaged in a pious struggle against tyrants and oppressors who through their sins became *kuffār.*

Islamic heresiographers and historians, many of whom lived at a time when the wider Islamic world had embraced what was essentially the Murji'ite stance on belief, miss the nuanced ways that the Muḥakkima, *shurāt,* and later the Azāriqa tied the language of *kufr* to that of oppression, sin, tyranny, and impiety and did so in ways that recalled certain Qur'ānic idioms as well as the postulated stance of the early "believers." Of course it is not difficult to see what is at stake for the heresiographers in their stark characterization of the Khārijites' use of *takfīr.* As a genre of Islamic writing that is dedicated to finding the one "saving sect" (*al-firqa al-nājiya*) amid those who are damned to hellfire, heresiography must draw contrasting images of true and false doctrines, and as such it is interested neither in ambiguity nor in the finer points of doctrinal development. Thus the Khārijites (all of them together) must for the heresiographers hold a strong and clearly defined notion of what *kufr* means as the opposite of belief, and they must compound their error by conflating sin and *kufr.* In this way emerging Sunnī or Shi'ite notions of belief and disbelief may be made clearer by contrast, just as the "proper" position of the sinner may be outlined.

Decoupled from their heresiographical caricature, the development of early *shurāt* boundary themes from the Muḥakkima to the Azāriqa may be reconsidered, as can the place of the Ibāḍiyya within it. Ibāḍī accounts of their origins openly connect their movement to that of the first Muḥakkima, and although the tribal affiliations of the first Muḥakkima and early *shurāt* do not match those who later adopted Ibāḍism as their own, it is here possible to see how certain foundational figures and their narratives—such as 'Abdullāh b. Wahb al-Rāsibī and Ḥurqūṣ b. Zuhayr—were embraced, along with their moderate quasi-theological stances toward non-Muḥakkima, by later groups such as the Ibāḍiyya.

It also seems fairly clear that it was the Azāriqa and Najdāt who adopted a particularly staunch interpretation of the Muḥakkima's actions against ʿAlī, and it was in their period that more formed theological notions of *kufr* and sin began to take root among certain groups of Khārijites (in accordance with trends in the wider Islamic world). This emerging Azraqī usage of the term *kuffār* would provide occasion for those who did not advocate constant and absolute warfare against the "enemies of God"—the quietists—to offer a counterdefinition of it. Thus the nascent Ibāḍiyya did two things at once: they cultivated their stance on *kufr* into the complex positions they hold today while criticizing in the process the violent excesses of the Azāriqa. According to this view, the moderate *shurāt*-cum-Ibāḍī claim that their interpretation of *kufr* also goes back to the original Muḥakkima remains justified. Indeed treating certain kinds of *kufr* as *kufr al-ni'ma* (à la the first ever elusive Ibn Ibāḍ) or casting non-Ibāḍī Muslims as *munāfiqūn, ahl al-qibla,* and monotheists though not full Muslims (à la Ibn Dhakwān and others) does hearken back to one of the plausible Muḥakkimite uses of *takfīr.* It was this refinement, in part, that allowed the Ibāḍiyya and other quietists to survive while the Azāriqa and other militants fought themselves to extinction.

Chapter 4

Ibāḍī Appropriations

Certain narratives of the Muḥakkima and early *shurāt* made their way into Ibāḍī sources through a complex process of appropriation, such that the Ibāḍiyya succeeded to and elaborated on the notion of *shirā'* and preserved in their discussions of it a concern with the rejection of the material world in favor of the hereafter as well as the attendant attitudes toward the human body/martyrdom that usually accompanied such an outlook. Of course the Ibāḍiyya used the concept of *shirā'* toward their own ends, and it is not helpful to overstate the comparisons that can be drawn between earlier *shurāt* materials (such as they survive) and later Ibāḍī texts. Ibāḍī concerns over the notion of *shirā'* differed in significant ways from that which can be reconstructed of the earlier groups, if for no other reason than the fact that by the end of the second/eighth century the Ibāḍiyya found themselves running polities in North Africa and Oman. Ibāḍīs developed their own ideas about the notion of *shirā'*, adapting it to their own purposes even when the earlier usages of the concept lived on in Ibāḍī literature.

The stories of the Muḥakkima and early *shurāt,* especially in their North African Ibāḍī iterations, owe a profound debt to Iraqi sources. In particular, Abū Mikhnaf's reports on these early groups, preserved in various Islamic historical sources (such as al-Ṭabarī and al-Balādhurī), match—often word for word—what comes via the reports of al-Fazārī and the *Kitāb Abī Sufyān.* Given such textual parallels, it is no surprise that Ibāḍī renderings of the Muḥakkima and early *shurāt* display profound resonances with other stories of the martyrs, ascetics, and saints in the hagiographical literature of late antique and early Islam.

The Emergence of the Ibāḍiyya

The movement that eventually came to be known as the Ibāḍiyya initially coalesced out of the quietist *shurāt* circles of the Basra and secondarily Kūfa and continued to develop as these moderates resisted the Umayyad and later the ʿAbbāsid authorities.[1] After several failed revolts, the Ibāḍiyya of the early ʿAbbāsid period established imāmates in the Arabian Peninsula and, along with their fellow quietists the Ṣufriyya, in North Africa. The term "quietist" or "moderate" is used here to designate those who did not rebel with or condone the actions of the more militant Khārijite groups of Azraqites and Najdites during the second *fitna*. From a doctrinal standpoint, "quietists" are defined as those who accepted the practice of *taqiyya* (prudent dissimulation), did not take a hard line on treating non-*shurāt* Muslims as unbelievers (that is, as *kuffār* or *mushrikūn* who could be indiscriminately fought), and did not require immigration (*hijra*) to their camp. However, it should not be assumed that the label "quietist" implies that these *shurāt* were pacifists; rather they seem to have counseled waiting for the proper moment to revolt and insisted on a higher standard for how enemies should be defined and treated than those of groups such as the Azāriqa and Najdāt.[2]

These terms are preferred to describe the first moments of the nascent Ibāḍī and Ṣufrī movements for several reasons. Chief among them is that although Islamic sources date the genesis of the Ibāḍiyya, Ṣufriyya, and Azāriqa to the supposed fragmentation (*tafrīq*) of the Basran Khārijites in 64/683, recent scholarship has shown that the Ibāḍīs and Ṣufrīs began to diverge into distinct sects only late in the Umayyad era and that this divergence was tied to alliances with specific tribes in the Arabian Peninsula and North Africa.[3] Initially those who became the Ibāḍiyya and Ṣufriyya likely constituted the same undefined masses of nonmilitant *shurāt* in Iraq. Indeed an anecdote from Ibāḍī historical sources reports that the first missionaries to North Africa in 105/723—one, ʿIkrima, identified as Ṣufrī, and the other, Salama b. Saʿd, an Ibāḍī—are said to have arrived in Qayrawān on the same camel. Although anecdotal, this report does point to a lack of strict denominational boundaries between the groups in this early period.[4]

As the Ibāḍiyya survived to the present era, it is possible to reconstruct their history due to the extensive sources that have survived.[5] The Ibāḍiyya seemed to have crystallized from the moderate scholarly circles of Basra and hailed from groups associated with Jābir b. Zayd (d. before 104/722), a *shārī* or a *shurāt* sympathizer originally hailing from Firq, a village near Nizwā, Oman. At an early age, Jābir settled with his family in Basra, where he became an important *ʿālim* and attracted a circle of students.[6] After Jābir's death, many of these students gave further definition to the moderate *shurāt* circles of Basra and attracted students of their own. Thus, Abū ʿUbayda Muslim b. Abī Karīma emerged as an important proto-Ibāḍī *ʿālim* in the mid-second/eighth century and epitomized the nonconfrontational, scholarly tendencies of the moderates. Ibāḍī sources remember him as the first Ibāḍī "imām," but it is clear that he did not enjoy exclusive authority and was surrounded by other important scholars. Another early Basran, for example, was the more activist-leaning Abū Mawdūd Ḥājib al-Ṭāī, who promoted the practice of *shirā'*.

In addition many later heresiographical traditions, including Ibāḍī writings, often posit 'Abdullāh b. Ibāḍ as the founder and eponym of the sect. However, biographical information on Ibn Ibāḍ is vague and often contradictory—later Ibāḍī writings identify him as a spokesperson for Jābir b. Zayd—and it is not altogether clear what role he may or may not have played in the formation of Basran Ibāḍism.[7] Ibn Ibāḍ may also have been associated with a rival proto-Ibāḍī group in Basra: Madelung suggests that he became the unwitting eponym of a contending Basran contingent of moderates after the 'Abbāsid caliph al-Manṣūr began calling them Ibāḍiyya. After Ibn Ibāḍ's rival group disintegrated, the main Basran Ibāḍīs accepted this name and absorbed the writings of their defunct rivals.[8] Whatever the case, it was under the direction of early proto-Ibāḍī scholars that the Basran moderates established a treasury (*bayt al-māl*) and used it to train the missionaries—those who would later be called the "carriers of knowledge" (*ḥamalāt al-'ilm*)—who would spread the nascent Ibāḍī doctrines throughout the early Islamic world.[9]

While the scholarly circles of Basran moderates provided the continuity and leadership that allowed for the emergence of the Ibāḍiyya, the alignment of the Basran moderates with southern Arabian tribal groups in Basra and the Arabian Peninsula as well as with Berber groups in North Africa was what truly transformed the proto-Ibāḍiyya into a fully recognizable group. In Iraq this alliance came about, in large part, due to the Umayyad dispossessions of prominent southern Arabian personalities in Iraq in the first half of the second/eighth century. For example, the Umayyad governor al-Ḥajjāj b. Yūsuf's defeat of the general from the Kinda tribe, 'Abd al-Raḥmān b. Muḥammad b. al-Ash'ath, in 83–84/702–3 proved extremely unpopular among the Kinda of Iraq, who found in Ibn al-Ash'ath a pious backer (he adopted the title "helper of the Muslims") and a tribal noble (*sharīf*). Likewise al-Ḥajjāj's machinations against the prominent Azdī family of Muhallabs in Iraq in the early part of the second/eighth century alienated the Azd. The Kinda and Azd tribes, especially those who had settled in Basra, had benefited from the political and economic patronage of Ibn al-Ash'ath and the Muhallabids. In fact ties between the Muhallabid family and the nascent Ibāḍiyya went back to the very emergence of the Ibāḍiyya in Basra, where proto-Ibāḍīs had made converts among the wives of some prominent Muhallabīs.[10] When the Umayyads removed Ibn al-Ash'ath and then the Muhallab family from power, the Kinda and Azd of Basra expressed their dissatisfaction by solidifying their ties to the proto-Ibāḍiyya, who represented a "home grown" (that is, Iraqi-Basran) form of the *shurāt* movement. In this way, by the early second/eighth century southern Arabian tribal groups such as the Azd and Kinda came to dominate a movement that had heretofore been populated by northern Arabian tribes (that is, Tamīm, Ṭayy, Rabī'a, Bakr, Shaybān, Yashkūr, and so forth).[11]

The tribal alliances forged in Basra eventually led to Ibāḍī-inspired rebellions in the ancestral homes of the Kinda and Azd—that is, southern Arabia and Oman. Though they failed at first, the uprising of ʿAbdullāh b. Yaḥyā (who became known as Ṭālib al-Ḥaqq) in Yemen and the Arabian Peninsula and that of al-Julandā b. Masʿūd in Oman represented successful Ibāḍī missionizing among the Azd and Kinda and set the stage for the ultimate success of Ibāḍism in these regions. Ṭālib al-Ḥaqq's rebellion erupted in 128/745 and subdued Yemen and much of Arabia including Makka and Madīna before being defeated in 131/748. Ṭālib al-Ḥaqq's successor, the Omani al-Julandā b. Masʿūd, defeated a rival group of Ṣufrī Khārijites before being overwhelmed and killed by an invading ʿAbbāsid army in 134/751.

Not daunted by their initial failures, the eastern Ibāḍiyya, in conjunction with several Omani tribes, rose again against the ʿAbbāsids in 177/793. In that same year a council of Ibāḍī *ʿulamāʾ* appointed Muḥammad b. Abī ʿAffān to the imāmate and thereby initiated the first successful Ibāḍī imāmate in Oman. The imāmate created profound changes in the articulation of Ibāḍism: for the first time the Ibāḍiyya controlled a region in which they resided, and consequently they could openly express religious convictions that previously needed to be veiled. The exercise of actual power also necessitated certain adjustments to inherited institutions; thus, for example, the ways that *shirāʾ* was understood and how the *shurāt* were organized evolved with the needs of the emerging Ibāḍī polity.

The Ibāḍī imāmate in Oman lasted until 280/893, when the discord caused by the unseating of the imām al-Ṣalt b. Mālik in 272/886 culminated in the defeat of the Ibāḍīs at the battle of Samad.[12] The ʿAbbāsids, who had been called to Oman by an opposing tribal group, ruled it for the next century, though actual control of the Omani coast passed to the Buyids, a Shi'ite dynasty that ruled in the name of the ʿAbbāsids. In the early fifth/eleventh century a new Ibāḍī imām, al-Khalīl b. Shathān al-Kharūṣī (r. ca. 407–20/1016–29 C.E.), consolidated Ibāḍī control in the interior. His successor, Rāshid b. Sa'īd al-Yaḥmadī, rid the Omani coast of the Buyids, so that by the middle of the fifth/eleventh century, the Ibāḍīs ruled Oman once more.

Within the nominally unified Ibāḍī polity, however, significant religious and tribal divisions existed. Two doctrinal "schools" of thought developed around the issue of al-Ṣalt b. Mālik's removal during the first Ibāḍī imāmate. On the one hand, the Rustāq group viewed those who supported his ousting as renegades, outside the fold of belief. They required dissociation (*barāʾa*) from the offenders. The Nizwā group, on the other hand, argued the compromise position by calling for a suspension of judgment (*wuqūf*) on the issue. In 443/1052 C.E. the Rustāq school, with the support of Imām Rāshid, issued a decree condemning the deposers of al-Ṣalt and compromising the possibilities of reconciliation between the parties. This intractability led the Ibāḍī community of the Ḥaḍramawt (in Yemen), who had traditionally recognized the authority of the Omani imāms, to break from them and establish their own imāmate under Abū Isḥāq Ibrāhīm b. Qays al-Ḥaḍramī (d. ca. 475/1082–83 C.E.). Abū Isḥāq's community lasted for a brief period, but the split eventually resulted in the disappearance of Ibāḍīsm from Yemen.

Underlying the doctrinal wrangling of the Rustāq and Nizwā schools lay simmering tribal rivalries. The Yaḥmad tribal group that had traditionally controlled the imāmate was first opposed by the *'ulamā'* of the Nizwā party, who attempted to establish their own line of imāms, and later by the moderate *'ulamā'* of the Rustāq party. By the beginning of the sixth/twelfth century moderate Rustāqī scholars began to support their own candidates for the imāmate in the Jawf region of Oman, further exacerbating the splits within the Ibāḍī community. The strain of this fragmentation proved too great, and the Ibāḍī imāmate collapsed at the end of the sixth/twelfth century as power passed to the Nabāhina of Azd, a tribal group that made no attempt to rule in the name of Ibāḍism.[13]

Just as the Ibāḍīs of the Mashriq spurred their movements with the help of alienated tribal groups, so too in North Africa, Umayyad mistreatment of the Berbers made certain tribes in the region more amenable to the *shurāt* missionaries coming from the Islamic East and inspired the North African "Khārijite" rebellions of the 120s/740s. These revolts seem to have been the impetus for the crystallization along tribal lines of moderates into distinguishable groups of Ibāḍīs and Ṣufrīs, though the differences between Ibāḍīs and Ṣufrīs before and even during these rebellions are difficult to discern. Indeed the *Akhbār Majmū'a,* for example, seems to conflate the two when it notes that the rebellions in North Africa were started by "Berbers of the Ṣufriyya and Ibāḍiyya sects."[14] Likewise a report in Latin in the anonymous *Chronica Muzarabica* identifies the perpetrators of the revolt as "Arures," a term that is likely a corruption of *Ḥarūriyya,* a generic Arabic name for the Khārijites.[15] Nevertheless as the revolts gave way to local polities in the early 'Abbāsid era, those who would become known as the Ibāḍiyya seem to have aligned themselves with the Berber tribes of the Hawwāra, Nafūsa, and some elements of the Zanāta; those who would become the Ṣufriyya elicited the support of the Miknāsa primarily but also the Barghawāṭa, Maṭghara, Maghīla, and Ifrān.

Umayyad efforts to enslave Berbers, even after the Berbers had converted to Islam, seem to have contributed to, if not initiated, the North African revolts of the 120s/740s, and missionaries labeled "Ṣufrī" appear to have been, at first, more successful than those identified as Ibāḍīs in the recruitment of Berbers to the *shurāt*'s cause. The moderates' insistence on the qualities of piety and justice in their leaders and its egalitarian bent likely appealed to the Berbers, who had suffered at the hands of the Umayyad governor ʿUbayd Allāh b. al-Ḥabḥāb and his subordinates.[16] Ibn al-Athīr reports, for example, that in the year 117/735 C.E. the Umayyad general Ḥabīb b. ʿAbīda wanted to enslave Berber Muslims as part of the *fay'* (tribute) that was regularly sent back to Damascus.[17] Similarly al-Ṭabarī's chronicle notes that the Umayyad governors of North Africa had long taken beautiful Berber girls as slaves, despite the prohibition against enslaving fellow Muslims.[18] Other factors, such as the poor treatment of Berber soldiers in the Umayyad army, surely contributed to the revolts as well.[19]

By 122/739–40 C.E. the Berbers of Tangier rose against the Umayyads, in the process spreading (*aẓhara*) their teachings throughout North Africa.[20] The revolt began under Maysara al-Saqqā' ("the water-carrier") al-Maṭgharī, who was described as a Khārijite and Ṣufrī. He was given the pledge (*bayʿa*) of the caliphate, and sermons (*khuṭab*) were said in his name using the caliphal title "Commander of the Faithful" (*amīr al-mu'minīn*). At his death Maysara was followed by another, Khālid b. Ḥumayd al-Zanātī, who met the Umayyad forces at the battle of the nobles (*ghazwat al-ashrāf*), named after the many highborn Arabs who died there. Yet another "Ṣufrī" victory came later that year near the Sabū River (in present-day Morocco).[21]

News of *shurāt*'s successes reached the Umayyad caliph Hishām b. ʿAbd al-Mālik, who vowed to send an army large enough to deal with them. This army, under the direction of Kulthūm b. ʿIyāḍ and Balj b. Bishr, took some time to organize, equip, and march into North Africa, and their campaign was not ultimately successful. Kulthūm was killed, and some of his army returned to Qayrawān. However, Ibn al-Athīr reports that in the year 123/740–41 C.E. ʿAbd al-Mālik b. Qaṭan allowed Balj b. Bishr to cross with some of the army in order to rid al-Andalus of the *shurāt,* whose North African revolt had spread to Iberia. Ibn Bishr's army met them at Shadhūna (Medina Sidonia/Sidon), where the rebels were routed.[22]

Several more "Ṣufrī" uprisings followed, harassing the Umayyads throughout the early 120s/740s. Ibn al-Athīr reports that in Qābis (Gabes), a Ṣufrī named ʿUkāsha b. Ayūb al-Fazārī rebelled to fight several battles against the remnants of the Umayyad army, who marched against him from Qayrawān. Again in 124/741–42 C.E. ʿUkasha and another Ṣufrite, ʿAbd al-Wāḥid b. Yazīd al-Hawwārī, converged to attack Qayrawān, where the Umayyad governor of Egypt Ḥanẓala b. Safwān al-Kalbī met and defeated them.[23] Yet Qayrawān and its environs were never fully controlled by the Umayyads: the Fihrid governor of Qayrawān was forced to deal with a series of Ṣufrī rebellions west of Tūnis in 130/748 C.E.[24]

Like the Ṣufriyya, Ibāḍīs (that is, those *shurāt* later claimed by the Ibāḍiyya as their own) were involved in resistance to Umayyad rule in North Africa and Iberia, but their rebellions were later than those of the Ṣufriyya and initially less effective. ʿAbdullāh b. Masʿūd al-Tujībī is said to have declared with the assistance of the Hawwāra Berbers the first Ibāḍī revolt in Tripolitania in 126/744 C.E. ʿAbd al-Raḥmān b. Ḥabīb, the Fihrid governor of

Qarawān, made the mistake of executing him, providing his successors—two Ibāḍīs, ʿAbd al-Jabbār b. Qays al-Murādī and al-Ḥārith b. Talīd al-Ḥaḍramī—with an excuse to oppose the Umayyads outright. They scored victory after victory in Tripolitania until mysterious internal rivalries caused them to run each other through with their swords in 131/749 or 132/750 C.E.[25] Their successor, Abū al-Zājir Ismāʿīl b. Ziyād al-Nafūsī, was declared imām in Tripolitania and extended his power to Qābis before being defeated and killed by Ibn Ḥabīb.[26]

Shurāt control of the Maghrib continued through the ʿAbbāsid revolution, and their continued resistance ultimately brought about the establishment of the Ibāḍī Rustumid and Ṣufrī Midrārid dynasties. An Ibāḍī-inspired uprising in 141/758 C.E. in what is today Libya and Tunisia under the leadership of Abū al-Khaṭṭāb al-Maʿāfirī captured several cities in the region, including Qayrawān. After four years an ʿAbbāsid army defeated the rebels, forcing many Ibāḍīs, under the leadership of Abū al-Khaṭṭāb's governor and fellow missionary ʿAbd al-Raḥmān b. Rustum, to flee to Tāhart (near modern-day Tiaret in Algeria). The remaining Ibāḍīs of Tripolitania recognized Abū al-Ḥātim al-Malzūzī as their leader. In 151/768 C.E. the Ibāḍīs of Tripolitania and Algeria joined forces with the Maghīla and Ifrānī Ṣufriyya Berbers. Earlier in 148/765 C.E. these groups had proclaimed one of their own, Abū Qurra al-Ifrānī, an imām and established a Ṣufrī polity centered in Tilimsān. Together the Tripolitanian Ibāḍīs and Ṣufrīs laid siege to the ʿAbbāsid outpost of Ṭubna. Their attack was unsuccessful, and the pursuing ʿAbbāsid army killed al-Malzūzī in 155/772 C.E., causing further migrations of Ibāḍīs to Tāhart.[27] In either 159/776 or 161/778 C.E. ʿAbd al-Raḥmān b. Rustum established himself as the first imām of the Rustumid dynasty—a dynasty that would flourish until the advent of the Fāṭimids in the early fourth/tenth century. ʿAbd al-Raḥmān married into the Ifrān tribe, absorbing into the Ibāḍī polity those Ṣufrī Berbers who did not migrate to the region of Tāfīlalt after the Idrīsids occupied Tilimsān in 174/790 C.E.[28]

The remaining Ṣufriyya in the Tāfīlalt region gathered at Sijilmāsa, which became the capital of the Ṣufrī dynasty of the Banū Midrār.[29] According to later North African geographers, the founding of the Midrārid dynasty began with the establishment of Sijilmāsa, which al-Bakrī and Ibn ʿIdhārī trace to Abū al-Qāsim Samghū b. Wasūl.[30] Abū al-Qāsim was said to be a Mikhnāsa Ṣufrī Berber and a participant in the first *shurāt* revolts in Tangiers. His father was reportedly an authority on ḥadīth, which he heard from Ibn ʿAbbās's *mawlā*, ʿIkrima. In 140/757 C.E. Abū al-Qāsim and forty of his followers began to construct the city of Sijilmāsa, and they elected ʿIsā b. Mazyad as imām. This ʿIsā was deposed some fifteen years later and replaced by Abū al-Qāsim. An alternate version in al-Bakrī of the founding of the Midrārid dynasty traces it to a certain Midrār, a blacksmith from the outskirts of Cordoba, who came to Sijilmāsa after the Umayyad Amīr al-Ḥakam I put down a rebellion in 202/818 C.E. in the suburb (*rabāḍ*) of Cordoba.

Though al-Bakrī favors the version of the story that features Abū al-Qāsim, he tacitly attempts to synthesize the two accounts by claiming that the Midrārids were descendants of the smith Midrār, who returned to Sijilmāsa later.[31] As these competing and confused accounts of the founding of the Midrārids suggest, the beginnings of the dynasty are ultimately unknown.

More certain is that under the Midrārids, and especially under Abū al-Qāsim's sons al-Yasā' (r. 168–74/784–90 C.E.) and Abū Muntaṣir (r. 174–208/790–823 C.E.), Sijilmāsa became an important way station on the north-south trade route between Islamic North Africa and West Africa. Not only did the Midrārids control the silver mines of the Dar'a region (that is, at Majjāna and near Tudgha, forty miles south of Sijilmāsa), but in addition they were important players in gold and slave trade coming up from West Africa in the second/eighth–third/ninth centuries. In fact *Kitāb al-Istibṣār* from the sixth/twelfth century notes that Sijilmāsa was known as the "gate of gold."[32] As rulers of an important economic hub, the Midrārids enjoyed strong trade and political relations with the Rustumids in Tāhart (who also engaged in the gold and slave trade) as well as the Umayyads of the Iberian Peninsula.[33] Despite the success of Sijilmāsa, internal strife and civil war plagued the city during the period 208–64/823–77 C.E. By the fourth/tenth century the Midrārids had become vassals of the Fāṭimids, and shortly thereafter they ceased to be a force in North Africa.[34]

Even as independent Ibāḍī and Ṣufrī polities developed North Africa and the Arabian Peninsula, Ibāḍīs and Ṣufrīs continued to remain active in Mesopotamia. Several "Ṣufrī" uprisings plagued the Umayyad governors of Iraq: the ascetic Ṣāliḥ b. al-Musarriḥ rose in 76/695, followed in the same year by Shabīb b. Yazīd.[35] Shabīb and his followers rampaged through the province of Mawṣil, threatened Kūfa, and were indecisively defeated by the Umayyad armies there. Shabīb's band moved south toward al-Ahwāz, where he was said to have drowned in the Dujayl in 77/697 or 78/698–99 C.E. Northern Iraq remained a center of Ṣufrī unrest, with nearly constant rebellion against the Umayyads and early 'Abbāsids (including a rebellion by Shabīb's son, Ṣuḥārī, in 119/737 C.E.).[36]

Another major uprising labeled Ṣufrī came after the murder of the Umayyad caliph Walīd II, and according to several reports in al-Ṭabarī, this inspired a series of "Ṣufrī" Khārijite uprisings in the Jazīra beginning as early as 127/744 C.E. The Khārijite al-Daḥḥāk b. Qays assumed leadership of a massive army after the leader of the Jazīran Ṣufriyya, Sa'īd b. Bahdal, died of the plague en route to Kūfa. Al-Daḥḥāk's army in 127/745 C.E. took Kūfa, where he remained until recalled to Mawṣil to eject the Umayyad governor from the city.[37] Al-Daḥḥāk's successor, Abū Dulāf Shaybān b. 'Abd al-'Azīz al-Yashkūrī, assumed control of the uprising after al-Daḥḥāk's death at the battle of Kafr Tūta at the end of 128/745 C.E.[38] Abū Dulāf withdrew the army to the eastern bank of the Tigris near Mawṣil, but after a long stand-off (during which Kūfa was wrested away from them), they were overwhelmed and, pursued south, eventually broke up. One faction was said to have left for India. The other, under Abū Dulāf, was defeated by the Ibāḍiyya of Oman under al-Julanda b. Masʿūd in 134/751 C.E.[39] These open hostilities between Ibāḍīs and Ṣufrīs in Mesopotamia point to an important difference between the groups: unlike the Ibāḍīs of Basra and Oman, the Ṣufriyya of Iraq had no connection with their alleged counterparts in North Africa, and (as per Lewinstein) do not seem to have constituted a coherent "subsect" of Khārijites in this region.

As the birthplace and first center of Ibāḍism, Basra continued to host an Ibāḍī community long after the establishment of the North African and Arabian imāmates. The Basrans enjoyed the leadership of three prominent scholars and imāms in the late first/seventh and early second/eighth centuries: al-Rabīʿ b. Ḥabīb, ʿAbū Ayyūb Wāʾil b. Ayyūb al-Ḥaḍramī, and Abū Sufyān Maḥbūb b. al-Ruḥayl (var. al-Raḥīl), who periodically provided guidance to the outlying Ibāḍī communities. Nevertheless by the early second/eighth century the Ibāḍī community at Basra was diminishing, and Abū Sufyān was said to have wound up the movement and relocated his family to Oman sometime in the 200s/820s.[40] Nothing is known of the fates of Ibāḍī communities outside of Basra (that is, in Kūfa and Khurasān), but it is presumed that they too fell into obscurity as the second/eighth century progressed.

Ibāḍī Appropriations: The Muḥakkima in Ibāḍī Sources

Concurrent with the emergence of the Ibāḍiyya in Basra and with their eventual establishment in North Africa and Arabia came the need to articulate a sense of Ibāḍī uniqueness and identity over and above their fellow Muslims. This need was undoubtedly felt in the wake of the Azraqite and Najdite uprisings during the second *fitna* and as the Ibāḍiyya operated alongside the various quietist (that is, "Ṣufrī") groups in Iraq, Arabia, and North Africa. Tribal alignments certainly played an important role in establishing certain kinds of identities for the nascent Ibāḍīs, but along with these tribal identities, and in accordance with how late antique religious communities fashioned a sense of community, early Ibāḍīs looked back on the narratives of the earliest Iraqi *shurāt* martyrs and ascetics to find an anchor for their movement.

The process of appropriation seems to have begun quite early: the Basran imām Abū Sufyān Maḥbūb b. al-Raḥīl (var. al-Ruḥayl), for example, was said to have written sometime in the latter part of the third/ninth century an important biographical work on the early *shurāt*/Ibāḍī community that illuminated a line of development from the Muḥakkima who seceded at Nahrawān to the Ibāḍiyya of Abū Sufyān's day.[41] Wilkinson suggests that Abū

Sufyān's work, which was probably commissioned by the Rustumid imām Aflaḥ b. ʿAbd al-Wahhāb (r. 250–55/864–68 C.E.), was actually compiled by another Iraqi Ibāḍī, Abū Ṣufra ʿAbd al-Mālik b. Ṣufra, and likely relied on Abū Yazīd al-Khwārizmī's (d. mid-second/eighth century as a contemporary of the Basran leader Abū ʿUbayda) earlier anecdotal and biographical treatment of the Muḥakkima and early *shurāt*.[42] Although both texts are now lost, large portions of the *Kitāb Abī Sufyān* survive in the works of the North African historians al-Darjīnī, Abu Zakariyya, al-Shammākhī, and al-Barrādī.

It is clear that the North African historians al-Barrādī and al-Shammākhī used early Iraqi sources when crafting their narratives of the early Khārijites. Al-Barrādī's work in particular displays profound textual parallels with what can be found in Abū Mikhnaf's writings on the Khārijites. Similarly al-Shammākhī's text preserves accounts of several Iraqi *shurāt* uprisings, the language of which matches to a high degree that which is related about them via Abū Mikhnaf in al-Ṭabarī and anonymously in al-Mubarrad, al-Balādhurī, and Ibn al-Athīr.[43] There are many possible explanations for the appearance of Iraqi sources in North African Ibāḍī materials. One is that Abū Yazīd and/or Abū Ṣufra/Abū Sufyān may have used Iraqi materials when crafting their own histories. Another possible source for such materials was the work of the second/eighth-century Kūfan Ibāḍī *mutakallim* ʿAbdullāh b. Yazīd al-Fazārī, who is quoted in several North African sources, including al-Barrādī.[44] Alternatively, Iraqi materials could easily have come to North Africa via Ibāḍī or Iraqi merchants; indeed the historian Ibn Ṣaghīr mentions the presence of enough Kūfans and Basrans living in Tāhart that they had their own mosques.[45] Whatever the case, it is certain that by the mid-third/ninth and likely as early as the mid-second/eighth century, Ibāḍīs had begun the process of appropriating the early Iraqi *shurāt* heroes and martyrs as their own and were doing so with the aid of Iraqi *shurāt* texts (including some Kūfan texts, which were some of the same ones used by Abū Mikhnaf and others).

As articulations of group identity often begin with a vision of noble and pious origins, so too Ibāḍī accounts of their origins—as with Muslims in general—usually commence with the event of revelation to the Prophet Muḥammad. Unlike Shīʿa accounts, Ibāḍī (and later Sunnī) narratives continue through the caliphates of Abū Bakr and ʿUmar, both of whom they consider righteous leaders to be emulated.[46] As the Ibāḍiyya have maintained that they preserved the truest and most correct form of Islam, such a focus remains unsurprising and underscores the notion that the Ibāḍiyya trace themselves to the very fonts of the Islamic venture.

Where Ibāḍī origins narratives often definitively diverge from their Sunnī and Shīʿa counterparts, of course, lies in their presentation of the events and personalities of the first *fitna*—specifically the incidents at and after the battle of Ṣiffīn. These episodes provide a crucial focal point for Ibāḍī identity by anchoring the group in a discursive argument and by tracing them to the pious Muslims who articulated and then died for it.[47] From the perspective of Ibāḍī distinctiveness, the stories of those who rejected ʿAlī's decision to arbitrate the battle of Ṣiffīn remained as important to Ibāḍī self-fashioning as the narratives of the Prophet and first two caliphs, for it was at Ṣiffīn, Ḥarūrāʾ, and later Nahrawān where the Muslims continued down what the Ibāḍiyya considered the straight and correct path of *islām*. They became in the process the only true and upright group, the *ahl al-istiqāma* (people of righteousness), whose followers throughout the generations have preserved the correct doctrine and protected truth so that it might survive to the present day.

There are several Ibāḍī sources for the story of the Muḥakkima and their demise at Nahrawān. The most elaborate and complete versions of this narrative are preserved in the Omani scholar al-Qalhātī's sixth/twelfth-century *al-Kashf wa al-Bayān*, the Omani al-Izkawī's *Kashf al-Ghumma* from the late eleventh to early twelfth/late seventeenth to early eighteenth centuries, the North African al-Barrādī's eighth/fourteenth-century *Kitāb al-Jawāhir*, as well as al-Shammākhī's tenth/sixteenth-century *Kitāb al-Siyar*. Additionally al-Darjīnī's seventh/thirteenth-century biographical dictionary, the *Kitāb Ṭabaqāt al-Mashāyikh bī al-Maghrib*, contains entries on some of the seminal figures of the early period. Although late in date, many of these sources rely on earlier materials: as noted above, the North African sources in particular preserve earlier materials from the *Kitāb Abī Sufyān* and from the early Kūfan Ibāḍī al-Fazārī.

Omani sources present a more complex situation. Wilkinson argues that before the sixth/twelfth century North African sources were not widely known in Oman but that after this period they became more and more incorporated into Omani Ibāḍī writings as part and parcel of the process of reimagining the Ibāḍiyya along the lines of a fully formed *madhhab* (a process initiated by increased contact with the norms of Sunnī scholarship).[48] Notably, Madelung too notes how al-Fazārī's works made little impact on the Omani Ibāḍīs of the early period.[49] Indeed this virtual absence of Iraqi and North African materials on the Muḥakkima in Omani works prior to the sixth/twelfth century is reflected in the Omani *siyar*: while early Omani Ibāḍī *siyar* do provide several (often scattered) references to the Muḥakkima, they offer no comprehensive historical narratives on the Muḥakkima to rival the post-sixth/twelfth-century works of al-Qalhātī and al-Izkawī. When al-Qalhātī and al-Izkawī penned their work, their overarching project remained similar to that of their North African Ibāḍī sources: namely, the reimagining of an Ibāḍī *madhhab* with an unbroken chain of legitimate authorities stretching back to the early period.

The prosopographical focus of these Ibāḍī materials remains telling of their particular method for establishing legitimacy. In general, Ibāḍī narratives present their arguments for the "correctness" of the Muḥakkima-cum-Ibāḍiyya's stance in two forms: outright defense of their position on the arbitration (*taḥkīm*) using the device of a formal debate (*munāẓara*) between Ibn ʿAbbās and/or ʿAlī and the Muḥakkima; and hagiographical depictions of figures associated with or appropriated for the early Muḥakkima.[50] This concern with pious originating figures reflects the Ibāḍī propensity to provide what Wilkinson has called "teacher lines" (lists of important personages who transmitted the Ibāḍī *madhhab*) as an integral aspect of authenticating the Ibāḍī view, and the inclusion of hagiographical descriptions of early personalities in Ibāḍī narratives about the Muḥakkima must be understood with regard to how Ibāḍīs viewed their particular interpretation of Islam as encompassing not only a collection of particular arguments, doctrines, and practices but also the accumulation of personalities whose piety and renown authenticated those doctrines and practices.[51] The place of hagiography therefore is vital to the project of Ibāḍī self-fashioning, and it is no accident that one of the first recognizable works of Ibāḍī "history," the *Kitāb Abī Sufyān*, was reportedly a collection of biographies. By establishing a group of pious founders to whom the later generations were connected, Ibāḍī authors bounded a community.

In order to provide the highest pedigree for those through whom the Ibāḍiyya traced themselves, Ibāḍī narratives make certain general claims about the slain at Nahrawān, and it is against such claims that the narratives of particular individuals gain prominence. For example, Omani sources relate that among those martyred were several of the best companions, including seventy who fought at Badr and four hundred from among a group called *al-Sawārī*. These narratives explain that the *Sawārī* were people who "were not absent from the mosque of the Prophet, such that their foreheads and knees were like calluses of a camel from the strength of their efforts [in prayer]."[52] Similarly al-Shammākhī notes that those who gathered at Ḥarurā', later to be killed at Nahrawān, were "the best people on the earth at that time, the [best in] recitation and asceticism (*qurrāʾuhum wa zuhhāduhum*) from among those who remained of the great Companions and Followers . . . people of Badr, and those about whom the Prophet bore witness that they would enter paradise."[53] In al-Qalhātī and al-Izkawī the departure of the Muḥakkima to Ḥarūrā' caused ʿAlī to ask why he did not hear the Qur'ān recited as he used to hear it, implying as it does that the Muḥakkima were zealous in their recitation of it.[54] Moreover, ʿAlī was shown to lament the killing of the people of Nahrawān, whom al-Barrādī and al-Shammākhī describe, using a phrase reminiscent of early Christian warrior-ascetics as well as early Islamic *ghaziyīn*, as "lions by day, monks by night."[55] Ibāḍī sources, then, elevate the slain at Nahrawān in ways that emphasize their piety, specifically their ascetic piety, and this background sets the stage for the specific narratives of individuals who embody such piety in their own particular ways. Moreover it is noteworthy how such depictions of piety resonate with the familiar tropes of late antique and early Islamic hagiography, even to the point of appropriating explicit phrases (for example, "lions by day, monks by night") from the lexicon of late antique/early Islamic hagiographical writings. Such resonance most surely comes via the textual sources on the Muḥakkima and *shurāt* that early Ibāḍī authors used to craft their narratives.

Beyond blanket statements on the piety of the Muḥakkima as a whole, Ibāḍī texts tend to focus on the narratives of certain individual figures, such as ʿAmmār b. Yāsir, Ḥurqūṣ b. Zuhayr, or ʿAbdullāh b. Wahb al-Rāsibī. ʿAmmār b. Yāsir, of course, perished not at Nahrawān but rather at Ṣiffīn, and it is with his narrative that Ibāḍī accounts of the battle of Ṣiffīn inevitably commence. In non-Ibāḍī (and mainly pro-ʿAlīd/Shiʿite) writings ʿAmmār is remembered as one of the first supporters (*shīʿa*) of ʿAlī. Abū Mikhnaf's narrative in al-Ṭabarī preserves several elements of ʿAmmār's story that also appear in Ibāḍī narratives. For example, Abū Mikhnaf relates the ḥadīth in which the Prophet Muḥammad predicted that ʿAmmār would be killed by a "rebellious party" (*al-fiʾa al-bāghiyya*) and that his last meal would be milk mixed with water.[56] Similarly, Abū Mikhnaf's account preserves several of ʿAmmār's exhortations to his fellows at Ṣiffīn, including his statement that he would "meet the loved ones—Muḥammad and his party" and his battle cry of "death is beneath the spears and paradise beneath the flashing swords."[57]

ʿAmmār is likewise portrayed with a dismissive attitude toward the world: he is quoted as saying of Muʿāwiya's followers that "if they have to accept the truth, it will be a barrier between them and the worldly things in which they are wallowing."[58] Of course Abū Mikhnaf's pro-ʿAlīd narrative portrays ʿAmmār as a loyal follower of ʿAlī, whose death at the hands of Muʿāwiya's army provokes consternation in the ranks of Muʿāwiya's army. Yet Muʿāwiya convinces his followers that, in fact, ʿAlī and his party are to blame for ʿAmmār's death because they were the ones who brought him to the battlefield.[59] In this way Abū Mikhnaf's account of ʿAmmār's death at the hands of Muʿāwiya—and thus the identification of Muʿāwiya's army as the "rebellious party"—serves as an occasion to confirm the piety of ʿAmmār, condemn Muʿāwiya for opposing ʿAlī, and highlight Muʿāwiya's powers of deception.

In Ibāḍī narratives ʿAmmār is similarly presented as a pious individual, about whom the Prophet predicted his death at the hands of the "rebellious party."[60] Yet unlike Abū Mikhnaf's pro-ʿAlīd portrayal of ʿAmmār, Ibāḍī depictions of ʿAmmār's death emphasize the juxtaposition between the Prophetic prediction of his death and the text of Qurʾān 49:9, which reads, "And if two factions among the believers should fight, then make settlement between the two. But if one of them oppresses the other, then fight against the transgressors (*al-lati tabghā*) until they return to the command of God." For Ibāḍīs as with the pro-ʿAlīds, ʿAmmār's death proved definitively that Muʿāwiya and his army were the "rebellious party" referred to by the Prophetic ḥadīth concerning ʿAmmār, but because 49:9 presented to the Ibāḍīs an unambiguous Qurʾānic directive to continue fighting rebels until they "returned to the command of God," Ibāḍī narratives strongly condemn 'Alī and his supporters for contravening a divine order by ceasing the fight against Mu'āwiya. In this way 'Ammār's death in Ibāḍī texts became a proof against the arbitration and for the Ibāḍī rejection of it.

Ibāḍī presentations of the *munāẓara* between Ibn 'Abbās/'Alī and the Muḥakkima make the connection between 'Ammār's death at the hands of the "rebellious party" and Qur'ān 49:9 explicit. In al-Qalhātī, the Muḥakkima argue, "did not 'Ammār b. Yāsir and the Muslims who accompanied him fight at Ṣiffīn, until they were killed practicing the principle of commanding good and forbidding evil, and fighting the transgressors until they comply with the command of God?"[61] They further reason, "how can 'Ammār be considered as a rightly guided man and [those] who follow his example as wrong-doers? If 'Ammār's fighting against the party of Mu'āwiya were right, then those who followed his example after his death would be right; and if it were wrong, then 'Alī and his followers must have gone astray by giving consent to this fighting [in the first place]."[62] Similarly in al-Barrādī the Muḥakkima ask during the *munāẓara,* "are we to bear witness that our combatants 'Ammār b. Yāsir and his companions fought in vain (*'alā bāṭilin*), that they are in hell and are the party of error (*ahl al-ḍalāla*) while [Mu'āwiya and his party] have fought truthfully?"[63] The rhetorical power of this question hinges on the reader's knowledge of 'Ammār's death at the hands of the "rebellious party." Driving home the Ibāḍī conviction that 'Alī was under a clear Qur'ānic command to continue fighting Mu'āwiya, the Muḥakkima of al-Barrādī's account state, paraphrasing 49:9, "battle, arms and the command regarding those who [unjustly] fight are not to be lain aside until [the unlawful combatants] return to the command of God."[64]

Ibāḍī accounts go even further than simply portraying 'Ammār's death as proof against the arbitration. Some sources—the earliest is likely in Ibn Ibāḍ's second letter—contain passages in which 'Ammār gives explicit warnings to 'Alī about the tactic of arbitration.[65] Munīr b. al-Nayyir's *sīra,* written for the Omani imām Ghassān b. 'Abdullah (r. 192–207/808–23 C.E.), too contains a description of 'Ammār's counsel to 'Alī against accepting arbitration.[66] Al-Qalhātī's much later version of this event renders Ibn Yāsir's cautionary to 'Alī in *kalām*-style argumentation: "Those people will say to you, 'Between you and us is the Book of God.' Say to them, 'We have fought you because you have abandoned the Book of God.' They will say to you, 'Let us appoint two arbiters between us and let us accept whatever judgment they give.' Say to them, 'Who can give better judgment than God for a people whose faith is assured?' [5:55] If they say, 'Let us appoint an armistice period in which to negotiate peace,' say to them, 'God Almighty has said: "Fight against the transgressors until they return to the command of God" [49:9].'"[67] In this passage 49:9 is unambiguously put in the mouth of 'Ammār as a warning to 'Alī against arbitration. Such narrative and rhetorical devices further drive home ʿAlī's complicity when he later acceded to arbitration and serve to clarify the rightness of the Muḥakkimite/Ibāḍī stance against it.

Beyond the arguments against arbitration, Ibāḍī sources provide further Prophetic proofs for ʿAmmār's righteous character. In a ḥadīth attributed to Ḥudhayfa b. al-Yamān, the Prophet was said to have related about ʿAmmār that "God filled his heart, hearing and sight with faith such that truth does not come to him but that he grasps it, and falsehood [does not come to him] except that he rejects it."[68] Another ḥadīth shows the Prophet defending ʿAmmār's veracity against polytheists who mocked him.[69]

Similarly, ʿAmmār's death is portrayed in terms that show his rejection of the material world for paradise. Al-Qalhātī's and al-Izkawī's narratives credit him with a martyr's death alongside twenty-five Anṣār and Muhājirūn, including Khuzayma b. Thābit al-Anṣārī (known as "he of two witnesses" because his testimony was declared the equivalent thereof by the Prophet Muḥammad).[70] In a widely preserved final speech to his companions (in which many of the statements attributed to ʿAmmār in non-Ibāḍī sources appear), ʿAmmār was said to have proclaimed, "ʿToday the Houris are adorning themselves, oh people! Turn back the water before you thirst, for I see paradise beneath the gleaming swords. Let us strike them today a blow that will drive doubt from those who do falsehood. By Him in whose hand is ʿAmmār's soul, even if they strike us so as to bring us to the palm leaves of Hajar, we will know that we hold to truth and they to falsehood,' and then he said, ʿWho is off to paradise before the arbitration of the arbiters?'"[71]

In al-Shammākhī's version of the story, it is only after ʿAlī has decided on arbitration that ʿAmmār invites his companions to martyrdom with the words "who is off to paradise?" and "today I will meet the beloved Muḥammad and his party."[72] In both cases the narratives are meant to underscore the rightness of the cause for which ʿAmmār died by explicitly celebrating ʿAmmār as a martyr and surrounding him with the symbols and language of martyrdom. Though his story was not necessarily as dramatic as some other martyrdom stories, Ibāḍī authors nevertheless crafted ʿAmmār's narrative around a core image of ʿAmmār as rejecting the world in favor of the hereafter, eagerly accepting his foretold death and thereby achieving his martyrdom. Yet it was not Ibn Yāsir's martyrdom per se but rather the Prophetic predictions about his death at the hands of the *fi'a al-bāghiyya* that made Ibn Yāsir into an important figure for Ibāḍī narratives of the Muḥakkima. In this perhaps Ibn Yāsir is a true *shahīd,* whose death bears witness to the actual nature of Muʿāwiya's army and illumines the fallacy of arbitration. Although the texts never describe his martyrdom in terms of *shirā',* ʿAmmār's narrative does contain a pinch of the basic ingredients and heralds more explicit references to come. Moreover it is abundantly clear that Ibāḍī authors had access to the same sources that undergirded Abū Mikhaf's accounts of ʿAmmār.

Close to the ideal of the ascetic martyr in Ibāḍī narratives on the Muḥakkima is the figure of Ḥurqūṣ b. Zuhayr al-Saʿadī, whose narrative reflects in many ways that of a Christian saint. Ibāḍī authors, for example, are unanimous in their preservation of the ḥadīth in which the Prophet declared Ḥurqūṣ one of the people of paradise.[73] Moreover al-Qalhātī's and al-Izkawī's narratives contain a curious anecdote about how Ḥurqūṣ was the one who buried the Prophet Daniel.[74] They mention that Daniel had prayed that he would be buried by "a person from the people of paradise" but that his body was kept unburied in its coffin by the "People of the Book," who treated it as a relic over which they prayed for rain. When Abū Mūsā al-Ashʿarī conquered Sūs (where Daniel was said to be not yet interred) he found the coffin and wrote to ʿUmar b. al-Khaṭṭāb requesting instructions on what to do with it. ʿUmar dispatched to him Ḥurqūṣ, who buried Daniel in secret, keeping the mantle that was found in the coffin and which ʿUmar bestowed upon him.[75]

Other Ibāḍī reports on Ibn Zuhayr emphasize his bravery and his asceticism. For example, a report in al-Barrādī, attributed to al-Fazārī, shows Ibn Zuhayr to be one of the Muḥakkima who challenged ʿAlī on the arbitration, calling him to repent for his "mistake" and his "sin."[76] In addition Ibn Zuhayr appears as one of the early figures who met in the house of ʿAbdullāh b. Wahb al-Rāsibī after ʿAlī proceeded with the arbitration. His speech to the Muḥakkima there assembled (preserved in al-Barrādī, again on the authority of al-Fazārī) warns his fellows of being tempted away from doing what is right by the fleeting delights of the world.[77] Moreover several entries on Ḥurqūṣ conclude with a quote from Abū Mūsā al-Ashʿarī emphasizing the sanctity of Ḥurqūṣ in the eyes of God: "if they had all agreed upon [killing him] with the spear that pierced him . . . they would all have entered the fire."[78]

Al-Darjīnī's entry on Ḥurqūṣ is devoted, in large part, to defending his character against some of the defamatory reports that can be found in non-Ibāḍī sources on the Muḥakkima. For his part, al-Darjīnī claims that Ḥurqūṣ was one of the "people of austerity and worship, mortification and asceticism (*ahl al-nusk wa'l-ʿibāda wa'l-taqashshuf wa'l-zahhāda*)."[79] He further claims that Ḥurqūṣ was one of the leaders of the army during the time of ʿUmar and that he conquered the Ahwāz, earning ʿUmar's thanks. For al-Darjīnī, Ḥurqūṣ's character and accomplishments belie the negative reports about him in non-Ibāḍī sources, which are shown not to stand up to the scrutiny of logic. Al-Darjīnī's treatment of Ḥurqūṣ thus remains somewhat unique in comparison with those of other Ibāḍī authors; nevertheless al-Darjīnī celebrates Ḥurqūṣ as an early martyr and ascetic and emphasizes his martial qualities.

Al-Darjīnī's explicit defense of Ḥurqūṣ shows the extent to which Ibāḍī authors were aware of (and even engaged in debate with) the narratives about the Muḥakkima that could be found in non-Ibāḍī writings. In this particular case it is possible to identify that source: a report in al-Barrādī attributed to al-Fazārī shows Ḥurqūṣ to be one of the Muḥakkima who challenged ʿAlī on the arbitration, calling him to repent for his "mistake" and his "sin."[80] The language of this report matches in profound ways a similar narrative preserved by Abū Mikhnaf in non-Ibāḍī sources.[81] Similarly, Ḥurqūṣ is presented as one of the early figures who met in the house of ʿAbdullāh b. Wahb al-Rāsibī after ʿAlī proceeded with the arbitration. Once again, Ḥurqūṣ's speech in al-Barrādī (again related by al-Fazārī) in which Ḥurqūṣ warns his fellows of being tempted away from doing what is right by the fleeting delights of the world matches exactly the language preserved by Abū Mikhnaf's report in al-Ṭabarī.[82] Indeed the entire episode of al-Rāsibī's election in both al-Fazārī and Abū Mikhnaf clearly hails from a shared, and likely Iraqi/Kūfan, source.

In Ḥurqūṣ, then, Ibāḍī authors found an ascetic of the highest moral fiber, a man promised paradise by the Prophet, a warrior and renowned conqueror—one cloaked literally in the mantle of the prophets. Such a person was willing to stand up to ʿAlī and to die a martyr's death at Nahrawān. In crafting their own presentations of Ḥurqūṣ, Ibāḍī authors most certainly drew upon materials that enjoyed a wider circulation and that likely came ultimately from an Iraqi/Kūfan text. Yet Ibāḍīs also had their own distinctive method of elevating him, such that Ḥurqūṣ emerged as a pivotal figure in Ibāḍī narratives, the paragon of the warrior-saint whose death underscored the righteousness of the Muḥakkimite cause.

In the figure of ʿAbdullāh b. Wahb al-Rāsibī Ibāḍī narratives found their first imām, a pious early ascetic described in al-Barrādī's narrative as "he of the calluses" (*dhū al-thafināt*).[83] Ibn Wahb al-Rāsibī's piety was underscored by his actions at his "election": at first he demurred accepting leadership of the Muḥakkima, but then he consented, saying, "I do not take it out of desire for this world, nor from fear of death."[84] Al-Barrādī's story preserves an oration delivered before his selection in which Ibn Wahb al-Rāsibī articulated the rejection of this world for the hereafter: "By God, a people who believe in God and stand up to the arbitration of the Qurʾān should not place their trust in this world nor should they prefer it. They should opt for commanding good and forbidding evil, and saying the truth. Surely for him who makes up his mind to suffer harm or injury in this world, his recompense is with God on the Day of Resurrection."[85] As with those of ʿAmmār b. Yāsir and Ḥurqūṣ b. Zuhayr, elements of ʿAbdullāh b. Wahb al-Rāsibī's narrative in Ibāḍī narratives find their reflection among non-Ibāḍī stories, especially what comes via Abū Mikhnaf, who preserves Ibn Wahb's nickname as well as versions of his declaration of consent to leadership (that is, "I do not accept it out of desire for this world") and his speech to the assembly who met in his house.[86]

Al-Darjīnī's narrative on Ibn Wahb al-Rāsibī too emphasizes his qualities of justice and truthfulness as well as his initial refusal to accept the position of leader.[87] Such qualities were reflected by early Omani authors, who recognized the importance of Ibn Wahb to the notion of Ibāḍī distinctiveness.

Munīr b. al-Nayyir's *sīra,* for example, attributes to Ibn Wahb a poignant rejection of the arbitration, which became "a proof against those who judged by other than what God had sent down."[88] Ibāḍī sources remember him as a *shārī:* he is so labeled by the Omani jurist Abū Bakr Aḥmad b. 'Abdullāh al-Kindī (d. ca. 557/1162 C.E.), and al-Izkawī included him at the beginning of his chapter devoted to "Imāms who sold themselves (*bā'ū unfusahum*) in forbidding evil."[89] In Ibn Wahb al-Rāsibī the Ibāḍiyya found a model for an early imām, a leader of unflinching integrity and ascetic praxis who was willing even to exchange his own life (as one of the *shurāt*) for the hereafter. As such, he became a link in the chain of early pious figures whom the Ibāḍiyya claimed as their own.

'Ammār b. Yāsir, Ḥurqūṣ b. Zuhayr, and 'Abdullāh b. Wahb al-Rāsibī are not the only personages claimed as founding figures and martyrs in Ibāḍī narratives on the early Muḥakkima; indeed there are many others.[90] However, considered together they represent three different types of persons through which Ibāḍī authors staked out and laid claim to three different and yet interrelated aspects of Ibāḍī identity: 'Ammār b. Yāsir, as the close early companion of the Prophet, linked the Ibāḍiyya to the earliest layers of Islamic authenticity; Ḥurqūṣ b. Zuhayr, the *ghāzī*-saint, evoked 'Umar b. al-Khattāb and the glories of the early Islamic conquests; while 'Abdullāh b. Wahb al-Rāsibī, the demurring leader of impeccably ascetic piety, outlined a prototype of the pious imām. Moreover all of them were tied together in Ibāḍī literature by their piety and martyrdom at the hands of the unrighteous. By associating themselves with such figures, the Ibāḍiyya made implicit claims about the authentic pedigree of their own group, linking themselves in a chain of legitimacy to the founding moments of the Muḥakkima, whom they regarded as the upright defenders of religion proper and as martyrs for the cause of truth.

Equally important to the process of Ibāḍī identity formation was the means by which the Ibāḍiyya linked themselves to such figures. As Wilkinson has shown, the tribal affiliations of the Muḥakkima and early *shurāt* (that is, Tamīm, Bakr, Shaybān, Yashkūr, among others) differed from those of tribes who later backed the Ibāḍiyya (that is, Azd, Kinda, and the various Berber tribes of North Africa).[91] As tribal affiliation could not provide a means to create connections, the Ibāḍīs early on found other ways to link themselves to the chain of pious figures whom they claimed as their predecessors. While this process of linking would mature into what Wilkinson has called "teacher lines" (lists of important personages who transmitted the Ibāḍī *madhhab*),[92] the Ibāḍī propensity to trace group identity through important personages seems to have been a relatively early practice: Munir b. al-Nayyir, for example, named 'Ammār b. Yāsir along with the *ahl al-nahr* ("People of the Canal") as examples of the "good models (*uswa ḥasana*) for [the person] who desires God and the last day, and [desires] to remember God much."[93] Shortly thereafter the third/ninth-century Omani scholar Abū

Mu'thir more explicitly included Ibn Yāsir, Ibn Zuhayr, and Ibn Wahb al-Rāsibī among the list of early martyrs and leaders of the Muslims (*ā'immat al-muslimīn*).[94] By the sixth/twelfth century these figures often appeared in more formalized Omani teacher lines, such that the Omani scholar Abū Bakr al-Kindī placed Ibn Yāsir and Ibn Wahb al-Rāsibī in a teacher line tracing those who preserved the true religion, and to whom the Ibāḍiyya trace themselves, while his contemporary and cousin Muḥammad b. Ibrāhīm al-Kindī presented in his *Bayān al-Shar'* an almost identical list.[95] Unsurprisingly al-Qalhātī's teacher line also included 'Ammār b. Yāsir and Ibn Wahb al-Rāsibī.[96]

So too North African Ibāḍī literature traced the line of true religion through figures such as Ibn Yāsir, Ibn Zuhayr, and Ibn Wahb. For example, anonymous Ibāḍī poetry that is preserved in al-Barrādī includes both Ibn Yāsir and Ibn Wahb in a litany of early figures whom the poet claims to follow in religion:

> We deposed 'Alī and Ibn 'Affān before him,
> And we don't go to extremes in what Ibn al-Azraq went to extremes,
> We keep to the religion of the Hāshmī, Muḥammad,
> And Abū Bakr and his Companion, the Pious [that is, 'Umar],
> And the religion of Ibn Mas'ūd and Ibn Yāsir,
> And the religion of Ibn Wahb al-Rāsibī, the successful.[97]

In placing Ibn Yāsir and Ibn Wahb among religious luminaries such as the Prophet, Abū Bakr, 'Umar, and Ibn Mas'ūd, the poet makes an important statement about the genealogy of the true religion. It is important to note as well that among North African Ibāḍīs, the biographical dictionary achieved an implicit teacher line with its generational (*ṭabaqāt*) structure, and it is no accident that authors who were interested in articulating a sense of Ibāḍī uniqueness, such as al-Darjīnī, al-Barrādī, and al-Shammākhī, wrote biographical dictionaries wherein they preserved the early Ibāḍī writings—such as that of Abū Sufyān and al-Fazārī—that were devoted to the same project.

Also noteworthy is how Ibāḍī texts on the Muḥakkima, either through design or through resonance with the texts that inform Ibāḍī narratives, reflect the same kinds of concerns with martyrdom and ascetic piety that illumined the stories of the early Muḥakkima as they were recorded in non-Ibāḍī texts. In part this focus can be attributed to the early Iraqi sources that Ibāḍī authors used to craft their own narratives—sources that were themselves steeped in the late antique and early Islamic ethos of asceticism and martyrdom. This textual resonance became even clearer when certain Ibāḍī authors moved to discuss the activities of the *shurāt* who operated after the battle of Nahrawān.

After Nahrawān: Iraqi *Shurāt* in Ibāḍī Texts

Just as Ibāḍī narratives on the Muḥakkima reveal profound textual parallels with non-Ibāḍī Iraqi materials—especially Abū Mikhnaf's reports—so too Ibāḍī texts on the post-Muḥakkimite *shurāt* betray the influence of Iraqi materials. Ibāḍī sources, of course, often mold this material for their own purposes, creating in the process a distinctively Ibāḍī pantheon of early martyrs and heroes. Ibāḍī appropriations of early *shurāt* materials, however, often present problems for Ibāḍī authors. For example, Ibāḍī narratives about ʿAlī's killer, ʿAbd al-Raḥmān b. Muljam, clearly rely on sources that valorized Ibn Muljam, and yet Ibāḍī authors treat him with some inconsistency. Al-Qalhātī, al-Izkawī, and al-Barrādī, for example, all preserve ʿImrān b. Ḥaṭṭān's poem praising Ibn Muljam;[98] however, he does not appear in al-Izkawī, al-Qalhātī, or any other Omani Ibāḍī teacher line. Al-Barrādī's short discussion of him aims to show that a certain Abū Ḥasan ʿAlī b. Muḥammad al-Bansāwī held Ibn Muljam among those with whom the Ibāḍīs associated in religion (*min ahl al-walāya*).[99] Al-Bansāwī's (and later al-Barrādī's) concern to include Ibn Muljam among those accepted by the Ibāḍiyya speaks to the fact that some Ibāḍīs either openly dissociated with him (that is, practiced *barā'a*) or refrained from making a decision (that is, practiced *wuqūf*). Both of these stances—*barā'a* and *wuqūf*—would place Ibn Muljam outside of those accepted as true believers and annul his status as a legitimate forebear of the Ibāḍiyya. This general dearth of information on Ibn Muljam combined with what was obviously a question among some Ibāḍiyya about his status in the community point to an overall ambivalence toward him among medieval Ibāḍī authors.

More acceptable to Ibāḍī historians were those who died at Nukhayla, making the narrative of the people of Nukhayla one of the more widespread stories in Ibāḍī histories. One source for this story is the second letter of Ibn Ibāḍ, which contains the main outlines of the account (minus the names of the Muḥakkima involved).[100] Al-Barrādī, however, preserves a most complete version, in which the remaining Muḥakkima were said to have organized at Nukhayla and elected Farwa b. Nawfal al-Ashjaʿī, or possibly Ḥawthara b. Wadāʿ (here an Azdī), as their leader.[101] Al-Barrādī reports that when Muʿāwiya approached Kūfa, he met the Muḥakkima encamped at Nukhayla and mistook them for al-Ḥasan b. ʿAlī's forces and that they attacked him. As in the second letter of Ibn Ibāḍ, the villain at Nukhayla was al-Ḥasan b. ʿAlī, who colluded with Muʿāwiya to attack those Muslims who resisted Muʿāwiya's seizure of Kūfa. Al-Ḥasan gathered his troops and rushed to Muʿāwiya's aid, and together their two armies crushed the Nukhaylites. An early Omani version of the story survives in Abū Qaḥṭān Khālid b. Qaḥṭān's *sīra,* which adds that it was al-Ḥawthara b. Wadāʿ who led the Nukhaylites.[102] The martyrs of Nukhayla, then, are somewhat unique in that their narrative was preserved among the early Omani Ibāḍīs as well as the usual later medieval sources.

Al-Barrādī further preserves two lines of poetry extolling the people of Nukhayla as *shurāt* to be emulated and as model ascetics. These lines closely match poetry that in non-Ibāḍī sources is attributed to the Azraqite al-Aṣam al-Ḍabbī, though al-Mubarrad credits the first two lines to ʿImrān b. Ḥaṭṭān:[103]

> We profess the religion to which the *shurāt* adhered
> on the day of Nukhayla, at the battle of Ḥūsan.[104]
> A people, who if reminded of God or if they mention [his name]
> Prostrate themselves in fear, chin and knees [to the ground].

Al-Shammākhī reports only that those who remained after Nahrawān gathered at Nukhayla and later notes that their leaders were Farwa b. Nawfal al-Ashja'ī and then ʿAbdullāh b. Abī al-Ḥisā' al-Ṭā'ī.[105] However, later in al-Shammākhī's narrative, he cites the poem recited by Muʿāwiya's ally ʿAbdullāh b. ʿAwf, expressing regret at killing a man—in al-Shammākhī's narrative it is Ibn Wadāʿ al-Asadī—who was known for his piety, prayer, and night vigils.[106] In non-Ibāḍī sources the poem and its backstory appear in the narratives of al-Balādhurī and Ibn al-Athīr.[107]

Al-Qalhātī and al-Izkawī provide an account of Nukhayla that matches al-Barrādī's in its outline, though their narratives are shorn of most of their details.[108] Nevertheless these Omani authors were aware of the early leaders at Nukhayla: later in his work al-Qalhātī remembers two of the three leaders at Nukhayla, "Farwa b. Nawfal and Wadāʿ b. Ḥawthara [*sic*]," in his teacher line;[109] and al-Izkawī mentions the leadership and martyrdom of Ḥawthara b. Wadāʿ at Nukhayla in his chapter on the "imāms who sold themselves forbidding evil."[110] From these references it is clear that Ibāḍī authors inherited and preserved—albeit in a fragmented fashion—the memory of the people of Nukhayla, who became an integral aspect of their founding narrative. While the essentials of this narrative are preserved in the earliest Omani sources, by the sixth/twelfth century it had become elaborated with other materials likely coming from North Africa.

Most Ibāḍī sources remain silent on the activities of the early Iraqi *shurāt* between the battle of Nukhayla and the revolt of Qarīb and Zuḥḥāf. The exceptions to this rule are al-Shammākhī and, to a lesser extent, al-Izkawī. Al-Izkawī's chapter on those who "sold themselves forbidding evil" provides only the briefest of details on the early *shurāt:* after Nukhayla he mentions a group that followed a leader named Mazāḥim, Ziyād b. Ḥarrāsh, an unknown Tamīm b. Muslima and his companions, and then ʿAlī al-Aʿraj, who was said to have rebelled from Ḥarūrā'.[111] In addition to al-Izkawī's brevity, both Mazāḥim and Tamīm b. Muslima are unknown to other authors, and al-Izkawī's source on them remains an open question.

Al-Shammākhī, in contrast, preserves far more material on the post-Nukhaylite *shurāt,* much of which is devoted to early Kūfan and Basran figures. It is clear that al-Shammākhī is using Kūfan and possibly Basran sources for his account. Al-Shammākhī's narratives on these early *shurāt* open with an abbreviated account of Ḥayyān b. Ẓabyān, Mustawrid b. Ullafa, and Mu'adh b. Juwayn. Al-Shammākhī includes a shortened version of a speech that in Abū Mikhnaf's account in al-Ṭabarī is attributed to Ḥayyān b. Ẓabyān and which matches Abū Mikhnaf's version in profound ways: both contain the allusions to "our brothers" who are killed at the "assemblies" (*al-majālis*) as well as God "healing the bosoms of the believers" through victory or, if they should be killed, finding "repose in parting from oppressors, while our predecessors have set an example for us."[112] The parallelism continues into the account of Mu'ādh and Juwayn's uprising, where again the language of al-Shammākhī's account matches that found in Abū Mikhnaf's narration of the same events.[113]

Al-Shammākhī then moves to the figure of Khālid b. 'Abbād al-Sadūsī, who in non-Ibāḍī sources appears only in the works of the Basran al-Mubarrad. As with the other figures mentioned in this section, al-Shammākhī's narrative follows more or less in wording and structure those found in al-Mubarrad's version: Khālid, an ascetic whose prayer marks are visible between his eyes, is betrayed to the governor Ibn Ziyād, who questions him regarding his whereabouts, to which he responds that he was "with brothers of mine, mentioning God and the imāms of guidance, and remembering the oppression among the people."[114] The governor then questions Khālid about their whereabouts and demands that he curse the people of Nahrawān. Khālid refuses to betray his brothers and says evasively of the Muḥakkima, "if they are the enemies of God, then God curse them." Khālid gives similarly ambiguous answers concerning 'Uthmān and 'Alī, to which a man from Ibn Ziyād's entourage accuses him of practicing *taqiyya.* No one wishes to kill Khālid, until a certain Muthallam b. Masrūḥ does so. Like al-Mubarrad's narrative, al-Shammākhī's includes Ḥurayth b. Ḥajl and Kahmas b. Ṭalaq al-Ṣarīmī's revenge killing of Muthallam as well as the story of how they buried the money found on him with his body.[115] As is obvious from the parallelism between al-Mubarrad's and al-Shammākhī's narratives, they are using the same (possibly Basran) source, one that valorizes Khālid al-Sadūsī as an ascetic and a martyr and frames his story using the classic martyrdom trope of interrogation.

Al-Shammākhī's story then moves to the uprising of Abū Layla and then to the Kūfan rebel Ziyād b. Ḥarrāsh al-'Ajalī (al-Balādhurī gives Ibn Kharrāsh).[116] These narratives are brief and provide scant detail, but what does appear matches what can be found in al-Balādhurī and, to a lesser extent, Ibn al-Athīr.[117] Al-Shammākhī then mentions, fleetingly, 'Alī al-A'raj (a figure unknown in non-Ibāḍī sources but known to al-Izkawī) before moving to the martyrdom of Ma'bad al-Muḥāribī. Ma'bad's narrative is far more substantial and matches that of Muʿayn b. ʿAbdullāh al-Muḥāribī in al-Balādhurī and Ibn al-Athīr: he is captured by al-Mughīra and then questioned on instructions from Muʿāwiya, who demands to be recognized as caliph in exchange for his freedom.[118] Maʿbad refuses to cooperate, antagonizing his captors until he is martyred.[119] As in the non-Ibāḍī versions of the narrative, his death is avenged by a fellow Muslim (an Omani in al-Shammākhī's version).

Textually speaking, then, al-Shammākhī's sources can be traced specifically to Kūfa and Basra. The Kūfan source was likely the same used by Abū Mikhnaf, while the Basran materials match what can be found in al-Mubarrad (himself of Basran origin) on the figure of Khālid b. ʿAbbād. Some of the materials cannot be so specified, though they also likely hail from Iraq: al-Shammākhī's narrative shares some structural and not a few textual parallels with those found about the early *shurāt* in al-Balādhurī (a Persian who lived in Baghdad) and Ibn al-Athīr (who hailed from Mosul). In other words, al-Shammākhī's narrative is undoubtedly using the same Iraqi sources that other writers on the early *shurāt* used, though it is ultimately unclear what the specific sources might have been. These writings collectively created something of an Iraqi "cycle" of martyrs, one that lived on into Ibāḍī writings long after other *shurāt* groups had ceased to exist. Up to the rebellions of Ṭawwāf b. ʿAllāq, Qarīb al-Azdī, and Zuḥḥāf al-Ṭāʾī, al-Shammākhī's source base remains the most accessible from the standpoint of textual comparison, and the narratives that appear in al-Shammākhī are more or less in conformity with what is found in non-Ibāḍī sources about the early *shurāt* martyrs. Moreover al-Shammākhī is the only Ibāḍī author to treat with any depth early *shurāt* figures such as Ḥayyān b. Ẓabyān, Mustawrid b. Ullafa, Muʿādh b. Juwayn, Khālid b. ʿAbbād, Abū Layla, Ziyād b. Ḥarrāsh, ʿAlī al-Aʿraj, and Maʿbad al-Muḥāribī.

Equally obvious is how al-Shammākhī's narratives perpetuate the early *shurāt* authors' concern for visible piety and present the early *shurāt* as ascetics and martyrs who rejected the world. In this way Ibāḍī texts reproduce the early *shurāt* narratives' nexus of piety, world rejection, and martyrdom, replicating in their own way those broadly held late antique tropes in later centuries and among new groups.

Nevertheless it is clear that al-Shammākhī and other Ibāḍī authors were not passive receivers of early materials. When faced with problematic narratives of early *shurāt,* as with the uprisings of Ṭawwāf b. ʿAllāq, Qarīb b. Murra, and Zuḥḥāf al-Ṭāʾī, Ibāḍī authors seem to have employed several strategies to overcome damaging the reputations of these early figures. For example, al-Shammākhī provides only abridged treatments of these rebellions: Ṭawwāf receives one line; while the narrative of Qarīb and Zuḥḥāf is shorn of most of its detail—for example, the narrative mentions only that they were cousins who were killed in the quarter of the Banī Rāsib when they were surrounded and thrown from the roofs of the houses.[120]

Given that al-Shammākhī had previously provided a wealth of details on the early *shurāt,* his cursory treatment of these figures remains curious and may indicate an attempt on his part to remove from their stories materials that he found questionable or offensive. It should be recalled that in non-Ibāḍī sources, Ṭawwāf was said to have killed his fellow *shurāt,* while Qarīb and Zuḥḥāf were said to have committed *isti'rāḍ,* earning the condemnation of Abū Bilāl for it; al-Shammākhī's (or his source's) reticence to reproduce such details would thereby be understandable. Al-Shammākhī's brevity thus allows him to pass over in silence some potentially complicating details of certain early *shurāt* uprisings while still acknowledging these early figures.

Other Ibāḍī presentations of Qarīb, Zuḥḥāf, and Ṭawwāf remain equally challenging, albeit for different reasons. Al-Izkawī's narrative, for example, confusingly unifies the two stories. It relates how after Qarīb and Zuḥḥāf witnessed the atrocities of 'Ubaydullāh b. Ziyād they rebelled but were pelted with stones by the locals.[121] It relates how they fought until Qarīb was killed but neglects to provide any information about Zuḥḥāf, shifting rather to the story of Ṭawwāf. This abrupt transition leaves much unanswered: was the manuscript damaged and part of the story lost? Did al-Izkawī intentionally run the two stories together?

Al-Izkawī's version of Ṭawwāf's narrative presents further difficulties insofar as it tells an entirely different story from that found in non-Ibāḍī sources. Ṭawwāf's guarantor is held by the governor and threatened with death if Ṭawwāf fails to present himself. Not wishing to cause harm to an innocent, Ṭawwāf returns to 'Ubaydullāh, accuses him of judging by "other than what God has sent down" (paraphrasing Qur'ān 5:44, 45, 47), and was put to death. Later, when 'Ubaydullāh orders that Ṭawwāf be killed, Ṭawwāf asks the executioner, "will you give 'Ubaydullāh the *fay'* but sin before God?" These "just words" cause the executioner to refuse the governor's order. However, a Bedouin appears and kills Ṭawwāf, after which two of Ṭawwāf's companions lure the Bedouin from the *sūq* (market) and kill him in revenge.[122] Al-Izkawī's narrative, then, presents Ṭawwāf's story using the somewhat standard martyrdom narrative, replete with an interrogation scene, as well as the revenge aspect that seems to be a part of certain early *shurāt* martyrdom narratives. Whether or not al-Izkawī is using an earlier source or providing this narrative himself is unknown, but what is clear is that Ṭawwāf's story has been sanitized of any offending detail and (re)presented in an immanently familiar fashion.

Later in al-Izkawī's text he provides two lines of poetry in reference to Ṭawwāf, the first of which is preserved in non-Ibāḍī sources and makes reference to the "people of the wall" (who, it will be recalled, are associated in non-Ibāḍī versions of the story with Ṭawwāf). However, in the text preceding the poem al-Izkawī establishes that the "people of the wall" refer not to Ṭawwāf and his comrades but rather to those who avenged Abū

Bilāl's death, and thus al-Izkawī's narrative frames the poem in such a way as to separate Ṭawwāf from the "people of the wall." Thus, as it stands in al-Izkawī's version, Ṭawwāf's story reflects none of the details that non-Ibāḍī versions of his story contain, even to the point of treating the "people of the wall" and Ṭawwāf as unrelated, representing separate entities to be celebrated for separate reasons. In this way al-Izkawī highlights the heroic while flattening out the details of Ṭawwāf's story.

Al-Darjīnī's narrative further complicates the picture of Ṭawwāf, Qarīb, and Zuḥḥāf in Ibāḍī sources by conflating the figures of Qarīb and Zuḥḥāf with what in non-Ibāḍī sources is Ṭawwāf's narrative and thereby casting aspersions on the persons of Qarīb and Zuḥḥāf. Without a doubt al-Darjīnī considers Qarīb and Zuḥḥāf as figures of a certain piety: he mentions, for example, that they were celibate. However, al-Darjīnī notes that they committed an error (*hafwa*) grievous enough to invalidate their martyrdom (*kafarathā al-shahāda*).[123] According to al-Darjīnī, whose source is Abū Sufyān, Qarīb and Zuḥḥāf along with another named Ka'b were among those early *shurāt* imprisoned by Ibn Ziyād. Ibn Ziyād ordered the *mawālī* among them to kill their Arab brethren, but they refused. However, when the governor ordered the Arabs to kill their *mawālī* brethren among them, the Arab *shurāt* did so. Having murdered their brothers and associates, they were set free but were consumed with guilt as well as ostracized by their fellows. Ka'b, the narrative states, would fall unconscious when he recalled the event, and no less than Abū 'Ubayda wished God's punishment on him for it. Qarīb and Zuḥḥāf, for their part, rebelled "in the path of God" and were killed.[124] Al-Darjīnī's narrative thus inserts Qarīb and Zuḥḥāf into what in non-Ibāḍī sources is essentially the story of Ṭawwāf, providing details (such as the story of Ka'b) that seem to tie the narrative to early Ibāḍī figures such as Abū 'Ubayda.

Elsewhere, however, al-Darjīnī provides a detail on Qarīb and Zuḥḥāf that indicates some familiarity with their story in non-Ibāḍī sources. An anonymous report informs us that Qarīb and Zuḥḥāf rebelled against Ziyād b. Abīhi and not against his son Ibn Ziyād (as in the report attributed to Abū Sufyān).[125] Al-Darjīnī also preserves some lines of their poetry that communicate the ubiquitous *shārī* desire to fight against tyrants but that nowhere indicate overwhelming regret at having (supposedly) slaughtered their *shurāt* brethren:

> They said to us: "give us space [to go] on our path."
> We replied to them: "No! by the Wise! The Generous!"
> Not until we pass you through with our swords,
> And cut in [your] heads every straight thing [that is, bones and so forth]
> Running with [horses'] bridals from the midst of our homes
> To the vengeful place of the oppressors (*al-ẓālimīn*).[126]

This poetry combined with the reference to Qarīb and Zuḥḥāf's rebellion coming during the time of Ziyād seem to indicate that al-Darjīnī (or his source) may have had access to at least some details of the narrative as told in non-Ibāḍī sources.

Early Omani Ibāḍī *siyar,* for their part, were aware of Qarīb and Zuḥḥāf as well as several other early *shurāt* figures. However, these sources offer only brief and enigmatic mention of them. Ibn Nayyir's *sīra,* for example, mentions Qarīb and Zuḥḥāf as well as the "companions of al-Khaṭm" (presumably al-Khaṭīm) in a list of early Muslims whose accomplishments preceded him.[127] Similarly, Abū Qahtān's *sīra* mentions the rebellion of Qarīb and Zuḥḥāf but only in the most superficial of ways: it simply states that they were killed before they had a chance to leave Basra; Abū Mu'thir's *sīra* offers little more than their names and the fact that they were killed by Ziyād.[128] Nevertheless, despite the fact that Abū Munīr and later Abū Qahtān and Abū Mu'thir do not provide the details of these stories, it is clear that by referencing early *shurāt,* they are drawing attention to figures who were known in some capacity to Ibāḍīs of Imām Ghassān's (and later Abū Qahtān and Abū Mu'thir's) era. Equally tantalizing is the mention of "Shahm b. Ghālib" (an obvious corruption of Sahm b. Ghālib), which comes from the mouth of Abū Bilāl in al-Izkawī's text.[129] However, Sahm b. Ghālib's story does not appear in al-Izkawī (nor in any other Ibāḍī text for that matter), and thus it must be assumed that al-Izkawī was selectively using an earlier source that made mention of Ibn Ghālib. In any case, what is clear is that early Omani Ibāḍī historians were aware of and had inherited the names of the early Iraqi *shurāt* and perhaps some of the details of their narratives, but they (just as their non-Ibāḍī counterparts) crafted this material to reflect their own concerns.

For early Omani Ibāḍīs, such concerns do not seem to have gone further than providing a list of early personalities, shorn of most of their details. Later North African and Omani authors betray a similar effort but imbue their narratives more fully and more obviously shape their materials to reflect Ibāḍī needs. Nevertheless their preoccupation was with continuity and with showing an unbroken chain of virtuous figures stretching back through the early *shurāt* to the people of Nukhayla and Nahrawān. These personalities were shown to have been pious, ascetic, and willing to die for their convictions. Unlike non-Ibāḍī sources, the Ibāḍī-authored *shurāt* stories make no mention of the practice of *isti'rāḍ* or other acts of random violence, as the Ibāḍiyya had long found these reprehensible. It is perhaps for this reason that the narratives of Ṭawwāf b. ʿAllāq, Qarīb al-Azdī, and Zuḥḥāf al-Ṭā'ī receive such brief mention in al-Shammākhī and become tailored or confused in al-Izkawī and al-Darjīnī. By shortening, reworking, or otherwise doctoring the stories of Ṭawwāf, Qarīb, and Zuḥḥāf, Ibāḍī authors attempted to ease the tension between the respect due to these early *shurāt* figures and some of the questionable actions attributed to them.

What is at once clear in this endeavor is that Ibāḍīs did indeed inherit a more or less coherent cycle of early Iraqi *shurāt,* along with the world-rejecting image of piety and asceticism that went with them. When the stories of these early *shurāt* did not tally with Ibāḍī understandings of proper Islamic behavior (as in the cases of Ṭawwāf, Qarīb, and Zuḥḥāf), Ibāḍī authors nevertheless found ways to present their stories. They did not simply ignore them, suggesting that the cast of early *shurāt* had been inherited and preserved at an early period and was by the medieval period something that Ibāḍī authors were compelled to acknowledge. Textual evidence suggests that the sources for Ibāḍī versions originated in Iraq, found their way to North Africa, and then trickled back to Oman by the sixth/twelfth century—a hypothesis first proposed by Wilkinson and one that seems to be borne out by the evidence. Of course early Omani Ibāḍīs were aware on some level of the early *shurāt* and even included some details about them in their writings. However, early Omani texts do not seem to preserve the same wealth of material that can be found, for example, in al-Shammākhī, al-Barrādī, and al-Darjīnī. This is not the case for the figure of Abū Bilāl Mirdās b. Udayya, whose narrative appears in virtually every Ibāḍī source and whose memory was preserved to such an extent that he appears alongside the alleged founder of Ibāḍism, Jābir b. Zayd, as a seminal figure among those claimed by the early Ibāḍiyya.

Abū Bilāl Mirdās b. Udayya: Model *Shārī*

As with non-Ibāḍī accounts of the early *shurāt,* the doyen of Ibāḍī narratives on the early martyrs is Abū Bilāl Mirdās b. Udayya, to whose narrative is usually appended that of his brother, ʿUrwa. Indeed, Ibāḍī texts elevate the Udayya brothers such that the stories of Ḥayyān b. Ẓabyān, Mustawrid b. Ullafa, Muʿādh b. Juwayn, Khālid b. ʿAbbād, Abū Layla, Ziyād b. Ḥarrāsh, ʿAlī al-Aʿraj, Maʿbad al-Muḥāribī, Ṭawwāf b. ʿAllāq, Qarīb b. Murra, and Zuḥḥāf al-Ṭāʾī appear but a preamble to their towering presence in Ibāḍī literature. The Udayya brothers, and especially Abū Bilāl, represented the model *shārī* warriors insofar as they embodied the piety, asceticism, and martial qualities that made their deaths at the hands of the Umayyads poignant moments of martyrdom and focal points for Ibāḍī memory. As such, their narratives became the locus for specifically Ibāḍī articulations of identity.

Abū Bilāl's narrative can be found in virtually every Ibāḍī text that treats the early *shurāt,* and it is clear that he was also known to early Omani Ibāḍīs. Just as with authors of other Ibāḍī narratives of the *shurāt,* Ibāḍī authors appear to have inherited the same materials that inform non-Ibāḍī versions of the Abū Bilāl cycle, such that the basic outlines of the narratives match in important ways. In fact, al-Darjīnī explicitly mentions al-Mubarrad's *al-Kāmil* as one of his sources; similarly al-Shammākhī quotes from a certain *Kitāb al-Aʿlām.* However, because of the importance of Abū Bilāl to the Ibāḍiyya, Ibāḍī authors preserve a wealth of materials that do not appear in non-Ibāḍī sources. Without the early texts, it is impossible to know whether this material represents a continuation of the earliest *shurāt* articulations of the Abū Bilāl cycle or a particular Ibāḍī version of that cycle.[130] In every case, however, it can be assumed that Ibāḍī versions of the Abū Bilāl narrative reflect the concerns of the authors who penned them.

Urwa's narrative in Ibāḍī sources matches almost exactly that which is given in non-Ibāḍī sources: he is remembered as the first to utter the *lā ḥukm* phrase and to draw his sword, as well as being the one who struck Ibn al-Ashʿath's riding animal at the announcement of the arbitration.[131] Al-Shammākhī, quoting the *Kitāb al-Aʿlām,* preserves a version of the story in which ʿUrwa accused Ibn Ziyād of five sins, for which Ibn Ziyād was eventually to cut off his hands and feet. As with Wahb b. Jarīr's version in al-Ṭabarī, ʿUrwa quotes Qur'ān 26:128–30 when he accuses Ibn Ziyād. Al-Shammākhī's version also preserves ʿUrwa's retort that he had ruined the next world for Ibn Ziyād as well as the fact that Ibn Ziyād killed his daughter along with him.[132] Moreover both al-Darjīnī and al-Shammākhī preserve al-Mubarrad's variant account of ʿUrwa's death (al-Darjīnī explicitly cites al-Mubarrad as his source) at the hands of Ziyād b. Abīhī, along with the comments of ʿUrwa's *mawla* concerning his ascetic practices.[133] To an extent, then, Ibāḍī sources have clearly preserved available materials on ʿUrwa and have done so in parallel with what can be found on him in non-Ibāḍī texts.

However, other aspects of ʿUrwa's story are either unique to Ibāḍī narratives or have been uniquely preserved in Ibāḍī narratives. Thus al-Shammākhī's version of the ʿUrwa story adds that Ibn Ziyād's guards saw a light on ʿUrwa's crucified body but that Ibn Ziyād considered them liars until he saw it for himself.[134] This detail, of course, has the effect of attributing sanctity to ʿUrwa—a project that remains distinctively *shārī*/Ibāḍī. Likewise both al-Darjīnī and al-Shammākhī preserve an anecdote surrounding ʿUrwa's arrest that places proof of his rectitude in the mouth of Ibn Ziyād. They tell of how Ibn Ziyād's secretary, when recording how ʿUrwa had come to them "from a group" (*min sirb*) of those who worshipped God, wrote that he had come from among those who "drink" [alcohol] (*miman sharaba*). Recognizing the mistake as well as the piety of ʿUrwa, Ibn Ziyād is recorded as saying to his secretary, "You have distorted and misread! How I wish that he were among those who drink."[135] Ibn Ziyād is thus shown to have borne witness to ʿUrwa's piety even as he condemned him to be killed.

As with ʿUrwa's narrative in Ibāḍī sources, Abū Bilāl's presents a colorful mixture of parallels with non-Ibāḍī versions and distinctly Ibāḍī details, all of which are put toward creating an image of the ideal *shārī* warrior. The elements of Abū Bilāl's core story all appear in various guises in Ibāḍī narratives: his public challenge of Ibn Ziyād and Ghaylān b. Kharash;[136] the interrogation of the female Khārijite al-Baljā' and her execution;[137] Abū Bilāl's subsequent rebellion with his stunning victory at Āsik;[138] and his ultimate betrayal and martyrdom at the hands of the Umayyad army.[139] Also to be found are familiar tales of Abū Bilāl's piety: his return to jail despite knowing of his imminent execution;[140] and his association of pitch on his garment with the pitch of hell mentioned in Qur'ān 14:50.[141] Such parallels remain unsurprising given al-Darjīnī's stated reliance on al-Mubarrad's *al-Kāmil* as well as al-Shammākhī's use of his source, the *Kitāb al-Aʿlām.*

Yet as with other Ibāḍī versions of *shurāt* narratives, Abū Bilāl's story in Ibāḍī sources contains certain distinctive details. For example, al-Shammākhī preserves how during al-Baljā''s interrogation, Ibn Ziyād attempted to pull off her veil and expose her shaved head—a mark that is clearly meant to identify her as one of the *shurāt.*[142] This detail confirms from the Ibāḍī perspective the importance of tonsure to some early *shurāt.*

Similarly, Ibāḍī narratives accentuate Abū Bilāl's piety and prowess through anecdotes meant to elevate his character and show divine blessing. One of the more prominent qualities that the various narratives highlight is Abū Bilāl's ascetic piety. Thus, for example, al-Shammākhī preserves a story about Abū Bilāl swooning in the face of various reminders of hellfire and the snares of the world. When questioned about them, he is said to have responded, "So turn away from what you have seen of [outward] forms, desires and amusements and seek assistance from your past wretchedness."[143] In addition al-Ikzawī gives numerous anecdotes that point to Abū Bilāl's piety. For example, one reads, "And he would not eat breakfast until he had separated [some food] from his breakfast to give it to the orphans or the needy."[144] A report from the same source tells that Abū Bilāl said on the day that he was killed, "Oh how I wish for two souls: one soul to fight in the way of God, and another soul to provide for the needs of the Muslims";[145] and another has him saying, "I would not stay in my house an evening when I had remembered a slip that I had done, but I would ask forgiveness for it. And I would guard everything about which I spoke, for I had become afraid to err."[146] Al-Izkawī also mentions that the impact of Abū Bilāl's *sujūd* could be seen on his face—a reference to a prayer callus on his forehead.[147]

Ibāḍī versions of Abū Bilāl's narrative also contain accounts of various miracles. Abū Sufyān narrates in al-Shammākhī an account of Abū Bilāl asking for confirmation of his decision to rebel under the rain spouts of the Kaʿba and receiving a couple of water drops in response.[148] Recalling some of the signs said to have accompanied Abū Bilāl and his companions in al-Mubarrad's version of the story, al-Izkawī's text has Abū Bilāl and his companions gather in the house of the Banū Tamīm to plan their rebellion, and there "they called to their Lord, and they asked Him, if He was pleased with what they desired, to grant them a sign. And [suddenly] the ceiling of the house in which they were located split so that they could see the sky, and then sealed up again as it was."[149] These miracles indicate divine favor as well as closeness with God, which Ibāḍī versions of Abū Bilāl's narrative attempt to demonstrate.

Moreover a little later in al-Izkawzī's text there is a story of a miraculous dream in which a heavenly ladder appears:

> And it was found that a man of the people of worship saw in his sleep, on the night in which Mirdās was killed, a ladder descend from the sky to the earth. And Abū Bilāl and his companions ascended to the sky. The man wished to ascend with them, but his face was struck and he was restricted from ascending. And it was said to him: "You are not of the people who go up with them, [those] who ascend the ladder." And when the man awoke, he broke from the way (*dīn*) of his people, and associated (*tawalla*) [with the practice of] Abū Bilāl and his companions, and fought on their path until he was killed.[150]

In this version of the story, the miraculous vision plays on the motif of the ladder to heaven, expressing divine favor for the actions of Abū Bilāl and his companions in a fashion strikingly similar to Christian narratives: the heavenly ladder is familiar in many a Christian story, not the least of which is that of Jacob's ladder or, more appropriately, the martyrdom of Perpetua.

Likewise the familiar late antique theme of dying to the world appears in certain iterations of Abū Bilāl's story. His address to those who wish to become *shurāt,* preserved in Ibn al-Nayyir's *sīra,* conveys an almost stoic acceptance of death combined with an ascetic hatred of "this life," even going so far as to inform the *shurāt* that they are, in fact, already dead in this world: "You go out to fight in the way of God desiring His pleasure, not wanting anything of the goods of this world, nor have you any desire for it, nor will you return to it. You are the ascetic and one who hates this life, desiring only the world to come, trying with all in your power to obtain it: going out to be killed and for nothing else. So know that you are [already] killed and have no return to this life; you are going forward and will not turn away from righteousness until you come to God."[151] By articulating the themes of world rejection, asceticism, and a desire to be killed for the sake of righteousness, Abū Bilāl became for Ibāḍīs the model *shārī,* articulating the essence of the concept of *shirā'* through his words and deeds. Indeed later Ibāḍī imāmate theory would postulate the existence of four imām types who corresponded to the different situations or "states" (*masālik*) in which the Ibāḍī community might find themselves: Abū Bilāl became the model for the *imām al-shirā',* who led those willing to "exchange" their lives for the establishment of an Ibāḍī polity.[152] Abū Bilāl's rebellion also shaped the ways that Ibāḍī legal scholars later articulated the legal framework for the "state" of *shirā'* among Ibāḍīs.[153] Indeed the above-quoted speech of Abū Bilāl appears in an epistle dedicated, in part, to clarifying certain questions surrounding the institution of the *shurāt* for Imām al-Ghassān: Ibn al-Nayyir treats the question of the amount of dower appropriate for *shurāt* who cannot refrain from marriage as well as the extent to which the Ibāḍī *'ulamā'* should function as their leaders.[154]

Ibāḍī versions of the Abū Bilāl narrative also function as sites where Ibāḍī authors articulate particularly Ibāḍī concerns through the details of Abū Bilāl's narrative. Thus, for example, Ibāḍī texts take great care to relate Abū Bilāl's meticulous restraint and his refusal to fight any but those who fought his group. Al-Izkawī offers the following description of Abū Bilāl and his band: "They did not call for *hijra,* nor did they adopt it. They did not threaten the peace, nor take spoils, nor take captives. They did not lower the people of the *qibla* [that is, their fellow non-Ibāḍī Muslims] to the level of idol worshippers."[155] These practices—separating from non-*shārī* Muslims (that is, practicing *hijra*), random killing (*isti'rāḍ*), and treating fellow non-*shārī* Muslims (the "people of the *qibla*") like unbelievers (*kuffār* or *mushrikūn*)—are famously associated with the Azraqite and Najdite Khārijites. The subtext for al-Izkawī's description of Abū Bilāl and his group, then, is a concern to portray Abū Bilāl and his followers, and thereby the Ibāḍiyya who looked to Abū Bilāl as one of their founding figures and heroes, as fundamentally different in their rebellion from the militant Khārijites. Al-Izkawī's passage, likely taken from the writings of Abū Sufyān (and possibly Abū Yazīd), reflects early Ibāḍī polemical writing against the Azāriqa and Najdāt. In fact it matches in sentiment and content Sālim b. Dhakwān's polemic against the Azāriqa and Najdāt as well as the anti-Azraqite passages from al-Ash'arī's *Maqalāt* that Lewinstein identified as coming from an Ibāḍī source.[156] In this way Abū Bilāl's portrait in Ibāḍī sources presents a complex mix of inherited material, itself heavily stamped by the late antique genre of hagiography, which Ibāḍī authors have shaped toward their own concern with Abū Bilāl as a model *shārī* and pious ancestor.

Ibāḍīs of North Africa and the Arabian Peninsula connected themselves to Abū Bilāl with different strategies. On the one hand, North African biographical dictionaries such as those of al-Darjīnī and al-Shammākhī implicitly created a sense of generational connection with their *ṭabaqat* structure and located Abū Bilāl in the earliest historical layer. This placement indicates the foundational importance of Abū Bilāl and underscores his role as one of the Ibāḍī *salaf.* On the other hand, Omani Ibāḍī thinkers made genealogical linkages to Abū Bilāl more explicit by delineating in list form the genealogy of the "true" religion. Thus, Abū Mu'thir includes Abū Bilāl in his list of the true martyrs and imāms of the Muslims, while Ibn al-Nayyir presents him as one of the pious predecessors to the Ibāḍiyya.[157] Ibn Qaḥṭān presents a shortened version of Abū Bilāl's martyrdom as a means to demonstrate how God "revives the traditions of Islam (*sunan al-islām*) through their deaths."[158] In all of these cases Ibāḍīs created links to Abū Bilāl as part of the process of delineating their group identity and showing themselves as the inheritors of the true religion. In so doing, they participated in a process with a long history in the ancient Middle East, one that their Christian and Muslim neighbors in Iraq also pursued when demarcating their own communal identities. Indeed, Ibāḍīs were not alone in appropriating the image and memory of Abū Bilāl: Nāfiʿ b. al-Azraq and the Azāriqa are said to have "followed" as a model (*yatawallūn*) the people of Nahrawān and Abū Bilāl;[159] al-Baghdādī associates the so-called Ṣufrī Khārijites with Abū Bilāl;[160] and, more interestingly, Muʿtazilites and Shiʿites are said to have laid claim to his memory.[161] It is therefore not surprising that the Ibāḍiyya should likewise ground their identity, in part, in his remembrance.

Transformations of the Ibāḍī *Shurāt*

Abū Bilāl represents the last of the early Iraqi *shurāt* to be appropriated by the Ibāḍiyya. That is to say, after Abū Bilāl those *shurāt* remembered as such in Ibāḍī sources hailed from the ranks of the emerging Ibāḍiyya, and their stories reflect in some senses the concerns and tribal affiliations of the proto-Ibāḍīs from whom they emerged. Wilkinson has shown how rebellions such as those of ʿAbdullāh b. Yaḥyā (Ṭālib al-Ḥaqq) and al-Julandā b. Masʿūd in the Arabian Peninsula were in many ways Yamani tribal affairs reflecting successful Ibāḍī missionizing among the Azd and Kinda.[162] They also capitalized on the strong anti-Quraysh feelings of these and other tribal groups in the peninsula: for example, having captured Makka and Madīna from the Umayyads in 130/747, Abū Ḥamza is reported to have said on the pulpit in Makka, "The sons of Umayya are a party of error, and their strength is the strength of tyrants. They seize people on suspicion, judge by caprice, and put them to death in anger. They rule by mediation, take the Law out of its context, and give the *zakāt* money to those who are not entitled to it."[163] By associating the whole of the Umayyads with the injustices of the caliphs, Abū Ḥamza employed the language of justice to mobilize tribal sentiments against them.

In addition these rebellions were explicitly aimed at establishing proto-Ibāḍī polities in the Arabian Peninsula. Accordingly, with figures such as Ṭālib al-Ḥaqq and al-Julandā b. Masʿūd the meaning of *shirā'* began to shift in important ways, as did the function of the *shurāt*. Although later Ibāḍī authors went to great lengths to portray an unbroken chain of authorities stretching from the first *shurāt* through Abū Bilāl to Ṭālib al-Ḥaqq and al-Julandā b. Masʿūd and then on to the Ibāḍīs of later generations, important changes occurred in the interval between Abū Bilāl's uprising and the proto-Ibāḍī uprisings of the mid-second/eighth century.

Most important to understanding the changes in the meaning and practice of *shirā'* is the gradual emergence of the Ibāḍiyya from the circles of moderate Basran *shurāt* and their affiliation with the Azd and Kinda tribes, a process that began some decades after Abū Bilāl's uprising and seems to have been quite advanced by the mid-second/eighth century. At that time something resembling the later Ibāḍiyya could be discerned amid the scholarly groups of Basra. Although, as Wilkinson observes, the origins of the Ibāḍiyya hail "from a far more amorphous background" than Ibāḍī sources tend to portray, by the mid-second/eighth century proto-Ibāḍī scholars (many of whom would retroactively be remembered as the first "imāms" of the movement, such as Abū 'Ubayda Muslim b. Abī Karīma and Abū Mawdūd Ḥājib al-Ṭā'ī) were providing religious and legal guidance for their peers, training missionaries to spread the doctrine, and organizing resistance against the faltering Umayyads.[164] The importance of these early scholars to the articulation and practice of *shirā'* can hardly be overstated, as it was these early figures—especially Abū Mawdūd Ḥājib al-Ṭā'ī—who began the process of transforming the *shurāt* into a fully articulated institution under the direction of Ibāḍī scholars and imāms.

Without a doubt, foundational proto-Ibāḍī figures, such as Jābir b. Zayd, perpetuated an earlier Muḥakkimite ideal of *shirā'* among the quietists of Basra: for example, in a report attributed to Jābir's pupil Ḍumām, Jābir chastises those who would hold on to their wealth and states that "there is no action greater in God's eyes than exchanging [oneself] (*shirā'*)."[165] However, other statements attributed to Jābir show his caution and his willingness to counsel secrecy and *taqiyya*—so much so that later Ibāḍīs associated the "state" of secrecy and the imām who led the Muslims during that condition (known as the *imām al-kitmān*) with Jābir b. Zayd.[166] Followers of Jābir and other early proto-Ibāḍīs, such as Abū 'Ubayda, were known to meet in secret and to go to great lengths to insure discretion in their activities. For this reason Wilkinson finds in Abū Mawdūd's promotion of *shirā'* a counterweight to quietist scholars such as Abū 'Ubadya.[167]

Indeed, Abū Mawdūd emerges from the pages of Ibāḍī histories as the organizer of the Basran end of Ṭālib al-Ḥaqq's uprising. Abū Sufyān's report, on the authority of a certain al-Mulayḥ, mentions him in conference with no less than Abū Ḥamza Mukhtār b. 'Awf and Balj b. 'Uqba, the two pillars of Ṭālib al-Ḥaqq's rebellion.[168] In fact Abū Ḥamza led a small band of *shurāt* to conquer Makka and then Madīna in the name of Ṭālib al-Ḥaqq, articulating in his *khuṭba* to the people of Madīna the ideal of *shirā'*. Describing his band, Abū Ḥamza said that they were "youths whose eyes were closed to evil and whose feet were slow to approach wrongdoing; exchanging with God the life that dies for the life that dies not, they mingled all that was theirs with their fatigue, and rose at night to watch and pray after fasting all day. They bent their backs over portions of the Qur'ān, and so oft as they came upon a verse [of fear, they were racked with terror of the Fire, and when they came upon a verse] of desire they were racked with longing for Paradise."[169]

Abū Ḥamza's description surely perpetuates the themes of ascetic praxis that were so profoundly associated with the ideal of *shirā'*, and his *khuṭba* continues on to describe the fearlessness with which the *shurāt* met the overwhelming number of their enemies. So too in the poetry of the early Ibāḍī poet ʿAmr b. al-Ḥuṣayn al-ʿAnbarī, a companion of Abū Ḥamza, the common *shurāt* themes of asceticism and martyrdom are duplicated. The poet describes his companions' excessive prayers, their night vigils, and the fear (expressed through sighing) of God and the impending Day of Judgment along with their desire to "exchange" themselves in battle against tyrants and enemies.[170]

While this image of *shirā'* is largely unchanged from earlier articulations, the hand of the proto-Ibāḍī *'ulamā'* can be seen directing the uprising in significant ways. Abū Mawdūd, for example, was said to have raised funds for weapons from among the Basran merchants and gone into debt to provide for them.[171] More to the point, Ṭālib al-Ḥaqq is remembered in Ibāḍī sources primarily as a pious imām who applied the *ḥudūd* penalties; although al-Darjīnī classes him among the *shurāt,* and a light was said to shine through his crucified body indicating his status as a martyr, his only battle was his final defeat at Ṣanaʿā', and it is more accurate to think of him as an able administrator, judge, and *'ālim.*[172]

Moreover, after Balj b. ʿUqba, Abū Ḥamza, and finally Ṭālib al-Ḥaqq's *shurāt* were successively defeated by the Umayyad general Ibn ʿAṭiyya, Abū Mawdūd traveled to the Ḥaḍramawt during the *ḥajj* season to settle a dispute among Ḥaḍramawtī proto-Ibāḍīs over whether or not they should engage in *shirā'* or accept a defensive imām. Mentioning the merits of *shirā'* over defense, he nevertheless stipulated that *shirā'* was incumbent upon only those who had the capacity for it, and he promptly ordered the *shurāt* out of the Ḥaḍramawt.[173] Unlike the early report attributed to Jābir b. Zayd, which provided an authoritative opinion on the merits of *shirā'* as a mode of ascetic living, Abū Mawdūd's decision provided an authoritative judgment for a specific group of petitioners. By his time, then, not only had the nature of *shirā'* become a topic of debate, but in addition proto-Ibāḍī scholars had asserted their authority over it. Indeed, Abū Sufyān's report in al-Shammākhī and al-Darjīnī emphasizes Abū Mawdūd's role as leader among proto-Ibāḍīs in matters of warfare (*al-ḥarb*) and his prowess in gathering funds for it (*jamʿ al-māl*). It is thus with figures such as Abū Mawdūd Ḥājib al-Ṭā'ī that proto-Ibāḍī scholars begin to exert their influence over the *shurāt.*[174]

North African sources offer little on the further history of the *shurāt* in North Africa after the revolt of Ṭālib al-Ḥaqq, despite the fact that proto-Ibāḍī and Ṣufrī rebels played an important role in wresting North Africa from the Umayyads and in later establishing Ibāḍī polities at Tāhart and Sijilmasa. There are several possible reasons for the relative silence of these sources with regard to actual *shurāt*. First, because North African chronicles and biographical dictionaries were written in the wake of the Nukkārite and Khalafite schisms that challenged the legitimacy of the Rustumids at Tāhart, these sources tend to focus on bolstering the authority and image of the Rustumid imāms as pious and just.[175] Second, after the establishment of their respective Ṣufrī and Ibāḍī polities, the Midrārids and Rustumids of North Africa enjoyed profitable and enduring relationships with the Umayyads of Spain as well as with the Muhallabid governors of Qayrawān and, to a certain extent, their successors the Aghlabids. In particular, the highly lucrative slave trade with the ʿAbbāsids created conditions of relative peace and stability from the late second/eighth century up to the Fāṭimid conquest of the early fourth/tenth century.[176] Under such conditions, the need for ascetic warriors (such as the *shurāt* presented) would be limited at best. Third, after the dissolution of the Rustumid imāmate in the fourth/tenth century, political and religious leadership of the Ibāḍī communities of North Africa fell to the local *ʿazzāba* councils consisting of scholars, relegating many prior Ibāḍī institutions (such as the imāmate) to the realm of theory. In fact the earliest recorded North African articulation of the "stages of religion" (*masālik al-dīn*) associates the communal condition (*maslak*) of *shirā'* with the long-dead figure of Abū Bilāl.[177] Likewise the sixth/twelfth-century scholar ʿAbd al-Kāfī outlines how *shirā'* was neither obligatory (*wujūb*) nor required (*farḍ*) but remained an option for those who chose to "exchange" their souls (*yashrī nafsahu*) to God and the Muslims for the cause of establishing an Ibāḍī imāmate. As a "stage" it was the closest to *ẓuhūr* (openness), and its stipulations would come into force for those who chose it for themselves, while the rest of the community remained in a state of *kitmān* (secrecy).[178] However, beyond these kinds of theoretical discussions, there is little actual evidence for the practice of *shirā'* or the existence of *shurāt* in later North African Ibāḍī contexts.

In the Arabian Peninsula, in contrast, the Ibāḍī imāmate survived as a functioning institution well into the modern period, and it is with Omani and Ḥaḍramawtī sources that the further history of *shurāt* and the articulation of the institution of the *shurāt* under the ostensible control of Ibāḍī imāms and *ʿālims* can be traced. As with the uprising of Ṭālib al-Ḥaqq, scholars again figured prominently in directing the practice of *shirā'* during the rebellion of al-Julanda b. Masʿūd. Wilkinson observes that al-Julandā b. Masʿūd and other early Omani imāms were *shārī* "in the sense that as leaders of the *shurāt* their function was to establish the Ibāḍī state, politically and militarily," but that they were known by the caliphal titular *amīr al-mu'minīn* among the soldiery.[179] Unlike Ṭālib al-Ḥaqq, who was primarily an *ʿālim* and secondarily a military leader, al-Julandā b. Masʿūd possessed the requisite martial prowess, but he was deemed to lack sufficient knowledge (*ʿilm*). For this reason his rule was supplemented by an advisory council of three Ibāḍī *'ulamā'*: Hilāl b. 'Aṭiyya; Shabīb b. 'Aṭiyya; and Khalaf b. Ziyād.[180]

Another indicator of the extent to which the Ibāḍī *'ulamā'* had gained a modicum of control over the institution of the *shurāt* comes from Ibn al-Nayyir's *sīra,* which outlines the structure and comportment of the *shurāt* during al-Julandā's uprising and likely relies on his father, al-Nayyir b. 'Abd al-Malik, for his information.[181] Ibn al-Nayyir intended this description to become a model for Imām Ghassān to follow in organizing the *shurāt* of Imām Ghassān's era. Ibn al-Nayyir thus explains how the *shurāt* were organized in groups of two hundred to four hundred persons under the command of a leader.[182] Importantly, he advises the imām, "Let there be among every group of ten a teacher from the people of knowledge to teach them religion, to educate them on what is acceptable, to stop them from deviation, to set them on the [right] road, and guide them on the path of righteousness."[183] Additionally those *shurāt* who could not maintain the ideal of abstinence could be allowed to marry only with the approval of the Iraqi-trained *'ulamā'*.[184] They were to shave their heads and generally refrain from the things of this world. From the above-quoted speech of Abū Bilāl in Ibn al-Nayyir, it is also clear that during the early Omani imāmate, those who opted to join the *shurāt* made a formal pledge (*bay'a*).[185] If Ibn al-Nayyir's *sīra* does in fact reflect the earlier practices of the *shurāt* during the uprising of al-Julandā b. Mas'ūd, then the Ibāḍī *'ulamā'* had by that time aspired to a high level of control over the actual affairs of the *shurāt* (the extent to which they actually achieved this control remains to be seen). Moreover, that Ibn al-Nayyir, some fifty years after the defeat of al-Julandā b. Mas'ūd's uprising, counseled Imām Ghassān to perpetuate this control betrayed an enduring belief among the Ibāḍī *'ulamā'* that the *shurāt* should properly be under their direction.

In addition to Ibn al-Nayyir, several other early Omani Ibāḍī scholars gave their authoritative opinions on the institution of the Ibāḍī *shurāt.* Abū 'Abdullāh Muḥammad Maḥbūb b. al-Raḥīl (that is, Abū Sufyān's son) (d. 260/873), in his *sīra* to the Tripolitanian Ibāḍīs of the Maghrib, mentioned that fighting an enemy was incumbent upon only those who had "exchanged their selves to God in order to command good and forbid evil" (*man sharā nafsahu li-lah 'alā al-amr bi'l-ma'rūf wa'l-nahī 'an al-munkar*) because they were the ones who had committed themselves to the Qur'ānic duty of "forbidding evil." The imām could not compel non-*shurāt* to fight, though it was meritorious for non-*shurāt* to assist those who did fight.[186] Coming several centuries later (and hailing from North Africa), Abū al-'Abbās Aḥmad b. Bakr (d. 504/1111) articulated several of the conditions for the *shurāt* when he stipulated that they

> agree that they sell themselves desiring God's pleasure, and show no claim for ruling, but to end tyranny and revive righteousness. They must not revolt with less [sic] than forty men, [and] they can

> complete that number with a woman. If their intention was not to return before ending falsity (*bāṭil*), they, therefore, must not return to their homes unless they ended falsehood or died. If they went out with the intention to return if they wanted, they can return at any time. Their homes are their swords, so if they return to their original homes for any purpose, they must pray short prayers (*qaṣr*) and pray complete prayers during their revolt even though they were far away from their original homes.[187]

Qaṣr prayers are typically done when journeying,[188] and thus Ibn Bakr implies that the "true home" of the *shurāt* is the battlefield. Additionally *taqiyya* was not permitted to the *shurāt*, and they chose their own leaders from among themselves.[189]

Later Ibāḍī *'ulamā'*, then, conceptualized the *shurāt* as a kind of volunteer force: chaste, tonsured, and ascetic; without fixed residences; and dead to the world, having exchanged their lives for the hereafter and devoted themselves to "commanding good and forbidding evil" once they reached the minimum number of forty persons. They elected and followed their own leader (who in later Ibāḍī literature became more and more associated with the *imām al-shārī*), but the *'ulamā'* and the Ibāḍī imām were to advise them. They imposed upon themselves a kind of *jus in bello* that involved fighting only proper enemies and taking only what could be properly considered theirs by right (and in so doing hearkened back to the model of Abū Bilāl).[190] In short, the spontaneous act of *shirā'* had become an institution, at least among those Ibāḍī *'ulamā'* who wished to see the *shurāt* come under some kind of control.

Reading between the lines of these idealized stipulations, however, it is clear that by the time of the first imāmate (and possibly earlier), the Omani *shurāt* had become a force that needed disciplining: they were not always under the direction of the imām or the Ibāḍī *'ulamā'*, and they were not following the standards that the Ibāḍī *'ulamā'* obviously found increasingly important to specify. In fact Ibn al-Nayyir's *sīra* suggests that by his era the *shurāt* had degenerated into tribal factions and that their commitment to the ascetic ideals of the institution, such as chastity, was less than uniform.[191] Wilkinson suggests that the tribalization of the *shurāt* may have begun as early as the revolt of al-Julandā b. Mas'ūd, and he views the execution of members of al-Julandā's family members at the *shurāt*'s hands as tribal meddling, reflective of their power in directing the course of Omani affairs.[192] The increasingly legislated and idealized institution of *shirā'*, then, is more properly understood as the *'ulamā'*'s attempt to rein in the ever more unruly *shurāt*. The Omani Ibāḍī *'ulamā'*, however, were embroiled in the tribal conflicts that underlay the first Omani imāmate. Indeed, Oman's tribal factionalism gradually brought different *shurāt* groups into alliance with different tribes and the *'ālims* who supported them, effectively turning the *shurāt* into tribal militias under the control of the variously affiliated *ʿālims*.[193] This sad state of affairs ultimately resulted in the civil wars that effectively ended the first Ibāḍī imāmate in Oman.

Ibāḍī narratives of the early *shurāt* provided the rich soil in which the nascent Ibāḍī community could cultivate its identity. These narratives, watered as they were by the late antique and early Islamic streams of hagiography, reflect the regional hagiographies of Mesopotamia but also show evidence of specifically Ibāḍī concerns. Ibāḍīs, of course, viewed themselves neither as products of their environment nor as an Islamic sectarian movement (*firqa*) but rather as the remnant of the original Muslim community, connected through the *shurāt* and Muḥakkima to the first two caliphs and thereby to God's last prophet, Muḥammad. The stories of their righteous martyrs occupied an important place in this chain of authenticity and articulated the piety, rectitude, and truthfulness that were the foundations of the Ibāḍī self-image as *ahl al-istiqāma* (people of righteousness). By collecting, narrating, and thereby focusing attention on the stories of the "very special dead," Ibāḍīs participated in a process of identity creation well known to the religious groups of late antiquity and early Islam, even as they turned those narratives toward their own ends.

Chapter 5

Ibāḍī Boundaries

The notion of boundary maintenance was critical to the ways that the early Muḥakkima and their followers articulated a sense of themselves and their mission in response to those they considered sinners, enemies, and tyrants. It was no accident that the period of the *shurāt* coincided with the era of the early Islamic civil wars in which one group's heroes became another's enemies. The Ibāḍiyya, as inheritors of the early Muḥakkima and *shurāt* movements, elaborated on this rich discursive tradition in their own distinctive ways, such that the notion of establishing boundaries became, along with other institutional features of Ibāḍism such as the imāmate, one of the distinguishing doctrines of the group. Accordingly the enemies of the Muḥakkima and early *shurāt* went on to populate Ibāḍī martyrdom narratives as antiheroes, clarifying in the process the sinfulness, tyranny, and oppression that came to characterize the antithesis of Ibāḍism. Just as in the *shurāt* literature of Iraq, Ibāḍī identity articulation functioned by defining the non-Ibāḍī, against which the emerging Ibāḍī self-image might become all the more clearly demarcated.

This work argues that the initial development of boundary themes among the Muḥakkima and first *shurāt* has been distorted in various ways, especially by non-Ibāḍī Islamic heresiographers, and that a comparative approach allows for some of these misrepresentations to be corrected. In particular it contends that the Muḥakkima and their successors among the early *shurāt* groups up until the point of the Azāriqa and Najdāt did not employ the term *kufr* or practice *takfīr* in the way that later Islamic heresiographers and historians have portrayed them as doing. The portrait of the Muḥakkima and early *shurāt* that comes through in later Islamic sources has been constructed in such a way as to portray a later and far more reified notion of what *kufr* meant and what *takfīr* implied. However, if careful attention is paid to the historical accounts of the Muḥakkima and *shurāt* movements, it is possible to see how their usages of *kufr* and accusations of *takfīr* fit into a broader (and far less defined) universe of terms that were used—often polemically—to designate enemies, sinners, and others who should be opposed or fought. Thus the idea of *kufr* and *takfīr* among the earliest Muḥakkima and *shurāt* was a far more ambiguous endeavor than it was (and is) usually made out to be. Moreover, from the evidence in the historical sources it appears as if the Azāriqa and Najdāt, by adopting a stricter notion of what *kufr* meant and *takfīr* implied, deviated in profound ways from the ways that the earlier *shurāt* had used the term and understood its implications. Quietist *shurāt* and the groups that emerged from among their ranks (such as the Ibāḍiyya), however, likely preserved in their own articulations of the boundary between the faithful and the faux some of the earlier senses of what *kufr* and *takfīr* may have meant.

Yet the Azāriqa and Najdāt had forced the question with their strong stance on how to treat non-Khārijites. Since the Ibāḍiyya (and proto-Ibāḍiyya and quietists before them) found the extremist position untenable, what was to be the proper doctrine? The Azāriqa and Najdāt stance on *takfīr* (such as it was) required refutation, but such rebuffs required their own clarifications on the question of proper boundaries. To some extent the question of boundary maintenance was addressed by the narratives of the early *shurāt,* and especially by that of Abū Bilāl. Ibāḍīs inherited and preserved earlier narrative traditions on the *shurāt,* even as Ibāḍī figures such as Abū Sufyān molded those stories toward their own ends. It is possible, therefore, to discern in the actions of the *shurāt* (as they were preserved by the Ibāḍiyya) models for how combatants should properly act in relation to those they fought. Abū Bilāl in particular became the model for the Ibāḍī *shurāt:* his tolerance and moderation during his rebellion were taken as emblematic of how the Ibāḍī *shurāt* should properly act toward non-Ibāḍīs. Simultaneously, Ibāḍī sources betray a measure of ambivalence toward some of the early *shurāt* figures who in non-Ibāḍī sources were often depicted as having engaged in questionable acts of violence: ʻAbd al-Raḥmān b. Muljam, Qarīb b. Murra, Zuḥḥāf al-Ṭāʾī, and Ṭawwāf b. ʻAllāq presented characters whose stories clearly posed certain problems for Ibāḍī authors. In attempting to make sense of this inherited tradition, these narratives often became (either by design or by accident) garbled, shortened, swapped, censured, or simply forgotten.

Also noted have been the strong textual parallels between Ibāḍī and non-Ibāḍī (especially North African and Iraqi) sources on the Muḥakkima and early *shurāt.* These textual parallels include certain shared passages that conceptualize ʻAlī's transgression in accepting arbitration using a variety of different terms: thus Ibāḍī sources—especially al-Barrādī—preserve the Muḥakkima's comment that the people of Syria and ʻAlī's supporters were "competing in *kufr* like betting horses";[1] Ḥurqūṣ b. Zuhayr's demand that ʻAlī repent his "mistake" (*khatīʾa*) and his "sin" (*dhanb*);[2] and Ibn Wahb al-Rāsibī's speech in which he called for the Muḥakkima to leave Kūfa, escaping "this misguiding innovation, these mistaken whims, and these tyrannous judgments" (*al-bid'a al-muḍilla wa'l-ahwā' al-muzilla wa'l-aḥkām al-jā'ira*).[3] Because of this parallelism, the same observations that can be made about the usage of the term *kufr* and the implications of *takfīr* in historical texts can be applied to Ibāḍī texts on the *shurāt* as well: Ibāḍī sources preserve the ambiguity of the Muḥakkima's usage of *kufr* and *takfīr* as well as the terms that seem to function as analogues for the notion of *kufr* (that is, *dhanb, shakk, khaṭī'a, bid'a,* and so forth) among them.

Material that is exclusive to Ibāḍī sources merely strengthens the observation that a range of terms (beyond *kufr*) was associated with 'Alī's acceptance of arbitration. On the one hand, al-Barrādī reports that a group of Iraqis challenged 'Alī over his status when he accepted the arbitration ("if you were a *kāfir* then we dissociate from you in your *kufr*") and refused to "bear witness among ourselves to *kufr*" by accepting arbitration.[4] On the other hand, another report (on the authority of al-Fazārī) mentions that those in 'Alī's army who detested the *taḥkīm* used to say to those who accepted it, "oh you enemies of God! You disobeyed God (*'aṣaytum Allāh*) and you judged in a matter of God, you doubted the religion of God (*shakkaktum fī dīn Allāh*) and you differed [in opinion] from the Book of God (*khāliftum fī kitāb Allāh*)."[5] A report in al-Qalhātī and al-Izkawī on 'Ammār b. Yāsir's reaction to the *taḥkīm* has 'Ammār say, "Should we doubt our religion, and forsake our discernment [*a'shakkaknā fī dīninā wa artadadnā 'an baṣā'irinā*]?"[6] As in non-Ibāḍī sources, other terms, such as *ma'ṣiya, shakk, irtidād* (though not in the sense of "apostasy"), and *khilāf,* appear alongside *kufr* as descriptors marking the transgression of arbitration, and it is not altogether clear the extent to which these concepts remain conterminous. The ambiguity of non-Ibāḍī sources regarding the exact nature of 'Alī's offense, it seems, finds its equivalent in Ibāḍī sources on the Muḥakkima.

In many ways it was precisely the ambiguity of these boundary themes in the narratives of the early *shurāt* that—in the aftermath of the Azraqite and Najdite uprisings of the late first/seventh century—begged the question for the nascent Ibāḍiyya of the proper stance toward non-Ibāḍīs. Narratives of the early *shurāt,* as it turned out (and with the exception of Abū Bilāl), did not offer much guidance on the precise definitions of non-Ibāḍīs or on how they should be treated. That such questions remained live issues for the early community can be seen in the example of Abū Muḥammad al-Nahdī, a contemporary of Abū 'Ubayda and Abū Mawdūd (Ḥājib al-Ṭā'ī) who held to the idea that wrongdoers (*ahl al-aḥdāth*) were neither believers nor polytheists but were *kuffār* and publically inveighed against the caliph Hishām, his governor Khālid b. 'Abdullāh al-Qasrī, and al-Ḥasan al-Baṣrī over the issue of God's *qadar.*[7] It was not al-Nahdī's stance that earned him the censure of his fellow proto-Ibāḍīs; the idea that sinners were *kuffār* but not *mushrikūn* was widely held, though not uniformly articulated, among proto-Ibāḍīs. Rather it was al-Nahdī's public abuse of these figures during a time when the proto-Ibāḍī community was in a state of secrecy, and practicing *taqiyya,* that brought down the community's criticism. The question of boundary maintenance and its implications for the community, then, occupied the nascent Ibāḍiyya in several different ways, and it is worth examining how the early Ibāḍiyya established their identity vis-à-vis non-Ibāḍīs.

Walāya and *Barā'a* in Early Ibāḍī Thought

Ibāḍīs discuss the proper boundaries of the community under the rubrics of *walāya* (association) and *barā'a* (dissociation)—two distinctive and early Ibāḍī doctrines that continued to receive attention in later Ibāḍī writings.[8] These concepts outline acceptance or rejection of an individual in the community of believers, the exercise of attendant duties toward those considered "associates" (*awliyā'*), as well as the identification and rejection of those considered outside the community.[9] Although characteristically Ibāḍī notions, the roots of *walāya* and *barā'a* can be found in sources that preceded the Ibāḍiyya: indeed *walāya* and *barā'a* can be said to be rooted in Qur'ānic (even pre-Islamic) notions of affiliation and dissociation.[10] Thus verse 3:28 cautions, "let not believers take disbelievers as allies (*awliyā'*) rather than believers"; 10:41 directs those who suffer the denials of the revelations to say, "For me are my deeds, and for you are your deeds. You are disassociated (*intum bar'ūna*) from what I do, and I am disassociated (*ana bari'un*) from what you do"; and 9:114 explains that "when it became apparent to Ibrāhīm that his father was an enemy of God, he disassociated himself from him (*tabarra'a minhu*)." While the root *w-l-y* has several layers of meaning, the relationship of *walā'* in the pre-Islamic and early Islamic periods designated an amicable affiliation that involved the responsibility of protection (thus *awliyā'* can even denote legal guardians).[11] *Barā'a* involved the severance of relations, often on the basis of evident sinfulness. In the Qur'ān such sinfulness was most often polytheism, as in the story of Ibrāhīm's father.[12]

Based as the ideas of *walāya* and *barā'a* were in early tribal and Qur'ānic notions of affiliation and dissociation, they became some of the means by which early Muslims in general negotiated the boundaries of the Islamic community. Non-Ibāḍī sources point toward the use of this terminology among early Muslims, including and especially the Muḥakkima and early *shurāt.* Abū Mikhnaf's account of the "split" (*tafrīq*) between the supposed founders of the Azāriqa, Ṣufriyya, and Ibāḍiyya recounts how a group of "Khārijites" sought out and questioned Ibn al-Zubayr in the interest of forming an alliance against the Umayyads. Giving his views on 'Uthmān, Ibn al-Zubayr was said to have declared, "I am an associate (*walī*) of Ibn 'Affān in this world and the next, and an associate of his associates (*walī awliyā'ihi*) and an enemy of his enemies." The Khārijites then broke with him, declaring, "may God dissociate himself from you (*bari' Allāhu minka*), oh enemy of God!" The same account tells of 'Abdullāh b. Ibāḍ's dissociation from Nāfi' b. al-Azraq for considering sinners to be the equivalent of polytheists, and 'Abdullāh b. Ṣaffār declared his dissociation from them both.[13] Although the historicity of Abū Mikhnaf's *tafrīq* account may be justly questioned, the narrative points to the importance of the language of *walāya* and *barā'a* in staking out claims of affiliation and establishing communal boundaries in the early Islamic period.

Later Khārijites too employed the language of *walāya* and *barā'a.* A follower of Shabīb b. Yazīd al-Shaybānī was said to have uttered to al-Ḥajjāj,

> I dissociate (*abrā*) before God from 'Amr [b. al-'Aṣ] and his supporters.
> And from 'Alī and from the Companions of Ṣiffīn
> And from Mu'āwiya the tempter (*al-ghāwī*) and his supporters,
> May God bless the fortunate people (*al-qawm al-mayāmīn*).[14]

The dichotomy between the early figures ('Amr, 'Alī, Mu'āwiya, and those at Ṣiffīn) from whom the poet dissociates and the blessing called down upon the "fortunate people" in the last stanza serves to establish clear lines of affiliation.

Given that the Ibāḍiyya inherited much from the early Muḥakkima movement and the *shurāt* who followed them, including their preoccupation with communal boundaries, it is small wonder that early Ibāḍī texts contain abundant discussions of *walāya* and *barā'a.* Even before the advent of the Ibāḍī movement in Basra, the question of conduct in relation to those not considered full Muslims was already complex. As a reflection of this complex inheritance, proto- and early Ibāḍī discussions of these concepts operated on several levels and negotiated identity in a number of different ways. Despite the strong rejection of the Azraqite stance on non-Azraqīs, Ibāḍī notions of communal boundaries remained far from uniform in their initial conceptualizations.

On the most basic level, *walāya* was conceived as a duty owed to fellow Muslims, and it could be determined on the basis of piety (including acceptance of certain key Ibāḍī tenets such as the rejection of illegitimate caliphs) and conduct; *barā'a* or suspension of judgment (*wuqūf*) was similarly required in relation to those who fell short. An early Ibāḍī *sīra* attributed to Abū Mawdūd Ḥājib al-Ṭā'ī, for example, says that *walāya* may be offered only to those who accept and act upon the truths of God's chosen religion for humankind (that is, *islām*).[15] *Barā'a,* in contrast, is given to a person who makes evident "rejection [of religion] (*al-kadhb*), hypocrisy (*al-nifāq*), uncertainty (*al-shakk*), and doubt in the truth (*al-rayb fi'l-ḥaqq*), because these characteristics do not describe the believer, and they do not confirm him in the [acceptance of the] truth (*lā tuḥaqqu 'alayhi*). It is not seeming that [a believer] should display [these characteristics]: a believer is not recognized by them, nor do they confirm *islām* upon those who are known by them whilst they do not repent."[16] Later in the manuscript Abū Mawdūd clarifies that "a person leaves *walāya* and enters *wuqūf* when they do [*sic*] something in which there is doubt; and they leave *walāya* for *barā'a* when there is proof of their opposing the truth that is known from the book of God, the *sunna* of His prophet, and the accumulated traditions of the righteous (*athār al-ṣāliḥīn*)."[17] A statement attributed to Abū al-Naḍr Bisṭām b. 'Umar b. al-Musayyib (d. latter half of the second/eighth century), an early convert from the Ṣufriyya, corroborates this basic view of the doctrines. When called to the Ibāḍī view, Abū al-Naḍr related that the Ibāḍiyya said, "we call you to *walāya* of those who you have known to declare the truth and act by it; and to *barā'a* of those who you have known to declare what differs from the truth and to act by it; and to reserve judgment (*al-wuqūf*) in what you do not know until you learn it."[18] A fragment of 'Abdullāh b. Yazīd al-Fazārī's *Kitāb al-Futyā* makes clear that association with believers and dissociation from unbelievers (*kāfir*) were obligations for Muslims since the time of the *fitna*.[19] When it was not possible to be sure which a person was, Muslims were obliged to abstain from judgment (*waqf*) until such time as it could be determined. In the *Kitāb fī man Raja' 'an 'Ilmihi*, al-Fazārī defines *wuqūf* as the relinquishing of both *walāya* and *barā'a*.[20]

Determining the status of a person, however, was not always straightforward. The early Maghribī Ibāḍī community, for example, was faced with such a dilemma after the two Ibāḍī rebels who conquered Tripolitania in 124/741 C.E., 'Abd al-Jabbār b. Qays al-Murādī and al-Ḥārith b. Talīd al-Ḥaḍramī, were found dead (around 131/748 C.E.) with their swords in each other.[21] As (proto-)Ibāḍīs, 'Abd al-Jabbār and al-Ḥārith had enjoyed *walāya*, but what was to be their status in the wake of their mutual murders? Was the community to dissociate from one or both of them, or to reserve judgment, or were they to remain in a state of *walāya* until it was proved that they merited *barā'a*? An epistle from Abū 'Ubadya and Abū Mawdūd on the subject counseled *wuqūf* in an attempt to preserve the unity of the community, and this became the stance of the Nukkārī Ibāḍī communities in North Africa.[22] However, those who followed the Rustumid line of imāms and who called themselves the Wahbī Ibāḍiyya ('Abdullāh b. Wahab al-Rāsibī) counseled that al-Ḥārith and 'Abd al-Jabbār should remain in their former state of *walāya* until it was known definitively (*yaqīnan*) that they merited *barā'a*.[23]

Walāya and *barā'a* also became means by which the early community enforced the parameters of proper belief. An account in al-Shammākhī narrates how Abū 'Ubayda dissociated from some youths who insisted that a Christian who had not heard of the Prophet Muḥammad was a believer but that the Zoroastrian (*rajul min al-majūs*) who had been converted to Christianity by this same Christian was a *kāfir*.[24] Distraught that Abū 'Ubayda had declared his *barā'a* from them, the youths went to Abū Mawdūd and asked him to intervene. Abū Mawdūd informed Abū 'Ubayda of their repentance, and they were allowed to rejoin the Ibāḍīs in their meeting (*majlis*).[25] In this way the concepts of *walāya* and *barā'a* also functioned as mechanisms of enforcing proper belief and action.

To the extent that it was possible, then, *walāya* and *barā'a* were to be based on a person's demonstrated piety and conduct. Al-Fazārī, summarizing the beliefs of "our companions" on the issue of *walāya* and *barā'a,* notes that they accepted anyone who acknowledged that allowing what God has forbidden renders a person no longer a believer (*ghayr mu'min*). A corollary to this requirement made *barā'a* a requirement for those who supported or condoned illegitimate caliphs or who otherwise committed forbidden acts. However, living as Muslims did in the "abode of monotheism and hypocrisy" (*dār al-tawḥīd wa nifāq*)—that is, for Ibāḍīs practicing *taqiyya* among non-Ibāḍīs who, because of their acceptance of and support for illegitimate caliphs, rendered themselves not fully Muslims—open dissociation was not practical.[26] Moreover, al-Fazārī noted, Ibāḍī scholars had required offenses (such as false beliefs) to be acknowledged only when they became apparent; in this way false beliefs among the general non-Ibāḍī population could be tolerated so long as they remained concealed. For his part, al-Fazārī self-consciously broke with past Ibāḍī precedent by arguing that deviant theological beliefs also excluded the holder of said beliefs from full status as a Muslim; in this way al-Fazārī excluded not only those who committed forbidden acts but also militant Khārijites and Qadarites who, in his view, did not merit *walāya* because of their deviant interpretations of the Qur'ān.[27] Al-Fazārī's view, however, was a departure from the general early Ibāḍī stance of either determining *walāya* or *barā'a* based on a person's demonstrated actions or, as was likely the most common case, refraining from doing so in the absence of evidence.

Ibāḍī emphasis on proper action as the determining factor in establishing a relationship of *walāya* or *barā'a* likewise becomes evident from Ibāḍī legal treatises from the early period. An epistle (*risāla*) on *zakāt* that is attributed to Abū 'Ubayda, for example, specifies those persons who may properly receive the *zakāt*—and thus those who would be considered members of the community—on the basis of their actions, specifically their piety or sinfulness.[28] Abū 'Ubayda declares that a person who sins against, curses, or leads astray a Muslim or who says to a Muslim, "Oh you enemy of God!" is not entitled to *zakāt* and is thus not considered a member of the community.[29] Abū 'Ubayda outlines several actions that would invalidate a potential recipient's ability to receive *zakāt,* and although this particular discussion does not use the terms *walāya* and *barā'a,* he is nevertheless plainly concerned with establishing the proper boundaries of the community on the basis of demonstrated piety. A similar opinion on *zakāt* is attributed to the Rustumid imām Aflāh b. 'Abd al-Wahhāb, though Ḍumām b. al-Sā'ib held that Ibāḍīs could give their *zakāt* to non-Ibāḍī relatives.[30] In a similar legal vein, a reference to *walāya* and *barā'a* in the *Futyā al-Rabī' b. Ḥabīb* contains the opinion of two late second/eighth-century scholars, 'Abdullāh b. 'Abd al-Azīz and Abū al-Mu'arrij 'Amr al-Sadūsī, on the status of one who wipes over his socks/sandals (that is, *al-masḥ 'alā al-khuffayn*) during *wuḍū'* instead of washing the feet.[31] Here again certain ritual actions determine the status of the actor with respect to the community. From a slightly later period, a statement attributed to the Rustumid imām 'Abd al-Wahhāb b. 'Abd al-Raḥmān in the *Kitāb Ibn Sallām* includes in a list of actions that comprise the act of submission (and thus the proper practice of Islam) "bearing witness to the people of guidance [on account of] their guidance, and association with them in it (*wa walāyatuhum 'alayhi*), and bearing witness to the people of misguidance (*ahl al-ḍalāla*) in their misguidance, and dissociation from them (*al-barā'a minhum*)."[32] Such references indicate that the concepts of *walāya* and *barā'a* were strongly connected to the performance of correct and pious deeds (in conformity with an emerging sense of what constituted *sharī'a* to Ibāḍī legal scholars) and thus found a place among those fundamental actions that comprised Islam, properly observed, or its rejection.

Other early Ibāḍī references to *walāya* and *barā'a* indicate that these concepts established a sense of community boundaries by connecting the Ibāḍiyya to or severing them from earlier generations. Ibn Ibāḍ's so-called "first letter" uses the concepts of *walāya* and *barā'a* to place the Ibāḍī community in a relationship of continuity with the Muḥakkima and *shurāt* movements and to specify those who lay outside of this relationship.[33] Thus, Ibn Ibāḍ claims that the Ibāḍiyya remain the "enemies of those who make them their enemies, and the affiliates (*awliyā'*) of those who affiliate with them."[34] He specifies, however, that "we dissociate (*nabra'*) . . . from Ibn al-Azraq and his followers." Elsewhere in some versions of Ibn Ibāḍ's letter, he adds, "when the believers saw what 'Uthmān did out of disobedience to God, they dissociated from him."[35] Similarly, Ibn Dhakwān claims that "we affiliate (*natawalla*) to Muslims who lived before our time and whom we have not seen, on the strength of the testimony of the Muslims; and we disown (*nabra'*) the imams of wrongdoing (*ā'immat al-ẓulm*) and their associates (*awliyā'ihim*) who lived before our time and whom we have not seen, on the strength of the testimony of the Muslims."[36] In this way *walāya* and *barā'a* could extend to past generations, becoming means by which Ibāḍīs established the pious pedigree of their group, forged a connection through the early Muḥakkima movement to the early caliphs, and rejected those whom they considered beyond the pale of proper religion. Indeed the roots of what would become the Ibāḍī "teacher lines" can be discerned in the creation of these lists of pious ancestors who merited *walāya*.

Later Ibāḍī writings expanded on this generational articulation of *walāya* and *barā'a* as means to establish the pious lineage of the Ibāḍiyya. The eighth/fourteenth-century North African Ibāḍī scholar Abū Ṭāhir Ismā'īl b. Mūsā al-Jayṭālī, for example, extended the duty of *walāya* to include (among others) all believers (among *jinn* and human beings) of every age up to the Day of Judgment, all the prophets, the priests and monks mentioned in Qur'ān 5:82–85, the people of the cave (*ahl al-kahf*), the people of the trench (*aṣḥāb al-ukhdūd*), the people of Yūnis (Jonah) mentioned in Qur'ān 10:98, as well as the "Sorcerers of Pharaoh" mentioned in Qur'ān 7:120–22.[37] Additionally al-Jayṭālī required *walāya* for Abū Ḍharr al-Ghifārī based on the Prophetic ḥadīth that described God's blessings toward him.[38] Al-Jayṭālī also mentions the *walāya* owed to the imāms of the Muslims: Abū Bakr, 'Umar, 'Abdullāh b. Yaḥyā al-Kindī, Abū al-Khaṭṭāb 'Abd al-A'lā b. al-Samḥ al-Ma'ārifī, al-Julandā b. Mas'ūd, and 'Abd al-Raḥmān b. Rustum and his progeny among the Rustumid imāms.[39]

In Oman the first methodical exposition of *walāya* and *barā'a* was the third/ninth-century legal work of Abū Jābir Muḥammad b. Ja'far, the *Jāmi'*, which treated the concepts in a chapter devoted to them.[40] Ennāmi notes that in North Africa the first systematic study was the fifth/eleventh-century *Kitāb al-Tuḥaf al-Makhzūna wa'l-Jawāhir al-Maṣūna* of Abū al-Rabī' Sulaymān b. Yakhlaf al-Mazātī (d. 471/1098).[41] Such works represent the attempt to gather and structure the scattered and varied opinions of earlier Ibāḍī scholars.

In these ways the early Ibāḍī concepts of *walāya* and *barā'a* established a notion of communal boundaries by building upon Qur'ānic, early Islamic and early Muḥakkimite, and *shurāt* notions of inclusion and exclusion. The community of believers was to include those held in *walāya;* all others were ultimately excluded, either explicitly so through the practice of *barā'a* or through the suspension of judgment, an action that nevertheless precluded full inclusion so long as a person's status remained undecided. The basis for determining *walāya* or *barā'a* remained, with some notable exceptions, the demonstrated actions of an individual, most importantly one's acknowledgment of the illegitimacy of the Umayyad caliphs insofar as this acknowledgment was connected with accepting that allowing forbidden acts (such as those perpetrated by the illegitimate caliphs) rendered one a non-Muslim. These concepts also allowed for a sense of historical boundaries, providing a connection to pious predecessors and rejecting past enemies.

Taxonomies of Unbelief

Conceptually linked to the question of *walāya* and *barā'a* and thus to the notion of communal identity were the classifications and treatment of non-Ibāḍīs. Those who did not enjoy full *walāya* were, by definition, not full believers, but what kind of nonbelievers were they? Beyond the dispensations allowed by the practice of *taqiyya,* what was to be done with those from whom one dissociated or with whom one had suspended judgment? Once it was determined that non-Ibāḍīs could not all be tarred—in the manner of the Azāriqa and Najdāt—with the brush of *kufr* or *shirk,* it remained to classify what sorts of non-Ibāḍīs existed in the world and how Ibāḍīs were to engage with them. This need to establish clear taxonomies of non-Ibāḍīs and to specify the proper responses to these groups undoubtedly became more pressing in the wake of the uprisings by Ṭālib al-Ḥaqq and al-Julanda b. Mas'ūd as well as those in North Africa, all of which forced Ibāḍīs into violent confrontations with and brought them into positions of power over non-Ibāḍīs.

Several non-Ibāḍī sources, namely histories and heresiographies, have attributed to the Ibāḍiyya, via Ibn Ibāḍ, a conceptualization of *kufr* into two aspects: *kufr al-shirk,* which denoted disbelief proper; and *kufr al-ni'ma,* which seemed to indicate a kind of sinful ingratitude that, while not rendering the offender the equivalent of a polytheist, nonetheless indicated that person's less-than-full status as a Muslim.[42] Allegedly this stance was the means by which the Ibāḍiyya distinguished themselves from other Khārijite groups, especially the Azāriqa and Najdāt, insofar as the doctrine of *kufr al-ni'ma* (var. *kuffār bil-ni'am/lil-ni'am/al-ni'am*) allowed the Ibāḍiyya to evade treating these *kuffār bil-ni'am* (and their children) as polytheists, to marry and inherit from them, and to live among them peacefully while practicing *taqiyya.* Such a view has been accepted widely among contemporary Ibāḍīs.[43]

Nevertheless, Crone and Zimmerman have shown that by and large, the terminology of *kufr al-ni'ma* was absent from early Ibāḍī sources before the epistle of Khālid b. Qaḥṭān (that is, ca. 287/900 C.E.) and thereafter appears in an unsystematic fashion. They also point out that *kufr al-ni'ma* was a pan-Islamic concept in use before the era of Abū Mikhnaf: although some Ibāḍīs may well have experimented with it, it was not exclusive to them, nor did it fully distinguish the way that they conceptualized non-Ibāḍīs.[44] Crone and Zimmerman note the prevalence of other terminology, especially the concept of *nifāq* (hypocrisy)/*munāfiqūn* (hypocrites), as the means by which early Ibāḍīs distinguished non-Ibāḍī Muslims and, citing Sālim b. Dhakwān, al-Rabī' b. Ḥabīb, Wā'il b. Ayyūb, and Munīr b. al-Nayyir as their earliest examples, implying that the language of *nifāq* became prevalent among Ibāḍīs beginning in the late second/eighth century. To this list can now be added al-Fazārī, who employs the term *kāfir munāfiq* in the *Kitāb fī man Raja'a 'an 'Ilmihi* to describe a person who will admit that the Qur'ān was originated in time but will not admit that it is created.[45]

Evidence from other Ibāḍī *siyar* points toward yet earlier taxonomies of unbelief—that is, even before the use of *nifāq/munāfiqūn.* Specifically, early Ibāḍī classifications of *kufr* and sin can be found in a *risāla* attributed to Abū 'Ubayda and Abū Mawdūd and in which the natures of faith and its opposites are discussed; in al-Sayfī's *siyar* collection this is called the *risālat Abī 'Ubayda wa Abī Mawdūd Ḥājib fī'l-radd 'alā al-Murji'a:* "Abū 'Ubayda and Abū Mawdūd Ḥājib's Epistle Refuting the Murji'ites," and it is hereafter referred to as the "Epistle Refuting the Murji'ites."[46] This *risāla* frames faith and *kufr* with a mytho-history of the creation whereby Iblīs's original act of disobedience opened the way for varieties of *kufr* to enter the world and become manifest among human beings. Abū 'Ubadya and Abū Mawdūd open their "Epistle Refuting the Murji'ites" by arguing that faithfulness to God was the original condition of the creation: "The genesis of faith came with the knowledge (*al-ma'rifa*) that God created in the totality of His creation."[47] The *risāla* implies that faithfulness is the natural state of created beings, quoting the Qur'ān to the effect that faithfulness was the "*fiṭra* of God by which he has created [all] people; no change should there be in the creation of God. That is the correct religion, but most of the people do not know" (30:30). However, the *risāla* continues, God tests his creation by what they choose to do with this knowledge so that he might know the sincere (*al-ṣādiqīn/al-ladhi ṣadaqū*) from the false (*al-kādhibīn*). In this way obedience (*al-ṭā'a*) and disobedience (*al-ma'ṣiya*) entered the realm of created things. Most of the creation—except some *jinn* and humans—chose obedience, and they were confirmed in the truth of their knowledge (*ṣidq al-ma'rifa*), in their being faithful, and in the reward that came with it. However, God's "test" (*al-balā*) also brought disobedience into the world as well as introducing *kufr* and the insistence on disobedience (*al-iṣrār*): "from disobedience began *kufr,* and by insistence in disobedience, *kufr* came [into being] before insistence."[48] Those who chose disobedience (the *ahl al-ma'ṣiya*) "left the sincerity of knowledge, its classification [as believers] and its reward, and entered into disbelief, confirming the classification of *kufr* and its recompense upon [themselves]."[49] This original act of disobedience, the *risāla* explains, was the origin of *kufr,* which was generated through the insistence on disobedience.

Leaving generalities, Abū 'Ubayda and Abū Mawdūd then specify that it was Iblīs who was the first to disobey, and so through him came the "genesis of disobedience" and the first act of *kufr* through insistence on disobedience.[50] Iblīs became the "imām of *kufr*" and based in this foundation of *kufr* instigated the path of the people of insistence (in disobedience) (*ahl al-iṣrār*). However, after Iblīs led Adam into disobedience, God, out of his mercy, opened the "gate of repentance" (*bāb al-tawba*) and established the means by which the people of disobedience could return from their *kufr* to true knowledge, to faith, and to its rewards.

Nevertheless, Iblīs continued to call human beings to *kufr,* trusting in his ability to lead them astray. Abū 'Ubayda and Abū Mawdūd then describe how Iblīs opened "the gates of disobedience" (*abwāb al-ma'ṣiya*) and introduced different types of sin that would "cause dissention among [human beings] (*yaftinuhum bihā*)."[51] Those to whom Iblīs made the world beautiful and alluring and who forsook the next world fell into disobedience, and Iblīs taught them insistence in it. By this insistence in disobedience "they entered the *walāya* of the enemy of God, Iblīs, and into the root of his *kufr*." For some, Iblīs opened "the gates of *bid'a,* of *shirk* and [other than *shirk*] among the gates of misguidance (*abwāb al-ḍalāla*)," making these ways appealing until they "snatched the religion that would have brought closeness to God." In this way Iblīs brought the various classifications of *kufr* and sin into the world.

Getting to their specific taxonomy of unbelief, Abū 'Ubayda and Abū Mawdūd elucidate that in Iblīs's religion (*da'wa*), *kufr* is of two types: one related to insistence in sin (*al-iṣrār*); and the other related to the allures of the world (*zayyina*).[52] *Kufr,* they assure their audience, remains singular, and its people are the people of disobedience. But the disobedience in which there is *kufr* is itself of two types: that of knowledge (*'ilm*); and that of ignorance (*jahāla*). Regarding the disobedience of knowledge, Abū 'Ubayda and Abū Mawdūd explain that because the knowledgeable person is aware of his/her sinfulness, *kufr* results from insistence on these sins.

As for the *kufr* that results from the allure of the world and the innovations (*zayyinat al-bid'a*) that snatch religion away from a person, it too is of two types: that of *shirk;* and that of "other than *shirk*" (*dūn al-shirk*). *Shirk* is to abandon God's call (*da'wa*) or the worship of God (*'ibāda*). The other type comes in what "the people of *tawḥīd* invented in [their] religion, in which they departed from the community of Muslims and made licit what was forbidden to them."[53] In this way Abū 'Ubayda and Abū Mawdūd introduce the Ibāḍī distinction between *kufr* that is *shirk* proper and *kufr* that relates to non-Ibāḍī Muslims—here called the "people of *tawḥīd*" to distinguish them from *mushrikūn.* Regarding the category into which the *kuffār* among the people of *tawḥīd* fall, Abū 'Ubayda and Abū Mawdūd introduce a further distinction: "the familiar nature (*al-'ahd*) of [this type of *kufr*] without *shirk* is of two types: the type involving the craving of the self (*shahwat al-nafs*) for the things of the world (*li-dhāt al-dunyā*); and the [final] type involving a hardness of heart, harshness, arrogance, and insolence for the command of God."[54] In this fashion Abū 'Ubayda and Abū Mawdūd lay out a taxonomy of *kufr* and its types that distinguishes between *kufr* that results from insistence in disobedience, *kufr* that comes from introducing inventions into religion and becoming enticed by the world, and *shirk* proper.

The "Epistle Refuting the Murji'ites" remains somewhat unique. Other *siyar* attributed to Abū 'Ubayda and/or Abū Mawdūd give descriptions of the nature of *kufr,* but they do not provide a comprehensive classification of *kufr* or distinguish between *kufr* and *shirk.* Nor do they provide their descriptions of faith and its opposites in the form of a mytho-history that discusses the genesis of disbelief as the result of the devil. Thus, Abū 'Ubayda assures in another *sīra* that "whoso wishes to alter the judgment of God, change what He has revealed, replace the Word with other than what He said, . . . he is ejected from Islam."[55] Likewise, Abū Mawdūd in his own *sīra* specifies that all "who commit great sins (*'āmil bi-kabīr al-ma'āṣī*) and hold to them (*qā'il 'alayhi*) without justification are *kāfirs*," as are those who "hold to other than the truth in His books and the *sunna* of His prophet, and in what His *awliyā'* follow (*bi-mā sunnahu awliyāuhu*) and profess (*dānū bihi*)," as well as those who "abandon the ritual actions (*farā'iḍ*) . . . or commit a thing from among the sins (*min al-ma'āṣī*) that disprove [adherence to] Islam by their commission."[56] While these descriptions tend to bolster Abū 'Ubayda and Abū Mawdūd's classifications of sin in their "Epistle Refuting the Murji'ites," they offer no distinction between *kufr* and *shirk*, nor do they no outline a comprehensive taxonomy of *kufr* or find its genesis in Iblīs. The "Epistle Refuting the Murji'ites" remains exceptional in providing a comprehensive taxonomy of unbelief.[57]

Notably, none of Abū 'Ubayda and Abū Mawdūd's early *siyar* employ the language of *nifāq* (as technical terminology) to describe non-Ibāḍī Muslims. While Abū Mawdūd's *sīra* mentions *nifāq* as a characteristic of those who merit *barā'a*, the word is given amid a long list of sins, and it is not used in a technical sense to define non-Ibāḍīs.[58] This absence seems to argue favorably for an early date to these *siyar:* slightly later Ibāḍī authors, such as Sālim b. Dhakwān, Khalaf b. Ziyād al-Baḥrānī, al-Fazārī, and Wā'il b. Ayyūb, used *nifāq* and its variants as the preferred means by which non-Ibāḍī Muslims were classified. Thus, Sālim b. Dhakwān argues that the Prophet Muḥammad divided *kuffār* into five categories, and it is these categories that Muslims must use when classifying non-Ibāḍīs of their own era: Arab polytheists (*mushrikū al-'arab*); Zoroastrians (*majūs*); People of the Book (*ahl al-kitāb*); hypocrites (*munāfiqūn*); and people of the *qibla* whom it has become lawful to kill.[59] Non-Ibāḍī Muslims fall into the last two categories, especially that of *munāfiqūn,* while the final category refers to those who have committed capital offenses.

Khalaf b. Ziyād al-Baḥrānī's *sīra* classifies people into six categories, one of which refers to Muslims while the remaining five refer to *kuffār* (of which one designates non-Ibāḍī Muslims): hypocrites; Jews; Christians; Zoroastrians; and polytheists (*mushrikūn;* also *ahl al-awthān*).[60] Each of these categories, along with the Muslims who comprise the first category, has associated beliefs (literally "professions" [*aqwāl*]) and actions (*af'āl*) through which they become known and by which their classification becomes fixed. Only slightly later in the same folio, Ibn Ziyād uses the words "the people of confirmed mischief from among the people of the *qibla* [*ahl al-aḥdāth fī'l-iqrār min ahl al-qibla*]" synonymously with "hypocrites." It is thus clear that "hypocrite" is the category that encompasses non-Ibāḍī Muslims, as they are the people whom the Ibāḍiyya consider to have sinned (*aḥdatha*) while sharing the same prayer direction.

Wā'il b. Ayyūb's *sīra* takes the category of *munāfiqūn* to refer to non-Ibāḍī Muslims, basing this in part on Qur'ān 9:77: "So He made the consequence [to be] hypocrisy in their hearts until the day when they shall meet Him, because they broke their word to God, that they promised Him, and because they lied." Explaining this category (and employing language similar to Ibn Ziyād's), Ibn Ayyūb states that the designation "people of *shirk*" brings together *mushrikūn* proper and "the people of confirmed mischief from among the people of the *qibla* [*ahl al-aḥdāth fī'l-iqrār min ahl al-qibla*]."[61] This is because *kufr* is of two kinds: *kufr shirk,* which makes incumbent the rules pertaining to the *mushrikūn* and clearly refers to polytheists proper; and the *kufr* of actions (*kufr bil-a'māl*), which refers to hypocrites. The *munāfiqūn* are those who "through affirmation [of their sins] enter the greater gate [of hypocrisy], leaving minor hypocrisy with their neglect of what God has commanded them to obey and has enjoined on them from His truth, [with their] doing what God has forbidden them (*mā ḥarama Allāh 'alayhim*) out of disobedience to Him, and committing what God has banned for them (*mā nahāhum Allāh 'anhu*) from the actions that He has prohibited (*min ḥaramātihi*). This is the *kufr* of the people of affirmation [of sin] (*ahl al-iqrār*), insofar as they judge by other than what God has sent down, and turn away from the command of God."[62] Hypocrites are thus different from *mushrikūn* but nonetheless possess a status as less than full Muslims through their willful persistence in sin.

From this brief cross-examination of early Ibāḍī taxonomies of *kufr,* it becomes abundantly clear that no consensus existed among early Ibāḍīs as to the precise terminology to be used to describe the many variations of *kuffār,* especially those *kuffār* who were non-Ibāḍī Muslims. Early authors, such as Abū 'Ubayda and Abū Mawdūd, spoke of non-Ibāḍīs as the people of disobedience or insistence, or as those entranced by the world into committing innovations in religion. Slightly later authors, such as Ibn Dhakwān, Ibn Ziyād, al-Fazārī, and Ibn Ayyūb, tended to use the term "hypocrite" to describe non-Ibāḍī Muslims. Nevertheless behind these various terminologies lies consent on a number of points. First, early Ibāḍīs clearly held that there was only belief and unbelief and nothing in between (as the Mu'tazilites would later argue). Second, all these early authors agreed that there was a difference between the *kufr* that resulted from polytheism (*shirk*) and the *kufr* that resulted from a believer's falling short of the mark, either through sin or by following a revealed religion that was not Islam. The first point allowed the nascent Ibāḍiyya to align themselves with the Muḥakkima and the early *shurāt,* while the second distinguished the Ibāḍiyya from the more militant of Khārijites. It also opened the door for Ibāḍī scholars to establish gradations of *kufr* and thereby to position themselves vis-à-vis the People of the Book, non-Ibāḍī Muslims, and polytheists proper.

Ibn Dhakwān provides perhaps the most elegant exposition of the duties toward and legal rights of those associated with each gradation of *kuffār.* His discussion begins with the polytheists, who enjoyed the least protection under Islam. Following the example of the Prophet Muḥammad, Muslims (meaning Ibāḍīs) were not to intermarry, inherit from them, eat the meat that they slaughter, or honor contracts with them. They were to be fought, without cessation, until they left polytheism, and during warfare their possessions could be treated as spoils.[63]

Zoroastrians (*al-majūs*), because they "claimed some remnant of knowledge" (paraphrasing Qur'ān 46:4), enjoyed better treatment at the hands of the Muslims. Allowed to pay the *jizya*, Zoroastrians gained protection for their lives and property. However, Muslims were not permitted to intermarry with them, inherit from them, or eat the meat that they slaughtered.[64] People of the Book (meaning Jews and Christians) stood one grade higher than Zoroastrians because they "professed some of what God had sent down to them."[65] They also paid the *jizya* in return for the protection of their lives and property. In addition Muslims could eat the meat that they slaughtered, and Muslim men could marry their women. But Muslims were not to inherit from or honor contracts with the People of the Book, and Muslim women were not to marry Jewish or Christian men.[66] What can be intuited from this exposition thus far is that *kuffār* enjoyed legal rights in relation to the degree to which they resembled (Ibāḍī) Muslims. Thus polytheists possessed no knowledge and acted at variance with how Muslims should act, and therefore they enjoyed the least protection under Islamic law, and Muslims were to have the least contact (in terms of marriage, inheritance, sharing meat, and so forth) with them. Zoroastrians and then People of the Book respectively displayed more traits in common with the Muslims, and thus they enjoyed respectively more legal protections and more contact was allowed with them.

The final category, that of non-Ibāḍī Muslims, meaning hypocrites, or what Ibn Dhakwān refers to as his *qawm*, most closely resembled true Muslims, and they therefore enjoyed the most legal rights due to "their use of [the Muslims'] *qibla*."[67] As the closest category to true Muslims, non-Ibāḍī *qawm* were also the most difficult to catalog. It is no great surprise that Ibn Dhakwān spills a great deal of ink discussing this classification; in fact the heresiographical nature of Ibn Dhakwān's epistle prefigures his ultimate discussion of how non-Ibāḍī Muslims should be treated. By scrutinizing the errors of the Azāriqa, Najdāt, the followers of Dāwūd, ʿAṭiyya and Abū Fudayk, and the Murji'a and Fatana, Ibn Dhakwān was better able to frame the truths to which the Ibāḍiyya, as the true Muslims, adhered. Non-Ibāḍī Muslims, thereby, enjoyed nearly all of the legal rights that full Muslims enjoyed: Muslims were permitted to intermarry with them, inherit from them, eat the meat that they slaughtered, and keep contracts with them, and they might not demand *jizya* from them; during times of peace they enjoyed the protection of the Muslims, while during a time of war they must first be summoned to accept the truth before they could be fought, and their property might not be taken, nor might their wives and offspring be treated as spoils.[68] They also could not be assassinated or killed in secret. Against the militant Khārijites, Ibn Dhakwān specifies that at no point might Muslims engage in indiscriminate slaughter (*istiʿrāḍ*), that there was no requirement to make *hijra* from the abode of their *qawm*, that minors could not be killed, and that it was proper to associate with those who chose to remain behind (*al-qā'id*) during fighting.[69]

Even though the distinction between Ibāḍīs and their *qawm* was affirmed through the process of demarcating those who merited *walāya* from those who merited *barā'a*, the guidelines discussed above created more or less normalized relations between Ibāḍīs and non-Ibāḍī Muslims. In fact Ibn Dhakwān's only real restriction on interactions with non-Ibāḍī Muslims related to serving "the kings of [the Muslims'] *qawm*," meaning non-Ibāḍī rulers. Such an action would have put a Muslim in the position of either approving of the cause of a ruler considered a *kāfir* or outright assisting him.[70] By the emerging Ibāḍī consensus on *barā'a*, either action would have been considered improper.

As Crone and Zimmerman have noted, Ibn Dhakwān's presentation of Ibāḍī doctrines tallies, for the most part, with what Islamic heresiographers have related concerning them. Two conclusions may be drawn from this fact: the first being that the heresiographers probably had good access to Ibāḍī texts; and the second being that Ibn Dhakwān's presentation of the ways that Ibāḍīs were to treat non-Ibāḍī Muslims remained representative of the general Ibāḍī thinking on the subject. Although still conferring the status of *kuffār* on non-Ibāḍī Muslims and dissociating from them or refraining from a decision, the Ibāḍiyya managed to establish clear boundaries for their group while still maintaining more or less amicable relations with non-Ibāḍīs. Such practicality undoubtedly contributed to the longevity of the Ibāḍī movement by allowing it the flexibility to survive as a minority.

Ibn Dhakwān's *sīra*, however, sits among a constellation of other Ibāḍī writings devoted to the issue of how to classify and treat non-Ibāḍīs, and its specific taxonomy of *kuffār* is therefore merely one among many early Ibāḍī attempts to do the same. Given the variations present in descriptions of how the Muḥakkima and early *shurāt* established similar boundaries as well as the exceptions in Azraqī poetry to the supposed Azraqite boundary scheme, the early Ibāḍī proliferation of writings on boundary themes may simply point to a discursive tradition in the process of coming to a consensus. In other words, it is only the fact that Ibāḍīs and their early writings survived that allows their multiple taxonomies of unbelief to be appreciated; presumably if more writings on the subject from the early *shurāt* or militant Khārijites had survived, then a similar variety of viewpoints might be in evidence from them as well. After all, it is often minority groups who require both a strong sense of identity and a practical sensibility when dealing with those outside of their group, if they are to endure, and yet it is often those same minority groups who, in the absence of political legitimacy, must struggle to establish the doctrines that unify them and give them definition.

Rather than there being just one means by which the early Ibāḍiyya established boundaries between themselves and others, a variety of different schemes were in evidence. Certainly the emerging doctrines of *walāya* and *barā'a* as well as the conviction that non-Ibāḍī Muslims could not be counted as full Muslims (though they were not to be treated as *mushrikūn* either) run through all of the early writings on the subject. However, these were the inheritance from earlier generations of Muḥakkima and *shurāt,* and they formed the foundation upon which the Ibāḍiyya elaborated the complex theological and legal frameworks that allowed them to survive as a distinctive group amid the masses of non-Ibāḍīs who surrounded them.

Conclusion

The ultimate aim of this study is to comprehend the textual accumulations and doctrinal trajectories that brought into being a distinctive sense of Ibāḍī identity, especially insofar as this identity was constructed and maintained through the inherited stories of their early ascetics and martyrs as well as the tyrants, oppressors, and enemies who persecuted them. It focuses on the early period, when the Ibāḍiyya were emerging from among the masses of quietists in Basra and crafting their own sense of uniqueness over and against the militant Khārijite groups who preceded them during the second *fitna*. In order to understand the constructed nature of early Ibāḍī identity, this study looks back through the recorded endeavors of the early *shurāt* toward the varieties of the late antique Middle Eastern hagiographical traditions, focusing in particular on Eastern Christian hagiography in its Mesopotamian context. The study argues that the early *shurāt* and the Ibāḍiyya who followed them crafted stories about their ascetics and "very special dead" in ways that resonated with how such stories were crafted in late antiquity. As such, their narratives functioned, as they did in late antiquity, to create group identity by focusing memory on the ascetics/noble dead, valorizing their "exchange" of this world for the next, and turning worldly defeat into ultimate victory in the hereafter.

Although the seam between late antiquity and early Islam is now more and more the object of scholarly inquiry, the so-called "Khārijites" have received but slight treatment, while the Ibāḍiyya have received virtually none. Rather the persistent weight of scholarship tends to view these groups as effectively sui generous—at best, products of Arab tribalism and Qur'ānic literalism. While denying neither the vital importance of Arab tribal ties and migrations nor the central role played by the Qur'ān in crafting the consciousness of the Muḥakkima and first *shurāt* (along with their followers among the militant Khārijites and quietist Ibāḍiyya), the aim of this study is to place these groups firmly within the context of late antiquity and to examine them in that light.

To be clear, this approach does not seek to find what "influence" the early Christians, Manicheans, "gnostics," Jews, or pagans may or may not have had on the early *shurāt* or on those who penned their hagiographies. Rather it seeks to keep the Muḥakkima and their followers firmly in the spotlight, with their own agendas and reasons for employing certain genres of late antique literature as well as their own variations on hagiographical themes. It superimposes the notion of "resonance" onto "influence," seeking to find the ways that the hagiographical genre reverberated across religious traditions, being employed for similar reasons and in similar fashions but always in concrete and unique situations. Similarly it uses language of proximity to locate the early *shurāt* amid the late antique and early Islamic communities who employed the hagiographical genre in their own ways, seeking thereby to preserve something of the originality of the various religious traditions so situated.

Such an approach can be justified when it is recalled that late antique groups treated the stories of their martyrs as an eminently public genre. As such, it was widespread and promiscuous, moving easily across the communities and geographies of late antiquity and early Islam. Evidence for the hybrid nature of the hagiographical genre in these periods is legion, even to the extent that the Ṣufrī rebel Shabīb b. Yazīd appears in the early Syriac Christian *Chronicle of 819* as an "illustrious horseman and mighty champion."[1] A method employed in this study is to focus in on geographically proximate hagiographical traditions of Mesopotamia and Arabia as the ones most likely to be familiar to the communities with whom the Muḥakkima and early *shurāt* mingled and from among whom they emerged. Without having to attribute direct "influence," then, it is argued that the *shurāt* authors wrote in the recognizable genre of hagiography in order to achieve the results that hagiography achieved, namely the establishment of group identity around the suffering of the saints and martyrs.

Indeed the stories and poetry of the Muḥakkima and early *shurāt* as they emerge from the pages of non-Ibāḍī sources such as al-Ṭabarī, al-Mubarrad, and al-Balādhurī betray familiar late antique hagiographical themes and structures: conversion scenes; ascetic practices; miracles; the inevitable confrontation with the authorities; and explicit and gruesome scenes of martyrdom replete with the images of the broken and mangled bodies of the martyrs. Of course *shurāt* narratives have their own unique elements, often including, for example, martyrdom on the battlefield as well as revenge scenes in which the martyrs' deaths are avenged by their surviving comrades.

Prominent among this literature is the trope of asceticism: as an extension of the world-denying ethos of the martyr, ascetic practice was part and parcel of the religious landscape of late antiquity and early Islam, and it is no surprise that it appears in the hagiographical literature devoted to the Muḥakimma and early *shurāt*. Indeed, fundamental to the very idea of *shirā'* as an "exchange" of this world for the pleasure of God was the notion of rejecting the lure of worldly pleasures. Thus *shurāt* narratives abound with images of bodies wasted from fasting, faces yellowed from extended prayers, shaved heads, and even celibacy, while exhortations to regard this life as but a passing fancy proliferate in their speeches. The phenomenon of *shirā'*, then, as a literary exercise imbibed the same waters as that of the late antique Christian, Manichean, and even pagan iterations of the genre of hagiography and did so for the purposes of group identity creation around the figures of the ascetics and noble dead.

In tracing the narratives of the early *shurāt* between non-Ibāḍī and Ibāḍī sources, the study argues that the *shurāt* first produced cycles of such stories and that these original prototypes formed the basis for the accounts of Abū Mikhnaf and his like, as well as in later Iraqi and North African Ibāḍī chronicles. In other words, the materials on the Muḥakkima and the early *shurāt* that appear in the sources (both Ibāḍī and non-Ibāḍī) originated with *shurāt* authors and poets, whose original works (in whatever hagiographical form they may have taken) are now lost. These works were first and foremost literary creations that employed the familiar genre of hagiography, and as such, they are here treated as literature rather than as history per se.

However, *shurāt* literature survives now only insofar as various Ibāḍī and non-Ibāḍī texts have preserved it, and this fact presents certain textual problems (albeit familiar ones) for researchers. In particular, non-Ibāḍī texts, with their openly hostile attitude toward the Muḥakkima and early *shurāt*, have inevitably introduced distortions into the narratives of these groups. Specifically, regarding the theme of boundary maintenance, this book attempts to show, through a comparison with heresiographical and historical accounts, that the ways the Muḥakkima and early *shurāt* went about conceptualizing their opponents looks far more varied and nuanced in historical sources than in Islamic heresiography. It was shown that the historical accounts preserve a far richer, far more varied and ambiguous vocabulary for opponents of the Muḥakkima and *shurāt*, such that the image in heresiographical texts of the prevalent use of *takfīr* by the *khawārij* must be viewed with extreme suspicion. That the early groups employed *takfīr* is without a doubt; what was meant by it and the implications of the appellation, however, most certainly remain in doubt. The term *kufr* sat within a conceptual universe populated with many other related concepts, such as *shirk*, *khaṭī'a*, *dhanb*, *ḍalāla*, *bidʿa*, *shakk*, *idhān*, *dhull*, and *irtidād*, that make it unlikely that *takfīr* in the early period constituted a theological indictment of existential unbelief in the way that such accusations functioned in later periods. In other words, it was not as a theological designation indicating unbelief proper that the early Muḥakkima and later *shurāt* employed the label; nor did the Muḥakkima and early *shurāt* seem to have treated their enemies as the legal equivalents of *kuffār*, despite the sometimes maladroit attempts in non-Ibāḍī sources to portray them as doing just that. In fact only in certain, specific groups of *shurāt*—and those viewed as exceptional by the sources—do we see the first glimmers of the practices that would characterize later militant Khārijism, such as *isti'rāḍ,* as well as the notion that the designation of *kufr* upon an enemy marked her as the absolute theological opposite of the believer.

Even with the Azāriqa—those first Khārijites who are almost universally condemned in the sources for considering, and then treating, their opponents and even their opponents' wives and children as the equivalent of *kuffār* and *mushrikūn*—their poetry contains not a small amount of ambiguity and contradiction when it comes to the actual application of the term *kufr.* Comparison of different kinds of Islamic sources, then, yields what numismatic evidence from the Azāriqa and so-called "Ṣufriyya" hints at: that these groups may not have universally adopted the harsh stances attributed to them in heresiographical literature.[2] If this is the case, then the Ibāḍī claim to have preserved the Muḥakkima and first *shurāt*'s stance on the notion of *kufr* over and against the deviations of the Azāriqa and Najdāt must be allowed more consideration. Of course the strong stance of the Azāriqa forced the Ibāḍiyya to clarify their own position on the nature of *kufr*—a process that took many generations and does not seem to have initially created much uniformity in terminology or taxonomy.

Ibāḍī sources do seem to have appropriated much earlier material from the Muḥakkima and early *shurāt,* preserving in the course of their own writings the image of the early *shurāt.* Thus, Ibāḍī texts abound with images of ascetic practice and martyrdom: the very same tropes that appear in non-Ibāḍī sources. Although the Ibāḍiyya were certainly preserving the image of such figures for their own purposes—such is evident from the way that certain problematic figures such as Ibn Muljam, Qarīb b. Murra, Zuḥḥāf al-Ṭā'ī, and Ṭawwāf b. 'Allāq are portrayed—they nevertheless left the ascetic image of the early *shurāt* largely unchanged. The Ibāḍiyya, it seems, saw themselves as preserving through the image of the *shurāt* their own version of the "primeval, conquest-era Muslim identity that had been abandoned by the Umayyads."[3] The figure of Abū Bilāl, in particular, comes across as a paragon of *shārī*-cum-Ibāḍī virtue: pious, ascetic even to the point of celibacy, and willing to die fighting tyranny, Abū Bilāl and his band are the prime examples of the *shurāt*'s many good qualities as they became refracted through the Ibāḍī lens. Such preservations are not surprising, as the earliest Ibāḍī articulations of such figures—at least insofar as they are preserved in North African Ibāḍī writings—seem to draw from the same *shurāt* sources that inform non-Ibāḍī Iraqi accounts of the early *khawārij.* Profound parallels exist between North African Ibāḍī sources and the writings of Abū Mikhnaf in particular but also those of al-Mubarrad and al-Balādhurī. Ibāḍīs, for their own part, seem to have used the *shurāt* image in ways similar to how the early *shurāt* used them—that is, as a means to focus identity on the righteous martyrs and saints.

Of course Ibāḍīs did manage this image for their own purposes, as is evident from the harnessing of the *shurāt* mythos for later Ibāḍī figures such as Ṭālib al-Ḥaqq and al-Julandā b. Mas'ūd. Both of these leaders presented able administrators, but their bravado and derring-do left something to be desired. Rather their importance lay in how their memories could be mustered by later Ibāḍī authors to establish a sense of identity based in a line of righteous forefathers. In this fashion, Ṭālib al-Ḥaqq and al-Julandā b. Mas'ūd joined the ranks of earlier *shurāt,* becoming links in a chain of legitimacy that stretched back to the Prophet Muḥammad.

Beyond the appropriation of the *shurāt* image in Ibāḍī sources, it is clear that the process of institutionalizing the *shurāt* soldiers was well under way on the ground: not only did the proto-Ibāḍī *'ulamā'* exert strong control over the uprisings of Ṭālib al-Ḥaqq and al-Julandā b. Mas'ūd, but in addition their *shurāt* seem to have been far more organized than the earlier bands of Iraqi martyrs, whose sole purpose (we are told) was to win paradise fighting overwhelming odds. Insofar as they both aimed to establish Ibāḍī polities in their respective areas, Ṭālib al-Ḥaqq's and al-Julandā b. Mas'ūd's methods of fighting tyranny were far more planned, structured, and controlled than was the glorified recklessness of their *shurāt* predecessors. That Ibāḍī authors chose to cast them as *shurāt* speaks more to the power of the hagiographical genre to snatch otherworldly victory from worldly failure than it does to the actual heroic exploits of their persons.

The institutionalization of the *shurāt* continued under later Omani Ibāḍī imāms, at least in theory; of actual *shurāt* in North Africa we have almost no information, though North African Ibāḍīs did continue to write on the theory of *shirā'*. In Oman, Ibn al-Nayyir's advice to Imām Ghassān makes it clear that the *shurāt* lacked discipline and that it was the Ibāḍī imām's and *'ulamā'*s job to enforce it among them. Ibn al-Nayyir envisioned a kind of volunteer army infused with the spirit of the first *shurāt* but answerable to proper authorities. Yet in reality it seems as if the *shurāt* soldiers had aligned themselves with various tribes and had become embroiled in their squabbles; indeed tribal differences would plague Omani Ibāḍism throughout its long history, bringing the downfall of more than one Ibāḍī polity.

Ibāḍī appropriations of *shurāt* themes extended to the ways that the Ibāḍiyya inherited and elaborated on the discussion of how to define themselves in relation to non-Ibāḍīs. In accordance with how early Muslims conceptualized group affiliation, the Ibāḍiyya preserved the language of *walāya* and *barā'a,* association and dissociation, elaborating these notions over the centuries into the complex theological-legal doctrines that continue to distinguish the Ibāḍiyya to this day. Closely connected to the concepts of *walāya* and *barā'a* were the classifications of non-Ibāḍīs as well as the guidelines for how they should be treated. In the wake of the Azāriqa and Najdāt, Ibāḍīs were forced to clarify much of the ambiguity that seems to have characterized early *shurāt* articulations on the classification and treatment of non-*shurāt*. Early Ibāḍī writings on the subject, contrary to the neat doctrinal formulations of the modern period, do not seem to have much consistency beyond the conviction that non-Ibāḍīs were not to be considered full Muslims but that users of the *qibla* (to employ Ibn Dhakwān's phraseology) were not to be treated as *mushrikūn*. Between these two positions, Ibāḍī authors formulated a number of taxonomical schemes to classify those considered *kuffār*. While this study aims to elucidate a few of the early taxonomies of unbelief, much work remains to be done on how such notions evolved into the late medieval period.

Also remaining to be studied properly is the transition in Ibāḍī prosopographical and historical literature from narratives about the martyrs to narratives about scholars and imāms. Both kinds of stories appear in Ibāḍī literature, often with the martyrs populating the first generational layers (*ṭabaqāt*) of Ibāḍī luminaries and the scholars and imāms of the community occupying those subsequent to them.[4] Insofar as Ibāḍī (and other) prosopographical literature chronicles the continuity of the Ibāḍī community, creating a collective sense of Ibāḍī identity through the presentation of important individuals, the strong implication is that later generations of scholars and imāms are the heirs to the martyrs.[5] Given the importance of ascetic piety to the ways that Ibāḍī scholars and imāms appear in these works, such continuities remain intriguing.

Early *shurāt* and Khārijite (and indeed Ibāḍī) poetry too awaits further study. This work utilizes this poetry for the purposes of elucidating the resonances between it and late antique/early Islamic tropes of martyrdom and asceticism and in how it articulates boundary themes. It explores the theme of the wine cup/poisoned cup of death as a means to contextualize the poems within their Arabian environs. This is but the surface of what these poems have to offer: far more insights remain to be gleaned from the stanzas of the *shurāt* and later Khārijites, to say nothing of the historiographical work that remains to be done in establishing how and why such poems were preserved in the first place. It is hoped that the insights presented here might serve as a foundation for further research.

Religious traditions accumulate in complex ways, gathering materials and falling into new courses as they pass through time. This study prefers the rather more chaotic metaphor of tradition as avalanche, in part because this image allows for early materials to be jumbled together with later ones, all of which are considered part of the whole at any given time. Thus in telling the story of the accumulation of Ibāḍī identity in the first few centuries of their existence, the late antique/early Islamic literary traditions of hagiography remain important indicators of the kinds of literary trajectories that would give rise to early *shurāt* literature, which would then become incorporated into non-Ibāḍī historical texts as well as being appropriated in a more active fashion by the hagiographical imagination of the nascent

Ibāḍiyya. Early Ibāḍī identity thus remained an ever-expanding memorial to those considered upright predecessors, whose asceticism and noble deaths were held to guarantee the veracity of the doctrines they passed on, the accumulation of which was (and still is) believed to constitute right religion. Insofar as the memories of the martyrs continue to provide a communal anchor and a source for inspiration, their stories persist long after the centuries have ground their skulls to dust.

Notes

Introduction

1. For introductions to the Khārijites, see Gaiser, "The Khārijites in Contemporary Scholarship"; Crone and Zimmerman, *The Epistle of Sālim Ibn Dhakwān;* Kenney, "The Emergence of the Khawārij"; Madelung, *Succession to Muḥammad,* 238–62; Madelung, *Religious Trends in Early Islamic Iran,* 54–76; Wellhausen, *The Religio-Political Factions of Early Islam,* 1–91.

2. al-Baghdādī, *Al-Farq Bayn al-Firaq,* 61–62; al-Ṭabarī, *Tārīkh,* 2:516–20; al-Mubarrad, *Al-Kāmil,* 3:194. See the variant account in al-Balādhurī, *Ansāb al-Ashrāf,* 3:114–15; and Ibn 'Abd Rabbih, *Al-'Iqd al-Farīd,* 1:283–84, 2:369–70 (which adds Abū Bayhas).

3. On the term *shārī/shurāt* as "exchanger(s)," see Higgins, "Faces of Exchangers, Facets of Exchange in Early *Shurāt* (Khāriji) Poetry," 8–9.

4. al-Ṭabarī, *Tārīkh,* 2:516–20; al-Mubarrad, *Al-Kāmil,* 3:194.

5. For introductions to the Ibāḍiyya, see Hoffman, *The Essentials of Ibāḍī Islam,* 3–53. For an exhaustive resource on Ibāḍī sources, both primary and secondary, see Custers's three-volume *Al-Ibāḍiyya.*

6. See, for example, Aṭfayyish, *Al-Farq bayn al-Ibāḍiyya wa'l-Khawārij,* 1–19.

7. Though the main activities of the Najdāt ended with their defeat in 73/692, there is evidence for the survival of the Najdāt up to the third/ninth century and possibly beyond. See Crone, "A Statement by the Najdiyya Khārijites on the Dispensability of the Imamate," 56.

8. An exception to this rule is the so-called first letter of Ibn Ibāḍ, wherein the term *khawārij* refers, positively, to those whom the author claims as his pious forefathers. Of course Ibn Ibāḍ is careful to specify that he dissociates from the Azraqites and disavows himself of their actions. See Kāshif, *Al-Siyar wa'l-Jawābāt,* 2:341–42.

9. al-Mubarrad, *Al-Kāmil,* 3:120; al-Iṣfahānī, *Kitāb al-Aghānī,* 18:115 ('Abbās, *Shi'r al-Khawārij,* 105–6 [no. 103]); Yāqūt al-Ḥamawī, *Mu'jam al-Buldān,* 2:215 (Jawsaq) ('Abbās, *Shi'r al-Khawārij,* 125 [no. 128]).

10. Sizgorich devoted a chapter of his *Violence and Belief in Late Antiquity* to comparing Khārijite notions of "militant devotion" with those found in the late antique and early Islamic worlds (and in particular, among Christians and early Muslims), focusing on investigating "why militant forms of piety and the figures associated with militant and aggressive modes of religiosity became such crucial resources for communal self-fashioning among early Christian and early Muslim communities" (4). While he makes an eloquent case for the importance of late antiquity to the study of early Islamic (and "Khārijite") forms of asceticism and martyrdom, he neglects Ibāḍī sources on the whole.

11. Markus, *The End of Ancient Christianity,* 85.

12. An admitted shortcoming of this metaphor is how it removes agency from the religious actors who shape any given religious tradition. Thus, while the metaphor of tradition as an avalanche can be helpful to an extent, it must never be taken as an absolute description of the myriad ways that traditions develop.

13. Sizgorich, *Violence and Belief in Late Antiquity*, 32.

14. Donner, *Narratives of Islamic Origins*, 125–229; Robinson, *Islamic Historiography*, 83–158.

15. See Gaiser, *Muslims, Scholars, Soldiers*, esp. chaps. 1 and 4; Wilkinson, *Ibāḍism*, esp. the first six chapters; Sizgorich, *Violence and Belief in Late Antiquity*, chaps. 5 and 6.

16. See Savage, *A Gateway to Hell, a Gateway to Paradise*, 96–105; Rushworth, "From Arzuges to Rustamids," 90–95; Talbi, "Un nouveau fragment de l'histoire de l'Occident musulman," 43.

17. Frend, *The Donatist Church*, 312–13. See also Tilley, *Donatist Martyr Stories*.

18. Lewicki, "Survivances chez les berbères médiévaux d'ére musulmane du cultes ancies et de croyances paiënnes," 7.

19. For an example and discussion of Maghribī Ibāḍī martyrs from the late third/ninth century, see Prevost, "Les enjeux de la bataille de Mânû (283/896)," 85–86.

20. Cobb, *Dying to Be Men*, 2.

21. Ibid., 9–10.

22. Castelli, *Martyrdom and Memory*, 29.

23. Ibid., 4.

24. Sizgorich, *Violence and Belief in Late Antiquity*, 147.

25. On the relation between history and rhetoric, see Meisami, *Persian Historiography to the End of the Twelfth Century*, 294–98.

26. al-Ṭabarī, *Tārīkh*, 1:3353.

27. Brock, "Saints in Syriac," 182.

28. Ibid., 187; Meisami, *Persian Historiography to the End of the Twelfth Century*, 296.

29. 18.3. On festivals for the martyrs, see Delehaye, *Les origines du culte des martyrs*, 24–49.

30. McCollum, *The Story of Mar Pinḥas*, 4–5.

31. On private reading of scriptural texts, see Gamble, *Books and Readers in the Early Church*, 203. On martyrdom texts specifically, see Kelley, "Philosophy as Training for Death," 724–25.

32. Brock, "Saints in Syriac," 185–87.

33. Morony, *Iraq after the Muslim Conquest*, 475.

34. 9:111 reads: "Indeed, God has purchased from the believers their lives and their properties [in exchange] for the attainment of Paradise. They fight in the cause of God, so they kill and are killed. [It is] a true promise [binding] upon Him in the Torah and the Gospel and the Qur'ān. And who is truer to his covenant than God? So rejoice in your transaction which you have contracted. And it is that which is the great attainment."

35. Morony, *Iraq after the Muslim Conquest*, 476–77.

36. Brock, "Early Syrian Asceticism," 2.

37. For references to the "Barbarian Plain," see Fowden, *The Barbarian Plain*, 1.

38. Brock, "Early Syrian Asceticism," 11–12; Koch, *Quellen zur Geschichte der Askese und des Mönchtums in der alten Kirche*, texts 1–19.

39. Cooper, *Plato*, 55, 57.

40. Klijn, *The Acts of Thomas*, 20–22.

41. Lewinstein, "The Revaluation of Martyrdom in Early Islam," 79.

42. Cook argues, for example, that 3:140 does, in fact, use the term *shuhadā'* in the sense of martyr. See Cook, *Martyrdom in Islam*, 16–17.

43. See also Ayoub, "Martyrdom in Christianity and Islam," 74–75.

44. Lewinstein, "The Revaluation of Martyrdom in Early Islam," 79.

45. See, for example, Heck, "Eschatological Scripturalism and the End of Community," 137ff.

46. Donner, *Narratives of Islamic Origins,* 143.

47. Watt, despite his own warnings, tends to reify the various programs of the Khārijite subsects, treating, for example, the Azāriqa, Najdāt, Ibāḍiyya, and others as coherent entities. See Watt, *The Formative Period of Islamic Thought,* 20–28; Lahoud, *The Jihadis' Path to Self-Destruction,* 61, 72–78, 82–88. Even though Lahoud notes on page 80 that the Khārijites "do not all seem to have shared a unified vision," she nevertheless persists in speaking about certain stances that the "Khārijites" (presumably all of them) had in common, as well as staking out the various doctrinal stances of the subgroups (based, for the most part, on heresiographical sources) as if they were also stable. See also Dabashi, *Authority in Islam,* 124ff; Heck, "Eschatological Scripturalism and the End of Community," 141ff, attributing to the Khārijites an "eschatological scripturalism."

48. Lahoud, *The Jihadis' Path to Self-Destruction,* 57ff. Dabashi, *Authority in Islam,* speaking of authority among the "Khārijites," states that they "did not establish any form of continuity with the Muhammadan charismatic authority and its legacy and, at the same time, categorically rejected the pre-Muhammadan mode of traditional authority, particularly in its political and administrative aspects" (126).

49. Dabashi, *Authority in Islam,* finds in the Azraqites "the representation of the original Kharijite position" (125). Lahoud, *The Jihadis' Path to Self-Destruction,* says that "the intrinsic flaw of the militant Khārijites is that they were over-qualified Muslims" (92). Heck, in "Eschatological Scripturalism and the End of Community," consistently conflates the actions of the militant Khārijites with the "first Khārijites" (by whom is meant the Muḥakkima and first *shurāt*); thus the Khārijites are viewed as "marauders" bent on the death of the "rest of the Muslim community" (137–38), the "first Khārijites" as attacking those who admitted human authority "with indiscriminate violence against men, women and children" (140), and as "examining people's theological commitments before slaughtering them" (a reference to the *miḥna* that was actually administered by the Azāriqa) (141).

1. Late Antique and Early Islamic Contexts

1. Jauss, "Literary History as a Challenge to Literary Theory," 7–37.

2. For a general discussion of the relations between pre-Islamic Arabs and Christians, see Andrae, "Der Ursprung des Islams und das Christentum," 155–80; Bell, *The Origins of Islam in Its Christian Environment,* 243ff; Trimingham, *Christianity among the Arabs in Pre-Islamic Times,* 33ff; Potts, *The Arabian Gulf in Antiquity,* 2:241ff.

3. Ostrogorsky, *History of the Byzantine State,* 58.

4. Ibid., 59–60.

5. Morony, *Iraq after the Muslim Conquest,* 360.

6. Toral-Niehoff, "The 'Ibād of al-Ḥīra," 339.

7. Ibid., 340.

8. Shahīd, "Ghassān," 2:1020.

9. Ibid.

10. Toral-Niehoff, "The 'Ibād of al-Ḥīra," 335.

11. Wilkinson, *Ibāḍism,* 70.
12. al-Ṭabarī, *Tārīkh,* 1:314–16; Peters, *Muhammad and the Origins of Islam,* 66.
13. Peters, *Muhammad and the Origins of Islam,* 66.
14. Ibid.
15. Kister, "Al-Ḥīra," 150ff.
16. See, for example, Jeffery, *The Foreign Vocabulary of the Qur'ān,* 43ff. This issue has become highly politicized since the publication of Luxemburg, *Die syro-aramaische Lesart des Koran,* a work that dramatically (and unconvincingly) overstates the case.
17. Fowden, *The Barbarian Plain,* 1.
18. Toral-Niehoff, "The 'Ibād of al-Ḥīra," 326. Savage has speculated on the possible connections between the 'Ibād of al-Ḥīra and the later Ibāḍī community. While this discussion of Christian "precedents" can be illuminating at times, it remains highly speculative. See Savage, *A Gateway to Hell, a Gateway to Paradise,* 91–96.
19. Quoted in Toral-Niehoff, "The 'Ibād of al-Ḥīra," 326.
20. See ibid., 328–29.
21. Quoted in ibid., 327.
22. Shahīd, *Islam and Oriens Christianus,* 25.
23. See Qur'ān, 85:4.
24. Finster, "Arabia in Late Antiquity," 71–72.
25. Ibid., 72.
26. Wilkinson, *Ibāḍism,* 70–71.
27. Finster, "Arabia in Late Antiquity," 72.
28. Toral-Niehoff, "The 'Ibād of al-Ḥīra," 335.
29. The examples are admirably gathered by Finster, "Arabia in Late Antiquity," 77–81, 107; Shahīd, "Byzantium in South Arabia," 29 (with map).
30. For a discussion of the problems surrounding the term "gnostic," see King, *What Is Gnosticism?,* 5ff.
31. Morony, *Iraq after the Muslim Conquest,* 402.
32. See Pagels, *The Gnostic Gospels,* 37; Holroyd, *The Elements of Gnosticism,* 37.
33. See Ephrem the Syrian, *Against Heresies, Hymn 22,* section 4.
34. Brock and Harvey, *Holy Women of the Syrian Orient,* 9.
35. Lieu, *Manichaeism in the Later Roman Empire and Medieval China,* 5–24.
36. Fakhry, *A History of Islamic Philosophy,* 22–26. See also Dillon and Gerson, *Neoplatonic Philosophy,* xiii–xxii.
37. Morony, *Iraq after the Muslim Conquest,* 306–7.
38. Ibid., 384.
39. Ibid., 400.
40. Cobb, *Dying to Be Men,* 4–8.
41. Brock, "Early Syrian Asceticism," 2.
42. Ibid., n4. See Ryan, *Irish Monasticism,* 197.
43. Brakke, *Demons and the Making of the Monk,* 25.
44. Ibid.
45. Ryan, *Irish Monasticism,* 197.
46. Brock and Harvey, *Holy Women of the Syrian Orient,* 64.
47. Ibid., 67.
48. For a guide to this literature, see Brock, *The History of the Holy Mar Ma'in,* 77ff.
49. Smith, "Constantine and Judah the Maccabee," 18.
50. Brock, "A Martyr at the Sasanid Court," 167.
51. Ibid., 179.

52. Ibid., 181.
53. Brock and Harvey, *Holy Women of the Syrian Orient*, 16–18.
54. On the issue of female martyrs, see Cobb, *Dying to Be Men*, 92–123.
55. Brock, *The History of the Holy Mar Ma'in*, 18; Fiey, *Saints Syriaques*, 130.
56. Elliot, *The Apocryphal New Testament*, 353; Fiey, *Saints Syriaques*, 186–87.
57. Fowden, *The Barbarian Plain*, 8ff.
58. Ibid., 11.
59. Walker, *The Legend of Mar Qardagh*, 164 ff.
60. Ibid., 171.
61. McCollum, *The Story of Mar Pinḥas*, 2; Fiey, *Saints Syriaques*, 153–54.
62. McCollum, *The Story of Mar Pinḥas*, 3, 19.
63. See Brakke, *Demons and the Making of the Monk*, 5–6.
64. Shahīd, "Byzantium in South Arabia," 28. See also Brown, *The Cult of the Saints*, 1–6.
65. Shahīd, *The Martyrs of Najrān*, 243–44.
66. See also ibid., 273.
67. Shahīd, "Islam and *Oriens Christianus*," 11n9.
68. Shahīd, *Byzantium and the Arabs in the Fifth Century*, 422–58.
69. Nebes, "The Martyrs of Najrān and the End of the Himyar," 46–47.
70. Shahīd, *The Martyrs of Najrān*, 49–51.
71. Nebes, "The Martyrs of Najrān and the End of the Himyar," 47.
72. Cf. Cobb, *Dying to Be Men*, 92ff.
73. Shahīd, *The Martyrs of Najrān*, 55–57.
74. Shahīd, "Byzantium in South Arabia," 42.
75. Finster, "Arabia in Late Antiquity," 75.
76. Shahīd, "Islam and *Oriens Christianus*," 19–20.
77. Sizgorich, "Become Infidels or We Will Throw You into the Fire," 135. See also Cook, "The *Aṣḥāb al-Ukhdūd*," 125ff.
78. Miller, *The Corporeal Imagination*, 15.
79. Comaroff, *Body of Power, Spirit of Resistance*, 6–7.
80. Brown, *The Cult of the Saints*, 70ff.
81. Castelli, *Martyrdom and Memory*, 32.
82. Miller has recently argued for a "material turn" beginning among fourth-century Christians in which sensibilities toward the signifying potential of the material world (and the human body) shifted toward the positive. See Miller, *The Corporeal Imagination*, 3.
83. Brock, "Early Syrian Asceticism," 4.
84. Ibid., 7.
85. See Acts 18:18.
86. Meyendorff, *St. Germanus of Constantinople on the Divine Liturgy*, 65, 69.
87. Klijn, *The Acts of Thomas*, (verse 37) 84.
88. Ibid., (verse 78) 106, (verse 95) 114.
89. Ibid., 35.
90. Ibid., (verse 15) 72.
91. Ibid., (verse 14) 71.
92. The notion of Jesus "selling" Thomas presents an interesting parallel with the concept of *shirā'*. However, this parallel is to be found only on the conceptual level, as the linguistic parallels cannot be made: the Syriac text uses the root *z-b-n* in the *peal* form (that is, the first verb form) to indicate buying and the same root in the *pael* form (that is, the second verb form) to indicate selling. Later on the same page, the text uses an

infinitive from the same root (*mzbnw*), which intensifies the meaning of the main verb. See Wright, *Apocryphal Acts of the Apostles,* 1:173.

93. Klijn, *The Acts of Thomas,* (verses 1–3) 65–66.

94. Ibid., (verse 168) 153.

95. Brock, "Early Syrian Asceticism," 9.

96. Theodoret himself was involved in the Christological controversies of the fifth century and was therefore retroactively associated with the Chalcedonian (that is, the so-called "Orthodox") articulation of Christianity that would emerge triumphant at Constantinople.

97. Brock, "Early Syrian Asceticism," 14–15; Canivet and Leroy-Molinghen, *Histoire des moines de Syrie,* 2:63 (section 19.3)—the Bible quotation is Galatians 2:20.

98. On the ways that *apatheia* came to be variously adapted and understood by late antique Christians, see Maier, "Clement of Alexandria and the Care of the Self," 737–39. Among Eastern Christians of later centuries, *apatheia* became associated with freedom from the body's urges or impulses: see Ware, "Apatheia," 18–19.

99. Brock, "Early Syrian Asceticism," 10.

100. Quoted in Miller, "Desert Asceticism and 'the Body from Nowhere,'" 141.

101. Brock, "Early Syrian Asceticism," 16; Miller, *Corporeal Imagination,* 36–37.

102. Quoted in Miller, *Corporeal Imagination,* 3.

103. Brock, "Early Syrian Asceticism," 18.

104. Ibid., 17.

105. Von Harnack, *Marcion,* 96.

106. Ibid.

107. Ibid., 87.

108. Gardner and Lieu, *Manichean Texts from the Roman Empire,* 231.

109. Ibid., 240.

110. Lieu, *Manichaeism in the Later Roman Empire and Medieval China,* 20.

111. Ibid., 143.

112. Gardner and Lieu, *Manichean Texts from the Roman Empire,* 231.

113. Ibid., 91–93.

114. Ibid., 242–43. Thecla is a heroine of the apocryphal *Acts of Paul* who rebuffs Alexander's advances and eventually achieves martyrdom; see Schneemelcher and Wilson, *New Testament Apocrypha, Volume 2,* 220–21. Drusiane is a figure from the apocryphal *Acts of John* who refuses to break her vow of chastity and dies of distress, to be raised from the dead by John; see Schneemelcher and Wilson, *New Testament Apocrypha, Volume 2,* 178–80. Maximilla appears in the *Acts of Andrew* refusing to have sexual relations with her husband, and Aristobula is mentioned "only in passing"; see Schneemelcher and Wilson, *New Testament Apocrypha, Volume 2,* 96n26.

115. Castelli, *Martyrdom and Memory,* 5.

116. See Royalty, *The Origin of Heresy.* 3ff, 119ff; Lyman, "Heresiology," 296–314.

117. Hawting, *The Idea of Idolatry and the Emergence of Islam,* 6.

118. Ibid., 49.

119. Ibid., 74.

120. On al-Ḥīra and Najrān, see Kister, "Al-Ḥīra," 143–69; Shahīd, "Byzantium in South Arabia," 23–94; Shahīd, "Islam and *Oriens Christianus,*" 9–31.

121. Shahīd, "Islam and *Oriens Christianus,*" 13–17.

122. Ibid., 24.

123. Ibn Hishām, *Al-Sīra al-Nabawiyya,* 1:147–49, 179.

124. See Qur'ān, 3:59–61.

125. Brock, "Early Syrian Asceticism," 15. Likewise, Wilkinson, *Ibāḍism,* 275, draws attention to the general Islamic awareness of Christological debates.

126. Qur'ān, 18:9–26; Brock, "Saints in Syriac," 183.

127. On Manicheanism and Islam, see Reeves, *Prolegomena to a History of Islamicate Manichaeism,* 15ff.

128. Ibn Isḥāq, *Al-Sīra al-Nabawiyya,* 2:170; Guillaume, *The Life of Muhammad,* 278.

129. Ibid., 2:171; Guillaume, *The Life of Muhammad,* 278.

130. Ibn Isḥāq, *Al-Sira al-Nabawiyya,* 3:245; 503.

131. al-Ṭabarī, *Tārīkh,* 1:1433.

132. Qur'ān, 18:46.

133. Ibid., 13:26.

134. Ibid., 4:77.

135. Ibid., 29:64.

136. Ibid., 18:28.

137. On whom, see al-Saḫḫāwī, *Rijḥān al-Kiffa fī Bayān Nubdha min Akhbār Ahl al-Ṣuffa,* 87ff; Ernst, *The Shambala Guide to Sufism,* 22.

138. al-Dārimī, *Sunan al-Dārimī,* 11:1:1 (no. 2168), 678.

139. Ibid., 11:3:3; (no. 2173), 680.

140. Sizgorich, *Violence and Belief in Late Antiquity,* 178–79.

141. al-Azdī, *Tārīkh Futūḥ al-Shām,* 115–16. See also Sizgorich, *Violence and Belief in Late Antiquity,* 161–64.

142. Quoted in Sizgorich, *Violence and Belief in Late Antiquity,* 180.

143. Bonner, "Some Observations Concerning the Early Development of Jihad," 19ff.

144. al-Azdī, *Tārīkh Futūḥ al-Shām,* 115–16; Sizgorich, *Violence and Belief in Late Antiquity,* 161–64.

145. See, for example, Ibn Ḥanbal, *Kitāb al-Zuhd,* 114–15; Sizgorich, *Violence and Belief in Late Antiquity,* 162.

146. Qur'ān, 9:111.

147. Ibid., 2:154, 3:169.

148. al-Ṭabarī, *Tārīkh,* 1:1321; translation by McDonald, *The History of al-Ṭabarī Volume VII,* 55 (with permission).

149. See also Cook, *Martyrdom in Islam,* 23–24.

150. On this story and its many versions, see the analysis of Cook, "The *Aṣḥāb al-Ukhdūd,*" 125ff.

151. Muslim, *Ṣaḥīḥ Muslim,* 1600–1601 (53:73, no. 3005).

152. al-Ṭabarī, *Tārīkh,* 1:1322; McDonald, *The History of al-Ṭabarī Volume VII,* 55–56.

153. al-Ṭabarī, *Tārīkh,* 1:1436; McDonald, *The History of al-Tabarī Volume VII,* 146. See also Cook, *Martyrdom in Islam,* 21–22.

154. Donner, "From Believers to Muslims," 12. There is much to commend Donner's thesis of a "believer's movement" at the early period of Islamic history, not the least being the way that this proposed movement seems to have put into practice the complex ways that the Qur'ān discusses the concepts of belief (and its opposites).

155. Qur'ān, 23:52–53.

156. Ibid., 6:159.

157. Ibid., 3:105. See also ibid., 3:103, 30:32, 42:13–14.

158. Waldman, "The Development of the Concept of Kufr in the Qur'ān," 442–43.

159. Ibid., 444. See also Izutsu, *Ethico-Religious Concepts in the Qur'ān,* 119ff, 204, on the connection between *imān* and *ṣāliḥāt.*

160. Waldman, "The Development of the Concept of Kufr in the Qur'ān," 445, 447.

161. Ibid., 445, 447, 451.
162. Ibid., 443.
163. Donner, "From Believers to Muslims," 13–14.
164. Ibid., 20; McDonough, "Iman and Islam in the Qur'an," 81.
165. See also Izutsu, *Ethico-Religious Concepts in the Qur'ān,* 187.
166. Bonner, "Some Considerations Concerning the Early Development of Jihad," 29.
167. Mingana, *Sources Syriaques,* 1:147, lines 1–6; quoted in Donner, "From Believers to Muslims," 44.
168. Sizgorich, *Violence and Belief in Late Antiquity,* 162ff.
169. Madelung, *The Succession to Muḥammad,* 48; Shoufani, *Al-Riddah and the Muslim Conquest of Arabia,* 102.
170. Madelung, *The Succession to Muḥammad,* 48–49.
171. Robinson, "Prophecy and Holy Men in Early Islam," 254.

2. *Shurāt* Battles, *Shurāt* Bodies

1. See Higgins, "Faces of Exchangers, Facets of Exchange in Early *Shurāt* (Khāriji) Poetry," 7–8.
2. al-Ṭabarī, *Tārīkh,* 1:3353.
3. On Arabic poetry, see Stetkevych, *The Zephyrs of Najd,* 1–49; Stetkevych, *The Mute Immortals Speak.*
4. Thus poems of the Azraqite Qaṭarī b. al-Fujā'a are included in the *Diwān al-Ḥamāsa,* a third/ninth century collection of mostly pre-Islamic poems that celebrate valor (*ḥamāsa*). See Cook, *Martyrdom in Islam,* 62; al-Tibrīzī, *Sharḥ Diwān al-Ḥamāsa,* 77–78 (no. 14), 101–3 (no. 21), 467–68 (no. 231).
5. Montgomery, "Dichotomy in *Jāhilī* Poetry," 6.
6. For a general account of the battle of Ṣiffīn and the emergence of the Muḥakkima, see Madelung, *The Succession to Muḥammad,* 238ff.
7. 'Abbās, *Shi'r al-Khawārij,* 33 (no. 5). Cf. translation by Gabrieli, "Religious Poetry in Early Islam," 10.
8. al-Mubarrad, *Al-Kāmil,* 3:177; Ibn 'Abd Rabbih, *Al-'Iqd al-Farīd,* 2:376; 'Abbās, *Shi'r al-Khawārij,* 48 (no. 25).
9. Lane, *An Arabic English Lexicon,* 1544–45.
10. On whom, see Juynboll, "The Qurrā' in Early Islamic History," 113ff; Juynboll, "The Qur'ān Reciter on the Battlefield," 11ff; Ja'yaṭ, *Al-Fitna,* 96–101; Shah, "The Quest for the Origins of the *Qurrā'* in the Classical Islamic Tradition," 2ff. A report in Ibn Qutayba, *Al-Imāma wa'l-Siyāsa,* includes 'Abdullāh b. Wahb al-Rāsibī among the *qurrā'* (104).
11. Lewinstein, "The Revaluation of Martyrdom in Early Islam," 78–79.
12. al-Mubarrad, *Al-Kāmil,* 3:118; 'Abbās, *Shi'r al-Khawārij,* 31 (no. 1).
13. Ibn A'tham al-Kūfī, *Kitāb al-Futūḥ,* 4:132; 'Abbās, *Shi'r al-Khawārij,* 31 (no. 2). Cf. translation by Donner, "Piety and Eschatology in Early Kharijite Poetry," 15.
14. Ibn A'tham al-Kūfī, *Kitāb al-Futūḥ,* 4:129–30; 'Abbās, *Shi'r al-Khawārij,* 33 (no. 3).
15. al-Ṭabarī, *Tārīkh,* 1:3365; Ibn al-Athīr, *Tārīkh Ibn al-Athīr,* 444 (3:334).
16. al-Ṭabarī, *Tārīkh,* 1:3363–64.
17. Ibid., 1:3364; Ibn al-Athīr, *Tārīkh Ibn al-Athīr,* 444 (3:334).
18. al-Ash'arī, *Maqālāt al-Islāmiyīn,* 1:206; al-Malaṭī, *Al-Tanbīh wa'l-Radd,* 53.
19. al-Ṭabarī, *Tārīkh,* 1:3457.

20. See also al-Tamīnī, *Kitāb al-Miḥan,* 78–81.

21. al-Ṭabarī, *Tārīkh,* 1:3466; 'Abbās, *Shi'r al-Khawārij,* 35 (no. 7); translation by Hawting, *The History of al-Ṭabarī Volume XVII,* 225 (with permission).

22. For example, Qur'ān 27:34, quoting the Queen of Sheba, reads, "She said, 'Indeed kings—when they enter a city, they ruin it and render the honor of its people humbled. And thus do they do.'"

23. al-Mubarrad, *Al-Kāmil,* 3:140–41 (gives the name as Qiṭām); al-Ṭabarī, *Tārīkh,* 1:3457–58 (gives the name as al-Qaṭamī bt. al-Shijna); Ibn Qutayba, *Al-Imāma wa'l-Siyāsa,* 130; Ibn A'tham al-Kūfī, *Kitāb al-Futūḥ,* 4:134–35 (Qiṭām bt. al-Aḍba').

24. al-Ṭabarī, *Tārīkh,* 1:3467; 'Abbās, *Shi'r al-Khawārij,* 35–36 (no. 8). Cf. translation by Hawting, *The History of al-Ṭabarī Volume XVII,* 225.

25. 'Abbās, *Shi'r al-Khawārij,* 38 (no. 13); Ma'rūf, *Diwān al-Khawārij,* 218 (no. 286).

26. Ibn al-Athīr, *Tārīkh Ibn al-Athīr,* 466 (3:409–10); al-Balādhurī, *Ansāb al-Ashrāf,* 5:169–71.

27. Ibn Khayyāṭ, *Tārīkh Khalīfa b. Khayyāṭ,* 123; Al-Ṭabarī, *Tārīkh,* 2:10 (gives the name 'Abdullāh b. Abī al-Ḥurr al-Ṭā'ī) al-Baghdādī, *Al-Farq Bayn al-Firaq;* 62 (gives his name as 'Abdullāh b. Jawshā al-Ṭā'ī).

28. Ibn 'Abd Rabbih, *Al-'Iqd al-Farīd,* 277.

29. Ibn al-Athīr, *Tārīkh Ibn al-Athīr,* 467 (3:411); al-Balādhurī, *Ansāb al-Ashrāf,* 5:171; Ibn Khayyāṭ, *Tārīkh Khalīfa b. Khayyāṭ,* 124; al-Mubarrad, *Al-Kāmil,* 3:170–71; Ibn 'Abd Rabbih (who gives his name as Ḥawthara al-Aqṭā'), *Al-'Iqd al-Farīd,* 1276–77.

30. Ibn al-Athīr, *Tārīkh Ibn al-Athīr,* 467 (3:411); al-Balādhurī, *Ansāb al-Ashrāf,* 5:172.

31. Ibn al-Athīr, *Tārikh Ibn al-Athīr,* 467 (3:411); al-Balādhurī, *Ansāb al-Ashrāf,* 5:171–72.

32. See also al-Mubarrad, *Al-Kāmil,* 3:171; Ibn 'Abd Rabbih, *Al-'Iqd al-Farīd,* 1:277–78.

33. Al-Mubarrad, *Al-Kāmil,* 3:168, attributes the first line of this poem to the Khārijite poet 'Imrān b. Ḥattān.

34. Yāqūt al-Ḥamawī, *Mu'jam al-Buldān,* 2:215 (Jawsaq); 'Abbās, *Shi'r al-Khawārij,* 125 (no. 128).

35. See, for example, 22:34–35: "And give good tidings to the humble [before their Lord], who, when God is mentioned, their hearts tremble (*wajalat qulūbuhum*)."

36. al-Mubarrad, *Al-Kāmil,* 3:181; Ibn Mūsā, *Tartīb al-Madārik,* 1:306; 'Abbās, *Shi'r al-Khawārij,* 56–57 (no. 37).

37. Ibn al-Athīr, *Tārīkh Ibn al-Athīr,* 467 (3:411); al-Balādhurī, *Ansāb al-Ashrāf,* 5:172; Ibn Khayyāṭ, *Tārīkh Khalīfa b. Khayyāṭ,* 128.

38. Ibn al-Athīr, *Tārīkh Ibn al-Athīr,* 467 (3:411); al-Balādhurī, *Ansāb al-Ashrāf,* 5:173.

39. Ibn al-Athīr, *Tārīkh Ibn al-Athīr,* 467 (3:411); al-Balādhurī, *Ansāb al-Ashrāf,* 5:173–74.

40. Ibn al-Athīr, *Tārīkh Ibn al-Athīr,* 467 (3:411); al-Balādhurī, *Ansāb al-Ashrāf,* 5:174.

41. Ibn al-Athīr, *Tārīkh Ibn al-Athīr,* 469 (3:420–21); 5:175; al-Balādhurī, *Ansāb al-Ashrāf,* al-Ṭabarī, *Tārīkh,* 2:19–21.

42. al-Ṭabarī, *Tārīkh,* 2:21.

43. Ibid., 2:18–19.

44. Ibid., 2:36; al-Balādhurī, *Ansāb al-Ashrāf,* 5:178; 'Abbās, *Shi'r al-Khawārij,* 45 (no. 20).

45. al-Ṭabarī, *Tārīkh,* 2:19; 'Abbās, *Shi'r al-Khawārij,* 44 (no. 19). Cf. translation in Morony, *The History of al-Ṭabarī Volume XVIII,* 23.

46. al-Ṭabarī, *Tārīkh,* 2:20–21.

47. Ibid., 2:40–41.

48. Ibid., 2:44.

49. Ibid., 2:64.

50. al-Balādhurī, *Ansāb al-Ashrāf,* 5:175–77.

51. al-Mubarrad, *Al-Kāmil,* 3:169–70.

52. al-Ṭabarī, *Tārīkh,* 2:181–82.
53. Ibid., 2:182.
54. Ibid., 2:183–84.
55. Ibid., 2:184.
56. al-Balādhurī, *Ansāb al-Ashrāf,* 5:179.
57. Ibid., 5:175–76.
58. On whom, see Madelung, *Streitschrift des Zaiditenimams,* 1–18; Van Ess, *Theologie und Geselschaft,* 1:406ff.
59. al-Mas'ūdī, *Murūj al-Dhahab,* 5:442–45.
60. al-Balādhurī, *Ansāb al-Ashrāf,* 5:179.
61. Ibn al-Athīr, *Tārīkh Ibn al-Athīr,* 468 (3:417–18); Ibn Khayyāṭ, *Tārīkh Khalīfa b. Khayyāṭ,* 124; al-Balādhurī, *Ansāb al-Ashrāf,* 5:179–81; al-Ṭabarī, *Tārīkh,* 2:19–21.
62. Ibn Khayyāṭ, *Tārīkh Khalīfa b. Khayyāṭ,* 128.
63. al-Balādhurī, *Ansāb al-Ashrāf,* 5:181.
64. Ibid., 5:180; 'Abbās, *Shi'r al-Khawārij,* 46 (no. 21).
65. al-Balādhurī, *Ansāb al-Ashrāf,* 5:181.
66. Ibid., 5:182. On the Basran *shurṭa,* see Ebstein, "*Shurṭa* Chiefs in Baṣra in the Umayyad Period," 106–12. I prefer the translation of *shurṭa* as "authorities."
67. Ibn Khayyāṭ, *Tārīkh Khalīfa b. Khayyāṭ,* 135.
68. al-Balādhurī, *Ansāb al-Ashrāf,* 5:183; Ibn Khayyāṭ, *Tārīkh Khalīfa b. Khayyāṭ,* 135–37; al-Ṭabarī, *Tārīkh,* 2:91. See also Ibn 'Abd Rabbih, *Al-'Iqd al-Farīd,* 1:281.
69. al-Balādhurī, *Ansāb al-Ashrāf,* 5:184.
70. Ibid.; al-Ṭabarī, *Tārīkh,* 2:91.
71. The Qur'ānic quote is 39:73.
72. al-Balādhurī, *Ansāb al-Ashrāf,* 5:184–85; al-Ṭabarī, *Tārīkh,* 2:91; Ibn Khayyāṭ, *Tārīkh Khalīfa b. Khayyāṭ,* 137.
73. al-Balādhurī, *Ansāb al-Ashrāf,* 5:184–85.
74. al-Mubarrad, *Al-Kāmil,* 3:193.
75. Ibid., 3:178, 194.
76. al-Balādhurī, *Ansāb al-Ashrāf,* 5:186; Ibn al-Athīr, *Tārīkh Ibn al-Athīr,* 495 (3:517–18). Ibn al-Athīr's version gives Jidār as the name of a person with whom the *shurāt* used to meet.
77. The reading I have chosen here is not that found in what has now become the standard Qur'ān for most Muslims (that is, the reading of Ḥafṣ b. Sulaymān b. al-Mughīra al-Asadī according to the recitation of 'Āṣim b. Abī al-Nujūd), which treats the verb *fatana* in the passive (that is, *futinū*) and therefore reads the line as "after they were persecuted." However, several commentators allowed the active reading of the verb *fatana,* and as this interpretation more accurately analogizes Ṭawwāf's situation, I have chosen to render the verse accordingly. See Yusuf 'Ali, *The Meaning of the Holy Qur'ān,* 666n2147.
78. al-Balādhurī, *Ansāb al-Ashrāf,* 5:186; Ibn al-Athīr, *Tārīkh Ibn al-Athīr,* 495 (3:517–18).
79. See also Ibn Khayyāṭ, *Tārīkh Khalīfa b. Khayyāṭ,* 161.
80. al-Balādhurī, *Ansāb al-Ashrāf,* 5:188; 'Abbās, *Shi'r al-Khawārij,* 59 (no. 40).
81. al-Balādhurī, *Ansāb al-Ashrāf,* 5:187; 'Abbās, *Shi'r al-Khawārij,* 59 (no. 41).
82. al-Jayṭālī, *Kitāb Qanāṭir al-Khayrāt,* 2:144; 'Abbās, *Shi'r al-Khawārij,* 50 (no. 27).
83. al-Balādhurī, *Ansāb al-Ashrāf,* 5:188; 'Abbās, *Shi'r al-Khawārij,* 55 (no. 35).
84. Van Ess, *Theologie und Gesellschaft,* 2:112.
85. Al-Balādhurī notes that Udayya was his mother, from the Muḥārib b. Khaṣfa; his father was Ḥudayr b. 'Amr b. 'Ubayd b. Ka'b, and he was one of the Rabī'a b. Ḥanẓala

from the Tamīm. See al-Balādhurī, *Ansāb al-Ashrāf,* 5:188; Ibn ʿAbd Rabbih, *Al-ʿIqd al-Farīd,* 1:278.

86. al-Mubarrad, *Al-Kāmil,* 3:129; Ibn al-Jawzī, *Talbīs Iblīs,* 134; al-Baghdādī, *Al-Farq Bayn al-Firaq,* 52; al-Shahrastānī, *Al-Milal wa'l-Niḥal,* 117–18.

87. al-Balādhurī, *Ansāb al-Ashrāf,* 5:189; Ibn Qutayba, *Al-Maʿārif,* 232; Ibn al-Athīr, *Tārīkh Ibn al-Athīr,* 495 (3:518).

88. al-Mubarrad, *Al-Kāmil,* 3:153.

89. Ibn al-Athīr, *Tārīkh Ibn al-Athīr,* 495 (3:518); Ibn Qutayba, *Al-Maʿārif,* 232.

90. Ibn al-Athīr, *Tārīkh Ibn al-Athīr,* 495 (3:517–18); al-Ṭabarī, *Tārīkh,* 2:186.

91. al-Mubarrad, *Al-Kāmil,* 3:129–30. See also the account at 3:182–83 as well as the alternate account given in Ibn al-Athīr, *Tārīkh Ibn al-Athīr,* 525 (4:95).

92. As per Lane, *An Arabic English Lexicon, zinya* indicates "a mode, or manner, of fornication or adultery" (1260).

93. al-Balādhurī, *Ansāb al-Ashrāf,* 5:189; al-Mubarrad, *Al-Kāmil,* 3:152–53; Ibn al-Athīr, *Tārīkh Ibn al-Athīr,* 495 (3:518); Ibn ʿAbd Rabbih, *Al-ʿIqd al-Farīd,* 4:113; al-Tamīmī, *Kitāb al-Miḥan,* 259–61.

94. There are many variations on her name: al-Balādhurī, *Ansāb al-Ashrāf,* 5:189, has al-Thabjā'; and Ibn al-Athīr, *Tārīkh Ibn al-Athīr,* 495 [3:518], gives al-Bathjā'.

95. al-Balādhurī, *Ansāb al-Ashrāf,* 5:189. The editors of the 1996 Dār al-Fikr edition of *Ansāb al-Ashrāf* believe that the term is properly rendered as *makhānīth* (hermaphrodites); Ibn al-Athīr, *Tārīkh Ibn al-Athīr,* says, "one of the *mujtahidāt*" (495 [3:518]). The reading of *makhānīth* is possible, as the text mentions how Abū Bilāl discouraged the rebellion (*khurūj*) of women and hermaphrodites are an ambiguous category. Nevertheless the root *kh-b-t* has connections to notions of humility before God, a concept embraced by the early *shurāt,* and it is therefore more likely that there existed among them a group devoted in some way to humbling themselves before God. Because women were discouraged from fighting, participation in this group would have been one means by which they could express their piety. In addition al-Balādhurī, *Ansāb al-Ashrāf,* later describes Thābit b. Waʿla al-Rāsibī as being one of the *makhābīt al-khawārij* (5:422).

96. See also al-Mubarrad, *Al-Kāmil,* 3:175.

97. al-Balādhurī, *Ansāb al-Ashrāf,* 5:189–90; Ibn al-Athīr, *Tārīkh Ibn al-Athīr,* 495 (3:518). Al-Tamīmī's *Kitāb al-Miḥan* (129–31) presents al-Baljā' as an example of patience (*ṣabr*) during her gruesome martyrdom.

98. al-Mubarrad, *Al-Kāmil,* 3:176.

99. al-Balādhurī, *Ansāb al-Ashrāf,* 5:190; Ibn al-Athīr, *Tārīkh Ibn al-Athīr,* 495 (3:518).

100. al-Mubarrad, *Al-Kāmil,* 3:180.

101. Ibid., 3:180–81.

102. Ibid., 3:181.

103. al-Balādhurī, *Ansāb al-Ashrāf,* 5:190; Ibn al-Athīr, *Tārīkh Ibn al-Athīr,* 495 (3:518–19).

104. al-Mubarrad, *Al-Kāmil,* 3:176; al-Balādhurī, *Ansāb al-Ashrāf,* 5:190; al-Ṭabarī (using the account of Wahb b. Jarīr), *Tārīkh,* 2:186–87.

105. al-Mubarrad, *Al-Kāmil,* 3:176.

106. al-Ṭabarī, *Tārīkh,* 2:187; Ibn al-Athīr, *Tārīkh Ibn al-Athīr,* 495 (3:519).

107. al-Mubarrad, *Al-Kāmil,* 3:176.

108. al-Balādhurī, *Ansāb al-Ashrāf,* 5:190; Ibn ʿAbd Rabbih, *Al-ʿIqd al-Farīd,* 1:278.

109. al-Mubarrad, *Al-Kāmil,* 3:177; Ibn ʿAbd Rabbih, *Al-ʿIqd al-Farīd,* 1:278.

110. al-Balādhurī, *Ansāb al-Ashrāf,* 5:191.

111. al-Mubarrad, *Al-Kāmil,* 3:177; Ibn Khayyāṭ, *Tārīkh Khalīfa b. Khayyāṭ,* 159; al-Balādhurī, *Ansāb al-Ashrāf,* 5:191; Ibn al-Athīr, *Tārīkh Ibn al-Athīr,* 495 (3:519); Ibn ʻAbd Rabbih, *Al-ʻIqd al-Farīd,* 1:279, 2:376.

112. al-Mubarrad, *Al-Kāmil,* 3:178; Ibn ʻAbd Rabbih, *Al-ʻIqd al-Farīd,* 2:376.

113. al-Mubarrad, *Al-Kāmil,* 3:178; al-Balādhurī, *Ansāb al-Ashrāf,* 5:191; Ibn ʻAbd Rabbih, *Al-ʻIqd al-Farīd,* 1:218–19. Al-Ṭabarī (on the authority of Wahb b. Jarīr) and Ibn Khayyāṭ give the name of the general as ʻAbdullāh b. Ḥisn al-Tamīmī or al-Thaʻlabī respectively; see al-Ṭabarī, *Tārīkh,* 2:187; Ibn Khayyāṭ, *Tārīkh Khalīfa b. Khayyāṭ,* 159.

114. al-Mubarrad, *Al-Kāmil,* 3:178; al-Balādhurī, *Ansāb al-Ashrāf,* 5:192; Ibn al-Athīr, *Tārīkh Ibn al-Athīr,* 495–96 (3:519); Ibn ʻAbd Rabbih, *Al-ʻIqd al-Farīd,* 2:377.

115. al-Mubarrad, *Al-Kāmil,* 3:179; Ibn ʻAbd Rabbih, *Al-ʻIqd al-Farīd,* 1:218–19; ʻAbbās, *Shiʻr al-Khawārij,* 54–55 (no. 34). Cf. translation by Hallaq, "Discourse Strategies," 147–48.

116. al-Balādhurī, *Ansāb al-Ashrāf,* 5:192; Ibn al-Athīr, *Tārīkh Ibn al-Athīr,* 525 (4:94). Ibn ʻAlqama's name is alternately given as ʻAbbād b. Akhḍar: according to al-Mubarrad, Akhḍar was the name of his mother's spouse. See al-Mubarrad, *Al-Kāmil,* 3:179; Ibn ʻAbd Rabbih, *Al-ʻIqd al-Farīd,* 1:279.

117. al-Mubarrad, *Al-Kāmil,* 3:179. Abū Mikhnaf in al-Ṭabarī, *Tārīkh,* 2:391; Ibn al-Athīr, *Tārīkh Ibn al-Athīr,* 525 (4:94); and Ibn Qutayba, *Al-Maʻārif,* 232, place them in Tawwaj.

118. al-Ṭabarī, *Tārīkh,* 2:391. Qur'ān 42:20 reads, "Whoever desires the harvest of the Hereafter—We increase for him in his harvest. And whoever desires the harvest of this world—We give him thereof, but there is not for him in the Hereafter any share."

119. al-Mubarrad, *Al-Kāmil,* 3:180; al-Balādhurī, *Ansāb al-Ashrāf,* 5:193; Ibn al-Athīr, *Tārīkh Ibn al-Athīr,* 525 (4:94–95).

120. al-Mubarrad, *Al-Kāmil,* 3:180; Ibn ʻAbd Rabbih, *Al-ʻIqd al-Farīd,* 1:279.

121. Abū Mikhnaf in al-Ṭabarī, *Tārīkh,* 2:391; al-Mubarrad, *Al-Kāmil,* 3:181–82; al-Balādhurī, *Ansāb al-Ashrāf,* 5:194; Ibn al-Athīr, *Tārīkh Ibn al-Athīr,* 525 (4:95).

122. al-Ṭabarī, *Tārīkh,* 2:391.

123. al-Balādhurī, *Ansāb al-Ashrāf,* 5:195; ʻAbbās, *Shiʻr al-Khawārij,* 53 (no. 33).

124. al-Balādhurī, *Ansāb al-Ashrāf,* 5:195; ʻAbbās, *Shiʻr al-Khawārij,* 61 (no. 44).

125. On battle imagery in the poetry of the Khārijites (but using the example of an Ibāḍī poet), see al-Qāḍī, "The Limitations of Qur'ānic Usage in Early Arabic Poetry," 178–81. See also Khalidi, "The Poetry of the Khawārij," 110ff.

126. ʻAbbās, *Shiʻr al-Khawārij,* 143–44 (no. 155); Maʻrūf, *Diwān al-Khawārij,* 132–33 (no. 182). Cf. translation by Hallaq, "Discourse Strategies," 139–40. See also Ibn ʻAbd Rabbih, *Al-ʻIqd al-Farīd,* 1:279–80; ʻAbbās, *Shiʻr al-Khawārij,* 141–42 (no. 153).

127. al-Mubarrad, *Al-Kāmil,* 3:200.

128. al-Baghdādī, *Al-Farq Bayn al-Firaq,* 61–62; al-Ṭabarī, *Tārīkh,* 2:516–20; al-Mubarrad, *Al-Kāmil,* 3:194. See the variant account in al-Balādhurī, *Ansāb al-Ashrāf,* 3:114–15. See also Ibn ʻAbd Rabbih, *Al-ʻIqd al-Farīd,* 1:283–84, 2:369–70, which adds Abū Bayhas.

129. al-Mubarrad, *Al-Kāmil,* 3:195–96; al-Balādhurī, *Ansāb al-Ashrāf,* 5:421–22.

130. al-Mubarrad, *Al-Kāmil,* 3:195; ʻAbbās, *Shiʻr al-Khawārij,* 69 (no. 50). Cf. translation by Donner, "Piety and Eschatology in Early Kharijite Poetry," 15.

131. al-Mubarrad, *Al-Kāmil,* 3:195–96.

132. Ibid., 3:120; al-Iṣfahānī, *Kitāb al-Aghānī,* 18:115 (which attributes the poem to ʻĪsā al-Khabaṭī); ʻAbbās, *Shiʻr al-Khawārij,* 105–6 (no. 103). Cf. translation by Gabrieli, "Religious Poetry in Early Islam," 13.

133. Yāqūt al-Ḥamawī, *Muʻjam al-Buldān,* 2:215 (Jawsaq); ʻAbbās, *Shiʻr al-Khawārij,* 125 (no. 128).

134. ʿAbbās, *Shiʿr al-Khawārij,* 123 (no. 125); Maʿrūf, *Diwān al-Khawārij,* 70–71 (no. 91).

135. Yāqūt al-Ḥamawī, *Muʿjam al-Buldān,* 3:228 (Sadhawwur); ʿAbbās, *Shiʿr al-Khawārij,* 127 (no. 131).

136. al-Balādhurī, *Ansāb al-Ashrāf,* 5:133; al-Ṭabarī, *Tārīkh,* 1:3365; Ibn al-Athīr, *Tārīkh Ibn al-Athīr,* 444 (3:334).

137. al-Baghdādī, *Al-Farq Bayn al-Firaq,* 57; Ibn Aʿtham al-Kūfī, *Kitāb al-Futūḥ,* 4:97.

138. Ibn al-Jawzī, *Talbīs Iblīs,* 133; Ibn ʿAbd Rabbih, *Al-ʿIqd al-Farīd,* 2:367–68.

139. Ibn al-Jawzī, *Talbīs Iblīs,* 132.

140. Ibn al-Athīr, *Tārīkh Ibn al-Athīr,* 467 (3:411); al-Balādhurī, *Ansāb al-Ashrāf,* 5:171; al-Mubarrad, *Al-Kāmil,* 3:171; Ibn ʿAbd Rabbih, *Al-ʿIqd al-Farīd,* 1:278.

141. Ibn al-Jawzī, *Talbīs Iblīs,* 138–39.

142. al-Mubarrad, *Al-Kāmil,* 3:169.

143. Ibid., 3:181 (verses 1–4); Ibn Mūsā, *Tartīb al-Madārik,* 1:306; ʿAbbās, *Shiʿr al-Khawārij,* 56 (no. 37).

144. al-Shahrastānī, *Al-Milal wa'l-Niḥal,* 118.

145. Ibn ʿAbd Rabbih, *Kitāb al-ʿIqd al-Farīd,* 3:297; ʿAbbās, *Shiʿr al-Khawārij,* 43 (no. 18).

146. On vultures as a common trope in pre-Islamic poetry, see Stetkevych, *The Mute Immortals Speak,* 67–70. In the *Qaṣīda Lāmiyya* by Ta'abbaṭa Sharrā, see Jones, *Early Arabic Poetry,* 260.

147. al-Balādhurī, *Ansāb al-Ashrāf,* 5:425; ʿAbbās, *Shiʿr al-Khawārij,* 71 (no. 53). Cf. translation by Hallaq, "Discourse Strategies," 137.

148. Fierro has suggested that references to the yellow faces of the Ṣufriyya may also have some connection to the South Arabian practice of physically dying the face yellow. See Fierro, "Al-Aṣfar Again," 204ff.

149. al-Ṭabarī, *Tārīkh,* 2:881; Ibn ʿAbd Rabbih, *Al-ʿIqd al-Farīd,* 1:285, 2:369.

150. ʿAbbās, *Shiʿr al-Khawārij,* 122–23 (no. 125); Maʿrūf, *Diwān al-Khawārij,* 70–71 (no. 91).

151. Ibn Aʿtham al-Kūfī, *Kitāb al-Futūḥ,* 4:89.

152. Ernst, *The Shambala Guide to Sufism,* 141.

153. al-Ṭabarī, *Tārīkh,* 2:31.

154. al-Mubarrad, *Al-Kāmil,* 3:193.

155. Ibid., 3:180.

156. Ibid., 3:208; ʿAbbās, *Shiʿr al-Khawārij,* 106 (no. 104).

157. al-Mubarrad, *Al-Kāmil,* 3:169.

158. al-Balādhurī, *Ansāb al-Ashrāf,* 5:188; Ibn al-Athīr, *Tārīkh Ibn al-Athīr,* 495 (3:518).

159. al-Mubarrad, *Al-Kāmil,* 3:180.

160. Ibid., 3:195.

161. al-Malaṭī, *Al-Tanbīh wa'l-Radd,* 51.

162. Ibn ʿAsākir, *Tahdhīb Tārīkh Dimashq al-Kabīr,* 5:413; ʿAbbās, *Shiʿr al-Khawārij,* 49–50 (no. 26). Cf. translation by Hallaq, "Discourse Strategies," 149.

163. Ibn Qutayba, *Al-Maʿārif,* 232.

164. Lafuente y Alcántara, *Colección de obras arábigas de historia y geografía,* 32; James, *A History of Early Al-Andalus,* 65.

165. Ibn Qutayba, *Al-Maʿārif,* 232.

166. Abū Dāwūd, *Sunan Abī Dāwūd,* 519 (nos. 4765, 4766).

167. Ibid., 519 (no. 4764). See the variant in Ibn al-Jawzī, *Talbīs Iblīs,* 133.

168. See Ibn al-Jawzī, *Talbīs Iblīs,* 133; al-Malaṭī, *Al-Tanbīh wa'l-Radd,* 51; Ibn Aʿtham al-Kūfī, *Kitāb al-Futūḥ,* 4:128.

169. al-Mubarrad, *Al-Kāmil,* 3:196.

170. See also Hallaq, "Discourse Strategies," 106ff.

171. al-Jayṭālī, *Kitāb Qanāṭir al-Khayrāt,* 2:143; ʻAbbās, *Shiʻr al-Khawārij,* 51 (no. 28).

172. al-Ṭabarī, *Tārīkh,* 2:827; ʻAbbās, *Shiʻr al-Khawārij,* 83 (no. 69).

173. al-Jayṭālī, *Kitāb Qanāṭir al-Khayrāt,* 2:144; ʻAbbās, *Shiʻr al-Khawārij,* 50 (no. 27). Cf. translation by Donner, "Piety and Eschatology in Early Kharijite Poetry," 16. Abū Bilāl modifies an earlier poem by ʻAbdullāh b. Abī al-Ḥawsā' al-Kilābī, who asks, "What do we care if our souls are collected? What did you do with limbs and bodies [anyway]?" See al-Balādhurī, *Ansāb al-Ashrāf,* 5:170. See also Ibn ʻAbd Rabbih (who attributes the poem to Farwa b. Nawfal), *Kitāb al-ʻIqd al-Farīd,* 3:297; ʻAbbās, *Shiʻr al-Khawārij,* 41 (no. 15). The *ḥanẓal* fruit mentioned in the poem is the colocynth (*citrullus colocynthis*), a common Mediterranean gourd sometimes known as bitter apple. I have reserved poetic license in translating it as "melon."

174. al-Mubarrad, *Al-Kāmil,* 3:181; ʻAbbās, *Shiʻr al-Khawārij,* 56 (no. 37). Cf. translation by Hallaq, "Discourse Strategies," 136.

175. Yāqūt al-Ḥamawī, *Muʻjam al-Buldān,* 2:215 (Jawsaq); ʻAbbās, *Shiʻr al-Khawārij,* 125–26 (no. 128). Cf. translation by Hallaq, "Discourse Strategies," 139.

176. Ibn ʻAbd Rabbih, *Al-ʻIqd al-Farīd,* 3:297; ʻAbbās, *Shiʻr al-Khawārij,* 43 (no. 18). Cf. translation by Hallaq, "Discourse Strategies," 135.

177. ʻAbbās, *Shiʻr al-Khawārij,* 51–52 (no. 29); Maʻrūf, *Diwān al-Khawārij,* 193 (no. 250). Cf. translation by Hallaq, "Discourse Strategies," 146.

178. al-Baghdādī, *ʻKhizānat al-Adab,* 3:150; ʻAbbās, *Shiʻr al-Khawārij,* 112 (no. 109). Cf. translation by Hallaq, "Discourse Strategies," 142–43.

179. al-Dīnawarī, *Al-Akhbār al-Ṭiwāl,* 253; ʻAbbās, *Shiʻr al-Khawārij,* 115–16 (no. 117).

180. Ibn al-Jawzī, *Talbīs Iblīs,* 138–39.

181. al-Jāhiẓ, *Al-Bayān wa'l-Tabyīn,* 1:269; ʻAbbās, *Shiʻr al-Khawārij,* 92–93 (no. 81). Cf. translation by Hallaq, "Discourse Strategies," 138.

182. al-Mubarrad, *Al-Kāmil,* 3:208; ʻAbbās, *Shiʻr al-Khawārij,* 107 (no. 104).

183. al-Dīnawarī, *Al-Akhbār al-Ṭiwāl,* 251; ʻAbbās, *Shiʻr al-Khawārij,* 72 (no. 55); translation by Donner, "Piety and Eschatology in Early Kharijite Poetry," 16.

184. Ibn Abī al-Ḥadīd, *Sharḥ Nahj al-Balāgha,* 4:133; ʻAbbās, *Shiʻr al-Khawārij,* 128 (no. 134).

185. ʻAbbās, *Shiʻr al-Khawārij,* 51 (no. 29); Maʻrūf, *Diwān al-Khawārij,* 193 (no. 250). See also the eulogy of al-Ḥuwayrith al-Rāsibī for Ṣāliḥ b. al-Musarriḥ in al-Balādhurī, *Ansāb al-Ashrāf,* 8:11; ʻAbbās, *Shiʻr al-Khawārij,* 177–78 (no. 209); al-Ṣāliḥī, "The Society, Beliefs and Political Theories of the Khārijites," 329–30.

186. al-Balādhurī, *Ansāb al-Ashrāf,* 5:416; al-Mubarrad, *Al-Kāmil,* 3:120; ʻAbbās, *Shiʻr al-Khawārij,* 142–43 (no. 154). Cf. translation by Gabrieli, "Religious Poetry in Early Islam," 14–15.

187. Kennedy, *The Wine Song in Classical Arabic Poetry,* 1.

188. For example, on the connections between wine imagery and blood vengeance, see Stetkevych, *The Mute Immortals Speak,* 71–73.

189. El Tayib, "Pre-Islamic Poetry," 81–85, 90–93; Kennedy, "Khamr and Ḥikma in Jāhilī Poetry," 97. See also Noorani, "Heterotopia and the Wine Poem in Early Islamic Culture," 219–21.

190. Sells, *Desert Tracings,* 41.

191. al-Tibrīzī, *Sharḥ al-Qaṣā'id al-ʻAshar,* 56–98; Izutsu, *Ethico-Religious Concepts in the Qur'ān,* 51.

192. Kennedy, *The Wine Song in Classical Arabic Poetry,* 91. See also Izutsu, *Ethico-Religious Concepts in the Qur'ān,* 48–50.

193. Some later Islamic poets, such as Qays b. ʿĀṣim, strongly rejected wine in favor of restraint. See Kennedy, *The Wine Song in Classical Arabic Poetry,* 154, 209–14.

194. Blachere, "ʿAntara," 1:521.

195. On ʿAntara and the ʿAntara legends, see Heath, *The Thirsty Sword,* 22ff.

196. ʿAntara b. Shaddād. *Sharḥ Diwān ʿAntara Ibn Shaddād,* 15; Kennedy, *The Wine Song in Classical Arabic Poetry,* 152.

197. ʿAntara b. Shaddād. *Sharḥ Diwān ʿAntara Ibn Shaddād,* 134; Kennedy, *The Wine Song in Classical Arabic Poetry,* 153.

198. ʿAntara b. Shaddād. *Sharḥ Diwān ʿAntara Ibn Shaddād,* 63; Kennedy, *The Wine Song in Classical Arabic Poetry,* 153.

199. ʿAntara b. Shaddād. *Sharḥ Diwān ʿAntara Ibn Shaddād,* 194; Kennedy, *The Wine Song in Classical Arabic Poetry,* 154.

200. Izutsu, *Ethico-Religious Concepts in the Qur'ān,* 48–52.

201. al-Ṭabarī, *Tārīkh,* 2:36; al-Balādhurī, *Ansāb al-Ashrāf,* 5:178; ʿAbbās, *Shiʿr al-Khawārij,* 45–46 (no. 20); translation by Morony, *The History of al-Ṭabarī Volume XVIII,* 41–42 (with permission).

202. al-Balādhurī, *Ansāb al-Ashrāf,* 5:422. Cf. translation by Donner, "Piety and Eschatology in Early Kharijite Poetry," 16; ʿAbbās, *Shiʿr al-Khawārij,* 70 (no. 52).

203. ʿAbbās, *Shiʿr al-Khawārij,* 109–10 (no. 107); Maʿrūf, *Diwān al-Khawārij,* 164–65 (no. 215). Cf. translation by Gabrieli, "Religious Poetry in Early Islam," 12–13.

204. al-Tibrīzī, *Sharḥ Diwān al-Ḥamāsa,* 467 (no. 231); ʿAbbās, *Shiʿr al-Khawārij,* 113 (no. 110).

205. Ibn ʿAbd Rabbih, *Al-ʿIqd al-Farīd,* 1:279–80; ʿAbbās, *Shiʿr al-Khawārij,* 141–42 (no. 153). Cf. Gabrieli, "Religious Poetry in Early Islam," 11.

206. Ibn ʿAsākir, *Tahdhīb Tārīkh Dimashq,* 3:125; ʿAbbās, *Shiʿr al-Khawārij,* 170 (no. 199).

207. al-Iṣfahānī, *Kitāb al-Aghānī,* 23:250–55; ʿAbbās, *Shiʿr al-Khawārij,* 226 (no. 279); translation from al-Qāḍī, "The Limitations of the Qur'ānic Usage," 169.

208. al-Qāḍī, "The Limitations of the Qur'ānic Usage," 167.

209. al-Iṣfahānī, *Kitāb al-Aghānī,* 23:234–36; ʿAbbās, *Shiʿr al-Khawārij,* 228–29 (no. 280). I am indebted to the late Annie Higgins for the translation.

3. *Shurāt* Boundaries

1. Donner, *Narratives of Islamic Origins,* 143.

2. Donner notes that certain types of boundary themes relate to their establishment within a given religious community; see ibid.

3. On the problems of Islamic heresiography as a source, see Watt, *The Formative Period of Islamic Thought,* 3–5; Lewinstein, "The Azāriqa in Islamic Heresiography," 251.

4. The difficulties posed by the genre of annalistic history (indeed of Islamic historiography in general)—i.e., layers of authors and editors, obscure motivations, and incomplete or contradictory accounts, to name but a few—are also well known to students of Islamic history. See Donner, *Narrative of Islamic Origins,* 125–229; Robinson, *Islamic Historiography,* 83ff.

5. See Lewinstein, "The Azāriqa in Islamic Heresiography," 251–68; Gaiser, "Source-Critical Methodologies in Recent Scholarship on the Khārijites," 1376–90.

6. al-Ashʿarī, *Kitāb Maqālāt al-Islamiyyin,* 1:167.

7. al-Baghdādī, *Al-Farq Bayn al-Firaq,* 55–56.

8. al-Shahrastānī, *Al-Milal wa'l-Niḥal,* 137, attributes the doctrine of *kufr al-ni'ma* to the founder of the Ṣufriyya. For a discussion of this problematic term, see Crone and Zimmerman, *The Epistle of Sālim Ibn Dhakwān,* 201.

9. al-Isfarā'inī, *Al-Tabbassur fī'l-Dīn,* 38.

10. See also Izutsu, *Ethico-Religious Concepts in the Qur'ān,* 124.

11. al-Shahrastānī, *Al-Milal wa'l-Niḥal,* 114–15. Ibn Ḥazm, *Kitāb al-Fisal fī'l-wa'l-Milal wa Ahwā` wa al-Niḥal,* simply states that "the Khārijites agree on . . . *takfīr* for those who commit serious sins" (1:370).

12. al-Shahrastānī, *Al-Milal wa'l-Niḥal,* 116–17.

13. al-Malaṭī, *Al-Tanbīh wa'l-Radd,* 47, 48–50.

14. al-Rāzī, *Kitāb al-Zīna,* 282. Al-Nawbakhtī, *Kitāb Firaq al-Shī'a,* 6, 14, explains that the Khārijites held the two arbiters to be *kāfirān,* and they anathematized 'Ali (*kaffara 'Alīan*) when he appointed them. Al-Nawbakhtī says that the Khārijites found justification for their actions in Qur'ān 5:47 and 49:9, explaining in regard to the latter that they held whoever abandoned fighting the "rebellious party" to be committing *kufr.* Al-Qummī's treatment is similar to that of al-Nawbakhtī; see al-Qummī, *Kitāb al-Maqālāt wa al-Firaq,* 12, 130.

15. Madelung and Walker, *An Ismaili Heresiography,* 20.

16. al-Baghdādī, *Al-Farq Bayn al-Firaq,* 57; al-Iṣfarā'inī, *Al-Tabbassur fī'l-Dīn,* 39, which pins the blame for the murder specifically on 'Abdullāh b. Wahb al-Rāsibī and Ḥurqūṣ b. Zuhayr.

17. al-Baghdādī, *Al-Farq Bayn al-Firaq,* 58; al-Iṣfarā'inī, *Al-Tabbassur fī'l-Dīn,* 39–40. In a similar fashion, Ibn al-Jawzī attempts to frame his discussion of the Khārijites by opening his section with a ḥadīth from the Prophet wherein the Prophet chastises his followers for doubting and wanting to kill a man who claimed to be a believer, saying, "I am not commanded to break open the hearts of people, nor to open their bellies"; see al-Jawzī, *Talbīs Iblīs,* 133. This is fairly standard Sunnī material that upholds the Sunnī (via the Murji'ites) line that belief is attested through words—bad deeds simply make one a sinner. Ibn al-Jawzī reinforces this dichotomy of *kufr/imān* by quoting an argument of the Khārijites in the context of their *munāẓara* that 'Alī had refused to let them take the spoils from the people of the Camel (to which 'Alī asks who would get 'Ā'isha) (136). Given Ibn al-Jawzī's late date, it is not inconceivable that he draws this material from earlier heresiographers.

18. al-Balādhurī, *Ansāb al-Ashrāf,* 3:130. See also a similar report in al-Mubarrad, *Al-Kāmil,* 3:150–51.

19. al-Balādhurī, *Ansāb al-Ashrāf,* 3:135.

20. al-Ṭabarī, *Tārīkh,* 1:3353.

21. Ibid., 1:3378, 3369; al-Balādhurī, *Ansāb al-Ashrāf,* 3:141. See also al-Dīnawarī, *Al-Akhbār al-Ṭiwāl,* 188, 190; Ibn al-Jawzī, *Talbīs Iblīs,* 137.

22. Ibn A'tham al-Kūfī, *Kitāb al-Futūḥ,* 4:90.

23. al-Ṭabarī, *Tārīkh,* 1:3351.

24. al-Balādhurī, *Ansāb al-Ashrāf,* 3:134. See also al-Dīnawarī, *Al-Akhbār al-Ṭiwāl,* 188.

25. Ibn Qutayba, *Al-Imāma wa'l-Siyāsa,* 114. Qur'ān 5:47 reads, "And let the People of the Book judge by what God has revealed therein. And whoever does not judge by what God has revealed—they are the transgressors (*al-fāsiqūn*)."

26. al-Mubarrad, *Al-Kāmil,* 3:129.

27. al-Minqarī, *Waq'at Ṣiffīn,* 513; al-Dīnawarī, *Al-Akhbār al-Ṭiwāl,* 179.

28. al-Ṭabarī, *Tārīkh,* 1:3361–63; al-Balādhurī, *Ansāb al-Ashrāf,* 3:128, 130.

29. al-Ṭabarī, *Tārīkh*, 1:3377.

30. al-Minqarī, *Waqʿat Ṣiffīn*, 518; al-Balādhurī, *Ansāb al-Ashrāf*, 3:114–15.

31. Ibn al-Jawzī, *Talbīs Iblīs*, 139.

32. Waldman, "The Development of the Concept of Kufr in the Qur'ān," 445–47; Izutsu, *Ethico-Religious Concepts in the Qur'ān*, 130–33.

33. al-Ṭabarī, *Tārīkh*, 1:3360; al-Balādhurī, *Ansāb al-Ashrāf*, 3:129; Ibn al-Jawzī, *Talbīs Iblīs*, 137; Ibn ʿAbd Rabbih, *Al-ʿIqd al-Farīd*, 2:367–68. See also Ibn Aʿtham al-Kūfī, *Kitāb al-Futūḥ*, 4:97 (in which the Khārijites chant *lā ṭāʿa li-man ʿaṣā Allāh* ("no obedience to those who disobey God").

34. al-Balādhurī, *Ansāb al-Ashrāf*, 3:130.

35. al-Ṭabarī (via Abū Mikhnaf), *Tārīkh*, 1:3361.

36. al-Balādhurī, *Ansāb al-Ashrāf*, 3:127–28; Ibn ʿAbd Rabbih, *Al-ʿIqd al-Farīd*, 2:367. See also Abū Mikhnaf's account in al-Balādhurī, *Ansāb al-Ashrāf*, at 3:137. Al-Mubarrad preserves a report in which the Muḥakkima were said to have borne witness to Ṣakhr b. ʿUrwā's misguidance (*fa-ḍallalathu*) after he refused to fight ʿAlī on the day of Nahrawān. See al-Mubarrad, *Al-Kāmil*, 3:195.

37. al-Balādhurī, *Ansāb al-Ashrāf*, 3:111.

38. al-Ṭabarī, *Tārīkh*, 1:3364; al-Balādhurī, *Ansāb al-Ashrāf*, 3:137. See also al-Sha'bī's version in al-Balādhurī, *Ansāb al-Ashrāf*, 3:134; al-Dīnawarī, *Al-Akhbār al-Ṭiwāl*, 188–89.

39. al-Balādhurī, *Ansāb al-Ashrāf*, 3:137.

40. Ibid., 3:145.

41. Ibid., 3:144.

42. Ibn Qutayba, *Al-Imāma wa'l-Siyāsa*, 120.

43. Likewise, in an anonymous version of the *munāẓara* in al-Mubarrad, *Al-Kāmil*, the Khārijites claim that ʿAlī left *imān* and chose *kufr* (3:118–19).

44. al-Dīnawarī, *Al-Akhbār al-Ṭiwāl*, 192. See also ibid., 191; ʿAlī's interaction with Ibn al-Kawwā' in al-Thaqafī, *Al-Gharāt*, 103–5; Ibn Aʿtham al-Kūfī, *Kitāb al-Futūḥ*, 4:95–97.

45. al-Ṭabarī, *Tārīkh*, 1:3366.

46. See Yaqūb and Abū Mikhnaf's versions in al-Ṭabarī, *Tārīkh*, 1:3373, 3374–76; al-Sha'bī and Abū Mikhnaf's accounts in al-Balādhurī, *Ansāb al-Ashrāf*, 3:136, 141–43; al-Mubarrad's anonymous version, which singles out Ibn al-Kawwā' as the murderer, *Al-Kāmil*, 3:134; Ibn al-ʿAbbās's version in al-Mubarrad, *Al-Kāmil*, 3:152; Ibn Qutayba, *Al-Imāma wa'l-Siyāsa*, 119; al-Dīnawarī, *Al-Akhbār al-Ṭiwāl*, 189–90; Ibn al-Jawzī, *Talbīs Iblīs*, 137; al-Tamīmī, *Kitāb al-Miḥan*, 121–23; Ibn Aʿtham al-Kūfī, *Kitāb al-Futūḥ*, 4:119; Ibn ʿAbd Rabbih, *Al-ʿIqd al-Farīd*, 2:368–69, 378. In the context of a *munāẓara* between the Caliph ʿUmar II and the Khārijite "Shawdhab," who was Bistām al-Yashkurī, see al-Ṭabarī, *Tārīkh*, 2:1348–49, 1375–79.

47. See al-Ṭabarī, *Tārīkh*, 3:142; al-Dīnawarī, *Al-Akhbār al-Ṭiwāl*, 189.

48. al-Ṭabarī, *Tārīkh*, 1:3379–80. See also al-Zuhrī's account in al-Balādhurī, *Ansāb al-Ashrāf*, 3:128, wherein ʿAlī predicts that the Khārijites will spill blood illicitly.

49. See also al-Sābiʿī's treatment of the Ibn Khabbāb episode in *Al-Khawārij wa'l-Ḥaqīqa al-Ghā'iba*, 124–31, 409.

50. al-Ṭabarī, *Tārīkh*, 1:3373; Ibn Saʿd, *Al-Ṭabaqāt al-Kubrā*, 5:189. See also Ibn ʿAbd Rabbih, *Al-ʿIqd al-Farīd*, 2:369; al-Tamīmī, *Kitāb al-Miḥan*, 122; Ibn Aʿtham al-Kūfī, *Kitāb al-Futūḥ*, 4:98.

51. al-Ṭabarī, *Tārīkh*, 1:3374; Ibn ʿAbd Rabbih, *Al-ʿIqd al-Farīd*, 2:369.

52. al-Balādhurī, *Ansāb al-Ashrāf*, 3:141. See also Ibn ʿAbd Rabbih, *Al-ʿIqd al-Farīd*, 2:369; al-Tamīmī, *Kitāb al-Miḥan*, 123.

53. See al-Balādhurī, *Ansāb al-Ashrāf,* 3:136, 142–43; al-Mubarrad, *Al-Kāmil,* 3:152; Ibn Qutayba, *Al-Imāma wa'l-Siyāsa,* 119; al-Dīnawarī, *Al-Akhbār al-Ṭiwāl,* 190.

54. al-Balādhurī, *Ansāb al-Ashrāf,* 3:179–81.

55. al-Ṭabarī, *Tārīkh,* 1:3457.

56. al-Mubarrad, *Al-Kāmil,* 140–41. See also Ibn Qutayba, *Al-Imāma wa'l-Siyāsa,* 129.

57. al-Mubarrad, *Al-Kāmil,* 140–41; al-Ṭabarī, *Tārīkh,* 1:3457–58; Ibn Qutayba, *Al-Imāma wa'l-Siyāsa,* 130; Ibn A'tham al-Kūfī, *Kitāb al-Futūḥ,* 4:134–35.

58. al-Ṭabarī, *Tārīkh,* 1:3460; ʿAbbās, *Shiʿr al-Khawārij,* 34 (no. 6).

59. al-Ṭabarī, *Tārīkh,* translation by Hawting, *The History of al-Ṭabarī Volume XVII,* 217 (with permission).

60. al-Dīnawarī, *Al-Akhbār al-Ṭiwāl,* 197.

61. As observed in Sizgorich, *Violence and Belief in Late Antiquity,* 112–14, 223–24, a clue to Ibn Muljam's attitude might be found in the behavior of certain late antique Christian monks, who took it upon themselves to patrol, often violently, the boundaries of their community. That is, these monks would insure that Christians, Jews, and Pagans did not mingle at, for example, public games, theaters, sacred spaces (temples, churches, synagogues), funerals, or weddings.

62. Sizgorich, *Violence and Belief in Late Antiquity,* 224–25.

63. See above on the narratives of Ibn Khabbāb, many of which show the "Khārijites" treating Christians with fairness (while abusing Muslims). Additionally an Ibn ʿIrbāḍ was said to have escaped the violence of some unnamed "Khārijites" by pretending to be Jewish. See Ibn ʿAbd Rabbih, *Al-ʿIqd al-Farīd,* 2:442.

64. al-Balādhurī, *Ansāb al-Ashrāf,* 3:114–15.

65. There is reason for skepticism regarding the dating of al-Dīnawarī's version of the story: in his version Ibn Muljam states that he would have "indiscriminately attacked them with my sword" (*li-istaʿraḍtuhum bi-sayfī*). The term *istiʿrāḍ* is more commonly used in later periods among the Azāriqa and Najdāt, and its presence in al-Dīnawarī's narrative therefore should give ample reason to question its full authenticity. See al-Dīnawarī, *Al-Akhbār al-Ṭiwāl,* 197.

66. There does seem to be a Qur'ānic connection between *kufr* and various other sins: whereas only God knows the inner state of a person, the *kāfir* can be known by his actions, such that the Qur'ān ties the term to those "who exceed the limits" by sinning. See Waldman, "The Development of the Concept of Kufr in the Qur'ān," 452–53; Izutsu, *Ethico-Religious Concepts in the Qur'ān,* 133. This association, however, is not the same as the outright conflation of *kufr* and sin found in heresiographical materials on the early Khārijites.

67. Izutsu, *Ethico-Religious Concepts in the Qur'ān,* 242–43.

68. ʿAbbās, *Shiʿr al-Khawārij,* 51–52 (no. 29); Maʿrūf, *Diwān al-Khawārij,* 193 (no. 250). Cf. translation by Hallaq, "Discourse Strategies," 146.

69. Madelung, "Ilḥād," 7:546. See also the later (probably Jazīran Ṣufrī) poem in which both *mulḥid* and *kāfir* are used: ʿAbbās, *Shiʿr al-Khawārij,* 139–40 (no. 150).

70. al-Ṭabarī, *Tārīkh,* 2:36; al-Balādhurī, *Ansāb al-Ashrāf,* 5:178; ʿAbbās, *Shiʿr al-Khawārij,* 45 (no. 20); translation by Morony, *The History of al-Ṭabarī Volume XVIII,* 41–42 (with permission).

71. Bearman et al., "Al-Muḥillūn," 7:470. Interestingly it is a term that was often used to denote those Umayyads and their supporters who had killed al-Ḥusayn b. ʿAlī at Karbalā': al-Mukhtār is said to have employed it in his *bayʿa* during his revolt in Kūfa. While it is doubtful that in this particular *shurāt* poem the term carries with it pro-ʿAlīd sentiments, the fact that Muʿādh was Kūfan remains intriguing.

72. al-Balādhurī, *Ansāb al-Ashrāf*, 5:182; ʿAbbās, *Shiʿr al-Khawārij*, 47 (nos. 22, 23).

73. al-Balādhurī, *Ansāb al-Ashrāf*, 5:171.

74. al-Mubarrad, *Al-Kāmil*, 3:170.

75. al-Balādhurī, *Ansāb al-Ashrāf*, 5:179.

76. The term also caused problems for the copyists of the manuscripts, one of which contains the variant *mustanṣirīn;* see al-Balādhurī, *Ansāb al-Ashrāf: Teil 4/1* (ed. Iḥsān ʿAbbās), 172n3. Following Qur'ān 29:38, the term may refer to *shurāt* who considered themselves "gifted with perception" but who did not allow the devil to tempt them from "the path" (as were the people mentioned in the verse itself). Later ʿAbbāsid era usage of the terms *ahl al-baṣā'ir* and *ahl al-baṣīra* to indicate "those with deep spiritual convictions" might also offer some clues as to its meaning. For example, see Kashshī, *Ikhtiyār Maʿrifat al-Rijāl*, 138–39 (no. 221); Sachedina, *The Just Ruler in Shiʿite Islam*, 47.

77. Al-Baghdādī's treatment of the pre-Azraqite *shurāt* includes several comments to the effect that they adhered to the views of the Muḥakkima before the Azraqī *fitna* occurred (al-Baghdādī, *Al-Farq Bayn al-Firaq*, 61–62). The language in the passage strongly suggests a quietist/possibly Ibāḍī source for these early rebellions, and it is interesting that these groups are conceptualized as continuations of the first Muḥakkima.

78. al-Balādhurī, *Ansāb al-Ashrāf*, 5:172; al-Mubarrad, *Al-Kāmil*, 3:173–74; al-Ṭabarī, *Tārīkh*, 2:90–91.

79. al-Balādhurī, *Ansāb al-Ashrāf*, 5:183; al-Mubarrad, *Al-Kāmil*, 3:173–74; al-Ṭabarī, *Tārīkh*, 2:91.

80. See Gaiser, *Muslims, Scholars, Soldiers*, 101–2.

81. Of course there remains the possibility that an Ibāḍī source—one that was interested in portraying the early *shurāt* as adherents to a quietist view that distinguished between *kufr* as unfaithfulness and *kufr* as sinfulness, and that rejected *istiʿrāḍ*—ultimately underlies the reports on Sahm, Qarīb, and Zuḥḥāf in the reports in al-Balādhurī, al-Mubarrad, and al-Ṭabarī. However, lacking clear citations to the sources of these reports, such a view remains speculative. Moreover, such a hypothesis would need to show why al-Balādhurī's, al-Mubarrad's, and al-Ṭabarī's reports neglect specifically Ibāḍī terminology (i.e., *kufr al-nifāq, kufr al-niʿma,* etc.) to describe the differences in various senses of *kufr.*

82. al-Ashʿarī, *Maqālāt al-Islāmīyyīn*, 1:169–74. Al-Shahrastānī is also fairly typical in this regard, claiming that the founder of the Azāriqa, Nāfiʿ b. al-Azraq (and by extension all Azraqites), anathematized and openly dissociated (i.e., *bara'a min*) from those who stayed behind and did not go into battle, those who did not join the Azraqite camp, and those who committed major sins (*aṣḥāb al-kabā'ir*), considering the wives and children of those so accused as equally guilty. See al-Shahrastānī, *Al-Milal wa'l-Niḥal*, 121–22.

83. Crone and Zimmerman, *The Epistle of Sālim Ibn Dhakwān*, 100–101.

84. Ibid., 102–3.

85. al-Balādhurī, *Ansāb al-Ashrāf*, 7:144–45.

86. Ibid., 7:145.

87. al-Mubarrad, *Al-Kāmil*, 3:202–3. See also ibid., 3:195; Ibn ʿAbd Rabbih, *Al-ʿIqd al-Farīd*, 372–75.

88. al-Mubarrad, *Al-Kāmil*, 3:200.

89. Crone and Zimmerman, *The Epistle of Sālim Ibn Dhakwān*, 100–103.

90. al-Mubarrad, *Al-Kāmil*, 3:201; Ibn ʿAbd Rabbih, *Al-ʿIqd al-Farīd*, 2:373.

91. al-Mubarrad, *Al-Kāmil*, 1:86; ʿAbbās, *Shiʿr al-Khawārij*, 86–87 (no. 73). Cf. translation by Hallaq, "Discourse Strategies," 144–45.

92. al-Marzubānī, *Mu'jam al-Shu'arā'*, 258; 'Abbās, *Shi'r al-Khawārij*, 58 (no. 39). Cf. translation by Donner, "Piety and Eschatology in Early Kharijite Poetry," 14.

93. See Qur'ān, 49:10, 61:4, 59:9.

94. Watt, *The Formative Period of Islamic Thought*, 37; Shaban, *Islamic History*, 96–98.

95. In this sense Savage overstates her case for Christian-Ibāḍī connections in Iraq and North Africa. See Savage, *A Gateway to Hell, a Gateway to Paradise*, 91–96.

96. al-Balādhurī, *Ansāb al-Ashrāf*, 7:151; 'Abbās, *Shi'r al-Khawārij*, 73 (no. 56). Cf. translation by Hallaq, "Discourse Strategies," 137.

97. al-Balādhurī, *Ansāb al-Ashrāf*, 5:423; 'Abbās, *Shi'r al-Khawārij*, 56 (no. 36). Cf. translation by Hallaq, "Discourse Strategies," 141.

98. al-Mubarrad, *Al-Kāmil*, 3:179; 'Abbās, *Shi'r al-Khawārij*, 54 (no. 34).

99. al-Tibrīzī, *Sharḥ Diwān al-Ḥamāsa*, 467 (no. 231); 'Abbās, *Shi'r al-Khawārij*, 113 (no. 110).

100. See al-Barrādī, *Kitāb al-Jawāhir*, 120–21; al-Izkawī, *Kashf al-Ghumma*, 1:578; al-Qalhātī, *Al-Kashf wa'l-Bayān*, 2:244ff.; Abū Qaḥtān Khālid b. Qaḥtān's *sīra* in Kāshif, *Al-Siyar wa'l-Jawabāt*, 1:107; Abū Mū'thir al-Ṣalt b. Khamīs's *sīra* in Kāshif, *Al-Siyar wa'l-Jawabāt*, 2:305.

101. 'Abbās, *Shi'r al-Khawārij*, 95 (no. 84); Ma'rūf, *Diwān al-Khawārij*, 93 (no. 123). See also Zayd b. Jandab al-Azraqī's poem, in which he uses the term to insult his fellow Azraqites (because they have split their ranks): al-Jāḥiẓ, *Al-Bayān wa'l-Tabyīn*, 1:38; 'Abbās, *Shi'r al-Khawārij*, 129–30 (no. 135).

102. 'Abbās, *Shi'r al-Khawārij*, 94 (no. 83); Ma'rūf, *Diwān al-Khawārij*, 96 (no. 130). Cf. translation by Hallaq, "Discourse Strategies," 145. See also a "Ṣufrī" poem in which Mu'āwiya is described as the "tempter" (*al-ghāwī*): 'Abbās, *Shi'r al-Khawārij*, 140 (no. 151).

103. al-Balādhurī, *Ansāb al-Ashrāf*, 7:151; 'Abbās, *Shi'r al-Khawārij*, 74 (no. 57). Cf. translation by Hallaq, "Discourse Strategies," 137–38.

104. al-Dīnawarī, *Al-Akhbār al-Ṭiwāl*, 253; 'Abbās, *Shi'r al-Khawārij*, 90–91(no. 78). Cf. translation by Hallaq, "Discourse Strategies," 141.

105. See Qur'ān, 2:26, 5:64, 5:68, 7:146, 7:178, 17:82.

106. al-Mubarrad, *Al-Kāmil*, 3:208; 'Abbās, *Shi'r al-Khawārij*, 106–7 (no. 104).

107. Lane, *An Arabic English Lexicon*, 556.

108. 'Abbās, *Shi'r al-Khawārij*, 102–3 (no. 100); Ma'rūf, *Diwān al-Khawārij*, 52 (no. 66). Cf. translation by Hallaq, "Discourse Strategies," 150.

109. al-Mas'ūdī, *Murūj al-Dhahab*, 5:315; 'Abbās, *Shi'r al-Khawārij*, 120–21 (no. 123). Cf. translation by Hallaq, "Discourse Strategies," 148–49; Gabrieli, "Religious Poetry in Early Islam," 14.

110. al-Ash'arī, *Maqālāt al-Islāmiyīn*, 1:174: "they [the Azāriqa] said: 'any who withdrew their hand from the fight after God, glorified and magnified be He, revealed the Exposition [that is, the Qur'ān] was a *kāfir*.'"

111. al-Shahrastānī, *Al-Milal wa'l-Niḥal*, 122–25.

112. Gaiser, "What Do We Learn about the Early Khārijites and Ibāḍiyya from Their Coins?," 174–83.

113. Waldman, "The Development of the Concept of Kufr in the Qur'ān," 452–53.

114. After all, had not Abū Bakr fought a two-year war against "*murtaddūn*" even though they technically had not refused ("gone back on") the basics of monotheism?

4. Ibāḍī Appropriations

1. For narratives on the emergence of the Ibāḍiyya, see Wilkinson, *Ibāḍism*, 122–210; Gaiser, *Muslims, Scholars, Soldiers*, 19–48; Hoffman, *The Essentials of Ibāḍī Islam*, 3–53.

2. See Wilkinson, *Ibāḍism*, 108.

3. Ibid., 165, 176. The term "Ṣufriyya" is itself problematic: Lewinstein, "Making and Unmaking a Sect," 77, concludes that Islamic heresiographers invented or possibly inherited an already invented category—the "Ṣufriyya"—into which they dumped all inconsistent or otherwise uncategorizable Khārijite material.

4. Abū Zakariyya, *Kitāb Siyar al-Āʾimma wa Akhbārihim*, 40–41.

5. The history of the Ṣufriyya is far more complicated to reconstruct due to the lack of sources as well as the confusion surrounding the term "Ṣufriyya." For an assessment of the sources for the study of the North African Midrārids, see Love, "The Sufris of Sijilmasa," 175–77.

6. See Wilkinson, *Ibāḍism*, 150–56.

7. Ibid., 150–54.

8. Madelung, "ʿAbd Allāh Ibn Ibāḍ and the Origins of the Ibāḍiyya," 51–57.

9. On a more literal level, the term *ḥamalāt al-ʿilm* might also be taken to denote those "pregnant" (*ḥāmila*) with knowledge. As Wilkinson has recently argued, this designation cannot be attested to in the earliest Ibāḍī literature and probably postdates the third/ninth century. See Wilkinson, "Hamalat al-Ilm" (paper presented at Cambridge University, Cambridge, U.K., June 16, 2014). It is nonetheless tempting to see in it a reflection of Socrates' description in Plato's *Theaetetus* (148e–151d) of philosophers (indeed Theaetetus himself) as pregnant with knowledge.

10. al-Shammākhī, *Kitāb al-Siyar*, 1:187, 201, 209.

11. Wilkinson, *Ibāḍism*, 157–60.

12. Gaiser, "Ibāḍī Dynasties," 2:477.

13. Ibid., 2:477–78.

14. Lafuente y Alcántara, *Colección de obras arábigas de historia y geografía*, 28; James, *A History of Early Al-Andalus*, 61.

15. Gil, *Corpus Scriptorum Muzarabicorum*, 1:45.

16. Blankenship, *The End of the Jihād State*, 204. On quietist notions of piety, justice, and egalitarianism, see Gaiser, *Muslims, Scholars, Soldiers*, 19ff.

17. Ibn al-Athīr, *Tārīkh Ibn al-Athīr*, 714 (5:191).

18. al-Ṭabarī, *Tārīkh*, 1:2816.

19. Blankenship, *The End of the Jihād State*, 204–5; Hrbek, *General History of Africa III*, 131.

20. Ibn al-Athīr, *Tārīkh Ibn al-Athīr*, 714 (5:191).

21. Ibn Khaldūn, *Histoire des Berbères*, 1:237; Lewinstein, "Ṣufriyya," 9:766 ; Blankenship, *The End of the Jihād State*, 213–14.

22. Ibn al-Athīr, *Tārīkh Ibn al-Athīr*, 714–15 (5:191–92), 730–31 (5:251–53); Ibn ʿIdhārī, *Histoire de l'Afrique du Nord et de l'Espagne musulmane*, 1:67–68.

23. Hrbek, *General History of Africa III*, 132.

24. Ibn al-Athīr, *Tārīkh Ibn al-Athīr*, 715 (5:192); Lewinstein, "Ṣufriyya," 9:766.

25. Lewicki, "The Ibādites in North Africa and the Sudan to the Fourteenth Century," 87.

26. Wilkinson, *Ibāḍism*, 216–17.

27. Ibn ʿIdhārī, *Histoire de l'Afrique du Nord et de l'Espagne musulmane*, 1:77–78.

28. Abun-Nasr, *A History of the Maghrib in the Islamic Period*, 43.

29. For a comprehensive overview of the Midrārids, see Love, "The Sufris of Sijilmasa," 177–86.

30. Ibn ʿIdhārī, *Histoire de l'Afrique du Nord et de l'Espagne musulmane,* 1:157–58; Pellat, "Midrār," 6:1037.

31. Levtzion and Hopkins, *Corpus of Early Arabic Sources,* 65–66.

32. ʿAbd al-Ḥamīd, *Kitāb al-Istibṣār fī ʿAjāʾib al-Amṣār,* 202.

33. Gaiser, "Slaves and Silver across the Strait of Gibraltar," 57.

34. Love, "The Sufris of Sijilmasa," 180–81.

35. Robinson, *Empire and Elites after the Muslim Conquest,* 114–24.

36. Robinson, "Shabīb b. Yazīd," 9:164.

37. al-Ṭabarī, *Tārīkh,* 2:1939.

38. Wellhausen, *The Politico-Religious Factions of Early Islam,* 81–82.

39. Ibid., 82. Al-Sālimī, *Tuḥfat al-Aʿyān,* 1:94, gives the name of the Ṣufrī leader as "Shaybān."

40. Wilkinson, *Ibāḍism,* 168, 269.

41. Ibid., 163.

42. Wilkinson, "Ibāḍī ḥadīth," 251. Wilkinson, *Ibāḍism,* 164, suggests that the *Kitāb Abī Sufyān* was unknown in Oman before the sixth/twelfth century and then only slowly began to become incorporated into Omani-Ibāḍī scholarship.

43. Gaiser, "North African and Omani Ibāḍī Accounts of the *Munāẓara,*" 69–71.

44. Madelung, "ʿAbd Allāh Ibn Yazīd al-Fazārī on the Abode of Islam," 53–54.

45. Ibn Ṣaghīr, *Akhbār al-Āʾimma al-Rustumiyyīn,* 32.

46. al-Barrādī, *Al-Jawāhir al-Muntaqāt,* 13ff; al-Shammākhī, *Kitāb al-Siyar,* 1:108ff; Crone and Zimmerman, *The Epistle of Sālim Ibn Dhakwān,* 58ff. Al-Izkawī is unique in some senses insofar as he begins his account with the period of the Jāhiliyya. Nevertheless he does devote a large section of his work to the Prophet: see al-Izkawī, *Kashf al-Ghumma,* 1:161ff.

47. Al-Fazārī considered the unity of the Islamic *umma* so irreparably sundered after the first *fitna* that it became necessary to abstain from judgment (*waqf*) in association (*walāya*) and dissociation (*barāʾa*), whereas before the *fitna* it was possible to consider all Muslims as associates and brothers (*awliyāʾ*). See Madelung and al-Salimi, *Early Ibāḍī Theology,* 152; Madelung, "ʿAbd Allāh Ibn Yazīd al-Fazārī on the Abode of Islam," 54.

48. Wilkinson, *Ibāḍism,* 419ff.

49. Madelung, "ʿAbd Allāh Ibn Yazīd al-Fazārī on the Abode of Islam," 53.

50. On Ibāḍī versions of the *munāẓara,* see Gaiser, ""North African and Omani Ibāḍī Accounts of the *Munāẓara,*" 64–71.

51. Wilkinson, *Ibāḍism,* 419.

52. al-Qalhātī, *Al-Kashf wa'l-Bayān,* 2:251; al-Izkawī, *Kashf al-Ghumma,* 582.

53. al-Shammākhī, *Kitāb al-Siyar,* 1:159.

54. al-Qalhātī, *Al-Kashf wa'l-Bayān,* 2:240; al-Izkawī, *Kashf al-Ghumma,* 573.

55. al-Barrādī, *Al-Jawāhir al-Muntaqāt,* 141; al-Shammākhī (who erroneously gives *aswad al-nahār*), *Kitāb al-Siyar,* 1:163. See also Sizgorich, *Violence and Belief in Late Antiquity,* 161.

56. al-Ṭabarī, *Tārīkh,* 1:3317, variant at 1:3320–21. See also al-Tamīmī, *Kitāb al-Miḥan,* 98–99, 101.

57. al-Ṭabarī, *Tārīkh,* 1:3318; al-Tamīmī, *Kitāb al-Miḥan,* 98.

58. al-Ṭabarī, *Tārīkh,* 1:3318.

59. Ibid., 1:3321.

60. al-Izkawī, *Kashf al-Ghumma,* 565; al-Qalhātī, *Al-Kashf wa'l-Bayān,* 2:234; al-Shammākhī, *Kitāb al-Siyar,* 1:156; al-Barrādī, *Al-Jawāhir al-Muntaqāt,* 149.

61. al-Qalhātī, *Al-Kashf wa'l-Bayān,* 2:249; al-Izkawī, *Kashf al-Ghumma,* 580.

62. al-Qalhātī, *Al-Kashf wa'l-Bayān,* 2:249–50; al-Izkawī, *Kashf al-Ghumma,* 580.

63. al-Barrādī, *al-Jawāhir al-Muntaqāt,* 121.

64. Ibid., 122.

65. al-Izkawī, *Kashf al-Ghumma,* 603. On Ibn Ibāḍ's second letter, see Madelung, "'Abd Allāh ibn Ibāḍ's 'Second Letter to 'Abd al-Malik," 7–17.

66. Kāshif, *Al-Siyar wa'l-Jawābāt,* 1:235. The anonymous *Sīra fī radd 'alā ahl al-shakk,* making a theological point against those who claim not to know if 'Uthmān was killed justly or unjustly, places 'Alī b. Abī Ṭālib and 'Ammār b. Yāsir on a similar footing as the two who called the people of Kūfa to fight against Mu'āwiya. See *Sīra fī radd 'alā ahl al-shakk,* Hinds Xerox, 379[2] (folio 411 by Crone and Zimmerman's renumbering; see Crone and Zimmerman, *The Epistle of Sālim Ibn Dhakwān,* 2–5).

67. al-Qalhātī, *Al-Kashf wa'l-Bayān,* 2:233–34; al-Izkawī, *Kashf al-Ghumma,* 565; al-Barrādī, *Al-Jawāhir al-Muntaqāt,* 149. See variant in al-Shammākhī, *Kitāb al-Siyar,* 1:157.

68. al-Qalhātī, *Al-Kashf wa'l-Bayān,* 2:234; al-Izkawī, *Kashf al-Ghumma,* 566; al-Barrādī, *Al-Jawāhir al-Muntaqāt,* 149.

69. al-Qalhātī, *Al-Kashf wa'l-Bayān,* 2:234; al-Izkawī, *Kashf al-Ghumma,* 565–66; al-Barrādī, *Al-Jawāhir al-Muntaqāt,* 149.

70. al-Qalhātī, *Al-Kashf wa'l-Bayān,* 2:235; al-Izkawī, *Kashf al-Ghumma,* 567.

71. al-Qalhātī, *Al-Kashf wa'l-Bayān,* 2:235; al-Izkawī, *Kashf al-Ghumma,* 566–67; al-Barrādī, *Al-Jawāhir al-Muntaqāt,* 150. See also al-Shammākhī, *Kitāb al-Siyar,* 1:157.

72. al-Shammākhī, *Kitāb al-Siyar,* 1:157.

73. al-Qalhātī, *Al-Kashf wa'l-Bayān,* 2:251; al-Izkawī, *Kashf al-Ghumma,* 582–83; al-Shammākhī, *Kitāb al-Siyar,* 1:159, 164; al-Barrādī, *Al-Jawāhir al-Muntaqāt,* 142.

74. al-Qalhātī, *Al-Kashf wa'l-Bayān,* 2:251–52; al-Izkawī, *Kashf al-Ghumma,* 582–83.

75. On the Prophet Daniel in Islamic sources, see Ibn Kathīr, *Qiṣaṣ al-Anbiyā',* 399–400.

76. al-Barrādī, *Al-Jawāhir al-Muntaqāt,* 147. See also al-Ṭabarī, *Tārīkh,* 1:3360–61.

77. al-Barrādī, *Al-Jawāhir al-Muntaqāt,* 148. See also al-Ṭabarī, *Tārīkh,* 1:3364.

78. See also al-Barrādī, *Al-Jawāhir al-Muntaqāt,* 142. In al-Shammākhī, *Kitāb al-Siyar,* 1:164, this quote refers to Zayd b. Ḥiṣn al-Ṭā'ī.

79. al-Darjīnī, *Kitāb Ṭabaqāt al-Mashāyikh,* 2:202.

80. al-Barrādī, *Al-Jawāhir al-Muntaqāt,* 147.

81. al-Ṭabarī, *Tārīkh,* 1:3360; al-Balādhurī, *Ansāb al-Ashrāf,* 3:129. See also Ibn al-Jawzī, *Talbīs Iblīs,* 137.

82. al-Barrādī, *Al-Jawāhir al-Muntaqāt,* 148; al-Ṭabarī, *Tārīkh,* 1:3364.

83. al-Barrādī, *Al-Jawāhir al-Muntaqāt,* 129.

84. al-Qalhātī, *Al-Kashf wa'l-Bayān,* 2:239; al-Izkawī, *Kashf al-Ghumma,* 573; al-Barrādī, *Al-Jawāhir al-Muntaqāt,* 129.

85. al-Barrādī, *Al-Jawāhir al-Muntaqāt,* 128.

86. al-Ṭabarī, *Tārīkh,* 1:3363–66. See variant in al-Mubarrad, *Al-Kāmil,* 3:117.

87. al-Darjīnī, *Kitāb Ṭabaqāt al-Mashāyikh,* 2:202.

88. Kāshif, *Al-Siyar wa'l-Jawābāt,* 1:235–36.

89. Abū Bakr al-Kindī, *Kitāb al-Ihtidā',* 237; al-Izkawī, *Kashf al-Ghumma,* 743.

90. Al-Barrādī gives an extensive list of those who left Kūfa for Ḥarūrā', including among others Shayth b. Rifā'a (the military commander), Farwa b. Nawfal al-Ashja'ī,

Zayd b. Ḥiṣn al-Ṭā'ī, Hamza b. Sinān al-Azdī, and Shurayḥ b. Awfā al-'Abasī. See al-Barrādī, *Al-Jawāhir al-Muntaqāt,* 118–19; al-Izkawī, *Kashf al-Ghumma,* 572.

91. Wilkinson, *Ibāḍism,* 156–60, 179.
92. Ibid., 419.
93. Kāshif, *Al-Siyar wa'l-Jawābāt,* 1:235.
94. Ibid., 2:313.
95. Abū Bakr al-Kindī, *Kitāb al-Ihtidā',* 237; Muḥammad al-Kindī, *Bayān al-Shar',* 3:271.
96. al-Qalhātī, *Al-Kashf wa'l-Bayān,* 2:479.
97. al-Barrādī, *Al-Jawāhir al-Muntaqāt,* 150.
98. al-Qalhātī, *Al-Kashf wa'l-Bayān,* 2:253; al-Izkawī, *Kashf al-Ghumma,* 584; al-Barrādī, *Al-Jawāhir al-Muntaqāt,* 146.
99. al-Barrādī, *Al-Jawāhir al-Muntaqāt,* 145.
100. al-Izkawī, *Kashf al-Ghumma,* 607.
101. al-Barrādī, *Al-Jawāhir al-Muntaqāt,* 146–47.
102. al-Kāshif, *Al-Siyar wa'l-Jawābāt,* 1:109.
103. al-Mubarrad, *Al-Kāmil,* 3:168; 'Abbās, *Shi'r al-Khawārij,* 125 (no. 128).
104. The end of this line could easily be a corruption: al-Barrādī gives *'and ḥūsan al-ḥarb,* while the line as it is attributed to al-Aṣam al-Ḍabbī/'Imrān b. Ḥaṭṭān is *'and jawsaq al-kharb.* See al-Barrādī, *Al-Jawāhir al-Muntaqāt,* 147.
105. al-Shammākhī, *Kitāb al-Siyar,* 1:168.
106. Ibid., 1:171.
107. Ibn al-Athīr, *Tārīkh Ibn al-Athīr,* 467 (3:411); al-Balādhurī, *Ansāb al-Ashrāf,* 5:171–72.
108. al-Qalhātī, *Al-Kashf wa'l-Bayān,* 2:255–56; al-Izkawī, *Kashf al-Ghumma,* 585–86.
109. al-Qalhātī, *Al-Kashf wa'l-Bayān,* 2:478.
110. al-Izkawī, *Kashf al-Ghumma,* 743.
111. Ibid.
112. al-Shammākhī, *Kitāb al-Siyar,* 1:168–69; al-Ṭabarī, *Tārīkh,* 2:18–19.
113. al-Shammākhī, *Kitāb al-Siyar,* 1:169; al-Ṭabarī, *Tārīkh,* 2:182–83.
114. al-Shammākhī, *Kitāb al-Siyar,* 1:170.
115. Ibid.; al-Mubarrad, *Al-Kāmil,* 3:193–94.
116. al-Shammākhī, *Kitāb al-Siyar,* 1:170–71.
117. al-Balādhurī, *Ansāb al-Ashrāf,* 5:175–76.
118. Ibn al-Athīr, *Tārīkh Ibn al-Athīr,* 467 (3:411); al-Balādhurī, *Ansāb al-Ashrāf,* 5:173.
119. al-Shammākhī, *Kitāb al-Siyar,* 1:171–72.
120. Ibid., 1:172.
121. al-Izkawī, *Kashf al-Ghumma,* 749–50.
122. Ibid.
123. al-Darjīnī, *Kitāb Ṭabaqāt al-Mashāyikh,* 2:233.
124. Ibid., 2:233–34.
125. Ibid., 2:235.
126. Ibid.
127. Kāshif, *Al-Siyar wa'l-Jawābāt,* 1:234–35.
128. Ibid., 2:314.
129. al-Izkawī, *Kashf al-Ghumma,* 745.
130. It is also possible that Ibāḍī versions of the Abū Bilāl cycle informed non-Ibāḍī texts.
131. al-Darjīnī, *Kitāb Ṭabaqāt al-Mashāyikh,* 2:215–16; al-Shammākhī, *Kitāb al-Siyar,* 1:179.

132. al-Shammākhī, *Kitāb al-Siyar,* 1:179–80.
133. al-Darjīnī, *Kitāb Ṭabaqāt al-Mashāyikh,* 2:224; al-Shammākhī, *Kitāb al-Siyar,* 1:179.
134. al-Shammākhī, *Kitāb al-Siyar,* 1:179.
135. Ibid., 1:180; al-Darjīnī, *Kitāb Ṭabaqāt al-Mashāyikh,* 2:224. See also al-Barrādī, *Al-Jawāhir al-Muntaqāt,* 168.
136. al-Shammākhī, *Kitāb al-Siyar,* 1:172–73; al-Darjīnī, *Kitāb Ṭabaqāt al-Mashāyikh,* 2:215.
137. al-Shammākhī, *Kitāb al-Siyar,* 1:173; al-Darjīnī, *Kitāb Ṭabaqāt al-Mashāyikh,* 2:216–17; in a highly elliptical reference, al-Izkawī, *Kashf al-Ghumma,* 744.
138. al-Shammākhī, *Kitāb al-Siyar,* 1:174–75; al-Darjīnī, *Kitāb Ṭabaqāt al-Mashāyikh,* 2:218–20; al-Izkawī, *Kashf al-Ghumma,* 745.
139. al-Shammākhī, *Kitāb al-Siyar,* 1:175; al-Darjīnī, *Kitāb Ṭabaqāt al-Mashāyikh,* 2:222. Al-Izkawī's version has Abū Bilāl pierced by a spear but allowing the spear to penetrate his body to the point where he could strike his assailant dead. See al-Izkawī, *Kashf al-Ghumma,* 747.
140. al-Shammākhī, *Kitāb al-Siyar,* 1:180; al-Darjīnī, *Kitāb Ṭabaqāt al-Mashāyikh,* 2:217.
141. al-Darjīnī, *Kitāb Ṭabaqāt al-Mashāyikh,* 2:217–18.
142. al-Shammākhī, *Kitāb al-Siyar,* 1:173.
143. Ibid., 1:178.
144. al-Izkawī, *Kashf al-Ghumma,* 2:749.
145. Ibid.
146. Ibid.
147. Ibid.
148. al-Shammākhī, *Kitāb al-Siyar,* 1:178.
149. al-Izkawzī, *Kashf al-Ghumma,* 2:744.
150. Ibid., 747–48.
151. Kāshif, *Al-Siyar wa'l-Jawabāt,* 1:236.
152. See Gaiser, "The Ibāḍī 'Stages of Religion' Re-examined," 211ff.
153. Gaiser, *Muslims, Scholars, Soldiers,* 105–9.
154. Kāshif, *Al-Siyar wa'l-Jawābāt,* 1:238–39.
155. al-Izkawī, *Kashf al-Ghumma,* 744.
156. Crone and Zimmerman, *The Epistle of Sālim Ibn Dhakwān,* 99–111; Lewinstein, "The Azāriqa in Islamic Heresiography," 253–55. See also al-Ash'arī, *Maqālāt al-Islāmiyīn,* 1:170.
157. Kāshif, *Al-Siyar wa'l-Jawābāt,* 2:314, 1:234, 236.
158. Ibid., 1:112.
159. al-Mubarrad, *Al-Kāmil,* 3:200.
160. al-Baghdādī, *Al-Farq Bayn al-Firaq,* 71–72.
161. al-Mubarrad, *Al-Kāmil,* 3:153.
162. Wilkinson, *Ibāḍism,* 178.
163. al-Jāḥiẓ, *Al-Bayān wa'l-Tabyīn,* 2:81; Williams, *The World of Islam,* 177. Later Ibāḍī writings bear out the Ibāḍī's anti-Umayyad sentiment, and it is not difficult to find examples of anti-'Uthmān, anti-Mu'āwiya, or other generally anti-Umayyad passages in Ibāḍī texts: for example, see the so-called first letter of Ibn Ibāḍ in al-Najjār, *Al-Ibāḍiyya wa Maddā Ṣillatiha bil-Khawārij,* 130–34; and Abū Mu'thir's *sīra* in which he portrays the people who killed 'Uthmān as righteous Muslims (Kāshif, *Al-Siyar wa'l-Jawābāt,* 2:303).
164. Wilkinson, *Ibāḍism,* 165.
165. al-Shammākhī, *Kitāb al-Siyar,* 1:201.
166. Gaiser, "Ibāḍī 'Stages of Religion' Re-examined," 212; al-Jannāwanī, *Kitāb al-Waḍ',* 29; al-Shammākhī, *Muqaddimat al-Tawḥīd wa Shurūḥihā,* 69–74.

167. Wilkinson, *Ibāḍism,* 175.
168. al-Shammākhī, *Kitāb al-Siyar,* 1:204; al-Darjīnī, *Kitāb Ṭabaqāt al-Mashāyikh,* 2:248–49.
169. al-Ṭabarī, *Tārīkh,* 2:2011; translation from Williams, *History of al-Ṭabarī Volume XXVII,* 116–17.
170. See al-Iṣfahānī, *Kitāb al-Aghānī,* 23:250–55; ʿAbbās, *Shiʿr al-Khawārij,* 226 (no. 279); translation from al-Qāḍī, "The Limitations of the Qurʾānic Usage," 165–70; al-Iṣfahānī, *Kitāb al-Aghānī,* 23:234–36; ʿAbbās, *Shiʿr al-Khawārij,* 228–29 (no. 280).
171. al-Darjīnī, *Kitāb Ṭabaqāt al-Mashāyikh,* 2:250, 262.
172. Ibid., 2:259–60; al-Shammākhī, *Kitāb al-Siyar,* 1:213.
173. al-Shammākhī, *Kitāb al-Siyar,* 1:205; al-Darjīnī, *Kitāb Ṭabaqāt al-Mashāyikh,* 2:251–52.
174. al-Shammākhī, *Kitāb al-Siyar,* 1:205; al-Darjīnī, *Kitāb Ṭabaqāt al-Mashāyikh,* 2:252. Of course Abū Sufyān was a Basran scholar, and it is worth questioning the extent to which Abū Sufyān's own depictions of Ṭālib al-Ḥaqq's uprising serve the purpose of bolstering the role of the *ʿulamāʾ* in directing the *shurāt.*
175. Savage, *A Gateway to Hell, a Gateway to Paradise,* 50–52.
176. Gaiser, "Slaves and Silver across the Strait of Gibraltar," 42–43.
177. al-Darjīnī, *Kitāb Ṭabaqāt al-Mashāyikh,* 2:364; Gaiser, "Ibāḍī 'Stages of Religion' Re-examined," 211.
178. ʿAbd al-Kāfī, *Arāʾ al-Khawārij al-Kalāmiyya,* 2:238.
179. Wilkinson, *Ibāḍism,* 213.
180. Ibid.
181. Ibid., 214.
182. Kāshif, *Al-Siyar wa'l-Jawābāt,* 1:238; al-Sālimī, *Tuḥfat al-Aʿyān,* 1:90.
183. Kāshif, *Al-Siyar wa'l-Jawābāt,* 1:239; al-Sālimī, *Tuḥfat al-Aʿyān,* 1:90.
184. Kāshif, *Al-Siyar wa'l-Jawābāt,* 1:239; al-Sālimī, *Tuḥfat al-Aʿyān,* 1:91.
185. Kāshif, *Al-Siyar wa'l-Jawābāt,* 1:236.
186. "Sīrat al-Shaykh al-Faqīh Muḥammad b. Maḥbūb (to the Maghribīs)," *Majmūʾ al-Siyar* (al-Sālimī library), folios 94, 98.
187. Quoted in Ennāmi, *Studies in Ibāḍism,* 233.
188. See Qurʾān, 4:101.
189. Ennāmi, *Studies in Ibāḍism,* 233.
190. Ibid., 234.
191. Kāshif, *Al-Siyar wa'l-Jawābāt,* 1:240ff.
192. Wilkinson, *Ibāḍism,* 214.
193. al-Salimi, "The Political Organization of Oman from the Second Imamate Period to the Ya'rūba," (Paper presented at the L'Ibandisme Dans Les Societes Islamiques Medievals: Modeles Politiques, forms d'Organisation et d'Interactions Sociales Colloquium, Madrid, Spain, Dec. 12, 2012)

5. Ibāḍī Boundaries

1. al-Barrādī, *Al-Jawāhir al-Muntaqāt,* 119.
2. Ibid., 127.
3. Ibid., 128.
4. Ibid., 126.

5. Ibid., 117.

6. al-Qalhātī, *Al-Kashf wa'l-Bayān*, 2:235; al-Izkawī, *Kashf al-Ghumma*, 567. See also al-Shammākhī, *Kitāb al-Siyar*, 1:157.

7. al-Shammākhī *Kitāb al-Siyar*, 1:210–11; Wilkinson, *Ibāḍism*, 173.

8. See, for example, Nāṣir b. Sālim b. 'Udayyam al-Rawāḥī's (d. 1339/1920) substantial chapter on *walāya* and *barā'a* from his *Al-'Aqīda al-Wahbiyya* ("Creed") in Hoffman, *The Essentials of Ibāḍī Islam*, 156–211.

9. For an extensive discussion of the concepts of *walāya* and *barā'a*, see Ennāmi, *Studies in Ibāḍism*, 207ff. For a discussion of the concept of *walāya* in a Shi'ite context, see Dakake, *The Charismatic Community*, 15ff.

10. On the tribal and early Islamic roots of the concepts, see also Ennāmi, *Studies in Ibāḍism*, 207–9.

11. Dakake, "The Myth of a Militant Islam," 6.

12. See Qur'ān, 6:19, 28:63.

13. al-Ṭabarī, *Tārīkh*, 2:516–21; Ibn 'Abd Rabbih, *Al-'Iqd al-Farīd*, 2:370–72.

14. 'Abbās, *Shi'r al-Khawārij*, 140 (no. 151). On Shabīb b. Yazīd, see Gaiser, *Muslims, Scholars, Soldiers*, 95; Robinson, *Empire and Elites after the Muslim Conquest*, 114–25.

15. "Sīrat Abī Mawdūd Ḥājib man Ḥamidu Allāh," *Majmū' al-Siyar* (al-Sālimī library), folio 577; "Sīrat Abī Mawdūd Ḥājib al-Ṭā'ī," *Al-Siyar al-Ibāḍiyya* (Aḥmad b. Nāṣir al-Sayfī library), folio 67.

16. "Sīrat Abī Mawdūd Ḥājib man Ḥamidu Allāh," *Majmū' al-Siyar* (al-Sālimī library), folio 577; "Sīrat Abī Mawdūd Ḥājib al-Ṭā'ī," *Al-Siyar al-Ibāḍiyya* (Aḥmad b. Nāṣir al-Sayfī library), folios 67–68.

17. "Sīrat Abī Mawdūd Ḥājib man Ḥamidu Allāh," *Majmū' al-Siyar* (al-Sālimī library), folio 579; "Sīrat Abī Mawdūd Ḥājib al-Ṭā'ī," *Al-Siyar al-Ibāḍiyya* (Aḥmad b. Nāṣir al-Sayfī library), folio 70.

18. al-Shammākhī, *Kitāb al-Siyar*, 1:227.

19. Madelung and al-Salimi, *Early Ibāḍī Theology*, 149–52; Madelung, "'Abd Allāh Ibn Yazīd al-Fazārī," 54.

20. See also Madelung and al-Salimi, *Early Ibāḍī Theology*, 206.

21. Torrey, *The History of the Conquests of Egypt, North Africa, and Spain*, 224–25; Abū Zakariyya, *Kitāb Siyar al-Ā'imma wa Akhbārihim*, 58; al-Darjīnī, *Kitāb Ṭabaqāt al-Mashāyikh*, 1:24–25; al-Shammākhī, *Kitāb al-Siyar*, 2:247–48; al-Barrādī, *Jawāhir al-Muntaqāt*, 170–71.

22. "Kitāb Muslim b. Abī 'Ubayda wa Ḥājib ilā Ahl al-Maghrib," *Kitāb Siyar al-'Umāniyya* (Muḥammad b. Aḥmad library), folios 275–81; "Kitāb Abī 'Ubayda Muslim wa Abī Mawdūd Ḥājib ilā Ahl al-Maghrib," *al-Siyar al-Ibāḍiyya* (Aḥmad b. Nāṣir al-Sayfī library), folios 50–55; al-Darjīnī, *Kitāb Ṭabaqāt al-Mashāyikh*, 1:24–25.

23. al-Darjīnī: *Kitāb Ṭabaqāt al-Mashāyikh*, 1:25.

24. al-Shammākhī, *Kitāb al-Siyar*, 1:199; al-Darjīnī, *Kitāb Ṭabaqāt al-Mashāyikh*, 2:242.

25. Abū 'Ubayda and Abū Mawdūd effected a similar excommunication when they forbade contact with Ḥamza, al-'Aṭiyya, and al-Ḥārith for their divergent views and for having "committed sins" (*aḥdatha aḥdāthan*). Pace Ennāmi, *Studies in Ibāḍism*, 211–12, the language of *walāya* and *barā'a* is not in evidence in the descriptions of these events. See al-Shammākhī, *Kitāb al-Siyar*, 2:198; al-Darjīnī, *Kitāb Ṭabaqāt al-Mashāyikh*, 2:243–44.

26. Madelung and al-Salimi, *Early Ibāḍī Theology*, 152.

27. Ibid., 149–50, 201–6; Madelung, "'Abd Allāh Ibn Yazīd al-Fazārī: On the Abode of Islam," 54–56.

28. Ibn Abī Karīma, *Risālat Abī Karīma fī Zakāt,* 19–22; Francesca, "Early Ibāḍī Jurisprudence," 261.

29. Ibn Abī Karīma, *Risālat Abī Karīma fī Zakāt,* 19.

30. Ennāmi, *Studies in Ibāḍism,* 218.

31. Francesca, "Early Ibāḍī Jurisprudence," 261.

32. Ibn Salām, *Kitāb Ibn Salām,* 107.

33. In fact Ibn Ibāḍ remains one of the few early authors to use the term *khawārij* when referring to these movements. See Crone and Zimmerman *The Epistle of Sālim Ibn Dhakwān,* 275-78

34. Kāshif, *Al-Siyar wa'l-Jawābāt,* 2:342.

35. al-Ḥārithī, *Al-'Uqūd al-Fiḍiyya,* 125.

36. Crone and Zimmerman, *The Epistle of Sālim Ibn Dhakwān,* 140–41.

37. al-Jayṭālī, *Qawā'id al-Islām,* 1:48–49.

38. Ibid., 1:59.

39. Ibid., 1:66–67.

40. Ibn Ja'far, *Al-Jāmi' li-Ibn Ja'far,* 1:147–253.

41. Ennāmi, *Studies in Ibāḍism,* 195.

42. Abū Mikhnaf's account in al-Ṭabarī, *Tārīkh,* 2:519; al-Balādhurī, *Ansāb al-Ashrāf,* 7:147; al-Mubarrad, *Al-Kāmil,* 3:204; al-Sharastānī, *Al-Milal wa'l-Niḥal,* 134–35. See also Crone and Zimmerman, *The Epistle of Sālim Ibn Dhakwān,* 198n9.

43. For example, see Mu'ammar, *Al-Ibāḍiyya fī Mawkab al-Ta'rīkh,* 1:89ff; Mu'ammar, *Al-Ibāḍiyya Bayn al-Firaq al-Islāmiyya,* 2:286–89.

44. Crone and Zimmerman, *The Epistle of Sālim Ibn Dhakwān,* 200.

45. Madelung and al-Salimi, *Early Ibāḍī Theology,* 211 (line 8).

46. "Risāla min Abī 'Ubayda wa Ḥājib Ayḍan," *Kitāb Siyar al-'Umāniyya* (Muḥammad b. Aḥmad library), folios 281–85; "Risālat Abī 'Ubayda wa Abī Mawdūd Ḥājib fi'l-Radd 'alā al-Murji'a," *al-Siyar al-Ibāḍiyya* (Aḥmad b. Nāṣir al-Sayfī library), folios 55–58.

47. "Risāla min Abī 'Ubayda wa Ḥājib Ayḍan," *Kitāb Siyar al-'Umāniyya* (Muḥammad b. Aḥmad library), folio 281; "Risālat Abī 'Ubayda wa Abī Mawdūd Ḥājib fi'l-Radd 'alā al-Murji'a," *al-Siyar al-Ibāḍiyya* (Aḥmad b. Nāṣir al-Sayfī library), folio 55.

48. "Risāla min Abī 'Ubayda wa Ḥājib Ayḍan," *Kitāb Siyar al-'Umāniyya* (Muḥammad b. Aḥmad library)

49. Ibid., folios 281–82; "Risālat Abī 'Ubayda wa Abī Mawdūd Ḥājib fi'l-Radd 'alā al-Murji'a," *al-Siyar al-Ibāḍiyya* (Aḥmad b. Nāṣir al-Sayfī library), folio 55.

50. Ibid., folio 282; "Risālat Abī 'Ubayda wa Abī Mawdūd Ḥājib fi'l-Radd 'alā al-Murji'a," *al-Siyar al-Ibāḍiyya* (Aḥmad b. Nāṣir al-Sayfī library), folio 55.

51. Ibid., folio 282; folio "Risālat Abī 'Ubayda wa Abī Mawdūd Ḥājib fi'l-Radd 'alā al-Murji'a," *al-Siyar al-Ibāḍiyya* (Aḥmad b. Nāṣir al-Sayfī library), 56.

52. "Risāla min Abī 'Ubayda wa Ḥajib Ayḍan," *Kitāb Siyar al-'Umaniyya* (Muḥammad b. Aḥmad library), folio 282

53. Ibid.

54. Ibid., folios 282–83; "Risālat Abī 'Ubayda wa Abī Mawdūd Ḥājib fī'l-Radd 'alā al-Murji'a," *al-Siyar al-Ibāḍiyya* (Aḥmad b. Nāṣir al-Sayfī library), folio 56.

55. "Min Kutub Abī 'Ubayda," *Kitāb Siyar al-'Umāniyya* (Muḥammad b. Aḥmad library), folio 279; "Min Kutub Abī 'Ubayda," *al-Siyar al-Ibāḍiyya* (Aḥmad b. Nāṣir al-Sayfī library), folio 61.

56. "Sīrat Abī Mawdūd," *Kitāb Siyar al-'Umāniyya* (Muḥammad b. Aḥmad library), folio 577; "Sīrat Abī Mawdūd Ḥājib al-Ṭā'ī," *al-Siyar al-Ibāḍiyya* (Aḥmad b. Nāṣir al-Sayfī library), folio 67.

57. Also noteworthy is how the cosmological unfolding of faith and *kufr* in the Abū 'Ubayda and Abū Mawdūd's *risāla* seems to resonate with the kinds of Neoplatonic schemes of emanation that were popular among Eastern Christian, "Gnostic," and Manichean groups in Iraq in late antiquity and the early Islamic periods. While, once again, no direct or specific "influence" can be detected on the *sīra,* the language of "genesis" as well as the metaphor of Iblīs opening various "doors" to allow different kinds of *kufr* into the world are strongly suggestive of an cosmological emanation scheme.

58. "Sīrat Abī Mawdūd," *Kitāb Siyar al-'Umāniyya* (Muḥammad b. Aḥmad library), folio 577; "Sīrat Abī Mawdūd Ḥājib al-Ṭā'ī," *al-Siyar al-Ibāḍiyya* (Aḥmad b. Nāṣir al-Sayfī library), folios 67–68.

59. See Crone and Zimmerman, *The Epistle of Sālim Ibn Dhakwān,* 195–96. For an analysis of how later Sunnī jurisprudence and tradition would classify these same types of persons, see Friedmann, "Classification of Unbelievers in Sunnī Muslim Law and Tradition," 163ff.

60. "Sīrat Khalaf b. Ziyād," *Hinds Xerox,* folio 304; "Sīrat Khalaf b. Ziyād al-Baḥrānī," *al-Siyar al-Ibāḍiyya* (Aḥmad b. Nāṣir al-Sayfī library), folio 108; "Sīrat Khalaf b. Ziyād al-Baḥrānī," *Majmū' al-Siyar* (al-Sālimī Library), folio 585.

61. Kāshif, *Al-Siyar wa'l-Jawābāt,* 2:59.

62. Ibid.

63. Crone and Zimmerman, *The Epistle of Sālim Ibn Dhakwān,* 68–69.

64. Ibid., 68–71. This treatment mirrors the ways that an emerging Sunnī consensus would also come to treat Zoroastrians. See Friedmann, "Classification of Unbelievers in Sunnī Muslim Law and Tradition," 180.

65. Crone and Zimmerman, *The Epistle of Sālim Ibn Dhakwān,* 70–71.

66. Ibid.

67. Ibid., 72–73.

68. Ibid., 132–33.

69. Ibid., 134–41.

70. Ibid., 134–35.

Conclusion

1. Robinson, *Empire and Elites after the Muslim Conquest,* 120; Barsaum, *Anonymi auctoris chronicon ad annum Christi 1234 pertinens,* 1:14.

2. Gaiser, "What Do We Learn about the Early Khārijites and Ibāḍiyya from Their Coins?," 186.

3. Robinson, *Empire and Elites after the Muslim Conquest,* 124.

4. Of course this is not always the case, as with the martyrs of the Battle of Mānū. See Prevost, "Les enjeux de la bataille de Mânû (283/896)," 85–86.

5. I am indebted to Paul Love for this insight into the community-building nature of Ibāḍī prosopographical literature.

Bibliography

Primary Sources

Arabic Manuscripts

Hinds Xerox. Florida State University Library, Tallahassee, Florida. FILM 9721.

Kitāb Siyar al-'Umāniyya. Sayyid Muḥammad b. Aḥmad b. Sa'ūd Library, Sīb, Oman.

Majmū' al-Siyar. Al-Sālimī Library, Bidiyya, Oman.

al-Siyar al-Ibāḍiyya. Aḥmad b. Nāṣir al-Sayfī Library, Nizwa, Oman.

Arabic, Syriac, and Translations

'Abbās, Iḥsān, ed. *Shi'r al-Khawārij: Jam' wa Taqdīm Iḥsān 'Abbās.* 3rd ed. Beirut: Dār al-Thaqāfa, 1974.

'Abd al-Ḥamīd, Sa'd Zaghlūl, ed. *Kitāb al-Istibṣār fī 'Ajā'ib al-Amṣār.* Alexandria: Université d'Alexandrie, 1958.

'Abd al-Kāfī al-Ibāḍī, Abū 'Ammār. *Arā' al-Khawārij al-Kalāmiyya: Al-Mūjaz li-Abī Ammār 'Abd al-Kāfī al-Ibāḍī.* Edited by 'Ammār Ṭālibī. Algeria: al-Sharika al-Waṭaniyya, n.d.

Abū Dāwūd Sulaymān b. al-Ash'ath al-Sijistānī. *Sunan Abī Dāwūd.* Riyadh: International Ideas Home, n.d.

Abū Zakariyya, Yaḥyā Ibn Abī Bakr. *Kitāb Siyar al-Ā'imma wa Akhbārihim.* Edited by Ismā'īl al-'Arabī. Algiers: Dār al-Maghrib al-Islāmī, 1979.

'Antara b. Shaddād. *Sharḥ Diwān 'Antara Ibn Shaddād.* Edited by 'Abd al-Munīm 'Abd al-Rawf al-Shalabī. Beirut: Dār al-Kutub al-'Ilmiyya, 1980.

al-Ash'arī, Abū al-Ḥasan 'Alī b. Ismā'īl. *Maqālāt al-Islāmiyīn wa Ikhtilāf al-Muṣallīn.* Edited by Muḥammad Muḥyā al-Dīn 'Abd al-Ḥamīd. Beirut: Maktabat al-'Aṣriyya, 1999.

Aṭfayyish, Abū Isḥāq Ibrāhīm. *Al-Farq Bayn al-Ibāḍiyya wa'l-Khawārij.* Rūwī: Maktabat al-Istiqāma, 1980.

al-'Awtabī, Abū Mundhir Salama b. Muslim. *Al-Ansāb.* Edited by Muḥammad Iḥsān al-Naṣṣ. Muscat: Maṭba'at al-Alwān al-Ḥadītha, 2006.

al-'Awtabī, Abū Mundhir Salama b. Muslim. *Kitāb al-Ḍiyā'.* Muscat: Wizārat al-Turāth al-Qawmī wa'l-Thaqāfa, 1991.

al-Azdī, Muḥammad b. 'Abdullāh al-Baṣrī. *Tārīkh Futūḥ al-Shām.* Edited by 'Abd al-Munīm 'Abdullāh 'Āmir. Cairo: Mu'assisat Sijil al-'Arab, 1970.

Badger, George Percy, trans. *History of the Imāms and Seyyids of 'Omān, by Salīl Ibn Razīk.* London: Printed for the Hakluyt Society, 1871.

al-Baghdādī, Abd al-Qādir b. 'Umar, Raḍī al-Dīn Muḥammad b. al-Ḥasan al-Astarābādhī, and Badr al-Dīn Maḥmūd b. Aḥmad al-'Aynī. *Khizānat al-Adab wa Lub Lubāb Lisān al-'Arab 'alā Shawāhid Sharḥ al-Kāfiya.* Beirut: Dār Ṣādir, 1968.

al-Baghdādī, Abū Qāhir b. Tāhir. *Al-Farq Bayn al-Firaq.* Beirut: Dār al-Afāq al-Jadīda, 1987.

al-Balādhurī, Aḥmad b. Yaḥyā. *Ansāb al-Ashrāf.* Edited by Suhayl Zakkār and Riyāḍ Zarkalī. Beirut: Dār al-Fikr lil-Ṭibā'a wa'l-Nashr wa'l-Tawzī', 1996.

al-Balādhurī, Aḥmad b. Yaḥyā. *Ansāb al-Ashrāf: Teil 4/1.* Edited by Iḥsān 'Abbās. Wiesbaden: Franz Steiner Verlag, 1979.

al-Barrādī, Abū al-Faḍl/al-Qāsim b. Ibrāhīm. *Al-Jawāhir al-Muntaqāt fī Itmām mā Akhalla bihi Kitāb al-Ṭabaqāt.* Cairo: Lithograph, 1885.

Barsaum, Aphram, ed., and Jean Baptiste Chabot, trans. *Anonymi auctoris chronicon ad annum Christi 1234 pertinens.* Paris: E. Typographeo Reipublicae 1920 (Corpus scriptorum Christianorum orientalium 81); Louvain: E. Typographeo Reipublicae, 1937 (Corpus scriptorum Christianorum orientalium 109).

Bedjan, Paul, ed. *Acts of Martyrs and Saints: Acta Martyrum et Sanctorum.* Piscataway, N.J.: Gorgias Press, 2007.

Būlruwāḥ, Ibrāhīm b. 'Alī, ed. *Mawsū'at Athār al-Imām Jābir b. Zayd al-Fiqhiyya.* Muscat: Maktabat Musqaṭ, 2006.

Cooper, John M., trans. *Plato: Complete Works.* Indianapolis: Hackett, 1997.

Crone, Patricia, and Fritz Zimmerman, trans. and eds. *The Epistle of Sālim Ibn Dhakwān.* New York: Oxford University Press, 2001.

al-Dārimī, Abū Muḥammad 'Abdullāh b. 'Abd al-Raḥmān. *Sunan al-Dārimī.* Edited by Maḥmūd Aḥmad 'Abd al-Muḥsin. Beirut: Dār al-Ma'rifa, 2000.

al-Darjīnī, Abū al-'Abbās Ahmad b. Sa'īd. *Kitāb Ṭabaqāt al-Mashāyikh bī'l-Maghrib.* Edited by Ibrahim Tallay. Algiers: Alger-Constantine, n.d.

al-Dīnawarī, Abū Ḥanīfa Aḥmad b. Dāwūd. *Al-Akhbār al-Ṭiwāl.* Beirut: Dār al-Arqam, 1995.

Ephrem the Syrian. *Against Heresies, Hymn 22.* Translated by Adam McCollum. http://www.roger-pearse.com/weblog/wp-content/uploads/2012/10/ephrem_contra_haer_22.mellel.pdf (accessed March 25, 2015).

Gil, Ioannes, ed. *Corpus Scriptorum Muzarabicorum.* Madrid: Instituto Antonio de Nebrija, 1973.

Guillaume, Alfred. *The Life of Muhammad: A Translation of Ibn Ishaq's Sirat Rasul Allah.* London: Oxford University Press, 1970.

al-Ḥārithī, Sālim b. Ḥamad b. Sulaymān. *Al-'Uqūd al-Fiḍiyya fī Uṣul al-Ibāḍiyya.* Muscat: Wizārat al-Turāth al-Qawmī wa'l-Thaqāfa, 1983.

Hawting, G. R., trans. *The History of al-Ṭabarī Volume XVII: The First Civil War.* Albany: State University of New York Press, 1996.

Ibn 'Abd Rabbih, Aḥmad b. Muḥammad al-Andalūsī. *Kitāb al-'Iqd al-Farīd.* Edited by Barkāt Yūsuf Habūd. Beirut: Dār al-Arqam, 1999.

Ibn Abī Karīma, Abū 'Ubayda Muslim. *Risālat Abī Karīma fī Zakāt lil-Imām Abī al-Khaṭṭāb al-Ma'ārifī.* Muscat: Wizārat al-Turāth al-Qawmī wa'l-Thaqāfa, 1982.

Ibn 'Asākir, Abu al-Qāsim 'Alī b. al-Ḥasan. *Tahdhīb Tārīkh Dimashq al-Kabīr.* Edited by 'Abd al-Qādir Badrān. Beirut: Dār Iḥyā' al-Turāth al-'Arabī, 1987.

Ibn A'tham al-Kūfī, Aḥmad. *Kitāb al-Futūḥ.* Hyderabad: Maṭba'at Majlis Dayrat al-Ma'ārif al-'Uthmāniyya, 1968.

Ibn al-Athīr, 'Izz al-Dīn. *Al-Kāmil fī al-Tārīkh.* Edited by Carl Johan Tornberg. Leiden: Brill, 1851.

Ibn al-Athīr, 'Izz al-Dīn. *Tārīkh Ibn al-Athīr.* Riyadh: Bayt al-Afkār al-Dawaliyya, n.d.

Ibn Ḥanbal, Aḥmad. *Kitāb al-Zuhd.* Beirut: Dār al-Kutub al-'Ilmiyya, 1976.

Ibn Ḥazm, Abū Muḥammad 'Alī b. Aḥmad. *Kitāb al-Fisal fī'l-Milal wa Ahwā` wa'l-Niḥal.* Edited by Aḥmad Shams al-Dīn. Beirut: Dār al-Kutub al-'Ilmiyya, 1999.

Ibn Hishām, ʿAbd al-Mālik. *Al-Sīra al-Nabawiyya*. Edited by Ibrāhīm al-Abyārī, Muṣṭafā al-Saqā, and ʿAbd al-Ḥāfiẓ Shabalī. Beirut: Dār al-Khayr, 1996.

Ibn ʿIdhārī, Muḥammad. *Histoire de l'Afrique du Nord et de l'Espagne musulmane, intitulée Kitab al-bayan al-mughrib, et fragments de la chronique de ʿArib*. Leiden: Brill, 1948.

Ibn Jaʿfar, Abū Jābir Muḥammad. *Al-Jāmiʿ li-Ibn Jaʿfar*. Muscat: Wizārat al-Turāth al-Qawmī wa'l-Thaqāfa, 1981.

Ibn al-Jawzī, Jamāl al-Dīn Abū al-Faraj ʿAbd al-Raḥmān. *Talbīs Iblīs*. Beirut: Manshūrāt Dār Maktabat al-Ḥayāt, 1989.

Ibn Kathīr, Abū al-Faḍāʾ Ismāʿīl. *Qiṣaṣ al-Anbiyāʾ*. Beirut: Dār al-Arqām, 1997.

Ibn Khaldūn, Walī al-Dīn ʿAbd al-Raḥmān b. Muḥammad al-Ishbīlī. *Histoire des Berbères et des dynasties musulmanes de l'Afrique septentrionale*. Paris: P. Geuthner, 1925–56.

Ibn Khayyāṭ, Khalīfa. *Tārīkh Khalīfa b. Khayyāṭ*. Beirut: Dār al-Kutub al-ʿIlmiyya, 1995.

Ibn Mūsā, ʿIyāḍ. *Tartīb al-Madārik wa Taqrīb al-Masālik li-Maʿrifat Aʿlām Madhhab Mālik*. Beirut: Dār Maktabat al-Fikr, 1968.

Ibn Qays, Abū Isḥāq Ibrāhīm. *Mukhtaṣar al-Khiṣāl*. Muscat: Wizārat al-Turāth al-Qawmī wa'l-Thaqāfa, 1983.

Ibn Qutayba, Abū Muḥammad ʿAbdullāh b. Muslim. *Al-Imāma wa'l-Siyāsa*. Beirut: Dār Kutub al-ʿIlmiyya, 1997.

Ibn Qutayba, Abū Muḥammad ʿAbdullāh b. Muslim. *Al-Maʿārif*. Beirut: Dār al-Kutub al-ʿIlmiyya, 1987.

Ibn Saʿd, Muḥammad b. Saʿd b. Manīʿ al-Hāshimī. *Al-Ṭabaqāt al-Kubrā*. Edited by Muḥammad ʿAbd al-Qādir ʿAṭā. Beirut: Dār al-Kutub al-ʿIlmiyya, 1997.

Ibn al-Ṣaghīr. *Akhbār al-Āʾimma al-Rustumiyyīn*. Edited by Muḥammad Nāsir and Ibrāhīm Bahhāz. Algiers: Dār al-Gharb al-Islāmī, 1986.

Ibn Salām. *Kitāb Ibn Salām al-Ibāḍī: al-Islām wa Tārīkhihi min Wijhat Naẓar Ibāḍī*. Edited by R. F. Schwartz and Sālim b. Yaʿqūb. Beirut: Dār Iqraʾ, 1985.

al-Iṣfahānī, Abū al-Faraj ʿAlī b. al-Ḥusayn. *Kitāb al-Aghānī*. Beirut: Dār Iḥyāʾ al-Turāth al-ʿArabī, 1994.

al-Isfarāʾinī, Shafūr Ibn Ṭāhir. *Al-Tabbassur fī'l-Dīn wa Tamyīz al-Firqa al-Nājiya ʿan al-Firaq al-Hālikīn*. Edited by Muḥammad Zāhid b. al-Ḥasan al-Kawtharī and Maḥmūd Muḥammad al-Khaḍīrī. Cairo: Maktabat al-Azhār lil-Turāth, 1940.

al-Izkawī, Sirḥān b. Saʿīd. *Kashf al-Ghumma al-Jāmiʿ li-Akhbār al-Umma*. Edited by Ḥasan Muḥammad ʿAbdullāh al-Nābudih. Beirut: Dār al-Bārūdī, 2006.

al-Jāhiẓ, Abū ʿUthmān ʿAmr b. Baḥr. *Al-Bayān wa'l-Tabyīn*. Beirut: Dār al-Kutub al-ʿIlmiyya, 1988.

James, David, trans. *A History of Early Al-Andalus: The Akhbār majmūʿa*. London: Routledge, 2012.

al-Jannāwanī, Abū Zakariyya Yaḥya Ibn Abī Khayr. *Kitāb al-Waḍʿ*. Muscat: Maktabat al-Istiqāma, n.d.

al-Jayṭālī, Abū Ṭāhir Ismāʿīl b. Mūsā. *Kitāb Qanāṭir al-Khayrāt*. Edited by ʿAmr K. Ennāmī. Cairo: Maktabat Wahba, 1965.

al-Jayṭālī, Abū Ṭāhir Ismāʿīl b. Mūsā. *Kitāb Qawāʿid al-Islām*. Edited by Baklī ʿAbd al-Raḥmān b. ʿUmar. Muscat: Maktabat al-Istiqāma, 1996.

Jones, Alan, trans. *Early Arabic Poetry: Select Poems*. Reading: Ithaca Press, 2011.

Kashīf, Sayyida Ismāʿīl, ed. *Al-Siyar wa'l-Jawabāt li-ʿUlamāʾ wa Āʾimmat ʿUmān*. Muscat: Wizārat al-Turāth al-Qawmī wa'l-Thaqāfa, 1989.

al-Kashshī, Abū ʿAmr ʿUmar b. ʿAbd al-ʿAzīz. *Ikhtiyār Maʿrifat al-Rijāl*. Mashhad: Faculty of Theology, University of Mashhad, 1964.

al-Kindī, Abū Bakr Aḥmad b. ʿAbdullāh b. Mūsā. *Kitāb al-Ihtidāʾ*. Muscat: Wizārat al-Turāth al-Qawmī waʾl-Thaqāfa, 1985.

al-Kindī, Muḥammad b. Ibrāhīm. *Bayān al-Sharʿ*. Muscat: Wizārat al-Turāth al-Qawmī waʾl-Thaqāfa, 1984.

Klijn, Albertus Frederik Johannes, ed. and trans. *The Acts of Thomas: Introduction, Text, and Commentary.* Leiden: Brill, 2003.

Lafuente y Alcántara, Emilio. *Colección de obras arábigas de historia y geografía, que publica la Real Academia de la Historia VI: Ajbar Machmua.* Madrid: M. Rivadeneyra, 1867.

Madelung, Wilferd. *Streitschrift des Zaiditenimams: Aḥmad an-Nāsir Wider die Ibaditische Prädestinationslehre.* Wiesbaden: Franz Steiner Verlag, 1985.

Madelung, Wilferd, and Abdulrahman al-Salimi, eds. *Early Ibāḍī Literature: Abu l-Mundhir Bashīr b. Muḥammad b. Maḥbūb* Kitāb al-Raṣf fi l-Tawḥīd, Kitāb al-Muḥāraba *and* Sīra. Wiesbaden: Harrasowitz Verlag, 2011.

Madelung, Wilferd, and Abdulrahman al-Salimi, eds. *Early Ibāḍī Theology: Six* kalām *Texts by ʿAbd Allāh b. Yazīd al-Fazārī.* Leiden: Brill, 2014.

Madelung, Wilferd, and Paul E. Walker, eds. and trans. *An Ismaili Heresiography: The "Bāb al-Shayṭān" from Abū Tammām's Kitāb al-Shajara.* Leiden: Brill, 1998.

al-Malaṭī, Abū al-Ḥasan Muḥammad b. Aḥmad. *Al-Tanbīh waʾl-Radd ʿalā Ahl al-Ahwāʾ waʾl-Bidʿa.* Cairo: Maktabat al-Azhariyya lil-Turāth, 1994.

Maʿrūf, Nāyif Maḥmūd. *Diwān al-Khawārij.* Beirut: Dār al-Masīra, 1983.

al-Marzubānī, Muḥammad b. ʿImrān. *Muʿjam al-Shuʿarāʾ.* Edited by ʿAbd al-Sattār Aḥmad Farrāj. Cairo: ʿĪsa al-Bābī al-Ḥalabī, 1960.

al-Masʿūdī, Abū al-Ḥasan ʿAlī b. al-Ḥusayn. *Murūj al-Dhahab.* Edited by Charles Pellat. Beirut: Publications of the University of Lebanon, 1966.

McCollum, Adam Carter, trans. *The Story of Mar Pinḥas.* Piscataway, N.J.: Gorgias Press, 2013.

McDonald, M. V., trans. *The History of al-Ṭabarī Volume VII: The Foundation of the Community.* Albany: State University of New York Press, 1987.

al-Minqarī, Abū al-Faḍl Naṣr b. Muzāhim b. Siyār. *Waqʿat Ṣiffīn.* Edited by ʿAbd al-Salām Muḥammad Hārūn. Cairo: Mu'assisat al-ʿArabiyya al-Ḥadītha, 1962.

Morony, Michael G., trans. *The History of al-Ṭabarī Volume XVIII: Between Civil Wars: The Caliphate of Muʿāwiyah.* Albany: State University of New York Press, 1987.

Muʿammar, ʿAlī Yaḥyā. *Al-Ibāḍiyya Bayn al-Firaq al-Islāmiyya.* Muscat: Wizārat al-Turāth al-Qawmī waʾl-Thaqāfa, 1992.

Muʿammar, ʿAlī Yaḥyā. *Al-Ibāḍiyya fī Mawkab al-Taʾrīkh.* Cairo: Maktabat Wahba, 1964.

Muslim, Abū al-Ḥusayn Ibn al-Ḥajjāj. *Ṣaḥīḥ Muslim.* Beirut: Dār Ibn Ḥazm, 1998.

al-Mubarrad, Abū al-ʿAbbās Muḥammad b. Yazīd. *Al-Kāmil fīʾl-Lugha waʾl-Adab.* Edited by Muḥammad Abū al-Faḍl Ibrāhīm. Beirut: Maktabat al-ʿAṣriyya, 2002.

al-Nawbakhtī, al-Ḥasan b. Mūsā. *Kitāb Firaq al-Shīʿa.* Istanbul: Maṭbaʿat al-Dawla, 1931.

al-Qalhātī, Abū Saʿīd Muḥammad b. Saʿīd al-Azdī. *Al-Kashf waʾl-Bayān.* Edited by Sayyida Ismāʿīl Kāshif. Muscat: Wizārat al-Turāth al-Qawmī waʾl-Thaqāfa, 1984.

al-Qummī, Saʿd b. ʿAbdullāh. *Kitāb al-Maqālāt waʾl-Firaq.* Tehran: Mu'assasat Maṭbuʿātʾī Aṭāʾī, 1963.

al-Rabīʿ b. Ḥabīb. *Al-Jāmiʿ al-Ṣaḥīḥ Musnad al-Imām al-Rabiʿ b. Ḥabīb.* Muscat: Maktabat al-Istiqāma, 2003.

al-Rāzī, Abū Ḥātim Aḥmad. *Kitāb al-Zīna.* In *Al-Ghuluww wa'l-Firaq al-Ghāliya fī al-Ḥaḍara al-Islāmiyya,* edited by Abdullāh S. al-Sāmarrāʾī, 229–346. Baghdad: Dār al-Ḥuriyya, 1972.

al-Saʿadī, Fahd b. ʿAlī, ed. *Ḥāshiyyat ʿalā Musnad al-Imām al-Rabiʿ b. Ḥabīb.* Muscat: Maktabat al-Anfāl, 2006.

al-Saḥḥāwī, Muḥammad b. ʿAbd al-Raḥmān. *Rijḥān al-Kiffa fī Bayān Nubdha min Akhbār Ahl al-Ṣuffa.* Riyadh: Dār al-Salaf lil-Nashr wa'l-Tawzīʿ, 1995.

al-Sālimī, Nūr al-Dīn ʿAbdullāh b. Aḥmad. *Tuḥfat al-ʿAyān bī-Sirat Ahl ʿUmān.* Cairo: Dar al-Kitāb al-ʿArabī, 1961.

Sells, Michael A., trans. *Desert Tracings: Six Classic Arabian Odes by ʿAlqama, Shanfara, Labid, ʿAntara, Al-Aʿsha, and Dhu al-Rumma.* Middletown, Conn.: Wesleyan University Press, 1989.

al-Shahrastānī, Abū al-Fatḥ Muḥammad ʿAbd al-Karīm. *Al-Milal wa'l-Niḥal.* Edited by ʿAbd al-ʿAzīz Muḥammad al-Wakīl. Beirut: Dār al-Fikr, n.d.

al-Shammākhī, Abū al-ʿAbbās Aḥmad b. Saʿīd. *Kitāb al-Siyar.* Edited by Muḥammad Ḥasan. Beirut: Dār al-Madār al-Islāmī, 2009.

al-Shammākhī, Abū al-ʿAbbās Aḥmad b. Saʿīd. *Muqaddimat al-Tawḥīd wa Shurūḥihā.* Muscat: Sulṭanat ʿUmān, 1988.

al-Ṭabarī, Muḥammad b. Jarīr. *Tārīkh al-Rusul wa'l-Mulūk.* Edited by M. J. de Goeje. Leiden: Brill, 1879.

al-Tamīmī, Abū al-ʿArab Muḥammad b. Aḥmad Tamīm. *Kitāb al-Miḥan.* Edited by Yaḥyā Wahīb al-Jabūrī. Beirut: Dār al-Gharb al-Islāmī, 1983.

al-Thaqafī, Abū Isḥāq Ibrāhīm b. Muḥammad b. Saʿīd b. Hilāl. *Al-Gharāt aw al-Istinfār wa'l-Gharāt.* Beirut: Dār al-Aḍwā', 1987.

al-Tibrīzī, Abū Zakariyya Yaḥyā b. ʿAlī b. Muḥammad. *Sharḥ al-Qaṣā'id al-ʿAshar.* Edited by Fakhr al-Dīn Qabāwa. Beirut: Dār al-Afāq al-Jadīda, 1980.

al-Tibrīzī, Abū Zakariyya Yaḥyā b. ʿAlī b. Muḥammad. *Sharḥ Diwān al-Ḥamāsa.* Beirut: Dār al-Kutub al-ʿIlmiyya, 2000.

Torrey, Charles, ed. *The History of the Conquests of Egypt, North Africa, and Spain: Known as the Futūḥ Miṣr of Ibn ʿAbd al-Ḥakam.* Piscataway, N.J.: Gorgias Press, 2002.

al-Warjlānī, Abū Yaʿqūb Yūsuf b. Ibrāhīm. *Al-ʿAdl wa al-Inṣāf fī Maʿrifat Usūl al-Fiqh wa'l-Ikhtilāf.* Muscat: Wizārat al-Turāth al-Qawmī wa'l-Thaqāfa, 1984.

al-Warjlānī, Abū Yaʿqūb Yūsuf b. Ibrāhīm. *Al-Dalīl wa'l-Burhān.* Muscat: Wizārat al-Turāth al-Qawmī wa'l-Thaqāfa, 1983.

Williams, John A., trans. *History of al-Ṭabarī Volume XXVII: The ʿAbbāsid Revolution.* Albany: State University of New York Press, 1985.

al-Wisyānī, Abū al-Rabīʿ Sulaymān b. ʿAbd al-Salām. *Siyar al-Wisyānī.* Muscat: Wizārat al-Turāth al-Qawmī wa'l-Thaqāfa, 2009.

Wright, William, ed. *Apocryphal Acts of the Apostles: Edited from Syriac Manuscripts in the British Museum and Other Libraries by William Wright.* London: Williams and Norgate, 1871.

Yāqūt al-Ḥamawī, Shihāb al-Dīn Abū ʿAbdullāh b. ʿAbdullāh al-Rūmī al-Baghdādī. *Muʿjam al-Buldān.* Beirut: Dār al-Kutub al-ʿIlmiyya, 1990.

Yūsuf ʿAlī, ʿAbdullah. *The Meaning of the Holy Qur'ān.* Beltsville, Md.: Amana Publications, 2004.

Secondary Sources

Abun-Nasr, Jamil M. *A History of the Maghrib in the Islamic Period.* Cambridge: Cambridge University Press, 1993.

Andrae, Tor. "Der Ursprung des Islams und das Christentum: I. Das Christentum in Arabien zur Zeit Muhammeds." *Kyrkohistorisk Årsskrift* 23 (1923): 155–80.

Ayoub, Mahmoud. "Martyrdom in Christianity and Islam." In *Religious Resurgence: Contemporary Cases in Islam, Christianity and Judaism,* edited by Richard Antoun and Mary Elaine Hegland, 67–77. Syracuse, N.Y.: Syracuse University Press, 1987.

Bearman, Peri, et al. "Al-Muḥillūn." In *The Encyclopaedia of Islam,* CD-ROM Edition, version 1.1. Leiden: Brill, 1999.

Bell, Richard. *The Origins of Islam in Its Christian Environment.* London: Macmillan, 1926.

Blachere, Regis. "ʿAntara." In *The Encyclopaedia of Islam,* CD-ROM Edition, version 1.1. Leiden: Brill, 1999.

Blankenship, Khalid. *The End of the Jihād State.* Albany: State University of New York Press, 1994.

Bonner, Michael. "Some Considerations Concerning the Early Development of Jihad on the Arab-Byzantine Frontier." *Studia Islamica* 75 (1992): 5–31.

Brakke, David. *Demons and the Making of the Monk: Spiritual Combat in Early Christianity.* Cambridge, Mass.: Harvard University Press, 2006.

Brock, Sebastian. "Early Syrian Asceticism." *Numen* 20 (1973): 1–19.

Brock, Sebastian. "A Martyr at the Sasanid Court under Vahran II: Candida." *Analecta Bollandiana* 96 (1978): 167–81.

Brock, Sebastian. "Saints in Syriac: A Little Tapped Resource." *Journal of Early Christian Studies* 16 (2008): 181–96.

Brock, Sebastian, trans. *The History of the Holy Mar Maʿin.* Piscataway, N.J.: Gorgias Press, 2008.

Brock, Sebastian, and Susan A. Harvey. *Holy Women of the Syrian Orient.* Berkeley: University of California Press, 1987.

Brown, Peter. *The Cult of the Saints: Its Rise and Function in Latin Christianity.* Chicago: University of Chicago Press, 1981.

Canivet, Pierre, and Alice Leroy-Molinghen, eds. *Histoire des moines de Syrie: Theodoret de Cyr.* Paris: Editions du Cerf, 1977–79.

Castelli, Elizabeth. *Martyrdom and Memory: Early Christian Culture Making.* New York: Columbia University Press, 2004.

Cobb, L. Stephanie. *Dying to Be Men: Gender and Language in Early Christian Martyr Texts.* New York: Columbia University Press, 2008.

Comaroff, Jean. *Body of Power, Spirit of Resistance: The Culture and History of a South African People.* Chicago: University of Chicago Press, 1985.

Cook, David. "The *Aṣḥāb al-Ukhdūd:* History and *Ḥadīth* in a Martyrological Sequence." *Jerusalem Studies in Arabic and Islam* 34 (2008): 125–48.

Cook, David. *Martyrdom in Islam.* Cambridge: Cambridge University Press, 2007.

Cook, Michael. *Early Muslim Dogma: A Source-Critical Study.* Cambridge: Cambridge University Press, 1981.

Crone, Patricia. "A Statement by the Najdiyya Khārijites on the Dispensability of the Imamate." *Studia Islamica* 88 (1998): 55–76.

Custers, Martin. *Al-Ibāḍiyya: A Bibliography.* 3 vols. Maastricht: Universitaire Pers Maastricht, 2006.

Dabashi, Hamid. *Authority in Islam: From the Rise of Muhammad to the Establishment of the Umayyads.* New Brunswick, N.J.: Transaction Publishers, 1989.

Dakake, David. "The Myth of a Militant Islam." In *Islam, Fundamentalism, and the Betrayal of Tradition,* edited by Joseph E. B. Lumbard, 3–37. Bloomington, Ind.: World Wisdom, 2004.

Dakake, Maria Massi. *The Charismatic Community: Shiʿite Identity in Early Islam.* Albany: State University of New York Press, 2007.

Delehaye, Hippolyte. *Les origines du culte des martyrs.* 2nd rev. ed. Brussels: Societe des Bollandistes, 1933.

Dillon, John M., and Lloyd P. Gerson, trans. and eds. *Neoplatonic Philosophy: Introductory Readings.* Indianapolis: Hackett, 2004.

Donner, Fred M. "From Believers to Muslims: Confessional Self-Identity in the Early Islamic Community." *Al-Abḥāth* 50–51 (2002): 9–53.

Donner, Fred M. *Narratives of Islamic Origins.* Princeton, N.J.: Darwin Press, 1998.

Donner, Fred M. "Piety and Eschatology in Early Kharijite Poetry." In *Fī Miḥrāb al-Maʿrifah: Festschrift for Iḥsān ʿAbbās,* edited by Ibrāhīm al-Saʿāfin, 13–19. Beirut: Dar Sader, 1997.

Ebstein, Michael. "*Shurṭa* Chiefs in Baṣra in the Umayyad Period: A Prosopographical Study." *Al-Qanṭara* 31 (2010): 103–47.

El Tayib, Abdulla. "Pre-Islamic Poetry." In *The Cambridge History of Arabic Literature: Arabic Literature to the End of the Umayyad Period,* edited by A. F. L. Beeston, T. M. Johnstone, R. B. Sergeant, and G. R. Smith, 27–109. Cambridge: Cambridge University Press, 1983.

Elliott, J. K., ed. *The Apocryphal New Testament: A Collection of Apocryphal Christian Literature in English Translation Based on M. R. James.* Oxford: Oxford University Press, 1993.

Ennāmi, ʿAmr K. *Studies in Ibāḍism (al-Ibāḍīyah).* Tripoli: Publications of the University of Libya Faculty of Arts, 1972.

Ernst, Carl W. *The Shambala Guide to Sufism.* Boston: Shambala Publications, 1997.

Fakhry, Majid. *A History of Islamic Philosophy.* New York: Columbia University Press, 2004.

Fierro, Maribel. "Al-Aṣfar." *Studia Islamica* 77 (1993): 169–81.

Fierro, Maribel. "Al-Aṣfar Again." *Jerusalem Studies in Arabic and Islam* 22 (1998): 198–213.

Fiey, Jean Maurice. *Saints Syriaques.* Princeton, N.J.: Darwin Press, 2004.

Finster, Barbara. "Arabia in Late Antiquity." In *The Qur'ān in Context: Historical and Literary Investigations into the Qur'ānic Milieu,* edited by Angelika Neuwirth, Nicolai Sinai, and Michael Marx, 61–114. Leiden: Brill, 2010.

Fowden, Elizabeth Key. *The Barbarian Plain: Saint Sergius between Rome and Iran.* Berkeley: University of California Press, 1999.

Francesca, Ersilia. "Early Ibāḍī Jurisprudence: Sources and Case Law." *Jerusalem Studies in Arabic and Islam* 30 (2005): 231–63.

Frend, W. H. C. *The Donatist Church: A Movement of Protest in Roman North Africa.* Oxford: Clarendon Press, 1971.

Friedmann, Yohann. "Classification of Unbelievers in Sunnī Muslim Law and Tradition." *Jerusalem Studies in Arabic and Islam* 22 (1998): 163–95.

Gabrieli, Francesco. "Religious Poetry in Early Islam." In *Arabic Poetry: Theory and Development,* edited by Gustave E. Von Grunebaum, 5–17. Wiesbaden: Harrassowitz, 1973.

Gaiser, Adam. "Ibāḍī Dynasties." In *Encyclopedia of the Islamic World,* edited by John Esposito, 2:476–79. New York: Oxford University Press, 2009.

Gaiser, Adam. "The Ibāḍī 'Stages of Religion' Re-Examined: Tracing the History of the *Masālik al-Dīn.*" *Bulletin of the School of Oriental and African Studies* 73 (2010): 209–22.

Gaiser, Adam. "The Kharijites in Contemporary Scholarship." *Oxford Bibliographies Online* (2013): 1–35. http://www.oxfordbibliographies.com/view/document/obo-9780195390155/obo-9780195390155-0159.xml [DOI: 10.1093/OBO/9780195390155-0159] (accessed March 25, 2015).

Gaiser, Adam. *Muslims, Scholars, Soldiers: The Origin and Elaboration of the Ibāḍī Imāmate Traditions.* New York: Oxford University Press, 2010.

Gaiser, Adam. "North African and Omani Ibāḍī Accounts of the *Munāẓara:* A Preliminary Comparison." In *L'ibādisme: Une minorité au cœur de l'islam,* edited by Cyrille Aillet, 63–73. Aix-en-Provence: Revue des Mondes Musulmans et de la Méditerranée, 2012.

Gaiser, Adam. "Slaves and Silver across the Strait of Gibraltar: Politics and Trade between Umayyad Iberia and Khārijite North Africa." *Medieval Encounters* 19 (2013): 41–70.

Gaiser, Adam. "Source-Critical Methodologies in Recent Scholarship on the Khārijites." *History Compass* 7 (2009): 1376–90.

Gaiser, Adam. "What Do We Learn about the Early Khārijites and Ibāḍiyya from Their Coins?" *Journal of the American Oriental Society* 130 (2010): 167–87.

Gamble, Harry. *Books and Readers in the Early Church: A History of Early Christian Texts.* New Haven, Conn.: Yale University Press, 1995.

Gardner, Iain, and Samuel N. C. Lieu, trans. *Manichean Texts from the Roman Empire.* Cambridge: Cambridge University Press, 2004.

Hallaq, Ghada Bathish. "Discourse Strategies: The Pervasive Power of Early Khārijī Poetry." Ph.D. diss., University of Washington, 1988.

Hawting, Gerald R. *The Idea of Idolatry and the Emergence of Islam: From Polemic to History.* Cambridge: Cambridge University Press, 1999.

Heath, Peter. *The Thirsty Sword:* Sīrat ʿAntar *and the Arabic Popular Legend.* Salt Lake City: University of Utah Press, 1996.

Heck, Paul L. "Eschatological Scripturalism and the End of Community." In *Archiv für Religionsgechichte,* edited by Jan Assmann et al., 137–52. Leipzig: K. G. Saur München, 2005.

Higgins, Annie. "Faces of Exchangers, Facets of Exchange in Early *Shurāt* (Khārijī) Poetry." *Bulletin of the Royal Institute of Inter-Faith Studies* 7, no. 1 (2005): 7–38.

Hoffman, Valerie. *The Essentials of Ibāḍī Islam.* Syracuse, N.Y.: Syracuse University Press, 2012.

Holroyd, Stuart. *The Elements of Gnosticism.* Dorset: Element Books Limited, 1994.

Hrbek, Ivan, ed. *General History of Africa III (Abridged Edition): Africa from the Seventh to the Eleventh Century.* Berkeley: UNESCO, 1992.

Izutsu, Toshihiko. *Ethico-Religious Concepts in the Qur'ān.* Montreal: McGill-Queen's University Press, 2002.

Jauss, Hans R. "Literary History as a Challenge to Literary Theory." Translated by Stetkevych, 219–40. Burlington, Vt.: Ashgate, 2009.

Ostrogorsky, George. *History of the Byzantine State.* New Brunswick, N.J.: Rutgers University Press, 1969.

Pagels, Elaine. *The Gnostic Gospels.* New York: Random House, 1979.

Pellat, Charles. "Midrār." In *The Encyclopaedia of Islam,* CD-ROM Edition, version 1.1. Leiden: Brill, 1999.

Peters, F. E. *Muhammad and the Origins of Islam.* Albany: State University of New York Press, 1994.

Potts, Daniel. *The Arabian Gulf in Antiquity.* Oxford: Oxford University Press, 1990.

Prevost, Virginie. "Les enjeux de la bataille de Mânû (283/896)." In *L'ibadisme, une minorité au cœur de l'islam,* edited by Cyrille Aillet, 75–90. Aix-en-Provence: Revue des mondes musulmans et de la Méditerranée, 2012.

al-Qāḍī, Wadād. "The Limitations of Qur'ānic Usage in Early Arabic Poetry: The Example of a Khārijite Poem." In *Festschrift Ewald Wagner zum 65. Geburtstag, vol. 2:*

Studien zur arabischen Dichtung, edited by W. Heinrichs and G. Schoeler, 168–81. Beirut: Kommission bei Franz Steiner Verlag Stuttgart, 1994.

Reeves, John. *Prolegomena to a History of Islamicate Manichaeism.* Sheffield: Equinox, 2011.

Robinson, Chase. "Shabīb b. Yazīd." In *The Encyclopaedia of Islam,* CD-ROM Edition, version 1.1. Leiden: Brill, 1999.

Robinson, Chase F. *Empire and Elites after the Muslim Conquest: The Transformation of Northern Mesopotamia.* Cambridge: Cambridge University Press, 2000.

Robinson, Chase F. *Islamic Historiography.* Cambridge: Cambridge University Press, 2003.

Robinson, Chase F. "Prophecy and Holy Men in Early Islam." In *The Cult of Saints in Late Antiquity and the Middle Ages: Essays on the Contribution of Peter Brown,* edited by James Howard-Johnston and Paul Antony Hayward, 241–62. Oxford: Oxford University Press, 1999.

Royalty, Robert M. *The Origin of Heresy: A History of Discourse in Second Temple Judaism and Early Christianity.* London: Routledge, 2012.

Rushworth, Alan. "From Arzuges to Rustamids: State Formation and Regional Identity in the Pre-Saharan Zone." In *Vandals, Romans and Berbers: New Perspectives on Late Antique North Africa,* edited by A. H. Merrils, 77–98. Burlington, Vt.: Ashgate, 2004.

Ryan, John. *Irish Monasticism: Origins and Early Development.* New York: Longmans, Green, 1931.

al-Sābi'ī, Nāṣir b. Sulaymān b. Sa'īd. *Al-Khawārij wa'l-Ḥaqīqa al-Ghā'iba.* Muscat: Maktabat al-Jīl al-Wā'id, 2003.

Sachedina, Abdulaziz Abdulhussein. *The Just Ruler in Shi'ite Islam.* Oxford: Oxford University Press, 1988.

al-Ṣāliḥi, 'Azmī Muḥammad Shafīq. "The Society, Beliefs and Political Theories of the Khārijites as Revealed in Their Poetry of the Umayyad Era." Ph.D. diss., School of Oriental and African Studies, University of London, 1975.

al-Salimi, Abdulrahman. "The Political Organization of Oman from the Second Imamate Period to the Ya'rūba: Rereading Omani Internal Sources." Paper presented at the L'Ibadisme Dans Les Societes Islamiques Medievales: Modeles Politiques, forms d'Organisation et d'Interactions Sociales Colloqium, Madrid, Spain, December 11–13, 2012.

Savage, Elizabeth. *A Gateway to Hell, a Gateway to Paradise: The North African Response to the Arab Conquest.* Princeton, N.J.: Darwin Press, 1997.

Schneemelcher, Wilhelm, ed., and Robert M. Wilson, trans. *New Testament Apocrypha, Volume 2: Writings Relating to the Apostles; Apocalypses and Related Subjects, Revised Edition.* Westminster: John Knox Press, 1992.

Shaban. M. A. *Islamic History A.D. 600–750 (A.H. 132): A New Interpretation.* Cambridge: Cambridge University Press, 1971.

Shah, Mustafa. "The Quest for the Origins of the *Qurrā'* in the Classical Islamic Tradition." *Journal of Qur'anic Studies* 7, no. 2 (2005): 1–35.

Shahīd, Irfan. *Byzantium and the Arabs in the Fifth Century.* Washington, D.C.: Dumbarton Oaks, 1987.

Shahīd, Irfan. "Byzantium in South Arabia." *Dumbarton Oaks Papers* 33 (1979): 23–94.

Shahīd, Irfan. "Ghassān." In *The Encyclopaedia of Islam,* CD-ROM Edition, version 1.1. Leiden: Brill, 1999.

Shahīd, Irfan. "Islam and *Oriens Christianus:* Makka 610–622 AD." In *The Encounter of Eastern Christianity with Early Islam,* edited by Emmanouela Grypeou, Mark Swanson, and David Thomas, 9–31. Leiden: Brill, 2006.

Shahīd, Irfan. *The Martyrs of Najrān: New Documents.* Brussels: Société des bollandistes, 1971.
Shoufani, Elias. *Al-Riddah and the Muslim Conquest of Arabia.* Toronto: University of Toronto Press, 1972.
Sizgorich, Thomas. "Become Infidels or We Will Throw You into the Fire: The Martyrs of Najrān in Early Muslim Historiography, Hagiography, and Qur'ānic Exegesis." In *Writing 'True Stories': Historians and Hagiographers in the Late Antique and Medieval Near East,* edited by Arietta Papaconstantinou, Muriel Debie, and Hugh Kennedy, 125–47. Turnhout: Brepols, 2010.
Sizgorich, Thomas. *Violence and Belief in Late Antiquity: Militant Devotion in Christianity and Islam.* Philadelphia: University of Pennsylvania Press, 2009.
Smith, Kyle. "Constantine and Judah the Maccabee: History and Memory in the *Acts of the Persian Martyrs.*" *Journal of the Canadian Society for Syriac Studies* 12 (2012): 16–33.
Stetkevych, Jaroslav. *The Zephyrs of Najd: The Poetics of Nostalgia in the Classical Arabic* Nasīb. Chicago: University of Chicago Press, 1993.
Stetkevych, Suzanne Pinckney. *The Mute Immortals Speak: Pre-Islamic Poetry and the Poetics of Ritual.* Ithaca, N.Y.: Cornell University Press, 1993.
Talbi, Mohammed. "Un nouveau fragment de l'histoire de l'Occident musulman (62–196/682–812): L'épopée d'al-Kahina." *Cahiers de Tunisie* 19 (1971): 19–52.
Tilley, Maureen A. *Donatist Martyr Stories: The Church in Conflict in Roman North Africa.* Liverpool: Liverpool University Press, 1996.
Toral-Niehoff, Isabel. "The 'Ibād of al-Ḥīra: An Arab Christian Community." In *The Qur'ān in Context: Historical and Literary Investigations into the Qur'ānic Milieu,* edited by Angelika Neuwirth, Nicolai Sinai, and Michael Marx, 323–47. Leiden: Brill, 2010.
Trimingham, J. Spencer. *Christianity among the Arabs in Pre-Islamic Times.* New York: Longman, 1979.
Van Ess, Josef. *Theologie und Gesellschaft im 2. und 3. Jahrhundert Hidschra.* Berlin: De Gruyter, 1991–95.
Von Harnack, Adolf. *Marcion: The Gospel of the Alien God.* Durham, N.C.: Labyrinth Press, 1990.
Vööbus, Arthur. *History of Asceticism in the Syrian Orient.* Louvain: Secretariat du Corpus SCO, 1958–88.
Waldman, Marilyn Robinson. "The Development of the Concept of Kufr in the Qur'ān." *Journal of the American Oriental Society* 88 (1968): 442–55.
Walker, Joel. *The Legend of Mar Qardagh: Narrative and Christian Heroism in Late Antique Iraq.* Berkeley: University of California Press, 2006.
Ware, Kallistos. "Apatheia." In *The Westminster Dictionary of Christian Spirituality,* edited by Gordon S. Wakefield, 18–19. Westminster: John Knox Press, 1983.
Watt, W. Montgomery. *The Formative Period of Islamic Thought.* Oxford: Oneworld Publications, 1998.
Wellhausen, Julius. *The Religio-Political Factions of Early Islam.* New York: Oxford American Elsevier Publishing Company, 1975.
Wilkinson, John C. "Hamalat al-Ilm." Paper presented at the Today's Perspectives on Ibadi History and the Historical Sources Conference, Cambridge, U.K., June 16–18, 2014.
Wilkinson, John C. "Ibāḍī ḥadīth: An Essay in Normalization." *Der Islam* 62 (1985): 231–59.
Wilkinson, John C. *Ibāḍism: Origins and Early Development in Oman.* Oxford: Oxford University Press, 2010.
Williams, John A. *The World of Islam.* Austin: University of Texas Press, 1994.

Index

Ḥanẓala b. Safwān al-Kalbī, 119
Ḥāritha b. Ṣakhr al-Qaynī, 59, 101
Ḥārith b. Jabala, 17
Ḥārith b. Ka'b (Arethas), 28, 108
Al-Ḥārith b. Talīd al-Ḥaḍramī, 120, 157
Al-Ḥarra, battle of, 59
Ḥarūrā', 47
Harvey, Susan, 21, 23
Al-Ḥasan b. 'Alī, 93, 133
Al-Ḥasan al-Baṣrī, 154
Al-Hathāth b. Thawr al-Sadūsī, 60–62
Ḥawthara b. Wadā' al-Asadī, 52, 71, 101, 133–34
Hawting, Gerald, 35–36, 89, 99
Ḥayyān b. Ẓabyān al-Sulamī, 54–57, 100, 135–36, 140
heresiography, genre of, 87–94, 98–100, 103–4, 110–12, 166–67, 171–72
Hilāl b. 'Aṭiyya, 149
Al-Ḥira. *See* Christians
Hishām b. 'Abd al-Mālik, 119, 154
Hishām b. al-Ḥakam, 58
Ḥudhayfa b. Yamān, 128
Ḥujayr al-Bāhilī, 60
Ḥujiyya b. Aws, 72
Ḥurayth b. Ḥajl, 60, 64, 135
Ḥurqūs b. Zuhayr al-Sa'dī, 50, 71, 94, 112, 126, 129–32, 153
Ḥuṣayn b. Ḥafṣa al-Sa'dī, 109–10
Ḥuṣayn b. Mālik, 107

'Ibād Christians. *See* Christians
Ibāḍīyya; and assimilation of Muḥakkima materials, 8, 40, 122–33; and assimilation of *shurāt* materials, 8, 40, 133–45, 145–51, 152–75; formation and identity construction of, 2–4, 6, 13–14, 113, 115–22, 146; imāmates of, 13, 115–22, 143, 146–51, 152, 157, 160, 174; "teacher lines" of, 125, 131–34, 159; tribal affiliation of, 131–32; *'ulamā'*, 13, 117–18, 144, 147, 149–50, 173
Iblīs, 162–63
Ibn 'Arfrā', 41
Ibn Khabbāb, 91, 95–96
Ibn al-Ṣaghīr, 123
Ibn Zur'a al-Kilābī, 60
imān (faith), 42–43, 94, 98–99, 101–2, 112
'Imrān b. Ḥaṭṭān, 67–68, 78, 84, 133, 134
India, 31
Iranaeus, 35
irtidād/*ridda* (apostasy)/*murtadd* (apostate), 44, 98, 154, 171
Isaac of Antioch, 33
'Īsā b. Fātik al-Khaṭṭī, 53, 61–62, 65, 72, 75, 105–7
'Isā b. Mazyad, 120
'Itrīs b. 'Urqūb, 54
'Izz al-Dīn b. al-Athīr, 53, 61–62, 64, 119, 123, 134–36

Jābir b. Zayd, 115, 116, 140, 146, 147
Jamāl al-Dīn 'Abd al-Raḥmān b. Jawzī, 71, 77, 93
Jews, 164, 166; contact with Muslims, 36–37, 42–43; in late antique Middle East, 1, 16, 22; use of accusations of unfaithfulness, 13, 35
jihād; and asceticism, 39–40; and martyrdom, 40–41; and *shirā'*, 55–56
jizya, 166
John the Baptist, 30
Al-Julandā b. Mas'ūd, 13, 117, 122, 145, 148–49, 150, 160–61, 173

Ka'b b. 'Amīra, 66
Kahmas b. Ṭalaq al-Ṣarīmī, 60, 64–65, 135
kalām (dialectic theology), 95, 127
Kaleb (Ella-Asbeha), 28
Kennedy, Philip, 81
Khalaf b. Ziyād al-Baḥrānī, 149, 164–65
Khālid b. 'Abbād ('Ubāda), 60, 72, 135, 136, 140
Khālid b. 'Abdullāh al-Qasrī, 154
Khālid b. Ḥumayd al-Zanātī, 119
Khālid b. Qaḥṭān, 161
Khalīfa b. Khayyāṭ, 58–59
Al-Khalīl b. Shathān al-Kharūṣī, 117
Khārijites (*khawārij*); in contemporary scholarship, 14, 88–89; definition and emergence of, 1, 47, 66, 70–71, 87–89; militancy, 2–5, 12–13, 68–70, 115, 144, 158, 166–67, 169, 172; in non-Ibāḍī sources, 2, 8, 15, 45, 90–99, 112; poetry, 46–47, 53 (*see also* poetry); subsects, 2, 12–14, 68–74, 87–89, 106–7, 144, 155, 161 (*see also* Azāriqa, Najdāt, Ṣufriyya); and tribal affiliations, 7, 106